VANGUARD

VANGUARD

The True Stories of the Reconnaissance
and Intelligence Missions Behind D-Day

DAVID ABRUTAT

Naval Institute Press
Annapolis, Maryland

A Unicorn Publishing Group / Naval Institute Press co-publication

Naval Institute Press
Annapolis, Maryland

Published and distributed in the United States of America and Canada by the
Naval Institute Press, 291 Wood Road, Annapolis, Maryland 21402-5043
www.nip.org

Published by Uniform
An imprint of Unicorn Publishing Group
5 Newburgh Street
London W1F 7RG

www.unicornpublishing.org

British Library Cataloguing in Publication Data
A catalogue record for this book is available from the British Library

Library of Congress Cataloguing-in-Publication Data
Library of Congress Cataloging Number: 2018966767

5 4 3 2 1

ISBN (UK): 978-1-912690-63-3
ISBN (USA): 978-1-68247-454-9

Cover design Unicorn Publishing Group
Typeset by Vivian@Bookscribe

Printed and bound by Fine Tone LTD

CONTENTS

'*Thus, what enables the wise Sovereign and the good General to strike and conquer, and achieve things beyond the reach of ordinary men, is foreknowledge.*'

Sun Tzu, 544–496 BC

〜〜

'*This vast operation is undoubtedly the most complicated and difficult that has ever taken place. It involves the tides, winds, waves, visibility, both from the air and the seas standpoint, and the combined employment of land, air and sea forces in the highest degree of intimacy and in contact with conditions that could not and cannot be fully foreseen.*'

Winston Churchill to the House of Commons, 6 June 1944

FOREWORD

The invasion of mainland Europe by Britain and her Western Allies under Operation Overlord remains arguably the greatest feat of arms ever recorded. The scale, complexity and ambition of the operation were unprecedented and matched only by the enormity of what was at stake for the Allied powers that embarked on it. Overlord's success was decisive, allowing the Allies to roll back the Nazi forces and bring about their defeat in Europe.

To the outside observer the way the modern British military deploys and employs its forces in the twenty-first century may look and feel very different to that which delivered military and strategic success during Overlord. Indeed, the character of conflict has changed significantly in just seventy years, as too have the societies and groups responsible for perpetuating it. Globalisation, rapid advancements in communicative and military technologies, population growth and dispersal, as well as shifting societal attitudes are just some of the many factors that have combined to create a battlefield and operating environment that is increasingly complex, congested, cluttered and contested.

Despite this marked evolution, and as many great military thinkers and strategists have famously observed, the nature of warfare remains unchanged, as do the fundamental principles relied upon for its successful conduct. The need for surprise, for concentration of force, effective deception and flexibility have all proven as important in the operations I have been a part of in Iraq and Afghanistan as they were to my predecessors planning and leading the amphibious and airborne assaults on to Normandy's beaches and defences in 1944.

Of equal and enduring importance for military planners and commanders is the ready access to timely and accurate intelligence. Through this, leaders and their forces can best prepare for the challenges their enemy will present, and so construct their plan in such a way as to pit their strengths against the enemy's weaknesses. This so called 'manouverist approach' should, if employed effectively, deliver maximum gain to one's force at minimal risk and cost. It may seem obvious to state but a military's ability to generate and then act against high-quality intelligence is nearly always decisive and therefore battle-winning.

Whilst the extraordinary scale of the task and the stakes involved in Overlord were what made it such an unprecedented military feat, the purpose of the operation was by comparison incredibly simple – to set the conditions to bring about the defeat of Nazi Germany in northern Europe. As a consequence, the focus of the intelligence effort was relatively narrow but remarkable, and since unmatched, for the depth and detail produced. As this book sets out with great care and precision, the Allied forces left little to chance and invested every possible resource in understanding their enemy, his intentions and the physical geography he occupied. This 'enemy-centric' approach was entirely appropriate for a total war that saw the application of hard conventional military power against the belligerent forces of another similarly configured nation state adversary.

By contrast, the late twentieth- and early twenty-first-century battlefields have been much harder to discern, requiring intelligence that allows us to persuade and influence as much as it does to defeat and destroy. Often branded 'wars amongst the people', the counter-insurgency campaigns we have fought in Northern Ireland, Iraq and Afghanistan have seen our forces pitched against an adversary that does not play by our rules and chooses to move and fight within a population not entirely unsympathetic to its cause. In response we have had to strike a fine balance between adapting our intelligence tactics, techniques and procedures to meet the evolving threat whilst remaining true to the guiding principles of intelligence-gathering that endure and were proven with such great effect during Overlord.

I highlight this comparison not so as to suggest either operating environment was any more difficult for the intelligence and reconnaissance practitioners who sought to understand it. Instead, I would emphasise that although a lot has changed in seventy or so years, a lot has also remained the same. I am proud to reassure you that the need for human ingenuity, determination, endurance and raw physical courage remain as essential in the intelligence and reconnaissance work of our Armed Forces and Security Services today as they were in the days and months leading up to 6 June 1944. As a result, there is a great deal in this work that makes it as much an invaluable case study for the modern practitioner as an excellent historical account for anyone wanting to understand the Allies' military success on D-Day and thereafter.

In closing, and most importantly of all, I would draw the reader's attention to the incredible human stories that the author weaves throughout this measured and meticulous account. As only someone that knows can, he brings to life the personal trials and tribulations as well as the great victories and bitter defeats that come with serving one's country and being willing to give all for the freedom and security of others. I strongly commend this work to you and hope you enjoy reading it as much as I did.

General Sir Gordon Messenger KCB DSO* OBE ADC
Vice Chief of Defence Staff

'The hopes and prayers of the Free World and of the enslaved
peoples of Europe will be with us ...'

Admiral Ramsay 5 June 1944

Quote from the

'Special Order of the Day to the Officers and Men of the Allied Naval
Expeditionary Force'

PREFACE

D-Day can be regarded as one of the greatest combined military operations ever undertaken. It was ambitious and on a size and scale that is, even to this day, almost unparalleled. Beyond the fabric of the operational plans was one of the most thorough cross-discipline intelligence collection efforts ever seen, mirroring the scale of the actual operation. Intelligence is an instrument of advantage to military commanders, be it in the jungles of Malaya, the beaches of Normandy or the streets of Helmand Province in Afghanistan.

As a former member of the Royal Marines Commando family, I have long been in awe of the fortitude and resilience of elite men who volunteered for special service during the early years of World War II and paved the way for one of the most auspicious and daring military invasions of all time. I have been privileged to meet some of these men who have shared some distant memories and experiences with me to shape this book. I have taken the time and patience of the last surviving member of the joint midget submarine X-Craft/COPP (Combined Operations Pilotage Parties) teams for Operation Gambit, Lieutenant Jim Booth, whom I have had the pleasure of interviewing several times. The humility, sheer courage and dedication to duty has been clear even now, more than seventy years later. This is a story of not just scale, but also of inspired individuals. The intelligence collection operations behind D-Day were not just the work of Bletchley Park or the Spitfire or Mosquito aerial reconnaissance missions, the field of scientific intelligence also made a significant difference. Scientists like Dr Reginald Jones and Professor Mason were critical to OVERLORD, but also Naval Hydrographers like Frank Berncastle and Special Forces officers like Major Logan Scott-Bowden and Lieutenant Commander Nigel Clogstoun-Wilmott, Royal Marines like Colonel Sam Bassett, and engineers like Tommy Flowers from the Post Office.

What they collectively achieved in the early 1940s would change the outcome of Operation Overlord and ultimately the course of history. These were renegades, free-thinkers and visionaries. But they were dedicated to one Mission – Normandy and the creation of a second front in Europe. They were given the trust by their senior commanders and bosses to do what they needed to do. For D-Day the leash was taken off the dog. Much of the story has been lost to the march of time but wherever I can, I have let the veterans of these operations speak for themselves, as there is no greater insight into the dedication, bravery and steadfast courage of these remarkable men.

Intelligence comes in many forms and real breakthroughs often come from the most unlikely of sources. The work the US signals intelligence community did against Japanese ciphers was to have a secondary effect, in exposing the traffic of the Japanese Ambassador to Berlin. In one of his forays to Normandy under the invitation of the Germany military, his report, covering in explicit detail the nature of the German defences and fortifications was to be a huge coup for Allied intelligence.

Global conflicts are often defined by significant battles or events and World War II was defined by many, but none so significant as what has become known since as D-Day. Operation Overlord and the naval amphibious plans defined in Operations Neptune pushed the Allied Expeditionary Force on to a bridgehead that spanned over 50 miles, deploying some 156,000 British, American and Canadian troops on to five beaches. The operation ultimately led to the Allied liberation of Western Europe.

The operational planners were very specific in the timings for the D-Day invasion of Normandy. They wanted a spring tide with a full moon, which honed in on only a few potential days, and 5 June 1944 was chosen. As is detailed in the book, this date slipped by twenty-four hours due to bad weather.

The Allied landings on the Normandy beaches on 6 June 1944 marked a turning point for World War II. It began the long road to Germany and the end of the War in Europe. It was estimated that in the region of two million soldiers, sailors and airmen were involved in Overlord, the biggest amphibious landing in history, utilising nearly 7,000 naval vessels. It was a veritable Armada. As Hitler most eloquently wrote in December 1943, '… the attack will come; there's no doubt any more. If they attack in the West, that attack will decide the war.'

As Churchill said in June 1944, 'much the greatest thing we have ever attempted', but little was it known at the time that two midget submarines and their COPP divers laid the groundwork for this invasion. In no small part was the success of D-Day down to their heroic actions in June 1944 and in the lead-up reconnaissance missions. Over 3,200 aerial reconnaissance missions took place prior to the invasion to acquire photographs of key installations and defences around the five landing beaches.

World War II was total war, and total war requires total intelligence. Operation Overlord was one of the boldest invasions ever mounted and for the four years prior to the 6 June 1944, the Allies developed a multitude of intelligence collection efforts and reconnaissance raids against the Normandy defensive positions. It was to be the most well-prepared invasion force of all time. Intelligence ranged from the almost industrial-scale collection and interpretation of aerial photographs at RAF Benson and RAF Medmenham, small naval teams undertaking hydrographic surveys under the noses of the German defences, to the small reconnaissance missions mounted by swimmer/canoeist teams from the COPP, who brought back samples from the beaches themselves.

The old military adage from Jasper Fforde (*Shades of Grey: The Road to High Saffron*) that '… time spent on reconnaissance is never wasted …' rings true and never more so with an operation as big and as complex as D-Day. The intelligence preparation of the battlefield is an important concept in modern warfare and the long build up to D-Day exemplifies the many avenues of intelligence strands that were employed to understand the target defences that could turn the tide against the Allied invasion of Normandy. It is often neglected, but the most important intelligence to the combat commander is that which is obtained by the fighting troops themselves. In a number of European operations before June 1944, the Allies developed a wide awareness of the capabilities of the German defensive forces that they would meet on the beaches and hinterland of Normandy.

Invasion plans for Europe had been created as early as 1942 by the Americans (Operations Roundup and the aptly named Sledgehammer) but these plans got sidetracked as Churchill pushed for military offensives across Italy and North Africa to secure the Mediterranean theatre.

One aspect apparent through researching this book was the industrial scale and breadth of the intelligence activity for Overlord. The planning warranted a scale of intelligence collection effort that had never been seen before, nor is it ever to likely be repeated. At Bletchley Park, in the run-up to D-Day some 18,000 encrypted German messages, some from Hitler himself, were being deciphered every single day. Normandy was an intelligence operation unparalleled for the detail, breadth, accuracy and scale of its collection effort alongside the creativity and guile of its deception strategies.

Much of the intelligence work was undertaken by eccentric and lone military units or individuals detached from centralised command structures and given the autonomy they needed. They all shared a collective belief in achieving the ultimate objective of the opening of a second front, in Normandy. What I have hoped to convey in this book is that small niche units that were established across the military command structures, often run by renegades and introverts but through guile and good fortune, made huge inroads in acquiring significant intelligence on the German defences and on the military dispositions. This was often at huge personal risk and many did not live to tell their tale.

I dedicate this book to my friend John Jeffrey whom I had the privilege to meet in 2009. He was a Lance Bombardier in the Royal Artillery and had been part of the 51st Highland Division, which went in with the Canadians at Juno Beach on 6 June 1944. He was fortunate to receive the *Legion d'Honneur* from the French government shortly before his death in December 2015.

This book, I hope, will serve as a permanent reminder of the courage, dedication and sacrifice of some extraordinary servicemen and women.

I salute you.

ACKNOWLEDGEMENTS

I would like to convey my thanks for the advice and guidance by:

Tony Comer GCHQ historian, and his assistant curators

Lieutenant Jim Booth, COPP9

Lieutenant Tony Byrd

Martyn Cox

Michael Mockford Medmenham Collection archives

Phil Hayes, Senior Colossus Engineer at Bletchley Park

Susan Killoran and Niall Sheekey at Harris-Manchester College, Oxford

Fred Bailey and John Sharp Jedburgh teams

Jane Harris, Kathryn Riddington and Jonathan Clatworthy at the Lapworth Museum of Geology, University of Birmingham.

Dr Ted Rose at the Department of Earth Sciences

Dr C.S. Knighton, archivist at Clifton College Bristol

Katharine Thomson at the Churchill Archives Centre, Churchill College, University of Cambridge

Mark Rowe

Tim Fryer at the Military Intelligence Museum archives in Defence Intelligence and Security Centre (DISC) Chicksands.

Joyce Hutton, Archivist and Assistant Curator at the Military Intelligence Museum

David Fowler and Dr Martin Maw at the Oxford University Press archives

Richard Callaghan and Mia Cameron-Dungey at the Royal Military Police Museum/Southwick Park

Dr Helen Fry and Fred Judge

Lord Paddy Ashdown

General Sir Gordon Messenger

John Bell

Patsy Cullen

Andrew Whitmarsh and James Daly at the Portsmouth History Centre/D-Day Museum

Geoffrey Pigeon

Lieutenant Colonel (retd) Ingram Murray

David Verghese

Martin Hutchinson at Malvern RADAR and Technology History Society (MRATHS)

Merlin Fraser

Hannah Ratford from the BBC archives in Caversham

Bob Hunt

Nick Catford for his Southwick graphic

John Taylor

Stewart Wardrop at the Royal Pigeon Racing Association (RPRA)

Sally Mason from the Centre of Buckinghamshire Studies, County Hall Aylesbury

Lee Richards

Claire Draper

Martin Hutchinson

Thanks to my publishers Ryan Gearing and Lord Ian Strathcarron from Unicorn Publishing Group for believing in me. And, finally, I would like to thank my family for tolerating me during this project, especially to Susan Moore for her tireless editing of my manuscript.

CHAPTER ONE
GREAT CRUSADE

*'We could take no chances; if we failed in Normandy the war might drag on for
years.'*

Field Marshal Bernard Montgomery, from
Field Marshal Bernard Montgomery, 1887–1976 A Selected Bibliography
(By Colin Baxter)

~~~

Shortly after the disaster of Dunkirk and the evacuation of thousands of Allied troops
from the beaches, Churchill was to create the foundation for the beginning of a second
front in Europe. He created a new position of Director of Combined Operations,
appointing Sir Roger Keyes as its immediate commander in his role as Admiral of the
Fleet. It was Keyes who started to bring together all the components of the Armed
Forces to develop combined amphibious operations and raids, and this continued
under Louis Mountbatten when he assumed the role in October 1942.

By the spring of 1943 the tide was beginning to turn against Hitler. The final
preparations for the invasion of Europe were proceeding with the formation of 21st
Army Group, which was created from the operational component of GHQ Home
Forces and Army Cooperation Command, which was converted to the 2nd Tactical
Air Force. This new formation had many RAF units at its core but it needed to be
supplemented by units from other parts of the world, including Army and Air Force
units from as far afield as the Middle East.

In May 1943 at the Trident conference in Washington DC, Churchill and Roosevelt
and their military commanders discussed the opening up of a second front in Europe
for the first time. But it was not until the following Quadrant conference in Ottawa
between 11 and 24 August 1943, hosted by the Canadian Prime Minister, William
Lyon MacKenzie King, that agreements were finally made to endorse the strategy.
This had been set by the Chief of Staff to the Supreme Allied Commander (COSSAC),
Lieutenant General Sir Frederick Morgan, and the objective would be the beaches of
Normandy. It was decided that the overall operation, Overlord, would be commanded
by General Dwight Eisenhower, assisted by a coalition of British and American senior
military officers. Morgan was to have an intelligence body, the Joint Intelligence
Committee (JIC), which he would use to harness the power of all the intelligence
structures at the Allies' disposal.

Later that year, two more conferences took place. The Sextant conference in Cairo between 22 and 26 November and the Tehran Eureka conference later that month would discuss the specifics of the invasion of France. The outcome from Eureka and Quadrant would be that Overlord would be mounted during May 1944 and coordinated with a near simultaneous invasion of southern France (Operation Dragoon) and the Russians would follow with a major offensive on the Eastern Front which would begin on 22 June 1944 (Operation Bagration). The Allies were keen to prevent any movement of German troops from the Eastern to Western fronts. When Churchill and his team arrived back in Britain after Quadrant, the Chiefs of Staff instructed the JIC to ascertain when the time was right for Overlord.

The part of the Normandy coastline from the Bay of the Seine west to the Cherbourg peninsula was to be the objective. It was a well-considered target, with long, expansive and lightly defended beaches, within reach of Allied aircraft from the airfields of southern England. The Germans had constructed their Atlantic Wall in this part of northern France with the misguided expectation that the Allies would need to take a key strategic port before a large-scale invasion could take place.

For a successful invasion to occur, the Allies would have to mount one of the greatest joint intelligence campaigns of modern history. It would need to cover the intelligence requirements of the operations and logistics behind Overlord but also the vital deception campaign. Intelligence needed to be gathered on the German defensive fortifications in Normandy on an unprecedented scale, along with information on the military strengths, communications, morale and dispositions in northern France. Militarily, the Allies would need to subdue the German *Luftwaffe* and the extensive RADAR systems that had been built along the Atlantic coastline. This was to be a secret war. It would include the work of special operation forces, including the Special Operations Executive (SOE), French Resistance, Special Air Service (SAS) and MI6, the acquisition of intelligence by an array of means including aerial reconnaissance and Signals Intelligence, and deception. Previous operations, such as Torch, in North Africa, had shown the value of a concerted deception campaign to fool the enemy. Overlord was also to involve psychological operations, using the combined efforts of the British Political Warfare Executive (PWE) and the American Office of War Information (OWI).

It was the JIC that was to provide the most overarching and strategic intelligence assessments for Overlord. From March 1944 these were considered so important to the planning of the Normandy campaign that the JIC assessments were produced on a daily basis. At the core of these assessments was Signals Intelligence (SIGINT). It was to be the most productive of intelligence providers to the JIC, and it was the ULTRA intercepts provided by Bletchley Park during the weeks leading up to June 1944 that were to be the crux of decision-making. SIGINT was to provide accurate estimates of the German forces, their locations and defences. Signals were also fundamental to the vast deception campaign that was being planned in parallel, to confuse the Germans into believing that the Allies were going to land in the Pas-de-Calais region, just across the Channel from Kent. The JIC Chairman, Victor Cavendish-Bentinck was to state that the deception plan would be the most, 'important and fruitful pieces of deception in the war'.

A security classification had to be introduced especially for Overlord, which kept operational detail held only at the highest level possible. Planning documents, letters and maps all featuring this mark restricted its distribution to only those with the special clearance. It was known as BIGOT, which stood for the British Invasion of German Occupied Territory. Several hundred individuals would have been given the clearance and access to the real details of the operation out of necessity. Those who had the clearance would have been put on the 'BIGOT list' and were banned from travelling outside the UK to avoid potential compromise of the Overlord plans. Those with the clearance became 'bigoted.' But secrecy went beyond documents. A top-secret transatlantic communications link was established, known as the Sigsaly or X-Ray telephone link, between Churchill and Roosevelt's office. It is alleged that Bletchley Park's most famous cryptologist, Alan Turing, worked on the security of the link.

As with all intelligence operations, Overlord was awash with codenames to obscure genuine objectives and placenames. In March 1944, SHAEF (Supreme Headquarters Allied Expeditionary Force) issued a directive to a number of command headquarters and government departments to disseminate to lower echelons of command. They were to be used in all communications, memoranda and over telephones instead of actual place names. The Normandy town of Caen, for example, was given the codename Camberley, Cherbourg became Yeovil, and Courseulles was referred to as Wicklow.

Befitting of its long line of famous military officers as former pupils, Clifton College in Bristol played a pivotal role in the planning of Overlord. Field Marshal Earl Haig and Field Marshal Lord Birdwood are two such alumni. Much of the coordination of the US First Army's share in the invasion and Normandy landings were made here during the early part of 1944.

Lieutenant General Sir Frederick Morgan was appointed into the role of Chief of Staff to the Supreme Allied Commander (COSSAC) in April 1943 to push forward the planning for Overlord. Initially a joint British and American headquarters was established, operating out of the former Lloyds Bank boardroom in Norfolk House on London's St James's Square. Its fledgling planning team presented an outline plan in the summer of 1943 to the Joint Chiefs of Staff which concluded that the Allied objective should be the poorly defended Calvados-Cotentin Peninsula. In the report Morgan was to comment, 'an operation of the magnitude of Operation Overlord has never previously been attempted in history. It is fraught with hazards, both in nature and magnitude, which do not obtain in any other theatre of the present world war. Unless these hazards are squarely faced and adequately overcome, the operation cannot succeed.'

Morgan was to recommend that the invasion force would comprise a three-division assault on to three beaches with a follow-up of a further two divisions to bolster the bridgehead. The plan set a date for May 1944.

When General Eisenhower was brought to Britain in January 1944 he took overall command of the invasion planning through SHAEF, which replaced the COSSAC role. The staff officers here had the onerous task of sifting through the wealth of intelligence now available to the Allies from multiple sources, such as the French Resistance and the Inter-Services Topographical Department (ISTD) based in Oxford.

It was Morgan's role to search for the most effective point on the French coastline to assault with sufficient force to have an established bridgehead. In May 1943 a Washington DC conference set out the framework for Overlord, for the invasion to occur in the spring of 1944.

General Eisenhower would refresh Morgan's plan but would keep much of his ideas alive in his plan for Overlord. 'Our main strategy in the conduct of the ground campaign was to land amphibious and airborne forces on the Normandy coast between Le Havre and the Cotentin peninsula and, with the successful establishment of a beachhead with adequate ports, to drive along the lines of the Loire and the Seine Rivers into the heart of France.'

It was under the US V Corps that a tactical headquarters was established in January 1942, under the command of Major General Russel P. Hartle and billeted at Clifton College. By July 1943, General Hartle was replaced by Major General Leonard T. Gerow, who led V Corps throughout the subsequent planning phases and eventual invasion of Normandy.

Each military command, such as SHAEF, follows a model aligned with a continental staff system to structure their respective staff functions:

1 – Personnel or manpower
2 – Intelligence and security
3 – Operations
4 – Logistics
5 – Plans
6 – Signals/Communications
7 – Training/Education
8 – Finance/Resource management
9 – Civil-Military cooperation

In original staff structures it was typical to just have 1–6 as branches, the latter three being relatively modern additions. The staff functions are typified with the prefix G, so the intelligence branch for SHAEF was designated G-2. But this staff structure applied to all three service arms, so A would refer to Air Force Headquarters, N for Navy Headquarters, G for Army Headquarters and J is often used for a joint headquarters.

As SHAEF began to mature, control of the various operational agencies came under the auspices of the G-2 Division, formed on 12 February 1944. It originally had a small intelligence staff. But the experiences of various senior officers, including Major General J.F.M. Whiteley, Assistant Chief of Staff, G-2 SHAEF, in the Mediterranean theatre with Allied Force Headquarters dictated that a merging of the Allied intelligence apparatus was necessary. This was to instigate the Theatre Intelligence Section (TIS) being integrated into SHAEF G-2 and was instrumental in providing detailed research intelligence for the Overlord planners. There was a pressing need for more detailed technical intelligence from the experiences the Allies had undergone in Italy. The Allies needed more effort and resource to examine and exploit enemy equipment and material.

The SHAEF G-2 Division was divided into a number of sub-sections to provide dedicated teams working on specific areas. The Naval Intelligence sub-division was formed in April 1944 to coordinate and disseminate Naval-focused intelligence. Another was the Operational Intelligence Sub-Division which 'was engaged in the collection, evaluation, and dissemination of intelligence of immediate tactical value as well as that of long-range strategic importance'. This was further divided into a series of sections:

a. **Enemy forces section**
   (1) German Army Sub-section – collated intelligence on German military dispositions, organisation and resources
   (2) Summaries Sub-section – published *Weekly Intelligence Summary* for G-2
   (3) *Fatherland* Sub-section – published *Fatherland*, a weekly publication covering intelligence on Germany (military, industry/economics and administration)

b. **Research section**
   (1) Engineer and Topographical Sub-section – terrain and topographical studies (such as water supplies, defences and health facilities) in collaboration with the Ministry of Economic Warfare (MEW), Inter-Services Topographical Department (ISTD), the Engineers at 21st Army Group, and MI10 in the War Office for intelligence on German communications
   (2) Operational Intelligence library – for collection and dissemination of intelligence for the sub-division
   (3) Defence Sub-section – intelligence on static German defences from all sources (POW, aerial reconnaissance, documents, SOE/SIS and French Resistance

31 St James's Square, London, home to General Eisenhower's SHAEF HQ or Norfolk House (© author)

agents). Worked closely with the Allied Central Interpretation Unit (ACIU) and ISTD

c. Enemy Plans and Logistics section

(1) Plans and Logistics Sub-section – assessed best value from strategic bombing. Collated intelligence on German military used of road, rail and water networks. Section worked closely with G-3 and G-4 SHAEF Divisions but also the Air Staff and Combined Services Strategic Targets Committee

(2) Enemy supply installations Sub-section – developed targeting material for Allied air forces, particularly on ammunition and fuel dumps. Worked closely with the ACIU at RAF Medmenham

(3) Enemy Communications Sub-section – worked closely with Air Reconnaissance elements to gather intelligence on German main supply routes, communications and rail systems

d. Air Reconnaissance Coordination section – coordinated all the demands on aerial reconnaissance resources

(1) Army Photographic Interpretation Sub-section – this key section for Overlord gathered photographic intelligence on coastal defences, supply dumps and inland defence structures and made it available to the various SHAEF staff divisions

e. Prisoner of War and Refugee section – receiving the bulk of its intelligence from the Combined Services Detailed Interrogation Centre (CSDIC), the Royal Patriotic School (RPS), MI19 and the Prisoner of War Interrogation Section (PWIS)

f. **Economics section** – gathered intelligence and advised on the German economic situation

g. **Enemy documents section** – established for the collection and exploitation of German documents

h. **Technical Intelligence section** – controlled the allocation of all captured enemy equipment and materials for technical intelligence assessment

i. **Circulation section** – distributed intelligence across the G-2 Division and across SHAEF

It was these staff functions established within SHAEF which created an effective intelligence dissemination structure. SHAEF Chief of Staff General Walter Bedell Smith was to state, 'the staff groups which contributed to the success of Overlord and the ultimate defeat of Germany were the exemplification of an idea of Allied unity, developed by General Eisenhower and perfected to such an extent that it has become the symbol of successful international cooperation.'

Operation Overlord was born out of some harsh lessons from previous operations. Operation Frankton, the raid on Bordeaux harbour by canoeists led by Major Blondie Hasler from the Royal Marines Boom Patrol Detachment (RMBPD) in December 1942 was marked a success but there was a parallel operation underway by the SOE to attack shipping in the same dock. At that time there was little operational coordination between the SOE and Combined Operations Headquarters. The lessons learned from this operation led to the creation of a Controller Office, to oversee operational activity and coordination between all components of the Armed Forces, covert Intelligence Agencies and Special Forces.

Operation Jubilee, the commando raid on the German occupied French port of Dieppe on 19 August 1942, was planned to probe the German defences to learn lessons which could be carried across to other commando raids and to the eventual invasion of Europe. This was a large-scale raid involving over 6,000, mostly Canadian, troops supported by Royal Marines Commandos. The force of 300 ships and 800 aircraft had as their mission to secure the heavily fortified town of Dieppe, which would show the Allies how serious Britain was in opening up a second front, and to some extent to be used as a propaganda tool. The attack commenced with an amphibious assault of the beaches either side of Dieppe, Puys and Pourville, to be followed thirty minutes later by a landing on the main beach by two Canadian infantry battalions – the Essex Scottish Regiment and the Royal Hamilton Light Infantry.

The raid was an experiment which was to go badly wrong. Allied planners and intelligence staff at Combined Headquarters had massively underrated the strength of the Dieppe defences and the topographical challenges encountered by an invasion force. The fundamental element of surprise was lost when the operation was delayed a month. It allowed German reconnaissance aircraft to undertake flights over the English coast, spotting the build-up of landing craft. They were aware an invasion force was targeting Dieppe from this aerial reconnaissance but also from signals intelligence. At the time the Allies did not have air supremacy over the Channel so the invasion forces would not have had sufficient aerial cover. The distinct lack of significant topographical intelligence for the beach and the hinterland meant that much of the heavy armour landed on the shingle beach floundered, denying the infantry heavy armour support. The naval fire support was also hopelessly inadequate to soften the hardened German defensive positions prior to the assault. But the lessons learned from Dieppe were to serve the Allies well for D-Day. Three months after Dieppe, the Allies landed in North Africa (Operation Torch), which forced the Germans on to the defensive. This successful invasion paved the way for the invasion of Sicily and then southern Italy.

One of the lessons Allied intelligence learnt from Jubilee was that for any future amphibious operations reconnaissance must be developed ahead of the development of a plan, to ensure that every detail and intelligence source was available to be supplemented by beach reconnaissance missions coordinated by the Navy. The Chief of Combined Operations, Mountbatten was to state 'for every one man who died in Dieppe in 1942, at least ten or more must have been spared in Normandy in 1944'.

Another mistake which emerged from the Dieppe raid post-mortem was focused on the Air Section at Government Code & Cipher School (GC&CS) Bletchley Park. The section had been informed of the raid just in time for one of the section's officers to be deployed to the Operational Headquarters, which gave no lead time for adjusting the communications service between the Headquarters and the Cheadle and Kingsdown intercept sites. There was also no time available to get Hut 6 or the Bletchley Directorate to assist with high echelon interception to cover the operation, so there was a clear void in valuable signals intelligence on the enemy reactions to the raid.

It was critical that the Allies should open a second front to relieve the pressure on the Russian army on the Eastern Front. In May 1943 the proposed invasion of Europe was given its name, Operation Overlord, and initial planning was undertaken by the COSSAC and superseded by the appointment of the Supreme Allied Commander General Dwight Eisenhower in January 1944.

The intelligence requirements of the Allies were vast – from what Hitler and Generalfeldmarschall Karl von Rundstedt were thinking, down to the technical specifications of the defensive RADAR systems, the gradient and slope of the beaches, even the composition of the concrete used for the gun emplacements, and the actual geological composition of the beaches. Every metaphoric stone needed to be turned for the invasion to be a success.

As the many forms of intelligence collected on German military activity in France began to mature, the JIC established the British Intelligence Objectives Sub-Committee (BIOS) to coordinate the multi-agency priorities around German targets. In parallel, the Americans developed the Field Information Agency Technical (FIAT) organisation to oversee target acquisition and intelligence prioritisation.

The hub of the initial planning for Overlord in 1943 and the early weeks of 1944 was Norfolk House, in St James's Square off one of London's most iconic streets, Pall Mall. It was at Norfolk House that the combined efforts of six different branches of Military Intelligence (MI), the Naval Intelligence Division (NID) at the Admiralty, the Allied Central Interpretation Unit (ACIU) at RAF Medmenham, and the Combined Operations HQ team came together and where all the strands of intelligence were being pulled together.

When General Eisenhower assumed the role of Supreme Allied Commander, the functions of COSSAC were morphed into SHAEF. Under Eisenhower's designated area of command, the European Theatre of Operations (ETO) meant he would have control over all the Allied forces for Overlord.

By March 1944 it was decided to move the SHAEF Headquarters to Bushy Park in West London, to a location called Camp Griffiss, a US Military base in the Teddington end of the Park. The HQ building became affectionately called *Widewing* and Eisenhower built himself a formidable team of seasoned British officers as his command team. One of his key officers was General Walter Bedell Smith who would directly oversee over 6000 men and 750 officers in the headquarters.

General Bernard Montgomery, the victor of El Alamein was to have command of the Land Forces, Admiral Bertram Ramsay was appointed the Naval Commander, and Air Chief Marshal Trafford Leigh-Mallory was put in command of the Allied Expeditionary Airforces. Sir Arthur Tedder became Eisenhower's Deputy ACM and General Walter Bedell Smith his Chief of Staff.

General Omar Bradley was withdrawn from the Mediterranean in October 1943 and assumed command of First Army Headquarters in Clifton College. Some of his dedicated II Corps staff from Sicily came with him. First Army Group was subdivided into three corps; V Corps, VII Corps in Plymouth and XIX Corps in Warminster. Intelligence activities within SHAEF were coordinated by the G-2 Intelligence Division commanded by a Major-General and his deputy, a US Army Brigadier-General. The division was sub-divided into five main sections:

1) Operational intelligence

2) Signals intelligence

3) Counter-Intelligence and censorship

4) Secretariat and organisation

5) Theatre intelligence

Intelligence policy and planning were the responsibility of the Assistant Chief of Staff. The divisions' main aims were to supply Eisenhower and his team with day-to-day operational intelligence.

One of its main functions, the collation of theatre intelligence, referred to detailed research intelligence during the planning stages of an operation like Overlord. This stream of intelligence would also be provisioned during operations, to continue 'to provide research intelligence as may be necessary, particularly with regard to interior defence lines and German dumps and lines of communication'.

The invasion forces for Overlord would eventually comprise the US First Army and British Second Army to make the 21st Army Group, which would be led by General Montgomery.

SHAEF HQ had no significant influence over the strategic bombing forces of the RAF Bomber Command and the US 8th Air Force who were concentrating their efforts on major German industrial areas and cities. They were not to shift their focus on Normandy until April 1944, but the impact they would have was considerable. A total of 76,200 tonnes of Allied bombs had hit the French railways, compromising the re-supply routes to the Atlantic Wall. By D-Day this had made 90 per cent of the French railway system inoperable.

On General Eisenhower's arrival in Britain in January 1944, the next four months would massively increase the workload of the operational commands and the demands for broad and wide-sweeping intelligence against a well entrenched enemy. Much of the key strategic Overlord decision-making was centred around SHAEF at Bushy and other London headquarters but in reality most of the actual planning was undertaken at Clifton College, as was the case for Operation Neptune, the naval invasion plan. The operations order for Neptune was issued to First Army Headquarters on 20 January 1944.

The nucleus of Bradley's planning offices was centred around the College's Council Room which housed the graphics and maps which adorned the walls and filing cabinets and desks full of troop dispositions and highly-classified top-secret BIGOT intelligence. Adjoining the Council Room was Wilson Tower, which housed the G-3 (Operations) and G-2 (Intelligence) offices. Further up the tower, in the crow's nest was the Headquarters Special Liaison Unit (SLU) which received top-secret ULTRA intercepts from GC&CS Bletchley Park. Most of this tower was under twenty-four hour armed guard. This ULTRA traffic was fundamental in assisting the planning

The Allies Chain of Command – July 1944

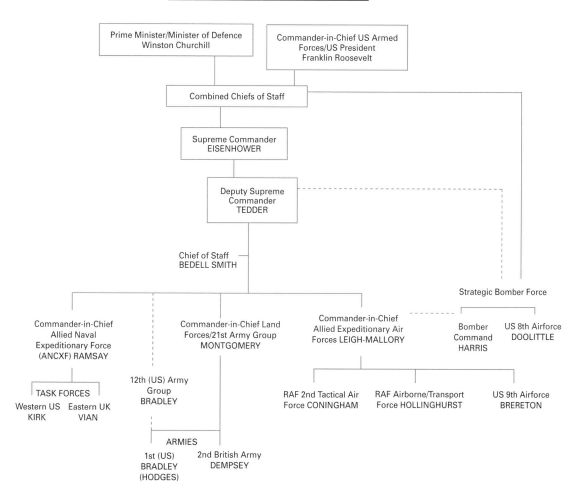

teams in making informed decisions around the German defensive positions in the Atlantic Wall and German troop dispositions in and around Normandy.

Before the Boer War, the British Army used to rely on forming temporary Military Intelligence structures during military campaigns to provide military commanders with timely intelligence and enemy information. The first permanent British intelligence agencies were established after the experiences in the Boer War. World War I reshaped military thinking and by the first years of World War II a sizeable military intelligence apparatus had evolved in Britain, under the War Office's Directorate of Military Intelligence control, to counter the threat from the Axis powers. Their roles

Southwick House, home to Overlord operational planners from April 1944 (© author)

and functions were markedly different and often changed over the course of the war.

MI1 – Codes & cipher (cryptography), which became GC&CS

MI2 – Russia and Scandinavia, Middle East, USA and Central/South America

MI3 – Germany, Eastern Europe and the Balkan states

MI4 – Aerial reconnaissance, transferred to military operations in April 1940

MI5 – Domestic intelligence and security

MI6 – Foreign intelligence and security

MI7 – Censorship and propaganda, transferred to the Ministry of Information in May 1940

MI8 – SIGINT, military interception/interpretation of enemy communications

MI9 – POW escape, escape and evasion behind enemy lines

MI10 – Weapons and technical analysis

MI11 – Field Security Police/Military security

MI12 – Military censorship

MI13 – Reconnaissance

MI14 – German specialists/intelligence

MI15 – Aerial photography, moved to Air Ministry in spring 1943

MI16 – Scientific intelligence, formed in 1945

MI17 – Secretariat body for Directorate of Military Intelligence (DMI), from April 1943

Admirals Ramsay, Vian and Creasy at Fort Southwick, May 1944 (© IWM London Photographic Archive – Reference A23719)

MI19 – POW debriefing unit, formed from MI 9 in December 1941

By February 1944, MI8(c) met its demise and the units work on collation and dissemination of technical information for telecommunications was transferred to MI8(a). This left a distinct void, and after continual protests from the Air Ministry due to the importance of this strand of intelligence, MI8(c) was reinstated by September 1944.

(MI18 remained classified and there was a supplementary independent organisation created called MI (JIS), as a sub-group of the Joint Intelligence Committee, to feed intelligence to the Allied planning staff.) All of these Military Intelligence sections were disbanded or dissolved into other organisations at the end of the war, bar MI5 and MI6 which still exists to this day.

There were a large number of agencies and departments which would feed intelligence into SHAEF HQ. On the American side this would include the usual military service teams at G2 Division of the War Department General Staff, the A2 Division of the USAAF, and the Office of Naval Intelligence in the Department of the Navy. It would also include the US State Department and the various US embassies and attachés. Because of the nature of Overlord, it was the British agencies and departments that were to dominate the intelligence domain for SHAEF. Intelligence was received from a vast array of sources including the Ministry of Economic Warfare (MEW), Joint Intelligence Committee (JIC), BBC Monitoring Service at Caversham, the Political

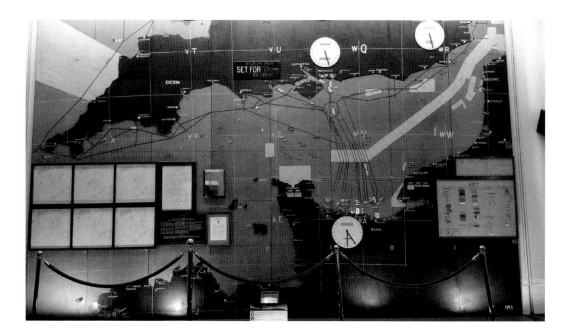

The D-Day wall map at Southwick House, as it was on 6 June 1944 (© author)

Warfare Executive (PWE) and Inter-Service Topographical Department (ISTD) based at the University of Oxford. The services intelligence arms were also integral to SHAEF, from the Director of Military Intelligence in the War Office, Naval Intelligence Division (NID) at the Admiralty and the Air Intelligence branch at the Air Ministry. With the number of commando raids that took place between 1941 and June 1944, the Combined Operations Headquarters also had a significant role in the supply of intelligence to SHAEF.

NID played a pivotal role in the collation of intelligence for Overlord and its naval phase, Neptune. By D-Day NID ranks had swollen to nearly 2,000 staff, based out of Room 39 in the Admiralty under the direction of Admiral Sir Reginald 'Blinker' Hall. It had over twenty separate sections which covered specific geographic or technical areas but its heartbeat was centred around the NID17 section which was in effect its clearing house. NID17 had senior officers involved in a number of Joint planning committees for Overlord /Neptune and contained some influential figures. These included Lieutenant Commander Ian Fleming (17F) (who was to go on to write the first James Bond books), who developed the idea that became 30 Assault Unit. He was to act as the liaison with the Special Operations Executive (SOE), the Secret Intelligence Service (SIS or MI6) and the Political Warfare Executive (PWE). Alongside Fleming was Commander Drake, who would represent NID at the Joint Planners meeting or JIC to discussed intelligence requirements, Lieutenant Commander Montagu RNVR who led on the deception operations for Naval Intelligence, including the infamous

Operation Mincemeat whereby a body was obtained and dressed up as a Royal Marines officer. After planting false documentation on him about an Allied invasion of Greece, his body was unceremoniously dumped into the sea off the southern coast of Spain, knowing that it would be picked up eventually by German intelligence.

NID17 also had a Commander Lewes RN, who acted as its link to the Inter-Service Service Board (ISSB) which liaised directly with MI5 and MI6. Fundamental to what was required for Normandy, the ex-Barrister Lieutenant Commander Christopher Shawcross RNVR provided a vital link to the ISTD, which was formed under the umbrella of naval sections NID5 and NID6 at the University of Oxford. He was to supervise the output of topographical intelligence and the production of their most valued geographical handbooks.

The Joint Intelligence Staff was the feeder for the JIC – as the top of the Intelligence hierarchy in Britain it required knowledge of enemy capabilities and intentions and all the MI organisations established were to provide this intelligence. From there the JIC would provide guidance and advice to the Prime Minister, Winston Churchill, and the Chiefs of Staff.

Montgomery's Chief Intelligence Officer from August 1942, Sir Edgar Williams, said, 'Military Intelligence is always out of date... there is a built in time-lag. Better the

MI Directorate – July 1944

best half-truth on time than the whole truth too late.... In battle, we deal not with the true but with the likely. Speed is therefore of the essence of the matter.'

One of the main British intelligence officers involved with the Overlord planning was Commander George Edmund Gonin who had lived and worked in Belgium during the inter-war years. As World War II unfurled, he was put in charge of a sub-section of the Naval Intelligence Division (NID) in the Admiralty, in charge of the provision of intelligence for operations in France, as well as Holland and German-occupied Belgium. He was responsible for the intelligence behind the commando raids on the port of St Nazaire in 1942 and the infamous raid on the Bruneval RADAR installation (Operation Biting). After his time at the Admiralty, Gonin was transferred to John Austin's Theatre Intelligence Section (TIS) assisting with the direction of the planning for Overlord.

In January 1943 NID produced a secret report highlighting the German preparations to defend the key ports in northern France. It made it clear that the German's intent was to deny the use of these ports to the Allied landing force wherever it was to go ashore. The report detailed a number of precautions which the Germans were instituting:

a) The laying of controlled minefields in approaches to certain ports. These may be worked in conjunction with shore detection units.

b) Considerable increase in the number and efficiency of booms, which are now placed across all important approach channels and harbour entrances. They are usually double or treble line booms, of both anti-submarine and anti-boat type. It is possible that some have warning devices attached thereto.

c) Preparations to block ports or approaches with blockships and with special concrete barges known as Bruges units.

d) The systematic mining of quays and port installations.

After the successful D-Day landings, Allied intelligence was filled with optimism, but this was to fade as the Normandy campaign went on into its first week and the Allies met a skilful and determined enemy. Normandy would become an attritional battle, resulting in the deaths or injury of 60,000 men in the first three weeks alone.

Towards D-Day, Allied intelligence had developed a good understanding of the strength of the German forces operating in France. At the Casablanca Conference in 1943, the intelligence estimates of the German divisional strength of fifty-eight divisions, which was only one off the actual fifty-nine divisions total.

Allied intelligence had much to learn about the defensive positions on the Atlantic Wall if Overlord was to progress and not turn into another Dieppe. Key to this was a broad and comprehensive collection of all sources of intelligence interwoven with one of the most detailed deception and propaganda plans ever devised. They had to convince the German High Command that the main thrust of the Allied assault would be in the Pas-de-Calais region. They also had to keep Overlord a secret from the outset. Security was vital.

However, intelligence is not a perfect science. It is often inconclusive in its assessments. There are flaws, there are mistakes, and the Normandy campaign was no exception. D-Day had to succeed.

CHAPTER TWO

BLUFF

'A belt of strongpoints and gigantic fortifications runs from Kirkenes (Norway) to the Pyrenees … it is my unshakable decision to make this front impregnable against every enemy.'

Adolf Hitler, 11 December 1941

By the spring of 1943 the tide was beginning to turn against Hitler. The Dieppe raid in August 1942 had changed the German mindset on its fortification strategy for Europe. Dieppe had been selected by the Allies, as it was one of the typical fortified ports along the stretch of coast that the Allies would be faced with when Overlord was to take place. They needed to probe the defences and ask questions of the German response. The German defences were successful in repelling the commando raid and it had demonstrated the need for the Atlantic Wall. Hitler had interpreted the Dieppe raid to be a failed Allied landing and he was convinced that the Allies would at first aim to seize the key Atlantic ports on the French coast.

The idea behind an all expansive Atlantic Wall, a series of defensive fortifications along the French coastline, was first muted in September 1941 by Generalfeldmarschall von Witzleben. There were over 3,000 miles of coastline stretching from the North Cape (Nordkapp) of Norway to the Brittany port of Brest. Von Witzleben was to point out that the only significant coastal batteries were the seven fortifications between Calais and Boulogne. But when Hitler issued his now famous *Küstenverteidigung* (Coastal Defence) Directive No. 40 on 23 March 1942, work began in earnest by *Organisation Todt* (OT) under the leadership of Generalfeldmarschall Karl von Rundstedt. In the Normandy region, his priority was to be the areas of coastline by the tidal rivers and to construct significant coastal batteries to cover the wide expanse of beaches on this stretch of coast.

Hitler wanted the wall to follow some key guidelines:

a) No interference with U-Boat traffic in and out of their bases. The U-boat bases had to be completed and prepared for defence.
b) Key strategic ports had to be made inaccessible to a landing force, drawing the

Allies to land on a less protected coastline, making logistical resupply more difficult.

c) Defensive positions and firepower had to be strengthened to maximise effect against a landing force. Coastal artillery would need to have sufficient range to hit Allied shipping.

d) Coastal batteries had to have reinforced concrete roofs as protection from aerial attack.

The contracts to build Hitler's Atlantic Wall had been given to OT, the civil engineering company under its founder Fritz Todt whom had previously built the infamous Siegfried Line between France and Germany. He was in charge of the early stages of construction of the wall until his death in February 1942 after his Heinkel 111 aircraft crashed. His successor was Albert Speer, who drove forward the design and construction of the Normandy wall.

Much of the work in this part of Normandy was choreographed by the *Oberbauleitung Normandie* (the Construction sector, OT HQ) based in St Malo. Labour was provided from foreign workers at camps, Belgian and Dutch deportees and localised French workers. Most Frenchmen were roped in to work on the defences through the *Service Travail Obligatoire* (STO) or compulsory labour service which was introduced nationwide by the Germans from October 1942. In Paris alone the STO scheme recruited 20,000 men every month for this forced labour.

The Reich introduced a compulsory labour scheme in occupied France, drafting in over 600,000 workers to construct these fortifications along the coastline of France. Many of the workers were free Russians and forced labour (*Zwangsarbeiter)* who were typically captured partisans. They were often under military escort, in comparison to the free Russians who moved around independently. In many areas they used Spanish Republicans (*Rotspanier*), or Dutch/Flemish (*Vlamen*) workers, which made up around 10 per cent of the workforce.

The Germans created a *zone interdite* (forbidden zone) extending 12 miles inland from the Normandy coast. Many of the feeder roads to the area had vehicle checkpoints and carriers manned by permanent German sentries.

Key German individuals involved with the shaping of plans for the Atlantic Wall with the German High Command and Hitler himself were Reich Minister Albert Speer, who was the then head of the OT and Generalleutnant Rudolf Schmetzer who was the Inspector of Land Forces for the Western Front. OT was not under the direct command of the *Wehrmacht*, but was, in many respects, considered a subsidiary or *Wehrmachtsgefolge*.

Concrete was the solution to Hitler's defensive impasse. The new Atlantic Wall was to involve the construction of 15,000 concrete fortifications which were to be defended by a force of over 300,000 men. Hitler wanted the defences completed by May 1943, but Speer was of the opinion that less than 40 per cent of the work would be completed by then. It was at this time during the war that there was a huge demand in Germany for enormous quantities of concrete and steel for the construction of submarine shelters and V1/V2 rocket launch sites. These had the priority from the German High Command, as it was thought these new weapons and submarine warfare in the Atlantic would win the war quickly for Hitler. The construction of the defensive positions would utilise nearly 1.2 million tonnes of steel and an estimated 17.6 million tonnes of concrete. The OT could produce a maximum of 450,000 cubic metres of concrete a month. Alongside the staggering concrete output, the preparation and groundwork of the construction sites involved moving over 25 million cubic metres of earth.

During World War II, Germany had two competing Intelligence departments. The German Military and Inter-Service Intelligence Service or *Abwehr* (which means 'Defence') was something of an anomaly in Germany, with many of its officers drawn from the upper classes – from the old Imperial Army and Navy. Established in 1920, it acted as the secret intelligence service for the German High Command. The other was the Nazi party's *Sicherheitsdienst* (SD), which was entirely separate from the *Abwehr*.

The organisation was centred on the *Tirpitzufer*, the *Abwehr* HQ in Berlin, which was led from January 1935 by Admiral Wilhelm Franz Canaris. In France, the *Abwehr* were headquartered at the Hotel Lutetia in Paris with a number of outstations around the country. The *Abwehr* often worked as the executive arm of other units such as the *Geheim Feld Polizei* (GFP) or military units.

The *Abwehr* had four departments or *Abteilungen* (Abts), each with a distinct role:

Abt 1 – Espionage
Abt 2 – Sabotage and Subversion
Abt 3 – Counter-Espionage and Protective Security
Abt Z – General Administrative department serving the whole organisation

The *Abwehr* was defined by its poor centralised control. It had the appearance of a functioning single organisation, but the reality was more of a loose conglomeration of differing groups which often competed against each other for power and influence.

The Nazi Party Intelligence organisation, the *Sicherheitsdienst* (SD), which fell under the direction and control of the *Reichsführer Schutzstaffel* (SS) was established from 1936 as both the State and Party intelligence service. One of its key figures was the

The German High Command

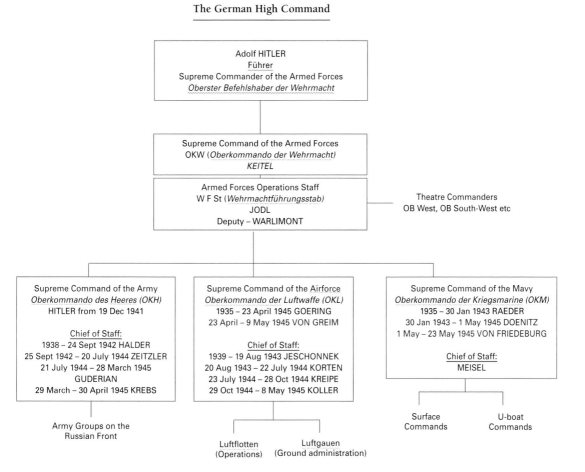

head of the foreign intelligence section in SD, Walther Schellenberg.

It was the OKW, the German Supreme Command (or *Oberkommando der Wehrmacht*) in Zossen, just outside Berlin, that was to collect and assess intelligence from the intelligence arms of the Army, Navy and Airforce, as well as the *Sicherheitsdienst* (SD) and *Abwehr*. When the Abwehr was absorbed into SD, Schellenberg would insist that all intelligence material would pass through his office to reach the OKW, and ultimately Hitler. He had argued this was to ensure the timeliness and accuracy of intelligence would reach the senior commanders, but in reality this was about the inter-service rivalries and Schellenberg exercising control.

The *Abwehr* changed markedly when Admiral Canaris was removed from his position by Hitler in January 1944, a critical period during the Overlord planning.

Hitler wanted to administer control and dominance over his disparate intelligence organisations after a failed coup attempt. His subsequent reorganisation caused the assimilation of both the *Abwehr* and SD. This founded the new *Reichssicherheitshauptamt* (RSHA) or Reich Main Security Office under the direction of Heinrich Himmler. This refurbished organisation was no more successful than any of its predecessors and these internal feuds and power games in German Intelligence helped the Allies effectively prosecute a successful invasion in Normandy.

In France, mirroring the RHSA structures, German intelligence and security was maintained through the German Security Police (*Sicherheitspolizei* or SIPO) and SD personnel. Paris was under the control of the *Höhere SS-und Polizeiführer* (Higher SS and Police Commander) or HSSPF. They controlled all the police services in France. Out in the regions the *Kommandeur der Sipo* (KdS) offices maintained security and order. In cities as widespread as Rouen, Paris, Bordeaux, Nancy, Rennes and Anger, KdS offices were established with a similar organisational structure. The offices, which were an amalgamation of SD, Kripo (Criminal Police) and Gestapo staff, were overseen typically by a Commander and Deputy Commander.

The OKW was split into two separate intelligence departments: the *Fremde Heere Ost* (FHO) and the *Fremde Heere West* (FHW). FHO dealt with the intelligence from the Eastern Front, FHW from the Western Front. FHW was commanded by a Prussian officer, Colonel Alexis Baron von Roenne, and heavily relied on signals intelligence from the German Y Service. In the beginning of 1944, FHW had been given the task of producing an order of battle for the Allied invasion force. Lieutenant Colonel Roger Michel was posted to Rommel's headquarters from FHW to assist with this work, and in January 1944 he forwarded an estimate to Hitler of the number of Allied divisions preparing for the invasion in southern England. Michel reported to von Roenne that the report had been intercepted at Schellenberg's office and the number of divisions halved. Schellenberg had wanted to emphasise to Hitler that the SD intelligence was more significant than that collected at FHW.

During the winter of 1943–4 Schellenberg's teams in SD were pursuing intelligence on the French Resistance networks and yielding some results. But none of this intelligence was shared with military units or commanders on the ground. This was contrary to FHO, under the leadership of General Reinhard Gehlen, which produced regular intelligence reporting and assessments on the Russian military capabilities on the Eastern Front. This disseminated through the chains of command and to individual military commanders.

One of the failures of German intelligence is reflected in what we had in Britain. The British Chiefs of Staff established a Joint Intelligence Committee (JIC) at the beginning of World War II. The OKW had no such body to oversee inter-service intelligence

German troops constructing landing craft obstructions (© Bundesarchiv_ Bild_1011-297-1716-28)

coordination. As Führer, Hitler was the top of the food chain for intelligence. His subordinates had access to constrained areas of Intelligence collection and analysis but he and only he would have access to all of it. The onus was upon him to make the key strategic decisions on that intelligence. In terms of Normandy, defence was dependent on good intelligence, and by June 1944 German intelligence was lacking in many areas of collection, analysis and assessment on the Allied invasion plans, which was exposed with the effect that the Allied deception operations would have.

A problem that undermined the German capabilities to defend the coast was its almost fractured and archaic command structures in command in northern France. In overall command of the German forces was Generalfeldmarschall Karl von Rundstedt but when Rommel arrived in January 1944 it led to a number of disputes between the two men. They were both of the same rank but von Rundstedt was the more senior of the two. However, Rommel was idolised by Hitler for what he had achieved in North Africa. Rommel had been taken in by German propaganda that the Atlantic Wall was Hitler's *Festung Europa* or Fortress Europe, but on seeing it firsthand he knew this was bluff.

The German *Wehrmacht* in Western Europe was divided into Army Groups and the various disparate command groups and military hierarchies meant there was a lack of coherent decision-making in Normandy. Group B stretched from the Netherlands to the Loire under the command of Rommel. Group G covered the region between the French Alps, Spain and the Mediterranean coast, and was led by Colonel General Johannes Blaskowitz. Both Army Groups were subservient to von Rundstedt's command. One of the most experienced World War II German officers in armoured warfare, General Leo Geyr von Schweppenburg, commanded another army unit in the region, the Armoured Forces in the West which comprised all the Panzer Divisions. Whilst he was directly subordinate to von Rundstedt, he was also accountable to Colonel General Heinz Wilhelm Guderian who carried the title of Inspector General of Armoured Forces.

Although von Rundstedt carried notable authority over the German forces in France, he had no command authority to coordinate the resources from the *Luftwaffe*, *Kriegsmarine* or Army. Both he and Rommel had little control over decision-making on the *Organisation Todt* in the construction of the defensive fortifications in Normandy. They took their direction directly from the OKW and Albert Speer, the Minister for Armaments and War Production. Von Rundstedt would have in the region of 850,000 *Wehrmacht* troops comprised of thirty-six infantry divisions, around half of which had no mobile artillery or even transport.

German Command in the West, January – August 1944

OKW

OKL

OKM

Luftflotte 3 SPEERLE

Oberbefehlshaber West (OB West)
1 May 1942 – 3 July 1944 VON RUNDSTEDT
Chief of Staff BLUMENTRITT
3 July 1944 – 17 Aug 1944 VON KLUGE

Chief of Staff BLUMENTRITT
17 Aug 1944 – 5 Sept 1944 MODEL
5 Sept 1944 – 10 Mar 1945 VON RUNDSTEDT
Cheif of Staff WESTPHAL
10 Mar 1945 – 7 May 1945 KESSELRING

Marinegruppe West KRANKE

Heeresgruppe B (Army Group B)
5 Nov 1943 – 17 July 1944 ROMMEL
Chief of Staff SPEIDEL
17 July – 17 Aug 1944 VON KLUGE (also OB West)
17 Aug 1944 – 21 April 1945 MODEL

Panzergruppe West
1943 – 5 July 1944
GEYR VON SCHWEPPENBURG
5 July – 10 Aug 1944 EBERBACH

Heeresgruppe G (Army Group G)
12 May 1944 – 17 Jan 1945
BLASKOWITZ
28 Jan – 2 Apr 1945 HAUSSER

7 Army
Channel coast, Brittany –
River Seine
1943 – 23 June 1944 DOLLMANN
29 June – 21 Aug 1944 HAUSER
22 Aug 1944 – 21 Apr 1945
EBERBACH

15 Army
Channel and North Sea
coast. River Seine to
Dutch/German border
VON SALMUTH

1 Army
Atlantic Coast
VON DER
CHEVALLERIE

19 Army
Mediterranean
Coast
VON
SODENSTERN

Both Guderian and Schweppenburg were protagonists of deploying reserve panzer divisions north of Paris to immediately deploy on the point of an Allied invasion to mount a massive armoured counter-attack. This went against Rommel's strategy of forward mounting a defence as close to the landing beaches as possible. Rommel had suspected the Allies were considering Normandy as their objective, even recognising the similarity of the beaches on the western fringes – which would become Omaha – being almost identical in features to the Italian landing sites at Salerno.

Rommel had been charged by Hitler to undertake an inspection of the coastal defences in the west and report back on their ability to repel an Allied invasion. Under guidance from his Chief of Staff, General Gausi, he was accompanied on the inspection tour with Vice-Admiral Friedrich Ruge, who was at that time the commander of German *Kriegsmarine* forces in Italy and had commanded minesweeper forces prior to that. Their inspection of the Danish section of the Atlantic Wall was to take ten days. Shortly after this Rommel moved the Army Group B Headquarters to Fountainebleau and with Ruge's assistance poured over maps and charts of the French coastal defences. Rommel had not set foot in France since 1940 and what he saw of the defences appalled him. He himself had been taken in by the German propaganda machine and had not realised how poor the defences were.

Rommel completed and submitted his report to Hitler on 22 April 1944. He provided some worthy praise on the speed of progress but was concerned that the defences were in need of bolstering to repel any concerted Allied invasion. Rommel stated that, 'our defences, together with the sea, represent one of the strongest defence lines in history … the enemy must be annihilated before he reaches our main battlefield … from week to week the Atlantic Wall will grow stronger and the equipment of our troops manning the defences will get better. Considering the strength of our defences and the courage, ability and the determination to fight being displayed by all our soldiers, we can look forward with the utmost confidence to the day when the enemy will attack the Atlantic Wall.'

Defensive coastal batteries had been constructed to protect the major ports on the northern coast of France and were linked to the Army Coastal Artillery. The inspection had found many of these Army artillery positions had no aerial cover so were very susceptible to attacks from the air, unlike the naval guns which were typically entombed in a steel cupola. There was also insufficient minelaying around the defensive positions. In over three years of construction just 1.7 million mines had been laid, no shallow-water mines had been laid below the low water mark. The obstacles to deter an amphibious landing were woefully inadequate and largely ineffective against the tanks in service.

After the high level inspections, Rommel was to issue orders to his subordinate

Construction of a
Normandy heavy
gun placement
(© ADM 202/599)

commands to bolster the defensive positions along the coast, and with a degree of urgency. Even then, he was to notice a distinct lethargy with units unwilling to carry out his orders. By April 1944 Rommel was to write, '… I noticed units that do not seem to have recognised the graveness of the hour and some who do not even follow instructions. There are reports of cases in which my orders that all minefields on the beach should be alive at all times have not been obeyed … in other cases my orders have been postponed to later dates or even changed … some units knew my orders but did not make any preparations to execute them.'

Rommel was to persuade Hitler, after his inspection tour, of the need for more concrete. The defensive batteries were to each have at least 6 ft of concrete overhead to protect from aerial attack. But even then, many of the batteries faced by the Allies in the Normandy landings still had no overhead cover, due simply to the supply shortages of concrete.

Regardless of concrete, Rommel and his team managed to bolster many of the Normandy defences in the early part of 1944, despite all the shortages of supplies. He was to increase minelaying across the whole region, laying an additional four million mines, many of which were just converted old or obsolete artillery shells. Rommel had a creative mind and conceptually designed some of the beach obstacles that were to face the Allies on the beaches themselves. Inland, farmers' fields were scattered with long wooden stakes, wired together with mines (the aptly named 'Rommel's asparagus') to impede airborne troops landing in gliders. By June 1944, the Germans had completed over 12,000 fortifications along the Atlantic Wall, including an estimated half-a-million individual obstacles.

The critical concept behind the German defensive systems in place in Normandy was the layering of obstacles. The beach obstacles themselves were arranged in order of height and often in rows of three, in parallel to the high and low tide marks. These were typically spaced evenly apart by 5 yards. The obstacles included triangular tetrahedral, and 'Czech hedgehogs', both steel girders welded together to rip the hulls of landing craft as they came ashore. Much larger 'Element C' or 'Belgian Gates', as they were more commonly referred to, were around 10 ft high and wide, and were the most impressive of the obstacles. These had been originally designed for the defence of the Maginot Line by French General Léon-Edmond de Cointet de Fillain.

The beaches were often strewn with rows of wooden stakes buried into the sand. Many of these obstacles would be mined, typically the common Teller mine or sometimes with French 75 mm artillery shells. Even offshore, the minefields would pose a significant challenge to the Neptune landing forces as they came close to the shoreline. The German *Kriegsmarine* had also built their own deadly obstacles, a makeshift wooden raft strapped together with several Teller mines. Beyond these rows of obstacles on the beach, Allied invaders would also have to contend with the barbed wire, machine gun nests, gun emplacements and pill boxes. It was a proverbial killing ground.

Rommel was convinced the invasion would come in the Pas-de-Calais region and he wanted control of his Panzer reserves so they could be moved when necessary to bolster his coastal defensive positions. He knew if the Allies could not get pushed back into the sea on the beaches then the war would be lost. Von Runstedt wanted the Panzer divisions nearer Paris so they could be deployed easier to where the invasion was to occur. This strategy by Rommel and von Rundstedt was to shape the thinking of Hitler, that the Germans would need strength in depth, a significant reserve force to mount a counter-attack.

The invasion would have to be repelled quickly before the Allies could establish a bridgehead. Rommel knew this: 'we must stop the enemy in the water and destroy his equipment while it is still afloat.' It was an enormous task. German forces had to defend over 3,000 miles of coastline with only fifty-nine divisions, many of them second-rate or convalescing from the Eastern Front and only ten being armoured. Rommel knew he would need strength in depth. Some of the key batteries that would defend the Normandy coast were to be a considerable barrier to the Allied advance during Overlord. The four 15 cm guns at the Merville battery laying half a mile inland would have impeded the British landings on Sword Beach, and Pointe du Hoc – with its six 155 mm French howitzers, with a range of 23 kilometres – could have scuppered the American landings at Omaha and Utah. Intelligence on these significant defensive batteries was going to be critical for understanding how they could be subdued during the assault phase of the operation.

Gen Rommel
inspecting the
German defences
on the Normandy
beaches, April 1944
(© Bundesarchiv_
Bild_101I-719-
0243-33)

But during the Normandy campaign the concerted efforts of the French Resistance and Allied special forces teams, such as the Jedburgh and Sussex teams, were to delay and impede some of the key German armoured divisions. The elite Panzer Lehr Division, under the command of General Bayerlein, 90 miles south of Caen took over three days to get to the frontline in Normandy, losing five tanks, 130 trucks and artillery pieces in the process.

Montgomery knew how his adversary and sparring partner from North Africa would operate in defending the French coast. He had witnessed a shrewd tactician and inspirational commander. 'On D-Day he will try (a) to force us from the beaches; (b) to secure Caen, Bayeux, Carentin. Thereafter he will continue his counter-attacks.... We must blast our way on shore and get a good lodgement before he can bring up sufficient reserves to turn us out. Armoured columns must penetrate deep inland and quickly … the air must hold the ring and must make very difficult the movement of enemy reserves by train or road towards the lodgement areas.'

What transpired was that individual Panzer divisions were put under the command of both Rommel and von Rundstedt. The delays in mobilising these defensive Panzer reserve divisions was ultimately to cost the Germans dearly and led to the final outcome of D-Day.

German military intelligence of Allied intentions for an invasion had glaring gaps in it. The bitter inter-service rivalries, the internal division within intelligence departments and lack of cooperation with the civil agencies was to have a marked effect on how much insight into Allied plans the German High Command would get before D-Day. It would also allow the Allied deception plans to get more traction within the German intelligence services.

Many of the German senior officers in northern France had little faith in the Atlantic Wall being significant enough to repel an Allied invasion. Von Rundstedt himself declared it a 'bit of cheap bluff'. He doubted his own defences would hold the Allies back for even twenty-four hours. Key defensive positions dotted along the coast, typically around the key strategic ports would be a formidable challenge. But in between these the defences were weak and there was little in terms of a continuous line. Where the Germans were expecting an Allied invasion, in the Pas-de-Calais region for example, there were ninety-three coastal batteries with a further thirty-nine mobile heavy guns available. In comparison, the stretch of the Normandy coast that the Allies were targeting during Overlord was covered by just twenty-seven coastal batteries and twenty mobile heavy guns.

CHAPTER THREE
PINPRICK

'No war can be conducted successfully without early and good intelligence.'

John Churchill, the First Duke of Marlborough

~~~

As Overlord planning progressed, raids needed to be more effectively managed, and Lord Mountbatten, as Chief of Combined Operations (CCO), would coordinate them through his delegated staff. As CCO, Mountbatten was ultimately responsible for obtaining approval for a raid from the Chiefs of Staff Committee of which he was a member. Invariably, the most significant agreement needed to come from the Naval Commander-in-Chief, as typically the raids involved some naval or amphibious component.

The raids on the French coast can be trailed back to as early as June 1940. These initial small-scale insertions by highly trained commando units were originated by the Combined Operations Organisation under the direction of Churchill's close confidant, Admiral of the Fleet Sir Roger Keyes. Towards the latter end of 1943, as the plans for Overlord were starting to mature, the Allied commanders needed to get specialist troops routinely on to the beaches to reconnoitre the defensive positions and establish what level of opposition the invasion forces might face. There is often no substitute for the 'Mark I' eyeball, seeing the land and defences at close-quarters. Whilst aerial reconnaissance from Medmenham was vitally important to Allied planners, having specialist troops ashore on the target beach would provide a localised sea-level view for which there was no substitute. Much of this intelligence-gathering work was tasked to the men of the No. 10 (Inter-Allied) Commando, who would also capture German soldiers if the opportunity arose.

These pinprick raids by highly trained commandos were a vital element of gathering close-hand intelligence on the beaches that would then be used for Overlord. Many of these raids were failures, but a few of them provided Allied planners with vitally important information on the landing beaches that would be used in June 1944. Keyes was succeeded in his role in October 1941 by Admiral Lord Louis Mountbatten

As CCO, Admiral Mountbatten formulated a request levied on all commando forces for probes of the German defences on the northern French coasts. He was told by Churchill, 'You are to plan for the offensive. In your headquarters you will never think defensively.' These raids had a number of key strategic objectives:

- to carry out vital reconnaissance of the invasion beaches for Overlord to better understand the beach defences
- to capture German prisoners for follow-on interrogation
- to gather equipment and documents for intelligence purposes
- or more generally to destroy defensive positions and harass the enemy.

Each beach was topographically very different, with varying geology and gradients. The beach obstacles, minefields and defensive positions all needed to be probed to find weaknesses. Their offshore tides and currents fluctuated. The hinterland needed to be assessed for its ability to support the construction of new airfields and nearby ports had to be researched to ascertain what capacity they would have to mount a sustained naval logistics link back to England.

The coastline between Cherbourg and Le Havre was pockmarked with defensive fortifications and casemates but this stretch of coast had no real port that the Allies could utilise during the invasion. It was one of the reasons why the German High Command thought the Allies would strike further up the coast, in the Pas-de-Calais region. They reasoned a large and sustained invasion force would need immediate access to a port to gain a foothold. The Allies would play to this game as part of the deception plan.

One of the first of these commando raids was Operation Chess on the night of the 27–28 July 1941 by sixteen raiders led by 2nd Lieutenant Philip Pinkney. The team from No. 12 Commando crossed the Channel in a Landing Craft Assault (LCA) to raid Ambleteuse just west of Calais. Although the commandos were only ashore for a short period of time, they managed to acquire numerous pieces of intelligence, including some wiring from the German defensive positions.

On the night of the 12/13 November 1941, a four-man team of commandos from No. 101 (Folbot) Troop, No. 6 Commando clambered ashore in the dead of night near the town of Houlgate in France. Operation Astrakan was the first significant beach reconnaissance operation in northern France and it set a benchmark for future commando raids and reconnaissance missions in the lead-up to D-Day. The Astrakan commandos fortunately did not encounter any German soldiers but they did gather information on the beach itself and its suitability for use by Allied landing craft.

Just ten days after Astrakan, 101 Troop undertook a further raid against a German coastal battery outside the town of Houlgate, east of the River Dives. Houlgate was to be a significant position thirty months later as the battery was used to cover the beaches which Overlord aimed to assault. The intelligence gleaned in this reconnaissance would help planners understand the defensive positions around the battery which was heavily bombed shortly before D-Day.

DATE	OPERATION	FORCE	TARGET
24–25 June 1940	COLLAR	No. 11 Independent Commando	Boulogne Le Touquet
27–28 July 1941	CHESS	No. 12 Commando	Ambleteuse
30–31 August 1941	ACID DROP	No. 3 Commando	Neufchâtel-Hardelot Merlimont
27–28 September 1941	CHOPPER	No. 1 Commando	Courselles/Saint-Aubin-d'Arquenay
27–28 September 1941	DEEP CUT	No. 1 Commando	St Vaast
12–13 November 1941	ASTRAKAN	No. 6 Commando	Houlgate
22–23 November 1941	SUNSTAR	No. 9 Commando	East of Houlgate
17–18 January 1942	CURLEW	V Corps of Raiding	St Laurent
17–18 February 1942	BITING	1st Parachute Battalion	Bruneval
27–28 March 1942	CHARIOT	No. 2 Commando (complemented by personnel from 1, 3, 4, 5, 9 and 12 Commando)	St Nazaire
5 April 1942	MYRMIDON	No. 1 and No. 6 Commando	Ardour estuary
11–12 April 1942	JV	No. 6 Commando	Boulogne-sur-Mer
21–22 April 1942	ABERCROMBIE	No. 4 Commando	Neufchâtel-Hardelot
3–4 June 1942	BRISTLE	No. 6 Commando	St Cecile
14–15 August 1942	BARRICADE	No. 62 Commando	Pointe de Saire
19 August 1942	JUBILEE	No. 3 and No. 4 Commando, 2nd Canadian Infantry Division	Dieppe
12–13 September 1942	AQUATINT	No. 62 Commando (SSRF)	Ste Honorine
11–12 November 1942	FAHRENHEIT	No. 12 and No. 62 Commando	Plouézec
15–16 November 1942	BATMAN	No. 12 and No. 62 Commando	Cherbourg
11–12 December 1942	FRANKTON	RMBPD	Bordeaux
3–4 July 1943	FORFAR EASY	No. 12 Commando	Onival
5–6 July 1943	FORFAR DOG	No. 12 Commando	Biville
3–4 August 1943	FORFAR LOVE	Special Boat Section (SBS)	Dunkirk
3–5 August 1943	FORFAR BEER	No. 12 Commando	Életot
2–3 September 1943	FORFAR ITEM	No. 12 Commando; No. 3 Tp, No. 10 Commando	St-Valery-en-Caux

DATE	OPERATION	FORCE	TARGET
3–4 September 1943	POUND	No. 12 Commando	Ushant
24–25 December 1943	HARDTACK 11	No. 10 (Inter-Allied) Commando	Gravelines
25–26 December 1943	HARDTACK 13	No. 10 (Inter-Allied) Commando, SBS	Bénouville
26–27 December 1943	HARDTACK 4	No. 10 (Inter-Allied) Commando	Biville
	HARDTACK 5	No.10 (Inter-Allied) Commando	Onival
	HARDTACK 21	No.10 (Inter-Allied) Commando	Quinéville
31 December 1943		COPP1	Courselles, Ver-sur-Mer
17–21 January 1944	POSTAGE ABLE	COPP1/X20	Vierville, Colleville and Moulins St Laurent
15–16 May 1944	TARBRUSH 5	No. 10 (Inter-Allied) Commando	Dunkirk
	TARBRUSH 8	No. 10 (Inter-Allied) Commando	Quend
16–17 May 1944	TARBRUSH 3	No. 10 (Inter-Allied) Commando	Bray-Dunes
17–18 May 1944	TARBRUSH 10	No. 10 (Inter-Allied) Commando	Onival

The Forfar raids between July and September 1943 were a sequence of deception Commando raids which fell under the banner of the broader Operation Starkey. Starkey was intended to draw out the *Luftwaffe* and enable the commandos to identify German defensive positions on the French coast and acquire what technical intelligence they could on German military equipment.

Operation Basalt, a Small Scale Raiding Force (SSRF) mission on the small Channel Island of Sark was the stimulus which prompted Hitler to issue the infamous *Kommandobefehl* or Commando Order on 18 October 1942, which led to many Allied commando troops being executed despite having being captured wearing a British military uniform or attempting to surrender. These Allied raids were to potentially come at a price.

Shortly before the Basalt raid on the Channel Islands in October 1942, the SSRF had been used in an unsuccessful raid referred to as Operation Aquatint, on what was to be part of Dog Sector on Omaha Beach, where the US invasion was to land. Its mission on the night of 12/13 September 1942 was to reconnoitre houses in the small town of Sainte-Honorine-des-Pertes. Some of the seafront houses in the town had been identified through Allied aerial reconnaissance missions to be German defensive positions.

This was shortly after the failed raid on Dieppe in August 1942 and the German forces in Normandy were on high alert. The raiding party commanded by the founder of the SSRF, Major Gus March-Phillipps, comprised five officers and men. The team initially landed in the wrong place on the vast expanse of beach and was then ambushed subsequently by a passing German patrol. In the firefight, the commandos were forced back to their supporting Motor Torpedo Boat (MTB), affectionately called 'Little Pisser'. It had been gifted the name due to the noise it used to make from the submerged exhausts. The shore batteries opened fire hitting the MTB, which sustained significant damage to its engines. March-Phillipps was killed as he attempted to get to the shoreline, alongside two of his men when the Goatley dinghy was riddled with machine-gun fire. Four of the group were captured.

A few weeks later, members of the same SSRF team went ashore on German-occupied Sark, under the mantle of Operation Basalt. The commandos intended to capture German soldiers and successfully managed to abduct one of the German engineers working on the defence constructions on Sark. *Obergefreiter* Weinrich hailed from the German Pioneer Corps Engineer Unit and would be a valuable commodity for the knowledge he held. Alongside an array of captured documents found in the German quarters, the prisoner was brought back to Portland after the operation and handed over to MI9 for interrogation.

A reconnaissance mission to Quinéville on the Cotentin Peninsula, called Operation Hardtack 21, provided some good in-roads into the understanding of the Normandy beaches' defences and topography. The commandos comprised an entirely French troop of five men commanded by Sub-Lieutenant Francis Vasrc'h. The mission was scheduled for the night of Christmas Day 1943 but it had to be delayed a day due to bad weather.

An MTB moved the team from Newhaven to Normandy, on to a target drop-off point that was to become known as the 'Peter' sector of Utah Beach. The team were inserted using a 20 ft dory with an outboard motor and during the hours of 2350 to 0245 hours they reconnoitered the whole stretch of beach and coastline for obstacles. It is regarded as one of the most successful Hardtack missions as they collected sand samples from the beach, investigated defensive obstacles such as the Element C/ Belgian Gates, and established terrain mapping and enemy defensive positions.

By January 1944, the Chief of Staff Supreme Allied Commander (COSSAC) put an abrupt end to all the raids coordinated under the banner of Operation Hardtack, due to the concerns it had of drawing any undue attention to the potential for Normandy to be used as a future area for invasion. Four of the remaining Hardtack raids, which were due to take place in the dark periods of January 1944, including Hardtack 14, 19, 24 and 27 were all aborted.

The responsibility for this decision ultimately fell to the SHAEF Raids and

Reconnaissance Committee, who clearly stated no further probing commando raids were to take place on the French coastline. SHAEF did exclude the work of the Combined Operations Pilotage Parties (COPP) teams in the early weeks of 1944, as they were pivotal in the clandestine reconnaissance of the key Normandy beaches.

Despite the SHAEF directive, a number of commando missions took place between 14 and 19 May 1944, as Operation Tarbrush was tasked with investigating the Allied concerns that the Germans were hardening their defensive positions, most notably with thousands of mines. Their clear mission intent was to 'obtain a beach mine from the enemy defended coast to obtain information of the nature of beach defences, and to withdraw unobserved'.

Operation Tarbrush was the name assigned to a series of clandestine raids and reconnaissance missions undertaken by No. 10 (Inter-Allied) Commando in May 1944. Lieutenant Colonel Lister handed over the command of the Commando Unit in 15 May 1944 to Colonel Robert Laycock, a man of some notoriety in Commando circles. Captain Brian Hilton Jones was duly promoted to Major and second-in-command. It was his role to directly manage the Tarbrush planning and to assign the men with the requisite experience from No. 3 (X) Troop to escort the Royal Engineers ashore in order to investigate any mines or beach obstacles in detail. With D-Day only three weeks away, knowledge of the operation was tightly held and secrecy throughout was vital to the mission's success. Hilton Jones commanded four of the missions himself.

There were originally eight proposed raids planned under the Operation Tarbrush umbrella during the period between 14 and 17 May 1944, but only five of them were successful. Lieutenant George Lane commanded three of the missions and during his team's incursions around Ault, where they had been tasked with investigating mines, they discovered that the Germans had been placing Teller mines on the tops of stakes submerged in the sea near the coast.

The Tarbrush 8 mission to undertake beach reconnaissance at Quend on the night of the 15/16 May 1944 also involved two Motor Torpedo Boats 354 and 359. The two-man commando team was led by Major Ernest Leigh Smith (then a Captain) who returned with vital intelligence about the beach obstacles, including an actual Teller mine which was brought back for examination. This vital mission to broaden the understanding of the mines themselves led to Smith being awarded a Military Cross.

On the night of 17/18 May 1944, Tarbrush 10 took place at the beach at Onival. The group was led by fluent German-speaking Lieutenant George Lane. He was born in Hungary as Lanyi Dyuri but had changed his name when he came to England. Lane was from X Troop 10 Commando, and his colleague Captain Roy Wooldridge from the 11 Field Company, Royal Engineers. Wooldridge had joined the Royal Engineers shortly after joining his University Officer Training Corps (OTC) in October 1939. He

Captain Roy
Wooldridge
RE MC
(© IWM
documents
19880)

had been inspired by one of his professors at Aberystwyth University, Professor Morton (the then Professor of Pure Maths) who had served with the Royal Engineers in the World War I. Morton was aware he would be losing some of his students to the call-up and gave them lectures in sound ranging and surveying methods to locate enemy artillery. These skills would serve Wooldridge well.

Wooldridge was called up in September 1940 and after his training served in North Africa, winning a Military Cross (MC) for his actions in the Battle of El Alamein. He was a specialist in mine disposal. An aerial attack on German coastal batteries that took place in April 1944 at Houlgate caused serious concern with Allied intelligence. A secondary explosion had taken place from a bomb that had dropped short and was noticed by some of the aircrew overhead. It was suspected the Germans were using mines on their beach obstacles, so a series of aerial reconnaissance missions were run over the area to acquire further intelligence.

George Lane had previously served with the Special Operations Executive (SOE) and his training was to be put to good use within X Troop. He was to shadow Wooldridge when they went ashore. The new mine was their objective, 'we didn't know whether it was electric or pressure release or magnetic. We didn't know anything about it, so someone had to go and bring it back.

'All I could find were old-knit Teller mines, which were fixed onto the top of stakes … driven into the sand, and I recognised them to be ordinary Teller mines and I took one off and brought it back, and they nearly died of fright when I presented it. Also they wanted to know all about these steel things that the Germans put about on the beaches, they were called tetrahedrons and things like that, and they wanted me to photograph them with an infrared camera.'

These aerial sorties identified rows of wooden stakes between 8-10 ft high, and on every sixth post there appeared to be a canister measuring around 3 ft long by 1 ft in diameter, suspected to be a new type of mine the Germans had developed. These sorties were flown at such a low level, one German officer was pictured firing at a plane with his pistol. The cost of these missions was high – three camera-fitted Mustangs were sent on the reconnaissance mission and only one returned. If this was a new device, it could cause serious damage to an amphibious force landing on the beaches, so Operation Tarbrush was born as a top priority mission, under the leadership of

Captain Hilton Jones. Four missions were planned between 14 and 19 May 1944, under the names of Tarbrush 3, 5, 8 and 10, all to take place simultaneously.

The teams were to be delivered on different sections of the Normandy coast. Tarbrush 10 was to strike on the beach at Onival with Captain Wooldridge being directly accompanied by Sergeant Bluff whose objective was to identify the mine. If it could not be identified then they were to attempt to bring one home to Dover for analysis. A subsidiary objective for Tarbrush 10 was to take measurements of the anti-tank obstacles, Element C. This was to gain essential structural measurements for the engineering teams in Britain to make calculations on the size and positions of charges required for the destruction of these obstacles on D-Day itself. The Prime Minister had taken a keen interest in the outcome of the Tarbrush raids. Prior to the mission, Wooldridge had access to a scale model of the Element C obstacles, constructed from aerial reconnaissance images, to identify the most significant measurements to take whilst ashore.

Before the Tarbrush teams departed Dover, they were given selective briefings by the Experimental Scientific Advisor to Combined Operations HQ, Professor John Bernal. Bernal suspected the mine 'might be magnetic, acoustic, contact, electrically controlled, voltaic or indeed something completely new'.

Wooldridge had sole responsibility for the mine and was equipped with a special infra-red camera which he had been trained to use by the RAF. Bernal had given Wooldridge an ingenious technique to test whether the new mine was magnetic, 'I was supplied with a small magnet, a plastic curtain ring and a hundred yards of twine. I would then climb up the post, attach the curtain ring to the top, thread the twine through it, take the twine back some fifty yards, attach to it the small magnet and, by pulling on the other end of the twine, cause the magnet to creep along the beach and up the post. If the device was magnetic it would explode.'

Wooldridge emphasised that Bernal did not convey what they should do if that happened, on the heavily defended Onival Beach, in the dead of night. The Tarbrush teams also had a mock-up post rigged up on a nearby beach to practise the Bernal routine, and they practised and practised transfers from MTB to dory and to dinghy.

'When dawn broke on the morning of 18 May '44 Lane and I had only managed to paddle the rubber dinghy about a mile out to sea. I realised that capture was inevitable. I started singing the German song 'Lili Marlene' … in the desert it was sung over the German radio each evening and we used to tune in to it. Lane had never heard it and I suppose I only sang it to keep our spirits up.'

According to the Tarbrush operational orders, an extraction plan was in place should the landing party fail to return. 'In the event of a landing party failing to return, the Flag Officer Commanding, Dover will arrange, if weather permits, to sail the necessary forces on the two nights following that of the operation to effect a rescue. The carrier MTB will be sailed so that the dory will be off the appropriate landing beach at 0200 until 0300 when, if contact had not been made with the landing party, the dory is to withdraw.'

Of the three raids prior to the night of the 17/18 May when they had been captured, one was aborted due to rough sea conditions (they were unable to lower the dinghy and dory for the raiding team). A second attempted raiding team landed too far south of their objective and on the third attempted landing the team was concerned about the amount of enemy activity and lights on the beach and turned back.

The Tarbrush teams were landed by Motor Torpedo Boat (MTB) 359 from 5th Flotilla to an area just short of a mile off the beach, where they were to be transferred to a powered dory which would carry them to within 100 yards of the beach. They would then be transferred into a rubber dinghy. The team members carried a Colt 45 pistol each and Lane had a grenade in case of being compromised by an enemy patrol on the beach. Wooldridge and his accompanying protector, Sergeant Bluff, carried the engineering equipment necessary for the task – mine detectors, wire cutters, pliers and reels of wire.

What was learned from the raid was that the cylindrical block at the top of the wooden stake was just the base to which a standard German Teller mine was fixed. This was the type of anti-tank mine which Wooldridge and others had seen in their thousands in North Africa. Wooldridge stated: 'Lane and I decided to set off along the beach towards Ault where we knew, from the aerial photographs, that there was a large number of Element C. We instructed Sgt Bluff and the commando to remain with the dinghy at the water's edge so that we would not miss them on our return. We estimated that we would be away for about one and a half hours. By this time it had started raining hard which at least had the effect of keeping the enemy sentries heads down and so we were able to keep up a brisk pace stopping only to examine briefly the Teller mines strapped to the tops of the wooden posts, the obstacles interspersed between the posts and to hit the deck whenever the beams of the searchlights sweeping the beach came too near.'

Lane and Wooldridge walked for three-quarters of an hour along the beach towards Ault, with no sign of the Element C obstacles, when they suspected a sentry had spotted them with a torch. They turned about and headed back to the dinghy and a subsequent firefight ensued, possibly with the MTB. They retraced their steps back to where they had left the dinghy and it was nowhere to be seen. Lane used his torch to flash their pre-arranged signal but with no avail. With dawn approaching, the pair walked further along the beach and found the abandoned dinghy, with no sign of the two occupants, suspecting they had been captured or killed.

Lane and Wooldridge had two options. First, to hide in the cliffs until the next night, but with limited time they would not have made the distance, or the second to push out to sea in the dinghy. 'Paddling and making headway in a rubber dinghy is not easy in the best of waters but with a choppy sea we managed only about a mile from the shore when dawn broke. Our chances of getting away now seemed remote and so we dumped all our equipment overboard except for escape outfits and pistols. As I dumped the infra-red camera overboard I couldn't help remembering how the RAF men had stressed that I must take great care of it in view of its value.'

The pair heard the sound of an approaching German motorboat patrol and while circling the dinghy the Commander onboard instructed them to raise their hands and surrender. Lane and Wooldridge from the Royal Engineers were both captured and taken ashore at Cayeux. They were taken away half an hour later by a German officer to a local gun emplacement where they were interrogated for a day. Lane recalled, 'they put me in an underground place which was very cold and damp, so I felt very unhappy and uncomfortable … then a good-looking chap came in, I think he was a Captain and he immediately started up by saying, "You know we'll have to shoot you, because you are obviously a saboteur, and we have very strict orders to shoot saboteurs and commandos".'

The following day they were both blindfolded, bound and transferred by car to a German Army facility in Abbeville where they were interviewed further and strip-searched. The next day they were moved to a country retreat where Wooldridge informed them that his hometown was Aberystwyth in Wales. He suspected this would be used by the German propaganda machine which regularly broadcast the names of Allied POW and where they came from.

They were then moved to a French château, the home of the Ducs de Rochefoucauld for over 400 years about 50 kilometres west of Paris and led into an ornate room and 'to my astonishment standing on the other side of a desk was Generalfeldmarschall Erwin Rommel and looking out of a window was Rommel's immediate superior Generalfeldmarschall von Rundstedt'. They both realised they had some important prisoners, with a pending Allied invasion of France.

Rommel was the first to ask a question. 'You are in a very serious situation, because we think you're a saboteur.'

Lane responded with a quick retort through the interpreter who was present, 'Please tell His Excellency that I know that if he thought I was a saboteur, he wouldn't have invited me here.'

Rommel laughed, and the atmosphere between the soldiers became convivial and more relaxed. Rommel asked, 'Are you an Engineer Officer?' Wooldridge responded with the rulebook reference to interrogation matters: 'Tell the Field Marshal that in accordance with the Geneva Convention I can give him my rank, name and number but nothing else.'

The invasion was clearly on Rommel's mind: 'Do you really think there's going to be an invasion? And the British will invade?... Well, where do you think the invasion is coming?' Lane remained resolute and responded intelligently to draw Rommel off the scent of what they both knew of Overlord, 'I certainly don't know, because I only watch what they tell junior officers on what the whole thing is about. But if it was up to me, I would do it across the shortest possible way, because that's the way you're going to get the least casualties.'

The conversation was coming to an end, and Rommel smiled and responded, 'Is there anything that you require?'

Wooldridge replied, 'I would like a pint of beer, a packet of cigarettes and a good meal.' Wooldridge was then dismissed from Rommel's company and led away. The pair were later served their first proper meal since they were captured, along with some tankards of beer and cigarettes.

'I found the interrogations a bit unnerving and the threat of being shot as a saboteur didn't help … counting the dummy run in Dover and the raids on the following four nights plus little sleep during the interrogations I hadn't had a good night's rest for some time.'

As Wooldridge recalled from his experiences of this Normandy interrogation and the time he had fought against Rommel in the desert, 'If it wasn't for Rommel, I'd have been executed. He was my foe, but he was an officer and a gentleman.'

Lane and Wooldridge were eventually transferred to the notorious Gestapo prison at Fresnes and onwards to Oflag IX A/H prison in Spangenberg in Germany.

Combined Operations, one of the two secret armies alongside SOE that Churchill set up to take the war to Germany, was instrumental in the gathering of intelligence on the Normandy defences. Aerial reconnaissance missions would keep the Allies informed of what was going on across the Channel but there was no substitute for having men on the ground. There were many incursions on this vital stretch of coast to capture prisoners or vital equipment, take soundings and measurements of the slope and gradients of the beach, take sand and soil samples, and examine the obstacles the Germans had devised to repel any Allied invasion attempts.

These high-risk clandestine operations along the French coastline from as far back as 1940 met with success and failure in equal measure. Good men were killed but intelligence critical to the outcome of the Overlord mission was gathered in the months and years leading up to the invasion. It was a precursor of what was to come.

SECRET

11 Jan 44

Cancels requirements
dated 17 Dec 43.

INTELLIGENCE REQUIREMENTS

OPERATION HARDTACK 24

TOPOGRAPHICAL.

Beach

1. Describe nature and firmness of beach where crossed.

2. Recover samples of sand from below and above high water mark.

3. Describe nature and dimensions of runnels on beach.

Wall.

4. Nature and dimensions of wall or bank between high water mark and dunes - is it an obstacle to infantry, MT and/or AFVs?

Dunes.

5. How easy is movement through the dunes for infantry, MT and/or AFVs?

6. How easy is it to recognise a given spot or skyline in the dunes from seaward?

7. How good is cover for infantry in the dunes?

Floods.

8. Limits of any flooded area met?

9. Exact depth of flooding (state places of measurement)?

10. Extent to which flooded or saturated ground forms obstacle to movement.

11. Are roads and tracks across flooding clear of water? If so how high, and by how wide and firm a verge?

12. Recover sample of mud from below flood water.

Roads.

13. What are dimensions and conditions of all roads and tracks? Are there any signs of prepared road or bridge demolitions?

DEFENCES.

14. Detailed description with measurements of any underwater obstacles, including details of apparent condition and method of fixing into ground.

15. Details of any wire fences encountered (size, layout, type and fixing of pickets); recovery of specimen wire strands and of any attached warning devices.

16. Details of any minefields encountered, giving:-

Type of mine
spacing
use of tripwires
marking and fencing-off.

56   484

Recovery of a specimen mine would be useful but is not essential.

CHAPTER FOUR
RACKET

The Croix de Lorraine, chosen by General Charles de Gaulle as the symbol of the French Resistance

'Securing the blueprint of the German Atlantic Wall was an incredible feat – so valuable that the landing operation succeeded with a minimum loss of men and material.'

General Omar Bradley talking of the René Duchez heist

'Without the networks of the French Resistance the invasion would not have been possible.'

Major-General Walter Bedell-Smith, SHAEF Chief of Staff in a letter to General Charles de Gaulle's Minister of Information, Jacques Soustelle

'The series of operations were of enormous importance in the liberation of France to which the Resistance made a great contribution by minimising the part played after D-Day by the two German Panzer divisions … which in Eisenhower's view, shortened the war by six months.'

Colonel Maurice Buckmaster, Head of SOE French Section writing about the 15th MGB Flotilla

The use and function of clandestine units are nothing new in warfare. Secret military units, operating behind enemy lines, have existed as far back as war can be traced. It is an effective method to unseat an army of occupation. Just two months after Germany invaded France, Churchill instituted the creation of the Special Operations

Executive (or SOE) and put his Minister of Economic Warfare, Hugh Dalton, at the helm. D-Day was to be the main SOE objective in France for the duration of the war. It was a difficult operating environment for the organisation due to the political divide with the Vichy Regime, under the direction of Marshal Pétain and the Free French operating out of London, under the command of General Charles de Gaulle.

There was a great deal of uncertainty when it came to the French Resistance in the early years of the German occupation, fuelled in part by the role General de Gaulle was playing. This was reflected in the SOE developing its work in France with two separate teams – the F and RF Sections. F Section worked independently of de Gaulle and was largely staffed by British officers. The RF Section was very different. It was organised in close consultation with the *Conseil National de la Résistance* (CNR) and was headed up by Colonel Hutchinson. The RF Section was the figurehead of the Free French and was often referred to as the '*Gaullists*'. F section was commanded by Major Maurice Buckmaster, who led the section for four years and was to make it the largest and most significant part of the SOE. Both sections were to become enveloped under the control of the EMFFI and SFHQ, with operational directives being levied on them from SHAEF.

The Oxford graduate Buckmaster had cut his teeth in the early years of the war fighting with the British Expeditionary Force in France, and his senior SOE officials were to refer to the organisation jokingly as 'The Firm' or the 'Racket'. From its early years the clandestine organisation had had some marked successes, such as the destruction of the heavy-water plant in Norway in 1943 scuppering the Nazis push to develop an atomic bomb. By 1944 it had grown to an organisation of nearly 13,000 staff.

Colin Gubbins was very much the energy behind SOE – he was a natural, charismatic and inspiring leader and he brought forward the militarisation of the organisation to good effect from 1942 to 1944, built around an effective air transport and logistics chain. It had the full backing of Churchill, who saw the value in irregular warfare. The organisation was to transform after an agreement in June 1942 with the Office of Strategic Services (OSS), its American sister organisation to carry out joint planning and have an integrated headquarters for the D-Day operations in 1944.

SOE derived a plan to air-drop over 50,000 attack packs into occupied Europe, which included a Liberator pistol, grenades and pocket incendiaries, under a project christened Operation Braddock. The initiative was abandoned, but the pistols were re-used in equipment drops to the French Resistance. The idea morphed into a joint SOE/ Political Warfare Executive (PWE) Operation Braddock II to disperse three million incendiary devices over occupied Europe to supply arson and sabotage efforts by the various Resistance groups. The PWE was hoping to synchronise the airdrops with some prolonged black propaganda. By May 1944, the Joint Intelligence Committee (JIC) approved the Braddock II plans and wanted it aligned with the Overlord plans if Eisenhower was in agreement.

As the organisation grew, it was to acquire a number of large English stately homes. The development and training of SOE agents was placed in a number of these houses, which the SOE referred to as the Special Training Schools (STS). The HQ-STS was in Room 98, Horse Guards, London. The STS were split into:

a)   Group A: Paramilitary Schools – all around Arisaig in Scotland
b)   Group B: Finishing Schools – also offered at some overseas schools, such as Massingham in Algiers, Italy and India
c)   Group C: Operational schools – preliminary training school at STS4/STS7; later designated 'Operational Holding Schools'
d)   Group D: Propaganda Training
e)   Group E: Code and Cipher training

There were ten Group B finishing schools, all in or around the Beaulieu estate (which SOE referred to as STS 27(b)):

STS31 – 'The Rings' and the 'House in the Woods'. The former became the HQ for Group B schools.

STS32 – Hartford House

STS32a – Saltmarsh

STS32b – Blackbridge

STS33 – The House on the Shore

STS34 – The Drokes

STS35 – The Vineyards

STS36 – Boarmans

STS37a – Warren House (micro-photography training and use of pigeons)

STS37b – Clobb Gorse (admin)

STS38 – Inchmery House, Hampshire (used by RF/BCRA, Poles (6th Bureau) and SSRF)

Many of the above were used by different nationalities at different times. Wanborough fell under Group A. Apart from the selection element of courses there, students also received training in fitness, explosives, CQB and other weapon training and map-reading. Many of the staff at these training schools were from the First Aid Nursing Yeomanry (FANY). They would often act as cooks and cleaners at the houses but their roles would evolve with the SOE and become intertwined throughout the organisation. The women would be trained as wireless operators, secretaries, teleprinter telegraphists, typists and coders. In fact, many of the famous female agents associated with the SOE, like Andrée Borrel and Violet Szabo, were actually from the FANY. Gubbins was always full of praise for them, '… to the organisation they were everything, and without them we just could not have done it…. I am proud to have been the means of their proving their great qualities. They have been magnificent and invaluable.' They were certainly to prove themselves in their roles as wireless operators. It has been estimated that up to two million words a week would be transmitted through the SOE wireless stations.

Many potential recruits to the SOE F Section were identified by links they had fostered with the Royal Patriotic School (RPS) in Wandsworth, the home of the London Reception Centre (LRC) where refugees from occupied Europe were processed and screened. MI5, MI6 and MI9 had a presence there and SOE had access to French exiles to interview and potentially select them for training if they were deemed suitable for SOE work.

Prospective SOE agents also had to undertake parachute training, as many were infiltrated into France by air, and this training was undertaken at RAF Ringway (STS 51), which is now Manchester Airport. The trainees were billeted close by at either Dunham House (STS 51a) or Fulsham Hall in Wimslow (STS 51b). Many of their drops were into Tatton Park. Agents destined for France were flown out of RAF Tangmere before RAF Tempsford became available as an operational airfield. The German military in northern France became very competent in their use of RADAR to identify Allied aircraft crossing the Channel. They were capable of plotting the speed and course of the aircraft, and when it slowed between two points they could pinpoint the potential Drop Zone (DZ) being used, which would initiate a localised search for Allied parachutists.

Led by Marie-Madeleine Fourcade, the Alliance network was one of the most extensive Resistance networks operating in northern France with over 145 agents at its disposal, providing a rich stream of high-quality intelligence to planners in England regarding German troop dispositions and movements. Much of the intelligence was from small snippets of information, often gathered in informal discussions or overheard conversations by German soldiers in French cafés. This material was all collated and interwoven with other strands of intelligence to complete a more rounded report.

Women were particularly sought after as agents, as they had notable advantages over their male colleagues. They could blend into the local population much more easily than men and were capable of using their attractive appearance and charm to deflect from their real identity if questioned. As Captain Selwyn Jepson (the SOE Senior Recruiting Officer) stated, 'in my view, women were very much better than men for the work. Women…have a far greater capacity for cool and lonely courage than men.'

Agents are often referred to as a Covert Human Intelligence Source (CHIS). A CHIS is someone who can establish or maintain a relationship for the covert purpose of using the relationship to obtain information or to provide access to any information to another person. This purpose is regarded as covert if one of the parties is unaware of that purpose.

The most powerful and largest French Resistance network operating in France by the spring of 1943 was the Prosper network, and as the planning for Overlord began in earnest it was to play a critical role.

Frustratingly for the SOE hierarchy, there was little interaction with the planners for Overlord. Not until 3 June was the full understanding of the operational detail apparent to SOE. This came about from a direct but brief fifteen-minute meeting between Bedell-Smith and the Commander-in-Chief at Southwick House. Bedell Smith came back from Southwick with a direct order to get the French Resistance to cause maximum disruption to the German army on the night of the invasion.

There was a huge logistical arm behind SOE operations in France. The organisation organised 3,733 parachute drops and 81 pick up operations into France by a variety of aircraft including Lysander, Dakota and Hudsons. Over 5 million kg of equipment was dropped into France during World War II to support SOE agent networks, which included a staggering 104,536 individual Sten machine guns, 409,224 grenades and 307,023 kg of explosives for sabotage operations. Many of the SOE agents were infiltrated into France by covert flights operated by two Special Duty squadrons, 138 and 161 Squadrons operating out of RAF Tempsford airfield. Prior to this, RAF Tangmere was used to deliver the SOE agents into France. Infamous SOE agents such as Violette Szabo and Wing Commander 'Tommy' Yeo-Thomas were both flown into France from Tempsford and played a critical role before D-Day in organising the French Resistance groups in northern France.

The 15th Flotilla based on the River Dart deployed a number of Motor Torpedo Boats (MTB) responsible for relaying Allied agents and equipment into northern France in the vital weeks before D-Day. The Flotilla was to be a vital cog in the gathering of intelligence on the Normandy defences.

MTB718 was a D-Class Fairmile boat, designed and built at the Robertson &

REMEMBER THE ENEMY IS LISTENING

FANY operators on W/T sets taken at Grendon Hall (SOE Station 53a), Grendon Underwood

Sons Sandbank yard on Holy Loch, tucked away on Scotland's rugged west coast. She had been given the nickname *Lone Wolf*, as she was to always hunt alone. MTBs had been built for speed, having had the burdensome torpedo tubes removed. They were equipped with four Rolls-Royce Packard engines which could produce a huge 6,000 horsepower, delivering a top speed of 35 knots. MTB718 was the fastest and most heavily armed boat in the flotilla. She had been commissioned on 24 February 1944 and subsequently joined the 15th Flotilla in March 1944 under the command of Lieutenant Ronnie Seddon RNVR, with Lieutenant Guy Hamilton RNVR as First Lieutenant and Lieutenant Tony Byrd RNVR, who was the Pilot or Gunnery Officer onboard. Hamilton was to become famous after the war as the Director of four of the early James Bond films.

MTB718 was one of five Coastal Forces craft assigned to the Flotilla, and she was the fastest of them. Her sister ship, MGB318, built at the Aldous Successors shipyard at Brightlingsea in June 1941 was partnered originally with MASB36. These two vessels were joined later by MGB502 and MGB503.

The Flotilla was based out of the upper floors of the Royal Dart Hotel in Kingswear, which was known as HMS *Cicala*. A number of Wrens worked long hours in the lead-up to D-Day in the Confidential Books (CB) section of *Cicala*. The hotel was originally built by Brunel when the railway arrived at the town in 1864. The upstairs floors were out of bounds to outsiders, but more importantly to the Royal Navy crewmen stationed in Kingswear, the bar remained open to public use. The Wrens were tasked with compiling the charts and secret codes which had come from the Naval Intelligence Division (NID) at the Admiralty. These all arrived by courier direct to the ships in dock. Some of these reports were signals intelligence decrypts from

Enigma intercept, on German naval recognition signals which the Allied crews could use to respond if challenged off the French coastline. The commanding officers of each boat of the flotilla was BIGOT security cleared and was privy to the movement orders for Overlord.

In the build up to D-Day, the American forces were moved into temporary camps not far from Kingswear. Those who were going to disembark from the Dart came on the train to Kingswear station. It was a hive of activity all based around the group of motorboats harboured up and veiled with secrecy. On 3 June 1944, some 485 ships and landing craft left the Dart estuary to join the Neptune invasion force three days later.

The 15th Flotilla was established in 1941 on the River Dart under the command of Captain Frank Slocum, the Deputy Director Operations Division (Irregular) or DDOD (I). Slocum was integral in masterminding the Flotilla's involvement in operations into northern France and supporting the established Shelburn escape line in western France. The Flotilla had been assigned 'Special Duties' to deliver SOE/MI9 or SIS agents, ammunition, equipment or mail ashore and return with downed airmen, returning agents or evaders. During 1943 and early 1944, these agents brought back vital information about the German defences in the run-up to the Normandy landings. MGB502 was responsible mostly for SOE tasks during this period, and MGB503 almost exclusively for MI9, working on the escape routes for downed airmen.

The vessels were moored midstream on the River Dart, next to their depot ship, the ageing paddle steamer *Westward Ho*, which had seen action during World War I as a minesweeper. It held the accolade of being the only paddle steamer to shoot down a *Luftwaffe* aircraft in World War II.

As Captain Slocum wrote aptly in his 1946 review, 'whether measured by the risks from the enemy or the navigational hazards of the long voyages involved, these were outstanding performances. At such distances from base special navigational aids do not function. Weather forecasts were imprecise and unreliable and no W/T contact could be maintained.'

Nearly 125 officers and men were to serve with the 15th Flotilla during the course of the war, and it would become the most highly decorated Royal Navy unit. The men of the 15th Flotilla were awarded a total of fourteen Distinguished Service Crosses (DSC) and twenty-seven Distinguished Service Medals (DSM) between them.

MTB718 had two missions to Plage Bonaparte on the north Brittany coastline. Its first was on 15 June 1944 and the second on 9 August 1944.

On 15–16 April 1944, MGB502 was accompanied by MGB718 on its first cross-Channel operation to Beg an Fry in one of the most important and successful missions carried out by the Flotilla before D-Day. It was marred by the death of Able Seaman Sandalls on MGB502.

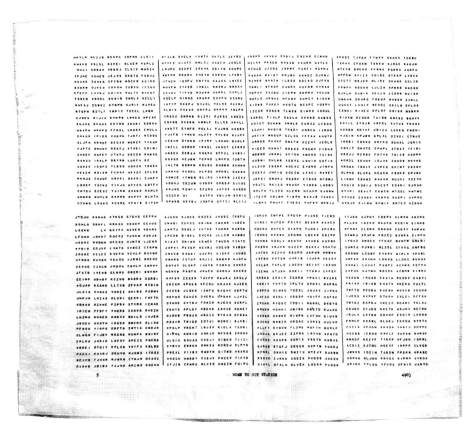

An SOE silk sheet One-Time Pad (© Crown Copyright, by kind permission of Director GCHQ)

Lieutenant Byrd, the Gunnery Officer, was born in 1925 in Evesham, Worcestershire to a wealthy family who grew fruit and vegetables in this garden of England. He was educated at the prestigious Bradfield College in Berkshire where he quickly excelled at sport, becoming the Captain of the Hockey team, playing water polo and boxing, which served him well when he joined the Royal Navy in 1942 as part of the 'Y Scheme'. This scheme was set up by the Admiralty for eighteen-year-olds with a secondary education who could be future RN officer material. Under the scheme the cadets had to undertake basic new entrant training in Class 48 at HMS Collingwood. Byrd found that he was not well respected on the course but his boxing skills got him some standing at least. After this ten-week long course, he went on to the twelve-week long course at HMS *King Alfred*, the RNVR Training Establishment in Hove, East Sussex, which is now a council-run leisure centre. Y Scheme and Commissioned & Warrant [CW] Officer cadets comprised the majority of the cadets at King Alfred. Out of the initial one hundred or so candidates on Class 48, Byrd was one of the half that went on to the next stage, a specialist signalling and navigation training course at Lancing College for six weeks.

By the end of the war, RNVR Officers accounted for 80 per cent of officers in Royal Naval active service.

During 1943 most of the communications with France in terms of agent and equipment drops had been undertaken using RAF Lysander and Hudson aircraft flying from airfields in southern England. Suspicions had been raised within the SOE and wider British intelligence about the security of this route, which was believed to have been compromised. A new strategy had to be invoked, which led to the creation of 15th Flotilla and the six months in the run-up to D-Day it became the only route in and out of northern France for the insertion of SOE or MI9 agents and the return of downed Allied airmen. The Shelburn line, as it became known, quickly became hugely significant to support field organisation and the French Resistance in providing the intelligence for D-Day.

When all the 15th Flotilla boats were lined along the Kingswear slipway, MTB718 stood out among the crowd. They all had distinctly different colour schemes dependent on the operational work they were tasked to do. MTB718 was painted 'Plymouth Pink' or more commonly known as 'Mountbatten Pink' a greyish-mauve camouflage colour.

One infamous mission for the crew took place a few days after D-Day. Lieutenant Seddon had been tasked to undertake the MTB's first solo cross-Channel mission to deliver equipment and three agents – Rauol Parent, Jean Tréhiou and the wireless operator Jean Hamon, on to Plage Bonaparte. When in position off the Brittany coast the derrick cranes offloaded the SN6 Dory dinghy to take the shore party onto French soil. Leading Seamen Albert 'Lofty' Dellow manned the 'Joey' to take the agents and equipment ashore from 800 yards out. It was a hard row with a loaded dinghy, the three agents, Lieutenant Hamilton and Able Seaman Rockwood, as the weather was beginning to close in. After a tense wait, the crew onboard continually attempted to establish radio communications with the shore party but had little success, the walkie-talkie VHF sets having been temperamental. With the associated storm swell, even with the anchored deployed the boat was dragging out of position. Due to the clandestine nature of the mission no light signals were to be used.

As the sun began to climb to the horizon and dawn began to break, the potential compromise of the whole operation and the danger to MTB718 anchored offshore was too big a risk for Lieutenant Hamilton to take and he ordered the crew to up anchor without his landing party.

Ashore, the cold and wet crewmen had struggled in vain to establish a radio communications link, and as the sun began to rise, they could hear Hamilton kick the silenced engines into gear.

The handpicked crew had worked together well and practised the French drops at Helford and Slapton Sands. They had become a well-drilled unit and a tight team. Lieutenant Seddon was one of the oldest crew members and as Commanding Officer of the boat was well respected, certainly after he had infamously rammed an E-Boat. Half-French, he had married a member of the French aristocracy. Lieutenant Hamilton was a good-looking, modest but very brave Royal Navy Officer. Lieutenant Tony Byrd was the junior officer onboard and as Pilot performed most of the navigational duties as well as being the Gunnery Officer.

Born in London in 1898, Valentine Blanche Charlet acted as a courier for the SOE French section during the early years of World War II. She was part of the Detective intelligence network or 'circuit' (*réseaux* to the French participants) of the SOE F Section. Codenamed Detective, she had been an active member of the circuit and was one of the first French agents to be landed, by a Polish felucca boat, on 1 September 1942. After picking up the work from fellow SOE agent, Virginia Hall, she worked closely on the ground with Brian Stonehouse, an SOE wireless operator.

In late October 1942, German radio direction finding teams picked up Stonehouse's transmissions while he was transmitting messages to his London controllers. The Germans tracked down his safe house and arrested both him and subsequently Charlet, who had come to a pre-arranged meeting by the *Milice* in Chateau Hurlevent close to Lyon.

Charlet was interned in November 1942 at the infamous *Centre de Séjour Surveillé* Prison in Castres. Over time she won the favour and trust of a prison wardress and managed to escape with a pistol and spare keys as part of a mass breakout of fifty prisoners on 10 September 1943. She escaped with Suzanne Henriette Warenghem, a young 'Pat Line' courier who was married to the organisation's main man in Lille, Harold Cole. The Pat Line was a network of safe houses and couriers in southern France. On 8 June 1942 they had both been arrested by the Vichy DST in Lyons. Cole was sentenced to death but Warenghem was acquitted.

After the prison break, Charlet and Warenghem managed to reach open country and following some assistance from a local farmer, they were sheltered by monks for two months at the Benedictine monastery of En Calcat. They had intended to escape over the Pyrennees to Spain but heavy winter snow scuppered that plan. In early April 1944, they got a message to SOE Headquarters in Baker Street, London and a pick-up by the 15th Flotilla was arranged from the Beg an Fry Beach in Brittany. The two travelled to Paris and subsequently left the city on 14 April 1944 alongside the crews from three downed aircraft.

The pick-up operation was known as Operation Scarf and took place on 15–16 April 1944 and the agents involved in this operation had a huge strategic impact on the forthcoming D-Day invasions. The then Head of the SOE French Section, Maurice Buckmaster stated 'the efforts of the Resistance in minimising the part played by the two German Panzer divisions had, in Eisenhower's view, helped to shorten the war by six months'.

Charlet travelled in the *Lone Wolf*, and Warenghem travelled on MGB502. As the boats embarked from the French coast they came across a number of enemy patrol vessels. The official report describes the operation: 'Lieutenant-Commander Williams was in command of a force consisting of MGB502 and MGB718 engaged on evacuating agents and evading airmen from a difficult pinpoint on the northeast coast of France. Having completed the embarkation he was standing out to sea along a narrow channel fringed by rocks and shoals whose only outlet was to the northward, when he found his way barred by three enemy patrol vessels waiting at the seaward entrance. By a judicious combination of speed and use of the special challenge and reply procedure provided by DDOD[I] for such emergencies, the enemy remained in doubt regarding his identity until they were abaft his beam. They then opened fire, but being still uncertain, ceased fire 15 seconds later, with the result that the force escaped with the loss of one rating killed and superficial damage to both ships.'

The most significant aspect of Operation Scarf was what was being carried by the young French agent Suzanne Warenghem. In her possession were two microfilms, which carried over fifty pages of detailed plans of Hitler's Atlantic Wall defences and plans for a significant RADAR station which had to be destroyed before the D-Day invasions.

A secondary part of Operation Scarf was to deliver three SOE F-Section agents and a number of French Secret Service agents ashore. MTB718 carried nine suitcases that accompanied the agents. The agents onboard MGB502 included Captain Pierre Duffoir (codenamed Amede, Diver, Felix or Pierre Dumartin as an alias) who was to be assigned to the new Racketeer circuit. Duffoir was accompanied by a Belgian national, Captain Maurice Henri Rouneau (codenamed Adolphe or Henri Robert Manguy as an alias). Rouneau was tasked with establishing the Racketeer network operating in Brittany ahead of the Allied landings.

The third SOE F-Section agent was Adher Arthur Watt, a wireless operator who was on his way to join another network in the Aube region. This network, the Diplomat circuit, was in preparation to isolate the town of Troyes when ordered.

The other two agents aboard MGB502 that night were assigned to General de Gaulle's Secret Service or *Direction Générale de Études et Recherches* (DGER) which was at that time based in Algiers. Colonel Ely (codename Algebre) was on route to replace Colonel Rondelay (codename Sapeur) who had recently been shot and killed while acting as the *Délégué Militaire* for the old occupied zone. Ely was accompanied by Sub-lieutenant Lazare Racheline (codename Socrate) who was tasked with shaping the CNR as a means to stemming any potential national reaction when the Overlord landings began.

Rouneau found it hard to get started with his new network, particularly without any wireless operator to support him. Time was also a big constraint, with only a few days to play with before the onset of Overlord.

Both Rouneau and Duffoir had been set the task by the SOE French Section to undertake sabotage in this northwestern part of France, to delay the deployment of German armoured forces in and around the town of Guers (Ille-et-Vilaine) as potential back-up troops to the German defensive positions in Normandy.

The nervous night time hours of the 5/6 June before the invasion forces hit the Normandy beaches were the time when the Rouneau and Duffoir partnership bore fruit. The teams they had equipped and trained over the preceding weeks cut the four main railway lines coming out of Guers, south of Rennes, destroyed fuel and ammunition dumps and cut telecommunications lines so that the German armoured divisions operating in this area of France took over nine days to reinforce the Normandy positions. These delaying tactics had a marked effect on the outcome of the Normandy invasion and similar SOE missions were being undertaken throughout northern France during this period. The 2nd SS Armoured Division or 'Das Reich' as they were known, was significantly delayed in its redeployment to Normandy from its home base of Montauban.

Over the course of the war, over 480 SOE agents were sent into France, deployed by aircraft, submarine or fishing vessels. 120 of them were killed and the operators involved with wireless/telegraphy (W/T) were the most vulnerable due to the risk of compromise. Some SOE and French Resistance W/T operators used multiple wireless sets to avoid detection by the German radio detection and Direction Finding (DF) or *Funk-Horchdienst* teams working in occupied France.

Deployed Special Forces and SOE personnel kept in touch with their respective London HQ using portable short-wave radios. In the early stages of the war, deployed SOE agents had to rely on the SIS communications network. SOE Headquarters in London had radio contact with 137 active deployed teams. During the summer of 1942, SOE developed its own signals organisation, overseen by four stations – two were located at Grendon Underwood (coded as 53A) and Poundon (coded as 53B) in Buckinghamshire.

Station 53a – Grendon Hall, Grendon Underwood the Communications HQ for SOE

Station 53b – Poundon House, joint OSS/SOE facility with over 350 US personnel and seventy British personnel

Thame Park – SOE Radio school where SOE agents trained in signals/morse code

Station 54a – Fawley Court, Henley on Thames, W/T training for the SOE, FANY and Jedburgh teams

Grendon Hall housed some 400 signallers and code specialists, most of whom were FANYs housed in Nissen huts in the grounds. They were typically posted there after their Morse code training at Fawley Court in Oxfordshire.

One such SOE wireless operator, who was deployed as part of the Farmer circuit in France, was Arthur Staggs. Prior to returning home to Britain at the outbreak of World War II, he had lived in France since the age of thirteen and was a fluent French speaker. During the early part of the war he was in the Intelligence Corps and was posted to Pembroke College, and appeared to have direct contact with the ISTD at Manchester College, giving them advice on the roads and waterways in northern France. After being noticed, due to his command of the French language, he was invited to the War Office and interviewed for the SOE by Major Maurice Gielgud. He carried out his initial training at Wanborough Manor and his parachute training at Ringway. This was promptly followed by Commando and other specialist training in Scotland, where he chose to take up specialist radio/Morse training, in Scotland and at Thame Park.

Staggs was deployed into France in November 1942. Moving around various towns and cities in France, he was to end up near Roubaix under the supervision of a woman called Gilberte Braem who had helped shelter British soldiers who had not managed to reach Dunkirk. He would work with Braem and entrust her with his safety.

'Her home became a safe house and I entrusted her with my codes which she kept in the family vault in the Cimetiere de Roubaix, her connections were spread far and wide this helped in so many ways greatly to my advantage.' He was able to cycle out to the countryside where he would transmit intelligence summaries back to Britain using his radio transmitter. He was also to take part in sabotage operations coordinated by the French Resistance. The largest of these was an attack on the railway workshops in Fives Lille. He was later captured and taken to Loos prison where he was imprisoned and interrogated for over two months. The Gestapo could not find any evidence of links to the Resistance or Britain, so he was released without charge. Reconnecting with some of his old network, he was redeployed to Aire-sur-la-Lys in the Pas-de-Calais region and renamed Capitaine Bebert to become the leader of the network there under the direction of the *Forces Française de l'Interieur* (FFI). For D-Day, his role was to get all the local groups to assemble in the pre-arranged area outside the town to undertake sabotage operations.

In October 1942 SOE created a black propaganda radio station called *Radio Patrie*, which was to provide a direct connection to the Resistance groups in France. Whilst it was successful, the broadcasts were to evolve over time and by the middle of 1943 a new radio station, *Honneur et Patrie* was turned on to replace *Radio Patrie*. It was to assist the *Conseil National de la Résistance* (CNR) set up by General Charles de Gaulle and Jean Moulin in London for the relay of information, directives and operational orders to the groups in France.

Leopold Samuel Marks was recruited at the age of twenty-three, was given the role as Cypher Security Officer for SOE and was instrumental in upgrading SOE's communications to effectively secure their backhaul back to Britain using cipher. He brought in the use of 'One-Time Pads' (OTP) or codebooks to encipher messages. He started cryptology at an early age, in the Marks & Co. bookshop which his Jewish father owned in London. His father had introduced a rudimentary cipher system to catalogue and price the books in the shop. Leo displayed a natural flair for breaking ciphers by attempting to decode his father's system, which took him just a few minutes.

Marks was called up in early 1942 and posted to Bedford as a cryptographer through contacts his godfather had in Special Branch. Apart from Marks, his entire intake was posted to Bletchley Park, but he was destined for the newly created SOE. He was soon to discover how vulnerable the SOE communications were to interception. The deployed agents were using poetry instead of ciphers to encode their messages, which could be exploited by educated Germans or through simple interrogation and torture on capture.

Leo Marks went along with this system and developed his own poems to encode messages. The most famous of these was the one penned at Christmas 1943, written in memory of his girlfriend Ruth Hambro who was killed in a plane crash in Canada:

> *The life that I have is all that I have*
> *And the life that I have is yours*
> *The love that I have of the life that I have is yours and yours and yours*
> *A sleep I shall have a rest I shall have*
> *Yet death will be but a pause*
> *For the peace of my years in the long green grass will be yours and yours and yours*

This particular code embedded within the poem was given to one of SOE's most famous agents, Violette Szabo, when she was deployed to France.

Marks helped in the recruitment of over 400 women for the First Aid Nursing Yeomanry (FANY) to assist with indecipherable traffic. The FANY teams were integrated throughout the SOE organisation across the world but he had a dedicated team based at Grendon Underwood in Buckinghamshire. Over 3,000 FANY personnel worked for SOE during World War II. FANY recruits were trained in four fields: W/T,

Codes, Motor Transport/Drivers or as general support. Of the fifty women deployed into France for SOE, some thirty-nine were FANYs. A total of thirteen of these were captured and murdered by the Gestapo.

Marks developed a one-off cipher system printed on silk, which the agent could stitch into their clothing. The silk cipher sheets were produced by GC&CS for SOE in bulk and were designed to be hidden in the lining of jackets.

The French Resistance graded their agents into distinct classes (the 'P' referring to 'person' in this context):

P0 – occasional agents
P1 – Agents devoting half their time to Resistance efforts
P2 – Full time agents

The networks covering the Normandy coastline were divided up into dossiers accordingly assigned to agents dependent on their skills, access and where they lived. These would cover the coastal and Anti-Aircraft (AA) batteries, beach obstacles, communications lines and infrastructure (railways/roads). The Caen network under Marcel Girard was on the frontline for intelligence gathering. Girard stated 'this is a mosaic job … putting together a thousand separate pieces … and the devil of it is we shall never know which piece it is that counts'. By mid-1943 London was developing an insatiable appetite for intelligence in the region. When the Resistance groups in and around Normandy were not coordinating arms and equipment airdrops or paramilitary training, they would be gathering intelligence and routing it through to their regional headquarters in Caen. The SOE mandate to support the Resistance was bolstered by a 1943 Directive issued by the Allied Chiefs of Staff, which was to articulate the requirements for Overlord.

Before World War II, Squadron Leader Forest Frederick Yeo-Thomas was a manager of the Molyneux dressmakers in Paris. During the outbreak of war in September 1939 he was to volunteer to join the RAF, remaining in France until he was evacuated out of Bordeaux in June 1940. In Britain he was attached as an RAF intelligence officer to act as an interpreter for a Polish Fighter Squadron and later transferred to the SOE RF Section in January 1942.

In February 1943, Yeo-Thomas was dropped into France by parachute for his first SOE mission, which was known as Seahorse under his covername of Shelley. He was to accompany General de Gaulle's intelligence chief André Dewavrin (aka Colonel Passy) and socialist leader Pierre Brossolette. Their collective aim was to organise ten inexperienced large groups and a dozen smaller groups of the French Resistance, uniting them under the leadership of General de Gaulle. During the deployment to

France, Yeo-Thomas was to save the lives of two Allied officers in the process, helping one of them return to Britain.

Brossolette and Yeo-Thomas would return to France later that year under another SOE liaison operation called Marie Claire, which was to establish how the various Resistance groups were faring after one of the highest profile members, Jean Moulin, was arrested by the Gestapo. Moulin had been instrumental in the creation of the unifying *Conseil National de la Résistance* (CNR). As he toured around the country attempting to recruit and bolster the Resistance efforts against the German occupation, Yeo-Thomas started to become known as the 'White Rabbit', which quickly gave him some notoriety both in the Resistance groups he worked with and with the German intelligence teams hunting him.

On the 21 March 1944, Shelley and his associate Brossolette were arrested on the steps of the Passy Metro station. Brossolette was to die soon after, after falling from the fifth floor of the Avenue Foch intelligence HQ. Yeo-Thomas was taken to the notorious Fresnes prison and was repeatedly tortured and interrogated. As the RF section second-in-command, he was one of the Gestapo's most valuable prisoners from SOE. It was on his direction that Churchill committed more airlifts and equipment for SOE and the French Resistance, which was to have a significant effect on the outcome for Overlord. Yeo-Thomas was always an advocate of the work and support the Resistance fighters could give to an Allied invasion, 'I was very much impressed by what I saw and if the camps I visited are a fair sample of the *Maquis* as a whole they promise to be one of our best assets for D-Day.'

Resistance groups in France played a hugely significant role in the gathering of intelligence in Normandy. The groups were to distribute over 1,000 telegrams a day to the BCRA Headquarters in St Stephen's House, London, and it has been estimated that these contributed nearly 80 per cent of the intelligence for D-Day.

In the early part of the German occupation of France the various Resistance groups did little in terms of cooperation with each other – there were communist groups, groups loyal to de Gaulle and groups aligned and tasked by SOE. It was not until March 1944 that General de Gaulle merged the fragments of the French Army into the Resistance to form the *Etat Major Forces Francaises de l'Intérieur* (EMFFI), although the communist FTP did not merge. The groups were collectively referred to as the '*Maquis*', which has connotations of outlaw behaviour and detachment from the regime. They were grouped according to the twelve regions of France and came under the official control of the *Comite d'Action contre la Deportation* (CAD). Around 10 per cent of their total complement were armed.

It was estimated there were 100,000 Resistance fighters operating in France by early 1944 who had serviceable weapons. But their main value for Overlord was not in offensive activity against the Germans but the intelligence gathering and sabotage that was undertaken on behalf of Allied intelligence. By the spring there were sixty intelligence cells operating whose sole mission was to gather intelligence. It has been estimated that in May 1944 alone they produced 3,000 written reports to Allied intelligence in England and transmitted 700 reports via wireless. The resupply of the *Maquis* was to put huge demands on the Allied Airforces and Navy in early 1944, but Churchill himself put pressure on military commanders to make these vital weapons and equipment drops. USAAF bombers from RAF Alconbury were re-directed exclusively for these missions.

The *Maquis* had a number of tasks to undertake on or around D-Day, their highest priority task being to interfere with the movement of troops and reinforcements by road and rail. They had a role to collect and relay tactical intelligence of relevance to the advancing Allied forces. Teams of up to thirty *Maquis* fighters in each district were instructed to be used as couriers to relay this important operational intelligence. They were to note details of bombing targets, the locations of enemy headquarters, troop concentrations and movements, ammunition dumps and enemy patrol locations.

Shortly after D-Day the independent Resistance circuits began to merge with the FFI and were put under the command of General Marie-Pierre Koenig, the Military Delegate of the French Committee of the National Liberation, and Commander-in-Chief of the French Forces in Great Britain. The EMFFI Headquarters was established in Bryanston Square, London and it was a subservient division of SHAEF HQ under Eisenhower.

One of the most significant of all Resistance groups operating in Normandy at the time was *Le Réseau Centurie* (or Century Network) which was part of the wider *L'Organization Civile et Militaire* (OCM) which had been set up by Marcel Girard from Caen but led by Gilbert Renault (aka Colonel Rémy). It provided the Allies with a plethora of maps, information and photographs on the German defensive positions on the Atlantic Wall. Guillaume Mercader was a network member and a professional cyclist before the war broke out. He had won 107 races and had opened up a bike shop in Bayeux. As he had a racing licence and looked the part, he could often get through the German checkpoints around the coastal defences with ease. He would stow sketches and maps which he had drawn in the tubing of his racing bike. Mercader also ran a mini-network of his own, with ninety-two agents operating in and around Bayeux, many of whom were farmers. One of the network's tasks was to monitor the movements of the German minesweepers and patrol boats coming in and out of Port-en-Bessin. Mercader would report the information daily back to London from his small Phillips transmitter radio set hidden in the basement of his bicycle shop. Mercader sold bicycles to many of the Germans deployed to Normandy and his estimate was that there were actually less than 1,500 German soldiers in the defensive positions on the 25-mile stretch of coastline between Grandcamp and Courseulles.

Another member of the Bayeux network was a blind French boy, Arthur Poitevin. He routinely used to walk along the Normandy cliffs around Port-en-Bessin. He would often get the opportunity to walk close to the defensive perimeters around the cliff batteries, pacing out each aspect of the perimeter. When he returned home, he would recall the figures to reconstruct the perimeter designs, which were conveyed to Allied intelligence via the group's wireless operator.

One of the Century Network was a painter and decorator, René Duchez. The forty-year-old was based in Caen and his group consisted of about forty Resistance operators. Shortly after the Dieppe raid, the network was tasked with acquiring intelligence on the German defences being built on the Normandy coast. During this period, Duchez applied for a painting job which had been advertised on the bulletin board in the Caen *Mairie*, or town hall. The decorating job was to be at the *Organisation Todt* offices on the Avenue Bagatelle, which in Caen were not strategically very important. The Germans would refer to it as a *Bauleitung* (works sub-sector), a subsidiary of the main offices in St Malo. One of the three buildings occupied by *Todt* in Caen was the *Abteilung Technik*, which oversaw work contracts and mapping.

Duchez immediately saw the opportunity to gather information for the network. He was hosted in the office by the site manager (*Bauleiter*), Faultier Schnedderer, with whom he discussed wallpaper patterns at length to use for papering two offices on the second floor. Agreeing on a price of 12,000 francs Schnedderer left the room briefly and Duchez took a look around the office. The desk was covered with maps and blueprints. He noticed one printed by the ozalide system of mimeograph, on deep blue cartographic paper which carried the bright red words '*SONDERZEICHUNGEN – STRENG GEHEIM*' (Special Blueprint – Top Secret). It appeared to have detailed construction plans for some of the Calvados coast batteries and fortifications. It covered in the minutest details all the military troop dispositions and coastal defensive positions between Quillebeuf and Cherbourg, a distance of over 100 miles on a scale of 1:50,000. Thinking quickly, Duchez folded up the 10-ft long plan and placed it behind a small mirror on the wall.

On his return the next day, Duchez wallpapered Schnedderer's office and rolled up the blueprint into one of his unused wallpaper rolls. On 13 May 1942, Duchez met Girard at the *Café des Touristes* in Caen where they exchanged the blueprint. The blueprint made its way to the leader of the network, Gilbert Renault. In Paris the plans were put in front of one of the leaders of the French Resistance networks, Colonel Alfred Touny, who commented, 'I think this may be the most important thing we have ever got hold of …'

Renault was aware of the value of the plans, and he asked some associates in Paris, including a skilled draughtsman, to copy the blueprint on a reduced scale so that they would have a copy to use and protect in case of compromise by German intelligence.

Renault knew the Gestapo was closing the net on him so he fled to Britain on a hired fishing boat with his family. The valuable blueprint had been folded up and placed inside a tin of *Crêpes Dentelles*, a Breton biscuit delicacy, waterproofed with some adhesive tape.

Schnedderer's office was appalled when the loss of the secret blueprint was noticed and being scared of the potential consequences of a Gestapo investigation, they covered everything up.

The stolen plans revealed the German defensive positions along the coastline between Le Havre and Cherbourg, and the subsequent gaps and weak points that could be exploited by an Allied amphibious assault. They displayed the gun emplacements with their effective ranges and fields of fire, the locations of Anti-Aircraft and machine gun positions, trench systems and supply depots. At this stage the Allies aerial reconnaissance efforts on Normandy were increasing as the plans for Overlord matured. What was critically important in terms of intelligence from the Duchez blueprint was that it highlighted some of the *Organisation Todt* defensive batteries and fortifications that had not even been built.

The blueprint originally made its way to the Combined Intelligence Section (CIS) of GHQ Home Forces under the command of General Bernard Paget. The CIS was a precursor to the Theatre Intelligence Section (TIS) in Storey's Gate in St James's Park, London, under the direction of John Austin. He was later to recall with regard to the value of the Duchez find, 'it scored a very great hit – it was the first genuine home-produced information about German defences that Britain received'.

The TIS intelligence staff, with some Royal Engineering support, merged the blueprint details with a contour map and the resulting 'Martian' report was distributed to a wide audience of the Overlord planners and intelligence teams. 'It turned their attention sharply to this weakly defended sector, showing that many earlier estimates of the strength had been alarmist and that a good deal of photographic interpretation had been in error.'

Duchez continued his work around Caen and another example of his opportunistic style was when he was relaxing in a café and met a St Aubin contractor who was supplying concrete for the defences in Ouistreham. He advised Chrêtian, the contractor, to alter the mixture of sand and cement to make the concrete more vulnerable. Eighteen months later, the US 9th Airforce launched bombing raids on Ouistreham and the concrete defences were damaged significantly more due to the structural weaknesses of the concrete.

The BBC *messages personnels* transmitted before D-Day were critical in getting the French Resistance operations coordinated. The night before D-Day on 6 June 1944 was a busy one for the Resistance. They carried out nearly a thousand sabotage operations, attacking telephone lines, railways, and the roads leading to Normandy, preventing the movement of German reinforcements once the Allies landed in the early hours.

General Eisenhower wrote after the war in his book, *My Crusade in Europe* (published in 1948) that the work of the French Resistance was the equivalent of fifteen divisions. By the end of June 1944 it is estimated that the French had in excess of 100,000 Resistance fighters operating against the Germans.

D-Day was the culmination of years of collective effort by the SOE and the Resistance groups in France. The groups were stimulated into action on 1 June 1944 by messages pumped out over the airwaves by BBC radio. It was to be a careful and meticulously planned call to arms. The SOE had been created almost from scratch in 1940 and General Eisenhower himself had recognised the value the organisation had brought to the Overlord plan in France. He was to state that the SOE 'played a very considerable part in our complete and final victory'. It refined itself as an effective subversive organisation by 1944 and swelled in numbers by D-Day with over 10,000 men and a further 3,000 women at its disposal.

The Resistance effort in Normandy had taken the lives of many Frenchmen. But they were a necessary sacrifice for the overall success of Overlord. Their intelligence-

Gilbert Renault on board the fishing vessel (N.51) en route to England, with his children Jean-Claude and Cécile Renault. Below the cardboard boxes is the biscuit tin containing the René Duchez Atlantic Wall blueprint (© Richard Collier – Ten Thousand Eyes)

gathering effort in 1944 demonstrated the value of local knowledge, opportunities that the Allies could never have imagined having. The Allies were to bolster these groups with small teams of highly trained special forces troops, which were called Jedburgh teams. It was their task to coordinate the Allied military campaign in France with the local Resistance efforts and arrange the supply of arms and equipment. The French Resistance had made huge strides forward in the year preceeding the start of Overlord, but the catalyst of the Jedburgh teams and other Allied special forces units were to turn the tide in northern France.

EMFFI Organisational structure 1944

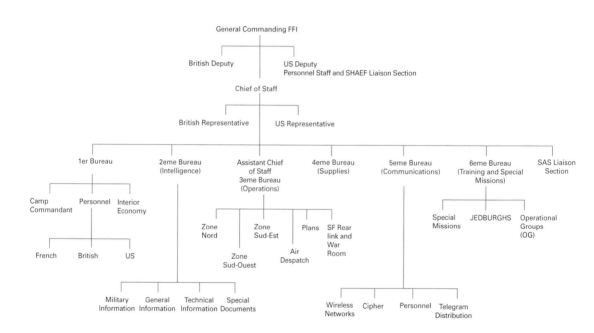

SOE F Section Organisational structure 1944

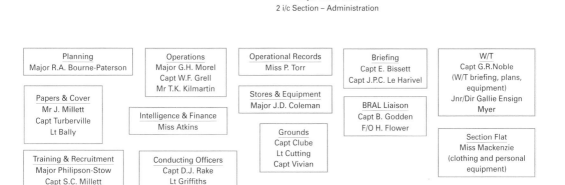

Lt. Colonel Maurice Buckmaster
Section Head

Major H.M. Fraser
2 i/c Section – Administration

Planning	Operations	Operational Records	Briefing	W/T
Major R.A. Bourne-Paterson	Major G.H. Morel Capt W.F. Grell Mr T.K. Kilmartin	Miss P. Torr	Capt E. Bissett Capt J.P.C. Le Harivel	Capt G.R.Noble (W/T briefing, plans, equipment) Jnr/Dir Gallie Ensign Myer

Papers & Cover
Mr J. Millett
Capt Turberville
Lt Bally

Stores & Equipment
Major J.D. Coleman

Intelligence & Finance
Miss Atkins

BRAL Liaison
Capt B. Godden
F/O H. Flower

Grounds
Capt Clube
Lt Cutting
Capt Vivian

Section Flat
Miss Mackenzie
(clothing and personal
equipment)

Training & Recruitment
Major Philipson-Stow
Capt S.C. Millett

Conducting Officers
Capt D.J. Rake
Lt Griffiths
Sub. Winser FANY
Ensign Minchin FANY
Ensign Wilen FANY

SOE RF Section organisational structure 1944

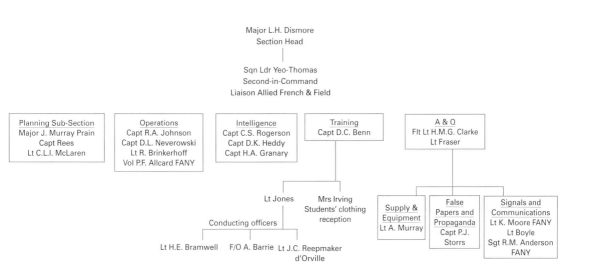

Major L.H. Dismore
Section Head

Sqn Ldr Yeo-Thomas
Second-in-Command
Liaison Allied French & Field

Planning Sub-Section	Operations	Intelligence	Training	A & Q
Major J. Murray Prain Capt Rees Lt C.L.I. McLaren	Capt R.A. Johnson Capt D.L. Neverowski Lt R. Brinkerhoff Vol P.F. Allcard FANY	Capt C.S. Rogerson Capt D.K. Heddy Capt H.A. Granary	Capt D.C. Benn	Flt Lt H.M.G. Clarke Lt Fraser

Lt Jones

Mrs Irving
Students' clothing
reception

Supply &
Equipment
Lt A. Murray

False
Papers and
Propaganda
Capt P.J.
Storrs

Signals and
Communications
Lt K. Moore FANY
Lt Boyle
Sgt R.M. Anderson
FANY

Conducting officers

Lt H.E. Bramwell   F/O A. Barrie   Lt J.C. Reepmaker
d'Orville

LEFT: SOE F Section wireless operator on Farmer Circuit, AAA Staggs passport photograph (© IWM Documents 12848 – FFI papers of AAG Staggs)

BELOW: SOE F Section wireless operator on Farmer Circuit, AAA Staggs FFI Identity card (© IWM Documents 12848 – FFI papers of AAG Staggs)

SOE Parachute drops April 1943 to September 1944
(from Secret Warfare – *The Arms and techniques of the Resistance* by Pierre Lorain)

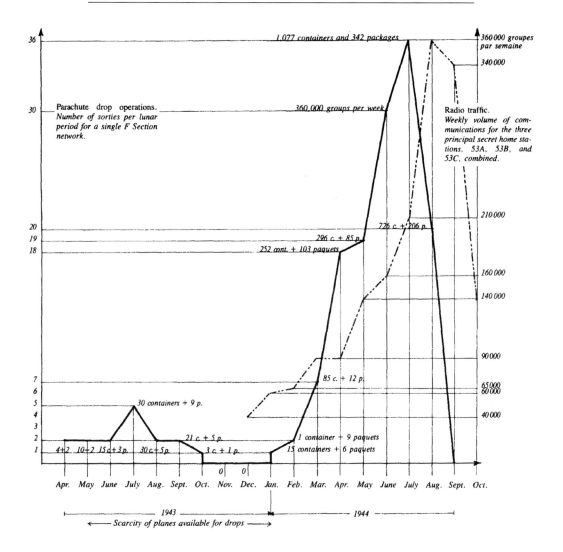

LEFT: Lieutenant Tony Byrd RNVR

ABOVE: MGB502 vessel involved in Operation Scarf (April 1944)

ABOVE: *Westward Ho* paddle steamer, which served as the 15th Flotilla HQ during 1944

LEFT: French agent Suzanne Warenghem

LEFT: French agent Blanche Charlet and SOE wireless operator Brian Stonehouse

RIGHT: The gravestone of Able Seaman William Sandalls, killed in action in Operation Scarf, 16 April 1944. His grave is in Charlbury village cemetery (© author)

CHAPTER FIVE
PERSUADERS

'Their patriotism was the purist essence, and the courage they showed will never be exceeded by the courage of any man.'

Colonel Francis Pickens-Miller

~~~

'They were, I believe, the best guerrilla fighters in the world.'

Lieutenant Colonel Frank Mills DSO

~~~

In the early stages of the German occupation of France, the French Resistance groups were in disarray, and had limited effectiveness against a professional army. Two major initiatives were developed during the latter part of 1942 to augment the Resistance, but also to provide the Allies with some much needed intelligence through putting eyes and ears on the ground to report on German army troop movements in northern France.

The Americans relied heavily on British intelligence between 1942 and 1943, and the ETOUSA (European Theatre of Operations, United States of America) teams knew they had to get in on the act. But they had no defined plan for producing their own intelligence. In the run-up to D-Day, Allied planners would need reliable, accurate and timely intelligence on the Germans in and around Normandy.

Joint work between SOE and their direct American counterparts, the Special Operations (SO) branch of the OSS began in earnest from around June 1942, and there was an agreement to establish a joint organisation to direct and support French Resistance groups.

After numerous tripartite discussions in the spring of 1943, OSS Captain Stacy Lloyd began to formulate a plan. The first OSS reference is in a branch report of 1 April 1943, which stated:

'As the month grew to a close, Captain Stacy Lloyd drew up a project for the organisation of a number of 2-man intelligence teams, equipped with W/T, to be dropped well behind the lines at the time a Continental bridgehead was being established.'

A further branch report dated 16 April 1943 refers to the project as 'one to drop 50 parties of observers and reporters behind enemy lines at the time of the Continental invasion'. This plan, which became known simply as 'Plan B', was submitted for approval to General Donovan, the then head of OSS. The plan outlined that the operatives would be wearing uniform. It was rejected '… while Captain Lloyd was to be commended for his foresight and efforts, the consensus of opinion was that reconnaissance intelligence groups constituted a combat intelligence function more appropriate to orthodox military organisations and personnel …'

A subsequent cable from OSS Headquarters in Washington in mid-April reinvigorated the plans to open new conversations with the French and British. This eventually led to the establishment of the Sussex Plan under the direction of three men, British SIS Commander Kenneth Cohen, American OSS Colonel Francis Pickens-Miller and the Frenchman BCRA operator Gilbert Renault. This was an intelligence operation to drop covert teams into France, north of the Loire Valley between January and September 1944 to spearhead the approach to the Overlord plan. It was to become the biggest intelligence operation of the entire war.

Their mission was succinctly put by Pickens-Miller: 'to secure strategic and tactical intelligence from rear areas'. At its outset this tripartite venture took some time to cement. 'The British were exceedingly reluctant to enter into such an arrangement. Eventually the British agreed, but it was quite clear that they desired to narrow the scope of such tripartite meetings.'

There were two main reasons for it to be established:

1. The fear that gathering of Allied forces for the invasion of Europe would rapidly increase German security measures in occupied France, where the existing 'reseaux' would become immobile, cut off from their communications, or penetrated and dismantled. The Plan would be a form of re-insurance to cover this possibility.
2. It was desirable to organise a chain of agents in certain areas as directed by the intelligence branch of the Combined General Staff, who would be capable of obtaining information of direct interest and value. This would be operational intelligence from the enemy rear areas, which could not easily be obtained through normal Army sources.

There were to be a total of fifty-six Sussex teams deployed, involving over 120 volunteers who would receive specialist training by SIS and OSS instructors at Praewood House in St Albans, and a week-long parachute training course at the Ringway School. The RAF dropped fifty-eight of the Sussex Plan agents into France during 1944, and the USAF 'Carpetbaggers' infiltrated some forty-eight agents. Many of the Carpetbaggers operations quirkily had names of car manufacturers, such as Bentley, Ellis, Lincoln and Plymouth. The Sussex Plan teams would fly out of RAF Harrington or Tempsford airfields after a period at the holding station of Farm Hall, on West Street in Godmanchester.

It was extremely dangerous work. Seven of the teams were caught during their operations and executed. The individuals selected for such an assignment had to be cherry-picked for the roles.

The W/T operators for the Sussex Plan teams were each supplied with the British Mark 7 or the American TR-1 radio sets and the cipher book, containing a double-transposition cipher with flash code. A flash code acts as a group of numbers which relay to a distinct phrase or word which carries significance. Some of the operators had come from Section VIII of SIS, based out of Whaddon in Buckinghamshire. They were to form up as Special Communications Unit (SCU) 9 and be dropped with the Sussex Plan teams.

The Berkshire town of Hurley became integral to the Sussex Plan communications. The OSS established a secret communications centre in the town to transmit and receive messages carrying vital intelligence on German military strengths and dispositions, particularly the Panzer divisions. Codenamed Station Victor, this acted as the communications hub for the deployed Sussex Plan teams.

One of the most famous Sussex Plan operations, due to the intelligence they provided to Allied forces, was undertaken by team Vitrail, which was deployed into Chartres on the 10 April 1944. It was the first deployed Sussex Plan team to send messages back to Station Victor. Soon after deploying they discovered the location of the Lehr Panzer division in Chartres. SHAEF HQ later commented that this message alone was worth the cost of the whole Sussex operational plan.

Another plan conceived by General Colin Gubbins in his role as Head of SOE was to run in parallel with the Sussex Plan. Operation Jedburgh would consist of around seventy highly trained special forces soldiers who would be parachuted into France to support the Resistance around D-Day in June 1944. They were to be controlled via the Jedburgh Section in Special Forces Headquarters (SFHQ) in Montagu Mansions, London.

A planning officer in the OSS Special Operations (SO) branch, Lieutenant Colonel Franklin Canfield, can take the credit for getting the OSS involved in the Jedburgh missions. As the date for D-Day progressed and drew near, he was subsequently moved across to SHAEF to act as the OSS Liaison. At this stage of the war, SFHQ was under the nominal command of SHAEF. This communications chain would assist with the transfer of the intent of General Eisenhower down to the French Resistance leaders.

On 6 July 1942, Gubbins described the concept:

'A project is under consideration for dropping behind enemy lines, in cooperation with an Allied invasion of the Continent, small parties of officers and men to raise and arm the civilian population to carry out guerrilla activities against the enemy's lines of communication. These men are to be recruited and trained by SOE. It is requested that "Jumpers" or some other appropriate code name be allotted to this personnel.'

The day after Gubbins scribed this memo, the code name Jedburgh was assigned to the group.

One of the key architects of D-Day, British Lieutenant General Frederick Morgan, gave approval for the Jedburgh proposal on 19 July 1943 in a report he drafted to the Chiefs of Staff:

'I have discussed with SOE their proposals for D-Day.

a. Small SOE staffs and Signal Sections at Headquarters of Armies, and SOE representatives at Headquarters of Army Groups and of the Supreme Commander, for controlling Resistance groups

b. Reserve teams of personnel (JEDBURGHS) to be kept in this country for use after D-Day, to provide, if necessary, suitable leadership and equipment for those Resistance groups found to be in need of them.

I have agreed in principle to these proposals, and request that the Chiefs of Staff instruct the War Office to prepare the detailed establishments and arrange at the appropriate time, for the transfer of SOE of any personnel necessary.'

The Chiefs of Staff Committee reviewed the proposal from General Morgan and gave it their tacit approval on 21 July 1943. They were to be an SOE strategic reserve – in that they could be directed by the Allied Commander as and when required. Both the Special Operations division of the OSS and SOE would act together to recruit and train selected officers and wireless operators. The SOE had drawn up plans to coordinate Resistance activities in northwest Europe in which the Jedburgh teams would play their part:

Plan Blue – sabotage against German army electrical supply systems

Plan Vert – railway sabotage

Plan Violet – sabotage against German telecommunications system

Plan Torture – sabotage against bridges/highways

A month later the D-Day plans were conveyed to SOE and OSS senior staff and planning began in earnest for the creation of a new secret army to augment the French Resistance.

During the latter months of 1943, the SOE and SO worked to develop the operational details for the Jedburgh deployments into France. It fostered the creation of the Jedburgh directive of 20 December 1943 which laid out the plans for how the units would operate and function:

'Jedburghs are specially trained three-man teams. They will be dropped by parachute at prearranged spots in France, Belgium and Holland on and after D-Day. Each Jedburgh team consists of two officers and a radio operator with his W/T set. One officer is a native of the country to which the team is going, and the other British or American. The members of the team are soldiers and will normally arrive in the field in uniform. There they will make contact with the Resistance groups, bringing them instructions from the Supreme Allied Commander, W/T communications, supplies, and if necessary, leadership.'

One such Jedburgh team was Team Citroen, led by the laid-back and athletic British regular Army officer Major John Smallwood. The three-man team also included the Frenchman Major Bloch and Sergeant Fred Bailey as the W/T operator. Major Bloch

Jedburgh W/T operators in training

(*nom de guerre* Rene Alcée) was a regular in the French Foreign Legion (he was later killed by a landmine after World War II, during the Algerian War of Independence) who did not speak any English. Sergeant Bailey admired Bloch but 'the Frenchman was more involved with the politics, there was a lot of politics with the *Maquis*. The Force Partisans were mainly Communist and the Forces Francaises de l'intérieur were the de Gaullists. So there was always a problem with politics. It used to get in the way sometimes. He sorted all that out. When we got prisoners he would do the interrogations.'

Many of the French volunteers for the SOE had come out shortly after the German occupation, but a lot came out of North Africa, especially Algeria, most notably the radio operators.

Bailey recalled that Smallwood 'was the only man I knew who was fluent in French but with an Oxford accent! He became an Aide-de-Camp to a French General after we finished in France. He was the active member, always looking for trouble. He went off with the *Maquis* to chase up the German rearguard when they were retreating.' He had to fight his way back to where the rest of the team was, which earned him an immediate *Croix de Guerre*.

Born in November 1923, Fred Bailey was only sixteen years old at the outbreak of the war. As soon as he could he joined up, coinciding with his eighteenth birthday. He was an enthusiastic and well-trained Radio Operator/Gunner within the Royal Armoured Corps but he had been posted into a dull and mainstream Armoured Car Battalion of the Green Howards in Scarborough, billeted in a seafront hotel. It was poorly equipped and poorly led, so Fred and many of his peers decided to volunteer out of the Battalion.

In 1943, a routine Part 2 orders notice came around his regiment about Special Duties involving parachuting and almost immediately he and two others volunteered.

Fred Bailey
(© Fred Bailey)

Bailey made his way to a camp just outside Oxford where they were interviewed by psychologists and had their rudimentary Morse skills tested. His radio work within the Royal Armoured Corps was mostly voice and they could only muster six to eight words a minute in Morse at this stage. They had little idea what they would be trained to do. After signing the Official Secrets Act, Bailey returned to his original regiment to gather his belongings and come back for the next phase of training.

The group was subsequently posted to the SOE's Fawley Court (the SOE referred to the site as STS 54a) just outside Henley-on-Thames, where they began their initial

Jedburgh wireless training under the direction of instructors from the Royal Corps of Signals. One such instructor was the overweight Signals Sergeant 'Busty' Lettuce who was superb at Morse. The site was also a training centre for the FANY wireless operators. It was here that the operators trained and operated on the B2 suitcase radios – with Morse skills of up to twenty words a minute. The volunteers were accommodated in Nissen huts in the grounds of Countess Gardens, a row of terraced cottages in Henley. There were no mess facilities, so they had to frequent the Catherine Wheel pub in Henley in order to have a drink.

As the operators became more proficient with the B-2 sets and Morse code, their training evolved to cover martial arts/close-quarter combat training, small arms/firearms training on weapons like the colt automatic and sten gun, physical training, silent killing techniques and further advanced training on the B2 radio. Henley was the non-commissioned officers wireless and clandestine warfare training school. They used to call the Colt, their issue sidearm, the 'Persuader'.

Bailey was to reflect that, 'the training was very intense but I stayed with it as I knew that I was doing something useful. There was a lot of work over vaulting horses and fences. We used to have a game called "all-in" played like rugger but with a medicine ball. There were no rules … anybody that wasn't up to scratch were weeded out and sent back to their unit.'

During training at the Fawley Court phase of training, the teams deployed up to Belhaven School not far from the barracks in Dunbar (which the SOE referred to as STS 54b), which was used as a training school for SOE wireless operators. The teams would practise sending messages back to Fawley Court, some 390 miles away to hone their Morse telegraphy and key operating skills. Bailey was to become an experienced W/T operator but 'people didn't have a clue who we were or what we were doing. We were never dressed like soldiers somehow. They didn't like us very much. We referred to ourselves as Jeds. We lived in what was an old school and there was a sign on the outside saying No Unauthorised WD Personnel.'

After Henley, the Jedburgh training became centred around the seventeenth-century ancestral home of Earl Fitzwilliam, at Milton Hall (known covertly by SOE as ME/65), 10 miles outside Peterborough, alongside contingents from the French BCRA and American OSS. There were a number of field exercises during the Milton Hall phase, explosives training, enemy weapons use, escape and evasion, intelligence gathering, language and the consolidated three-day parachute training.

'We met up there with the Americans and French. That was when we first realised there was something serious going on. We found ourselves on American rations, smoking American cigarettes. We all trained together and lived together. We all got on, as we were all under similar circumstances. This is where we all got into our teams. We formed mutually agreeable teams. Smallwood came over to talk to me and asked to set up a team.'

Parachute training was undertaken at the infamous RAF Ringway No. 1 Parachute Training School at what is now Manchester Airport. Bailey recalls: 'I used to hate it. I remember the first jump from a balloon, from a cage underneath a barrage balloon at 800ft. I always remember, we were about to go up onto the balloon and a Flight Lieutenant roared up on a motorbike and he said "Right I'm the Dispatcher, and I'm on a 48 hour pass after this so I don't want any buggering about up there."

'The second jump, the next day was a daylight jump from a Whitley Bomber. The third jump was a night jump also out of a Whitley Bomber. That was the training. That was it.'

The Jedburgh teams were ready to deploy into France, long before D-Day but were not tasked. Bailey stated, 'everybody was ready but somehow the plans just seemed to get delayed, and we couldn't quite get off the ground…. We had spent a lot of time and sweat training for this very thing but we all went in just before D-Day.

'We had been trained to land at 800 feet but we were dropped at 1800 feet. I landed in a disused brick yard, but luckily landed in a good position, uninjured.

'We were supposed to send back intelligence, organise supply drops to local Resistance forces and carry out any subversive operations that were available to us, such as bridge blowing, ambushes and general harassing of the enemy. We went in just before D-Day but in my view we went in far too late. We should have gone in at least 3 months before. We went in too late to be effective. It takes time to organise sabotage, raids and ambushes. We could have achieved greater confidence from the local Resistance forces. We didn't really get enough time to know them well, to know the good from the bad. We could have arranged substantially greater supply drops in the places where they were required and we would have had more time to assess the enemy's strength and to carry out subversive operations.'

Bailey's Team Citroen sailed to Algiers on the *Capetown Castle* in the early part of 1944 from Southampton, via Gibraltar. After the three-week voyage, the teams were based at El Riyaf, an old French Cavalry Officers' facility in the middle of a nectarine orchard a short distance from the SOE headquarters in Algiers. After a short period of training in the mountains of Algeria, they became one of the fifteen Jedburgh teams who were parachuted into France under the cover of a moonless night. The teams were given little in the way of briefing on local intelligence or on the Overlord plans, briefings were given by some of the FANY operators in Algiers on local topography (largely from textbooks) but it was a very poor and limited preparation for them. Bailey was given a silk scarf printed with an escape map of France in case they were ever compromised.

Much of the intelligence Citroen gathered was fed back via their B2 wireless sets to the FANY wireless operators deployed to Massingham, the SOE Headquarters in Algiers which had responsibility for operations in southern France.

The B2 set was used for transmitting and receiving Morse. 'We had two sets, one in a suitcase that you could plug into a light socket and another one in a canvas pack which you could use a hand generator to operate. When I went in, the parachute which was attached to the container which held the suitcase set and some of my personal equipment failed to open... we had small arms, a Colt .45 automatic revolver and an American carbine with the associated ammunition. The policy was, as far as possible, that the radio operators were kept away from the enemy because they were the only means of communication. The aggressive activities were carried out by the two commissioned officers in conjunction with the local *Maquis*.

'It was important to be on the air as short a time as possible, because if you got zoned in on a direction-finding team the Gestapo would be round knocking on the door. The main thing was to keep the messages short and to move the transmission area as much as you could. We usually had two schedules a day. You had to send the information back, however long it took.

'We were dropped about 20 miles north of Aix-en-Provence in a town called Apt and from there on the following day we travelled to a town just northeast, a town called Pertuis about and I lived there in various addresses until we were overrun by the Americans.'

Citroen was dropped in on 13 August 1944 in the South of France from an American Liberator aircraft, just prior to the invasion. There was a bit of anti-aircraft fire as it neared the coast. It was dropped slightly off target. The French Resistance had laid-on a reception committee of signal torches in the shape of an arrow pointing in the direction of the wind.

Bailey was understandably apprehensive about the mission, 'the DZ where we were dropped wasn't meant for personnel, only equipment and it was the last mission for the Liberator crew and they were quite convinced they weren't going to get back so instead of dropping us at 800 feet they dropped us at 2,000 feet. It took us an age to get down. We've no idea where the ground is because it's pitch dark. I landed in a disused brick yard. I suddenly saw someone running towards me. I got my parachute off and wrestled to get my Colt .45 out and I was embraced by a Frenchman with about 3 months growth of beard and I offered a handshake but he insisted on kissing me and he stank of sweat and garlic.'

The Jedburgh teams, as they were in uniform, were entitled to be treated as Prisoners of War, but they suspected that would not be the case. If the team was ever to be picked up by the Germans:

'The primary instruction, whatever pressure you were under, was to hold out for at least 48 hours, so the rest of the circle that you were connected with had a chance to disappear and make the appropriate arrangements.'

Daphne Park

The soldiers in the area where Citroen was deployed were very weak, as they consisted mostly of troops convalescing from the Eastern Front. 'If they'd have had one armoured division down there the Americans wouldn't have been able to get off the beach.'

Each Jedburgh W/T operator had a cipher book, or One-Time Pad, which was used to encode and decode the transmitted or received traffic. Much of the training on this was delivered by FANY Daphne Park, a Cambridge graduate at Milton Hall. She had joined the FANY in 1943 and during her selection she had come to the attention of the SOE, due to her natural ability with codes and ciphers. She was quickly promoted to Sergeant and trained the Jedburgh teams. After the war, she went on to have a long and successful career with the SIS.

These One-Time Pads were been printed at the Oxford University Press (OUP) under direction from the GC&CS staff at Mansfield College.

Most of the messages Citroen transmitted back were about troop movements in the area and operations that had been undertaken. Smallwood actually received a *Croix de Guerre* whilst Citroen was in southern France, which was fairly unusual. If operating behind enemy lines was not a tough enough challenge, both Bailey and Smallwood had almost permanent bouts of dysentery the whole time they were in France!

On one particular operation they managed to capture about half a dozen German

Wehrmacht soldiers who were subsequently interrogated. One was a Lieutenant who had a map sewn into his jacket sleeve, which showed the German army southern escape route up towards Lyon and on to Germany. Citroen transmitted the information back to HQ and an air strike took place the next day using Halifax and Liberator bombers deploying from Algiers to attack the retreating convoys. The raid caused a lot of devastation.

Citroen remained in Pertuis in the Vaucluse district until September 1944, when the US forces arrived in the town, and the team moved into Avignon where the Jedburgh teams in the South of France congregated at the Hotel Creyon. Bailey was then deployed in a group of 3 W/T operators to Bari in southern Italy. A few months later he deployed to Ceylon and became part of the SOE's Force 136 in the Far East.

Lieutenant Colonel James Riley Holt Hutchison was the son of a Scottish shipbuilder. He was assigned the *nom de guerre* 'John Hastings' but was not actually categorised as a Jedburgh operator, He had served in World War I in the Lanarkshire Yeomanry, and was the only serving Jedburgh in World War II to have fought in Gallipoli in 1915. His face and identity were widely known to the Gestapo, as Resistance interrogations and captured documents had exposed him as a senior SOE officer. They had nicknamed him the 'Pimpernel of the *Maquis*' in his role as the head of the SOE RF Section.

To disguise himself further, Hutchison had facial plastic surgery undertaken by one of the leading plastic surgeons in the country at the time, New Zealander Rainsford Mowlem. He operated on Hutchison at the London Clinic in Marylebone, reducing the size of both his ears and nose, and altering his chin.

Hutchison spent over four months in France with the Jedburgh team and was subsequently awarded the Distinguished Service Order (DSO) and the French *Croix de Guerre*. After the war, Hutchison enjoyed a fourteen-year Parliamentary career as a Unionist MP for Glasgow, and during this period was appointed Financial Secretary and Under Secretary of State for the War Office between 1951 and 1954.

The second member of ISAAC was the Frenchman Lieutenant Colonel F.G. Viat from the BCRA. The team was complimented by the British W/T operator Sergeant John Sharp.

Sharp joined the Army just before his nineteenth birthday in March 1942. He volunteered for the Royal Armoured Corps and did his initial training at Bovington, where he first met Fred Bailey. Sergeant John Sharp joined the Jedburgh teams from his parent unit of Royal

Sergeant John Sharp

Armoured Corps aged twenty-one. He left Britain aboard a Sterling bomber at D+3 with Lieutenant Colonel Hutchison from 22 SAS. It was intended that they be dropped into France at D-7 but the plan was aborted. Their mission was to delay the infamous *Das Reich* panzer division which was positioned outside Dijon, to prevent it moving up to Normandy. There were twelve operators blind-dropped from this aircraft near Nièvre, in the Morvan Region national park, including near the town of Aubingy-sur-Nère. The team was dropped from far too high, at over 3,000 ft and they were carried far from the proscribed Drop Zone (DZ). Sharp, who had been last to jump, landed in a tree but managed to scramble quickly to the ground. Hutchison was found two fields away and had broken a bone in his foot.

One of the most decorated French agents involved with the Sussex Plan was Jeanette Guyot. She had been involved with the French Resistance with her parents from the onset of the German occupation through the Amarante network as a *passeur*, smuggling people across the demarcation lines. Towards the end of 1941 she became the liaison officer for Gilbert Renault (codename Colonel Rémy), chief of the Parisien network Confrérie Notre-Dame. Guyot was captured by the Germans in February 1942 and imprisoned at the Chalon-sur-Saône and Autun prisons, where she was routinely interrogated and tortured. She was released three months later, but further activity with the Resistance in Vichy France put her under the Gestapo spotlight and she was extracted during a rescue mission launched by Lysander aircraft from the RAF's 161 Squadron.

In London Guyot met back up with Colonel Rémy and enlisted into the Free French forces and was volunteered for the Sussex Plan. On 8 February 1944, Guyot was parachuted back into France, as part of the Calanque team. This team acted as the Sussex Plan pathfinders, scouring the French countryside for parachute drop zones and safe houses for the following Sussex Plan teams. Over the course of seven months the Calanque team organised a score of drop zones with the French Resistance and nearly a hundred safe houses for Sussex Plan agents.

In the Montmartre area of Paris, Guyot recruited one of her cousins, Mme Andrée Goubillon, to hide the team's wireless operator at the Café de l'Electricité, which she owned. 'I knew which kind of work she had come to make, and when she asked me … if I were ready to help her, I answered yes without the least hesitation. Although the café was located beside an office of the Gestapo … I was not afraid.' The café was later renamed the *Café des Sussex*, in honour of its wartime role.

The Special Air Service (SAS) were also involved in Overlord. Their original request to 1 and 2 SAS Regiments was for ten separate parties consisting of five men each to be dropped on the night of D-2/D-1. They were to be a combined unit – with soldiers from the 3rd and 4th French Parachute battalions, to provide interpreters. They were to lie low until the next night of D-1/D. They had numerous tasks to fulfil:

i)   Special tasks – the destruction of a specific bridge, or installation
ii)   Roads – prevention of movement along roads by all available means
iii)   Railways – derailment of trains, damage to signals, rolling stock
iv)   Telecoms – destruction of underground cables, cutting of overhead telephone/telegraph lines
v)   Contact with Partisans – raising the flag of revolt among the local inhabitants and assistance to existing Resistance groups
vi)   Offensive jeep patrols

The training and exercises for the teams were coordinated in the run-up to D-Day by the founder of the SAS, Lieutenant Colonel David Stirling and his French counterpart M. Le Capitaine Conan. At these final stages of the Overlord planning, it was critical that no military personnel who were exposed to the detailed strategic plans behind the invasion were dropped into occupied Europe before D-Day to prevent any information being seized on capture and interrogation. In the Operational instructions for Overlord it stated 'no personnel who have been concerned in planning, or who know the date or area of seaborne assault will be permitted to operate before D-Day'.

1 SAS Regiment had some quite specific tasks to undertake, notably to prevent the movement of enemy reserve divisions in:

1. Lisieux area – prevent ten SS Panzer Division Frundsberg moving toward Caen
2. Alencon area – elements of seventeen SS Panzer Grenadier Division Goetz Von Berlichingen. 'There is almost certainly a division in this area on D-Day, and it is vital that the movement of this Division towards Caen and St. Lo should be delayed to the maximum extent.'
3. Mantes area – prevent twenty-one Panzer Division moving towards Lisieux.

The teams were deployed to raise havoc with German reinforcements moving towards Normandy, carry out sabotage, and gather information on German military movements and dispositions, and French Resistance activity. They were also briefed to identify targets that might be suitable for Allied bombing. The units were to 'assume command in the area and endeavour to convert it into a major centre of Resistance to which supplies can be regularly sent and from which parties can continue to operate'. At about D+4 the units would be reinforced depending on the information they sent back. If it was impossible to operate because of the strength of the German reactions, the SAS troops could be evacuated by sea.

Each SAS unit carried a 'Biscuit Tin' MCR.1 (Midget Communications Receiver) unit, so called because it was so small it could fit in a biscuit tin, built by Philco (UK) which was used to receive broadcasts from England. It had a battery set that could last one hundred hours of continual use. Each unit also carried a pigeon which was to be despatched on D+1 or D+2 with information on the operations.

By the end of June 1944, a total of 585 SAS soldiers had been dropped by 38 Group RAF into France, nearly a third of the Brigades operational capacity. On the crucial night of the 5/6 June, forty-three SAS troops were dropped in the early hours, being among the first Allied soldiers to re-enter Europe on Eisenhower's second front.

As part of the Operation Titanic deception operation, two SAS officers and four other ranks dropped west of St Lo with hundreds of dummy parachutists, rifle fire simulators and Verey lights to distract the Germans away from the US Airborne divisional landings north of Carentan.

Following D-Day, American Staff Headquarters wanted to bolster the number of Sussex intelligence teams operating in France. The OSS was tasked with pulling together the surplus agents within the Sussex Plan and in conjunction with the French BCRA a bilateral operation was hatched, known as the Proust Plan.

The plan would hinge on the BCRA recruiting volunteers in North Africa and this began in earnest in March 1944. The new recruits would often arrive into the UK individually. In charge of the Proust Plan was the US Colonel Neave, and the training for the group would take place at an established OSS school located in Horsham, Sussex.

The training centre for Proust was at the thirteenth-century Drungewick Manor in Horsham (covername Freehold), which was owned at the time by the American film producer Gilbert Miller. The teams were to be infiltrated into France mostly via parachute airdrop by the Carpetbaggers from RAF Harrington. The 801st/492nd Bomb Group at Harrington were responsible for dropping Proust, Jedburgh, SOE, OSS and Sussex Plan teams into France. Between the months of January and September 1944 they had undertaken 2,263 missions, of which 1,577 were deemed successful. Forty-six of the Proust team agents were airdropped by the USAF Carpetbaggers teams in 1944.

Many of the new recruits did not make it over to England or did not make the grade during the initial selection phases of training. The much larger, and now operational, Sussex Plan eventually sucked in many of the more able recruits but by April 1944 the training began in earnest to shape the team of fifty selected agents.

The intelligence-gathering work of the Sussex Plan was very significant for the collection of situational awareness of the German forces before and after D-Day. By the end of August 1944, over thirty Sussex Plan teams were deployed into France and they had transmitted over 800 radio messages with key intelligence on the German troop dispositions. But it came at a price. Over ten agents lost their lives.

CHAPTER SIX
CAGES

'If any German had any information we wanted, it was invariably extracted from him in the long run.'

Lieutenant Colonel Alexander Scotland, London Cage

~~~

'Since its inception in September 1939, CSDIC has proved one of our most valuable sources of intelligence ...'

JIC Subcommittee Report – CAB81/93 JIC (45) 54 (O), 15 February 1945

~~~

Prisoner of War (POW) intelligence has always played a critical part in intelligence gathering in war. World War II was no exception. Interrogation, or the systematic longer-term questioning of an individual, is an important component of the processing and exploitation of a POW. Pre-D-Day vital intelligence was gleaned from the work undertaken by MI9 at the 'cages' or interrogation centres. It could be said that the contribution this intelligence made was as significant as the work done at Bletchley Park in the run-up to June 1944. Without a doubt, military intelligence from POW interrogations has been very much undervalued by historians. Over 10,000 POWs had their conversations monitored at a network of covert facilities around the country, providing over 100,000 intelligence transcripts which led to MI19 issuing over 2,000 formal interrogation reports.

The first POW camps to emerge were at Glen Mill Camp, a disused cotton mill in Oldham, Lancashire and Camp No. 1 at Grizedale Hall a forty-room mansion near Satterthwaite in the Lake District. As the war progressed, so did the flood of prisoners from Europe, to a point near the end of the war where Britain had 600 POW camps. It has been estimated over half-a-million Axis prisoners were being held in Britain by the end of World War II. Many thousands of these went through the interrogation centres. What developed over the course of the war was a complex and very professional global network of facilities producing high-grade intelligence for the Allied intelligence machine.

In the early stages of the war the three services had a degree of independence and autonomy when it came to prisoner of war interrogations. The RAF had a specific team, AI1(K) under Flight Lieutenant Felkin, established to conduct the detailed interrogations of *Luftwaffe* pilots shot down in Britain. Naval Intelligence had its own interrogation specialists in NID11, created in 1940 and run by Lieutenant Colonel Trench. By January 1942 NID11 was split into NID1(P/W) and NID3(P/W) which would deal with the interrogations of German and Italian naval prisoners of war respectively. The Army was initially centred around manpower provided to the Combined Services Detailed Interrogation Centre (CSDIC) and the Prisoner of War Interrogation Section (Home) or PWIS(H). Each service orchestrated its own POW intelligence collection but prospective prisoners held by any service who were deemed of intelligence value were transferred to CSDIC (UK).

Around this time AI1(K) also set up a Document Section, to assess and analyse documents found in downed aircraft, such as logbooks, maps and diaries. They even valued savings books, which would assist with the tracking of Axis pilots' movements. Identity papers and field-posting papers were often significant in informing Allied intelligence as to the whereabouts of German divisions. Interrogators often looked for postcodes (*Feldpostnummera*) in the men's paybooks. The Air Ministry also had ADI(K) or Assistant Director Intelligence (K Section) set up to be responsible for interrogating shot-down *Luftwaffe* aircrew. The section was also on the distribution for the ULTRA deciphered signals traffic from Bletchley Park.

In 1939, Field Marshal Sir Gerald Templer set up MI9. It was led by Major Norman Crockatt DSO MC and operated out of Room 424 in the Metropole Hotel (now the Corinthia Hotel), in London's Northumberland Avenue. It was largely focused on the movement of Allied prisoners and evaders, and dealt with captured enemy POWs.

MI9 had a number of roles, one of which was to collect and disseminate intelligence from POWs. MI9 was divided into two distinct sections: MI9a dealt with enemy POW and oversaw the work of the CSDIC and MI9b, which dealt with British and Allied prisoners and evaders. Before the war started all three of the military services established a combined services interrogation centre, which was initially located in the Tower of London. On 12 December 1939, CSDIC moved to Trent Park in Cockfosters, north London. This tri-service collaboration and joint approach to POW intelligence gathering stayed firm until the end of the war.

MI9(a) was responsible for the following duties:

a)   The general policy and Intelligence administration of the Combined Services Detailed Examination Centre for Enemy Prisoners of War, at Cockfosters Camp.

b)   The provision and maintenance of special apparatus required by the three services at Cockfosters Camp.

c) Liaison with GHQ, British Expeditionary Force (BEF) on arrangements for the examination of enemy Prisoners of War.

d) Organisation of examination of Internees in conjunction with Commandants and Interpreters of Alien Camps and of persons arriving from enemy countries.

e) Obtaining from the Service or other interested Departments interrogatories for use at the Combined Services Centre and the distribution of reports in accordance with the requirements of these Departments.

f) Coordination of policy on questions affecting Alien Camps and Prisoners of War Camps from the point of view of censorship, propaganda and MI5.

Organisational structure of MI19 (from WO 208/4970)

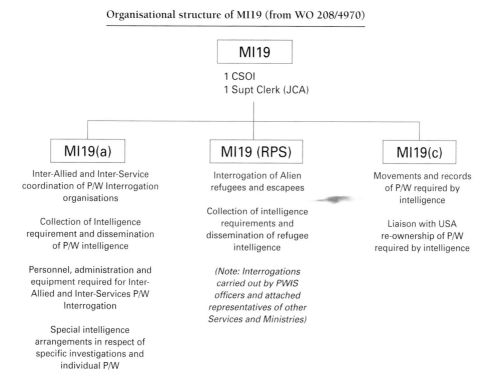

Its counterpart section MI9(b) had the following remit:

a) General questions on behalf of the three Services affecting British Prisoners of War and Internees in enemy countries.

b) Arrangements in conjunction with Military Attachés in neutral countries for the collection and despatch to this country of escaped British Prisoners of War (hitherto dealt with by MI1).

German prisoners being off-loaded from a train to the centre at the PWIS facility at Kempton Park racecourse

Men taken prisoner by 30 Assault Unit from surrender of German Naval HQ in Octeville, Normandy, 26 June 1944 (© ADM 202/599)

c)   The interrogation of escaped British Prisoners of War, and the distribution of Military Information so obtained.

By 1944, CSDIC was one of the most vital and important sources of intelligence prior to D-Day, through the interrogation of Prisoners of War. It was a highly secretive unit, and staff deployed to any of the facilities had to sign the Official Secrets Act. The Prisoner of War Interrogation Section (PWIS) supported this effort with running the nine 'cages' or specialist interrogation facilities established from southern England to Scotland in each of the command areas, which came under the jurisdiction of the Directorate of Military Intelligence. The PWIS (H) first screened the prisoners at the cages before they were sent onwards to other facilities run by CSDIC for further interrogation. The cages were dotted around the country. Racecourses were often used, such as the cages at Kempton Park, Lingfield and Doncaster. The cages at Loughborough and Catterick were built in farmers' fields. Another was built on the ground of the Preston North End Football Club. These PWIS(H) run facilities were where POWs would be identified, processed, graded and have initial interrogation carried out to establish the value of the prisoner. CSDIC (UK) was very much the second line, where selected prisoners would be sent if PWIS considered them to be of special intelligence value.

CSDIC (UK) organisational chart

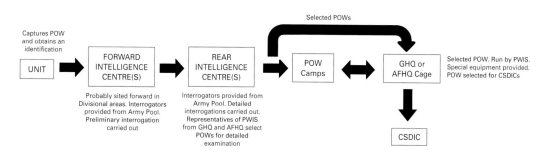

POW processing chain through from Unit to CSDIC

Latimer House (picture taken in 1929) (Ref PHO1842 © Amersham Museum)

CSDIC only had three of these cages assigned to it – one at Wilton House (known as No. 2 Distribution Centre or No. 2 DC) near Beaconsfield and another at Trent Park. The third CSDIC facility, Latimer House (known as No. 1 Distribution Centre or No. 1 DC) in Buckinghamshire became the CSDIC HQ from 1942. Both Wilton House and Latimer House had thirty cells and twelve interrogation rooms equipped with covert microphones. No. 2 DC would be used predominantly for Italian prisoners and No. 1 DC for German senior officers.

Another facility, Latchmere House, came under the control of MI5 who referred to it ignominiously as 'Camp 020'. It was used for lower profile German officers, which played a pivotal role in the 'Double Cross' deception plan.

One of the most infamous cages resided in one of the salubrious and grandiose Victorian villas in Kensington Palace Gardens, one of the most exclusive streets in the capital, if not the world. Its properties regularly exceed £50 million in today's value. Numbers 6, 7 and 8 Kensington Palace Gardens became known colloquially as the 'London Cage', and these three houses belonged to the London offices of CSDIC between July 1940 and September 1948.

The London Cage was run by Lieutenant Colonel Alexander Scotland, an Englishman who, at the turn of the century, had previously served in Namibia with the German Army and had a good command of the German language. He had spent most of World War I interrogating German POWs, which had earned him an OBE. At the outbreak of war in 1939, aged fifty-seven, he was recalled for service as he was so highly thought of and was put in charge of the PWIS from 1940. He had ten officers working under him directly and around a dozen NCOs who did much of the interrogations and interpreting. At the regional commands cages, Scotland was responsible for training all the officers.

The London Cage comprised just five interrogation rooms, and with appropriate accommodation could house sixty prisoners at a time, who were guarded by soldiers from the Guards regiments. They were typically held two prisoners to a cell. In total, some 3,573 prisoners passed through the London Cage. There have been numerous allegations of systemic torture and abuse of prisoners at the facility during World War II. Shortly after opening the cage, both MI5 and MI6 were caught in little-needed publicity about the employment of torture techniques and violence at the facility. Colonel Robin Stephens, who ran Latchmere House, once stated '... violence is taboo for not only does it produce answers to please, but it lowers the standard of information ... never strike a man. In the first place it is an act of cowardice. In the second place, it is not intelligent. A prisoner will lie to avoid further punishment and everything he says thereafter will be based on a false promise.'

On the other side of London, the CSDIC facility at Trent Park had a massive influence on the gathering of intelligence on Normandy before the invasion in June 1944. Over fifty-nine high-ranking German generals were held there, some of whom were long-standing prisoners who had been held for over three years. The interrogations of these Generals helped to extract some of Hitler's most valuable secrets.

Known locally as a supply depot to No. 1 Distribution Centre to hide its real activities, Latimer House became the CSDIC HQ from May 1942. Many of the most senior German Generals were sent here amongst the thousands of other prisoners. The site and CSDIC in its entirety was run by Colonel Thomas Kendrick, an MI6 officer. As CSDIC grew in importance between 1942 and 1944, the unit grew to over 1,000 staff. At any one time, the unit could house 392 POWs.

Opportunities for gathering intelligence also arose when prisoners were transferred in between camps. Four thirty-two-seat coaches were converted into semi-mobile listening and interrogation units.

There were numerous methods employed to extract information from the prisoners. Many of the POW cells had concealed microphones, often housed in the light fittings, to glean information from them when they might be off-guard or dotted around the camp by staircases or outside in trees. They were often put in cells with prisoners from different services or units, which would naturally engender talk between them of their experiences. The microphones were monitored by teams of six in a separate room (referred to as the M-Room or Monitor Room), where they had the ability to monitor two or three cells simultaneously, by switching from one cell to another to establish whether any interesting conversations were taking place. The monitors had an ability to record distinct conversations using record-cutting equipment.

Another method was to deploy a Stool Pigeon (SP) into the cell, that being a prisoner who had been turned to work for the Allies, either through political conviction or bribery. A great deal of preparation was done on these SP prisoners to make them knowledgeable about the person to help them steer the conversation to something of real intelligence value. Even the SP would be unaware of the hidden microphones in the cells. Forty-nine SPs were employed by CSDIC (UK) during the war, who were used against around 15 per cent of all prisoners.

Interrogation through direct questioning is a tried and tested way to extract information and intelligence from prisoners. At Trent Park they utilised a fake welfare officer for German senior officers to draw out relevant information that could be used, or a fake newspaper would be placed with the prisoner to guide the conversations.

Prisoners were always interrogated multiple times, but many of the best strands of intelligence came from conversations they had in their cells with fellow inmates. Some of the intelligence collected was useful for psychological warfare purposes and used to good effect by the lead protagonists in this, the Political Warfare Executive (PWE). Allied radio stations purporting to be German would broadcast material over the airwaves to undermine the morale of the German soldiers and public. To develop further exploitation of German prisoners morale, a psychiatrist (Henry Dicks from the Royal Army Medical Corps) was attached to CSDIC between the autumn of 1942 to mid-1944. Morale is something SIGINT or aerial reconnaissance can have little effect on.

The way CSDIC (UK) evolved into a complex, but well-run intelligence outfit in its own right was built around a three-stage process for all Axis prisoners. The three stages were:

1. Interrogation in the field (identification, preliminary interrogation, detailed interrogation up to the level of Army Headquarters)
2. Detailed examination of selected POWs (theatre of war headquarters)
3. Long-term interrogation

Used by the War Office during World War I as a hospital for shell-shocked officers, Latchmere House, a Victorian mansion near Ham Common in southwest London, was operated as an interrogation centre by MI5 during World War II. The house, with thirty rooms converted into cells, was run by the legendary Colonel Robin 'Tin Eye' Stephens. He was so named as he wore a monocle in one eye, as a result of exposure to

Italian mustard gas whilst working as a volunteer for the British Red Cross in Abyssina in the mid-1930s. He was supported by Harold Dearden, a psychiatrist who helped Stephens devise a regime of sleep and sensory deprivation to break the prisoners. The facility was expanded by Stephens with an additional ninety-two-cell extension. Latchmere's first residents were members of the British Union of Fascists (BUF).

Every wartime German spy identified operating in Britain during World War II was sent to Latchmere House by MI5. Many of them were turned into long-standing double agents. Information for the Allied code breakers at Bletchley Park was also extracted at the camp providing vital assistance for the work against Enigma. One such agent who was turned at Camp 020 was the Danish citizen Wulf Dietrich Christian Schmidt (aka Harry Wilkinson). Schmidt, a Danish fascist, entered Britain as a German spy in September 1940 by parachute. On landing in the Cambridgeshire countryside, he sprained an ankle and limped into the nearest village of Willingham. Wearing a blue suit and talking in an unmistakeable foreign accent, he was almost immediately arrested. He resisted initial interrogation attempts but began to cooperate with his CSDIC interrogators and was turned to work as a double agent, under the covername 'Tate', after the 1940s comedian, Harry Tate. He became the longest-serving double agent and was instrumental in the double-cross deception plan which preceded D-Day.

Civilian refugees arriving in Britain were often good potential sources of intelligence. Recognising this, in January 1941 the London Reception Centre (LRC) was established at the Royal Patriotic School (RPS) in Wandsworth. The facility was used as a screening facility for civilians entering Britain and MI5, MI6 and MI9 had a permanent presence in the LRC, helping develop an 'Information Index' of valuable intelligence from the 33,000 people that passed through the site during the war. The RPS allowed for the Intelligence services and Armed Forces to get up-to-date intelligence of life in German-occupied France. It was also to act as a fertile ground for the SOE and SIS to recruit potential agents to deploy. Many would agree to work for them and subsequently sign the Official Secrets Act.

One such example of the value of the RPS interrogations of refugees was that of Tadeusz Salski, a Polish civil servant born in October 1910. He had left Poland on 13 October 1943, bound for France via Germany and had left France on 15 November 1943. He arrived in Britain in December 1943 and was subsequently moved to London and interviewed by the RPS. Salski was an important target, as he had been an engineer with the *Organisation Todt* (OT) civil engineering firm, the builders of Hitler's Atlantic Wall. He was posted to the *OT Einsatzgruppe West* in Paris and then their offices in Bayonne. 'Informant … gives exact location of the head offices of OT Einsatzgruppe West in Paris as being at the corner of the Avenue des Champs Élysées and Rue de Marignan, on the south side of the former and the east side of the latter, by

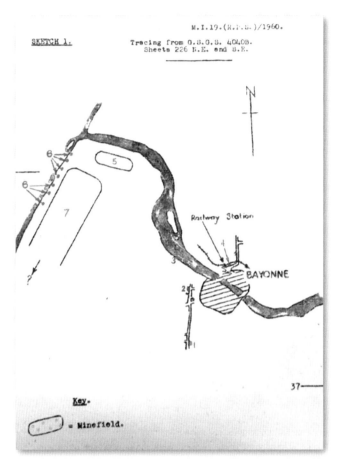

M.I.19.(R.P.S.)/1960.

SKETCH 1.

Tracing from O.S.G.S. 4040B.
Sheets 226 N.E. and S.E.

N

5

7

Railway Station

4

3

BAYONNE

2

1

37—

Key.

= Minefield.

Sketch from the RPS interrogation of Tadeusz Salski, a Polish civil servant who had worked for Organisation Todt in Bayonne in 1943 (© WO208/3720)

Marbeuf metro station.' This information was confirmed by the TIS as being correct. He was to give details of OT barracks, stores and offices. He was to also provide detailed intelligence on the OT rank structures and uniform insignia. 'All German OT personnel, but NOT non-Germans, wear also the swastika emblem on the upper left arm.' He also conveyed the poor state of much of the equipment and machinery being used by the OT in that part of France. Only 60 per cent of the machinery was working and in good order. He worked with a number of nationalities including French and Belgian volunteers and a number of Czech and Serbian workers.

Because of the wider nature of RPS reports, they would be disseminated to a much wider distribution of readers from MI3a, MI5, MI6, MI9, MI10, MI14a, MI19, TIS, NID (1 & 6), ETOUSA HQ, ADI(K), MEW, CCO, JIS, PWE, SOE, COSSAC and even to the Deputy Director Operations Division (Irregular) or DDOD(I) for short, nominally a Captain Frank Slocum whom commanded the 15th Flotilla on the River Dart which ran agents on to the French coast.

The D-Day plan for processing the thousands of German POW (from WO208/4970)

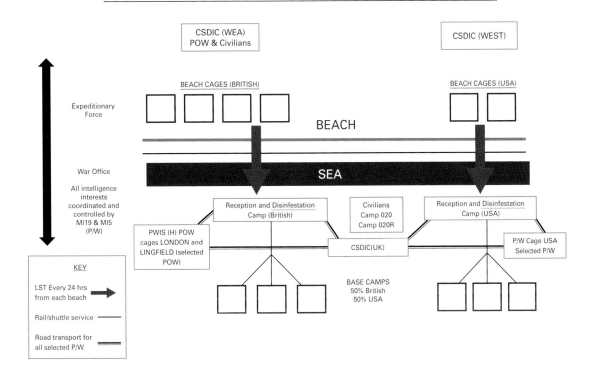

It was fully expected that the invasion of Normandy under Overlord would produce a flood of German prisoners. Under the direction of SHAEF and 21st Army Group, a process was agreed whereby PWIS(H) would have immediacy for processing the prisoners and transport them to two holding centres, at the cages at Kempton Park racecourse near Sunbury-on-Thames and a facility in Devizes for US-captured prisoners. Kempton Park alone was preparing to process over 2,000 prisoners a day. After initial processing and assessment, if the prisoner was deemed to be of intelligence value he would be transported to either the London Cage in Kensington Palace Gardens or the cage at Lingfield racecourse.

The CSDIC transcripts from the secret cages were always marked 'Top Secret' and were a vital component in decision-making by the Allied planners in the run-up to D-Day. The German specialists in MI14 received valuable intelligence in early 1944 from the CSDIC, which helped them to understand the German army hierarchy and equipment which would be facing them in Normandy. By 1944 POWs were a firm source of reliable intelligence, giving away knowledge of command and control, equipment and capabilities of the German defence forces in and around northern France.

In a CSDIC (UK) summary in 1942, the organisation wrote of German prisoners' viewpoints on a prospective invasion of Europe:

'The possibility of an Allied invasion of the continent has been increasingly discussed … opinion appears to be about equally divided between the view that if the British attempted an invasion they would suffer a second Dunkirk, and the view that German forces in the West are inadequate to repel an invasion and would have to be reinforced by troops from Russia, where their withdrawal might prove fatal to Germany. The majority of speakers, however, incline to the belief that the threat of a "second front" is more bluff, that if the British really intended to invade they would not talk about it so much in public, and that they are either too cowardly, or too incompetent to put such a plan into effect. Towards the end of the period there was some mention of actual preparations against a British invasion, runways were said to have been mined, fighter aerodromes moved back from the coast, a state of readiness to have been ordered at aerodromes and large-scale anti-invasion manoeuvres to have taken place.'

The number of CSDIC (UK) Prisoners and reports issued September 1939 to October 1945 (taken from WO208/4970 The History of CSDIC (UK)

Date	Prisoners Handled	Records cut	SR REPORTS								Army Interrogation Reports
			SRN	SRM	SRA	SRX	SRGG	GRGG	Extracts	Total	
Sep – Dec 1939	169	x	3	x	10	16	x	x	x	29	x
1940	1083	x	166	13	1081	152	x	x	141	1553	109
1941	980	5328	572	1	1320	456	x	x	85	2434	13
1942	700	9008	653	142	1061	755	x	x	283	2894	86
1943	1288	18060	1143	258	1274	442	732	109	499	4457	203
1944	4007	21003	1954	725	890	191	376	129	171	4436	1220
Jan – Nov 1945	1968	11028	335	115	159	64	197	88	199	1157	569
TOTAL	10195	64427	4826	1254	5795	2076	1305	326	1378	16960	2200

KEY:

SR reports are listening reports

SRN – Listening reports on Naval POW

SRM – Listening reports on Military POW

SRA – Listening reports on Air Force POW

SRX – Listening reports on POW from Navy, Military and Air Force mixed

SRGG – Listening reports from Senior Officer POW

GRGG – Omnibus report on Senior Officer POW combining material obtained by direct and indirect means.

Allied planners were desperate for intelligence on the German defensive positions in Normandy as the momentum behind Overlord began to pick up in mid-1943. POW interrogations, often from prisoners captured a long way from France, would help illuminate some of the defensive structures the invasion forces would face in June 1944. One such prisoner, PW M359, an *Unteroffizier* from 146th Infantry Regiment, was captured in Italy on 2 December 1943. He had previously been responsible for the coastal defences between Villers-sur-Mer and Honfleur. He had given precise details of the defences at Trouville, as his company was responsible for them. His interrogators said of him that 'he is efficient and appears fairly reliable'.

Much of the intelligence gleaned from this German prisoner had been extracted through the comparisons with maps and aerial photographs, and the CSDIC drawing staff would sketch the diagrams of the defensive locations. It was immediately clear the beaches were to be a formidable proposition.

'There was a double belt of barbed wire extending right along the coast from Villers-sur-Mer to Honfleur. Every position was surrounded by a similar belt. PW had no certain knowledge of mines except at Trouville.... PW stated that mines laid in the sand were usually anti-personnel mines, but that mines laid further inland where tanks might operate included T-mines. PW stated that before he left Trouville the OT was already at work and that eventually all the dugout emplacements would be concreted ... the four emplacements on the front at Deauville were concreted ... the general principle was to permit the concentration of maximum fire power at any given point. Nevertheless there appears to be evidence of a special strengthening of the defences round Trouville.'

The individual had borne witness to some of the procedures and routines around coast, which was of as much use to the intelligence community as some of the detailed defensive information, 'twice every night a patrol usually consisting of one section armed with MPs went out at unspecified times and remained out for approximately 1½ hours ... on being challenged by a sentry, the patrol leader would shout the password which was generally the name of a town eg. "Berlin", "München" etc. PW stated that the procedure was sometimes very loose and that the sentries on hearing the approach of the patrol would not challenge ... on occasion PW had known the same password to be used on two consecutive nights.

'As well as the telephone, there was an automatic device which was connected to the barbed wire in front of each site. If touched this wire would set off a rocket which would illuminate the area around ... rockets were sited at intervals of

30 to 40 m. Where there were no strong points PW stated that the wire was connected to S-mines.

'There were four sentries on each of the strong points on the front. Two sentries remained on the site and patrolled the interior. The other two patrolled round the exterior of the site and along the promenade....'

Interestingly, the colleagues of the POW arrested a purported British agent when he had tried to get access to one of the coastal positions in the area.

Another prisoner taken in Italy a few weeks earlier, in November 1943, also provided valuable POW intelligence for the CSDIC on the Atlantic Wall defences. The prisoner, PW M358, had been stationed on the Normandy defences from January to April 1943. His interrogators noted he was 'observant to a point, and the sketches attached should give a general impression of layout, but not necessarily a picture accurately dimensioned and proportioned, or exactly correct in detail'. Although stationed further up the coast near Ostend, the CSDIC teams would have noted consistency from their questioning. Passwords and challenges by sentry guards were the same all the way along the French coastline. Passwords 'had to be very simple in the POWs unit because so many men were of non-German origin. Names of German cities were used, eg, Berlin, Königsberg, Warschau. Passwords were changed every 24 hours. He obtained the password and passed it on to the company CO who informed the rest of the unit.'

This particular POW report highlighted the common practice of positioning rifle and machine gun pits dug into the edge of the sea wall and along the coast road. 'The pits themselves may be reached by underground passages leading from the houses situated directly to the rear of these posns. These houses are used by 3 Coy as billets. The front covered by 3 Coy was approximately 250m long. By day this area is open to traffic. At 2100hrs, however, all traffic through this area ceases. The area is closed off by obstacles across the road. One guard is stationed on each of these barriers from 2100hrs to daylight.'

Not all POW were captured during land campaigns, such as the battles on the Italian peninsula which would precede the Normandy campaign. German sailors were fairly routinely captured off the British coastline whist on Naval operations. In April 1944, the German E-boat, S-147, from the German 9th Flotilla was sunk off Beachy Head and the crew were captured and processed through CSDIC (UK). The interrogation of the crew was to provide useful intelligence on the German military strength and dispositions in Cherbourg in the vital weeks before D-Day. S-147 and its crew had been based in

Cherbourg from 25 February 1944. 'Naval artillery was seen only occasionally…. Army infantry was much in evidence. One POW stated that he saw "some" Russian volunteers wearing a shield flash with the letters POA on their left arm. Approx. 100 men, all over 40, and known as the "Wach und Schliessgesellschaft" guard the port area.' Another gauge for the interrogation team was the numerical superiority at the local brothel. It was the S-Boat crews who were to lead the way there.

CSDIC intelligence was reported to typically three main agencies – MI19a at the War Office, the Naval Intelligence Division (NID) at the Admiralty, and ADI(K) at the Air Ministry. Cherbourg was going to a critical port for the logistical supply routes for the offensive.

'It is fairly well established that the western harbour waters including the approaches to the arsenal are unmined. There is no indication that the quays and the outer and inner moles have been prepared for demolition. The Passé de l'Est is barred by boom and guarded by contact mines to the north and by a field of electric mines just inside the Grande Rade. Control point for the electric mines is at the eastern extremity of the Digue du Homet. The entrance to the Petite Rade has been narrowed by a boom. The remaining gap is about 50 m wide and is closed nightly between 2200 and 0800hrs by a second boom. In the morning this boom is submerged to leave a depth of about 8m for entering ships.

'Single 8.8cm AA guns are sited on the NW and NE corners of the pier W of the Darse Transatlantique. Several PW consider the slope heading down from the Fort du Roule 147221 the most heavily defended point in the Cherbourg area. The guns cover the harbour and the E and W approaches to the city. They never fired on aircraft.

a) The Fort itself mounts several guns, number and calibre unknown

b) Three or four heavy guns, calibre 24-28cm, are sited in concrete posns along the northern and western slopes on approx the 90m contour. The sites are well camouflaged but not dug in.

c) About twelve to fifteen guns, possible calibre 8.8 cm, are sited along the northern, eastern and western slopes in a strip from the 40m to the 80m contour. The gun sites are staggered at different heights and at intervals of about 30m. Emplacements in this case were blasted into the mountain and are well protected against air attacks. PW maintain that the sites do not permit sufficient elevation to fire against aircraft. Camouflage is excellent.'

Rocket alarm device for barbed wire defences in the beaches by Trouville (© WO208/3585 – SIR136)

ROCKET ALARM DEVICE

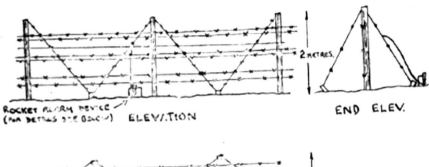

ROCKET ALARM DEVICE
(FOR DETAILS SEE BELOW)   ELEVATION

END ELEV.

2 METRES.

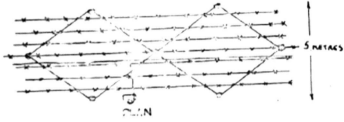

5 METRES

PLAN

DETAILS OF ROCKET ALARM DEVICE

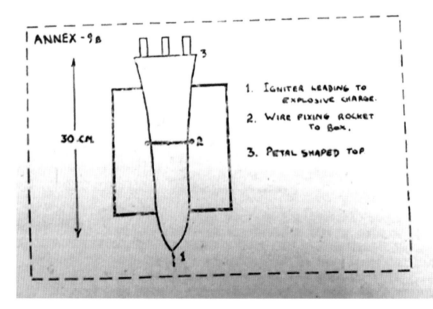

ANNEX - 9B

30 CM.

3

2

1

1. IGNITER LEADING TO
   EXPLOSIVE CHARGE.

2. WIRE FIXING ROCKET
   TO BOX.

3. PETAL SHAPED TOP

Sketch of the rifle pits from the CSDIC interrogation of a German POW
(© WO208/3585 SIR127)

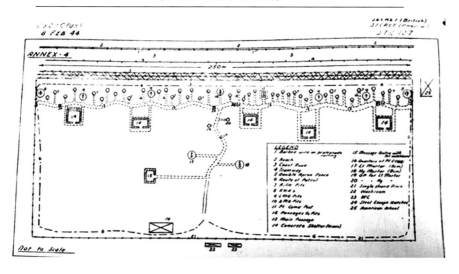

Sketch of Notre Dame – location of Panzer Grenadier Regiment 21 – from CSDIC interrogation of a
German POW, approximate scale 1:50,000 (© WO208/3584 SIR99 Annex 5A)

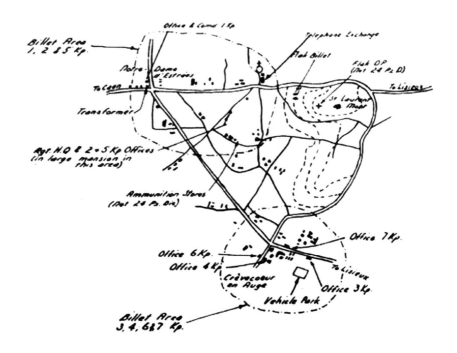

The interrogation report goes on to list obstacles that might impede the Allied advance on the port. One POW in the group had even gone so far to suggest that the south of the peninsula would be flooded if the invasion was to occur.

A POW who deserted from Le Havre in September 1943 after stealing an officer's motor launch to cross the Channel, provided some insight into the defences at le Havre. The CSDIC assessed him as being 'not intelligent but he is tough and brave'. They believed he might be a valuable recruit for the SOE: 'he has expressed his desire to return to Germany or France in a sabotage crew or as an agent'. He had been stationed in Le Havre for eighteen months in the Navy. His desertion highlighted he was a capable individual, 'On 31st August 43 PW noticed that an officer's motor launch was being loaded up with 500 litres of fuel and he decided to attempt his escape that night. He joined some comrades in a drinking bout and at 2230hrs, feigning extreme drunkenness, excused himself to two minesweepers that were putting to sea, managed to pass through the harbour entrance. He knew the password and had a lamp which he used to answer the signal station. He had no compass and guided the boat by the North Star. About 0600hrs the next morning the engine broke down while POW was still 10 miles from the English coast. He states that he drifted up and down off the Isle of Wight for five days without food or drink. He was finally spotted by an aircraft and later picked up by a flying boat.'

The prisoner provided useful intelligence of the defence scheme by the German defenders of the town, and that only the '*Abschnitt Hafon Mitte*' would be defended in case of a frontal attack on the harbour, although the morale of the defending troops was extremely low, so it would be unlikely they would put up much of a fight. Much of the port areas had been mined with naval TMC 42 mines, typically at 4-5 ft in depth and at 10 ft intervals. They were all controlled from the Harbourmaster's command post and could be set off from this location. The prisoner stated, 'The navy has also mined the waters just off the south mole and south breakwater, as well as the beaches near Le Havre.'

One critical intelligence requirement was the strength and location of the reserve Panzer Divisions that Rommel would need to respond quickly to any Allied invasion in Normandy. CSDIC intelligence would again provide some useful insight, through the interrogations of prisoners in early 1944. They were to elucidate that the Headquarters of 24 Panzer Division was in the town of Lisieux and provided their interrogators with a detailed sketch of the town and the various locations used by the Division's officers and other ranks, along with many other towns in the area. They also provided some knowledge of the roads in Normandy, which was to be useful for logistical planning for which road could carry heavy armour efficiently.

ROADS IN NORMANDY (Annex 11 SIR 99 WO208/3584)

From	To	Width	Surface	German Designation
Lisieux	Livarot	8/10m	Concrete	A4
Paris	Cherbourg	12m	Part concrete Part Tarmac	Heeres-strasse V
Lisieux	Trouville	8m	Tarmac	BI
Lisieux	Orbeck	6m	Tarmac	QII or GII
Lisieux	Le Havre (via Pont Audemer)	8m	Part concrete Part tarmac	13
Honfleur	Trouville	6m	Asphalt	Küsten-strasse

One of the prisoners 'stated that their Div formed part of the II SS Pz Korps, and that this Korps belonged to the new 6th Army being reformed in the North of France. According to their statements this Army was commanded by Rommel who arrived in the North of France after the fall of Tunis.'

These Panzer Divisions were critical for Rommel's strategy for the defence of Normandy but by early 1944 the Allies' aerial bombardment of logistical supply chains had significantly diminished the potential of these Divisions to operate. 'The training of the whole Div seems to have been handicapped by the lack of petrol. During its six months' stay in Normandy (March–August 1943), the the Div was reformed, only one large exercise involving the whole Div was held.' The one exercise that did take place had been reconnoitored by Allied spitfires, 'at the beginning of the exercise some Spitfires suddenly swooped down low on to POW's unit without attacking and apparently gave the nerves of the Abt Comd a severe shock'.

D-Day would bring about a deluge of German prisoners and the role the CSDIC beach camps would play on the beaches would be extremely significant for the efficient processing of valued POWs. Prisoner number KP/2 (M) Hptm Gundlach, attached to the 716th Infantry Division, was captured in the town of Ouistreham on D-Day itself. His quick local interrogation yielded a huge amount of timely intelligence on the German defences at Caen. Gundlach had been the Director of the Battle School in Caen. Although regarded as 'intelligent and thoroughly indoctrinated in Nazism', he was at first security-conscious, but over time became cooperative. He informed his interrogators from the CSDIC that the 'chief German troop concentrations are at Falaise. He heard that the Germans planned to allow us to take most of the Cherbourg Peninsula and then counter-attack in force.'

Caen was a key stronghold that the Allies would need to capture quickly to gain the advantage and move through the hinterland of Normandy. Any current knowledge of the Caen defences would have been gold dust to Allied intelligence. 'The defences of Caen are based on an elastic plan, which embraces eight points of *Resistance*.' Caen's main defence was listed as Caserne Lefevre, and with its 8-10m deep moat, bridges and gates for access across and seventeen machine gun (MG) positions it was the main strongpoint in Caen. Gundlach was to tell his captors 'within the Burg itself there are earthworks, two anti-tanks and two 8.1cm mortars ... three flamethrowers at the N gate, three at the E gate and two at the S gate. The roadways to each gate are mined for about 15m distance.'

Intelligence from POWs was to grow in importance over the course of the war. For the invasion of Europe in 1944, it was an integral component of all the intelligence arms in the military and government. It was to grow more valuable as it was to grow in volume. Overlord was to almost overwhelm the POW interrogation facilities in the scale of prisoners taken on or near the beaches. It was the skills and ingenuity of the interrogation teams who could work on an individual's background, his linkages to the military hierarchy and planning, which could yield vital information on military dispositions and equipment. The ability of an interrogator to exert his personality over the prisoner was the key to a successful interrogation. The old adage of knowledge breeds knowledge rings true with interrogation, whereby a prisoner is induced to talk by making him think he is not saying anything that is new.

The scale and volume of POW intelligence could not be underplayed, but the thousands of German prisoners taken before and after D-Day helped build an extremely comprehensive picture of the defensive positions in Normandy. Without it, the Allies' intelligence picture may have been plagued with gaps which could significantly have changed the outcome of the initial phases of the operation.

CHAPTER SEVEN
BLACK LIST

Recent military history research has unearthed some evidence that the Dieppe raid in August 1942 was a diversionary activity for a pinch operation mounted by an elite commando unit assigned as 30 Commando Assault Unit (30AU) to target a number of key locations in and around Dieppe. These included the Hotel Moderne by the port housing the German Naval HQ, and Allied intelligence had also convinced itself that trawlers moored in Dieppe harbour were acting as secret German signals intelligence collection platforms. It has been suggested that 30AU's main target was to obtain spare parts for the new four-rotor wheel version of the Enigma cipher machine and associated codebooks, to aid the work being done by GC&CS at Bletchley Park.

The team was put ashore acting as No. 40 Royal Marines Commando on HMS *Locust*, which failed to breach the inner channel in Dieppe harbour, so the 30AU troops had to go ashore aboard a landing craft. Strategically, the Dieppe raid was a disaster. Over 900 Canadian soldiers were killed, 586 injured and 2,000 captured. The 30AU team returned to England empty handed.

Bletchley had been successful at breaking the three-rotor wheel Enigma machines which provided Allied planners with some rich streams of German intelligence, up until 1 February 1942 when a fourth rotor-wheel was introduced. Ian Fleming, the PA to the then Director Naval Intelligence (DNI), Admiral John Godfrey in Naval Intelligence Division (NID), who helped set up 30 Assault Unit, routinely visited Bletchley to understand how significant the exploitation of the Enigma traffic would be to the war effort in Europe.

30AU was the brainchild of the now famous Lieutenant Commander Ian Fleming RNVR. He was affectionately known as 17(F), which is how he appeared in Naval Intelligence files. His role was to act as the NID liaison to the Head of SIS (MI6) and SOE. One of the Royal Navy officers in No. 36 Section, Commander Patrick Dalzel-Job RN was said to have been the inspiration for the lead character in his later James Bond novels. Fleming was also in contact with elements of MI5's deception operations and was a regular visitor to Bletchley Park, and also Medmenham, and once a week he would drop into the ISTD at Oxford. The secret team from 30AU were under the command of Lieutenant Huntington-Whitely, a close friend of Fleming and the grandson of the former Prime Minister Stanley Baldwin.

The Germans had their own specialist intelligence-gathering unit which deployed ahead with forward troops and it became the model for what Ian Fleming was suggesting. The proposal was backed by a Major Geoffrey Cass, who was attached to MI5 and Jim Granville, an SOE agent who had operated in Yugoslavia. Cass and Granville had become two of the earliest recruits to 30AU.

A branch of the Abwehr, known as the *Marine Einsatz Kommando* (shortened to MARES) and was commanded by Kapitaen Leutnant Obladen. The unit had the following objectives:

- the seizure of secret documents, charts, naval stores and supplies and fuel and lubricants
- counter-demolition duties in captured harbours
- the transmission by W/T of operational intelligence concerning the state of harbour location of wrecks and minefields, and manpower requirements for the operation of port installations
- the interrogation of POWs and civilians, and counter-espionage work

MARES would accompany the assault waves of a naval force and comprised in large part by personnel from the Lehr Regiment Brandenburg, who typically were Germans who had lived abroad. During the German advance in Greece, MARES proved its worth in the capturing of valuable intelligence materiel from the British in Athens and Crete. The German army also had its own equivalent, the *Abwehrtruppen*, who had a similar role and function to the MARES units.

Originally the Joint Intelligence Committee (JIC) had doubts about 30 Assault Unit, but the DNI's persistence won through. The unit formed on 30 September 1942 and fell under the cover term of the Special Engineering Unit, which later became the 30 Commando. The success of a small unit such as 30AU in World War II can be attributed to the blend of having technical and scientific staff deploying with highly trained and highly skilled commandos.

A memo written at the time, outlined that the unit was 'on an experimental basis … designed to provide a force of armed and expert "authorised looters" who will operate in small groups which will move with the assault troops to fight and capture enemy material and documents of special importance; in some cases they may be required to work behind the enemy lines in advance of assault troops. During an assault and advance the local Gestapo HQ in some port or town might be seized before papers can be destroyed. Enemy black lists would then become our white lists and vice-versa; we should know at once who can be trusted and who must be arrested. Thus in occupied territory our Security Police would be provided with information which would enable them to strike deep and quickly at the enemy's organisation and suppress espionage and political warfare. The importance of seizing the enemy's codes and ciphers needs no emphasis and is one of the reasons why this unit has been so strongly pressed for by the Admiralty.'

30AU was originally named as the Special Intelligence Unit (SIU). It was later renamed 30 RN Commando (Special Engineering Unit) and later designated 30 Assault Unit in December 1943. The unit initially reported to the Chief of Combined Operations as its chain of command but in reality it came under the direct authority of DNI. The number 30 is alleged to have come from the door number for NID in the Admiralty. The term 'Assault Unit' was to act as a veil to cover up the covert intelligence remit for the teams.

By September 1942 the unit was composed of a number of sections:

No. 33 Section, Royal Marines (established 1943) – comprised two officers and twenty other ranks, developing through 1944 to six officers and 144 other ranks

No. 34 Section, Army – comprised four officers and twenty other ranks

No. 35 Section, RAF – comprised just two officers

No. 36 Section, Royal Navy – comprised between five and ten officers

Also attached to 30 Assault Unit was a Forward Interrogation Unit (FIU) from the Royal Navy. Deployed teams would often work in close collaboration with the Intelligence Corps Field Security sections. A typical team would a Royal Navy officer in command, a technical officer/attached scientist, a German-speaking officer from the RN FIU, a Royal Marines officer or a SNCO with a section of Royal Marines, vehicles and a W/T (Wireless Telegraphy/radio) section. Cooperation with the FIU interrogators was invaluable to the unit when it deployed into Normandy, 'a very high percentage of success obtained by 30AU was due to interrogation under operational conditions'.

The Littlehampton headquarters for the unit was established in a property at St Augustine's Road in the town. Much of the administration and organisation of the HQ fell to its secretary, Miss Margaret Priestley, a history academic from Leeds University who had transferred to 30AU from the Department of Naval Research (DNR). Priestley is believed to be the inspiration for Fleming's Miss Petty Pethaval, the original character name that became Miss Moneypenny.

One of the key planning tools for the unit was their 'Black List'. This was ostensibly a set of military, political or industrial targets derived from all sources of intelligence available to the unit. Detailed plans and requirements were shaped by DNI from the numerous Admiralty divisions that had a vested interest.

The Black List was exactly that: a list. Little information could be gleaned from a list in learning about the appearance of documents and materiel. There was no

30 Assault Unit HQ
in Littlehampton,
as it is today
(© author)

substitution for short lectures, films, slides or the inspection of previously gathered materiel. For major target locations, such as naval bases and major headquarters buildings, the unit relied on the Theatre Intelligence Section (TIS) for much of its insight. For the more minor targets they would have to rely on a wide range of intelligence sources. 30AU had two liaison officers, Captain Cunningham and Captain Hargreaves-Heap, attached to TIS in the build up to Neptune. Within TIS they were 'furnished with day to day appreciations of the German order of battle, with interpretations of air photographs of the area, and with all other information likely to have any bearing on 30AU's operations'. Lieutenant Glanville also liaised frequently with TIS to gather naval intelligence on the movements of German Headquarters in Normandy, or new RADAR or W/T stations being established.

The Black List would rely on information from topographical models, maps or reports from *the* Inter-Services Topographical Department (ISTD) at Manchester College in Oxford, SOE, PWE, aerial photography, Signals Intelligence (SIGINT), BBC Monitoring radio reports, Ministry of Information press analyses, Prisoner of War interrogation reports from the Combined Services Detailed Interrogation Centre (CSDIC) or the Royal Patriotic School (RPS), Secret Intelligence Service (SIS) (CX) reports and captured documents. It was widely appreciated that the most valuable and accurate sources of information to 30 Assault Unit came from the CSDIC reports and captured documents.

Target locations in Normandy from the Black List were first transferred to 'Target Lists' and annotated on maps specially prepared by the ISTD for the unit. These target maps would be based on available published town plans. Lieutenant Bailey and a number of other ranks from the Royal Marines Intelligence section worked at the ISTD to assist with their work on sand table models of target areas in Normandy.

A priority system was devised for the targets on the list, which were to be pondered upon by a Committee, but in reality the decisions were on the discretion of the senior officer in charge of the list. The priorities were:

A1	Materiel and documents of the highest operational priority, the importance of which is sufficient to justify the mounting of special operations and the incurring of heavy casualties on the part of 30 Assault Unit
A2	Requirements of high priority, sufficiently important to justify casualties and to be regarded as the first targets (after A1 priorities) to be considered when planning the participation of 30 Assault Unit in large scale operations
B1	Materiel and documents whose importance will justify the presence of detachments of 30 Assault unit in front line areas and their crossing the enemy's lines, subject to no extraordinary risks being taken
B2	Miscellaneous requirements to be dealt with by 30 Assault Unit in cleaning up operations
C	Requirements, generally of a scientific nature, whose importance is largely contingent on the development by the enemy of new weapons and devices. Materiel of this nature, being for the most part highly technical, can usually only be recognised and handled by specialists. When seized, it is to be guarded until such time as a detailed examination can be made on the spot by specialist officers

The Black List often listed locations which had no connection to an objective with which they had been associated. Whilst this did cause some consternation within the unit, 'it should be emphasised that no major operation was laid on, or extreme risk taken, before an appreciation of the situation had been obtained from TIS, NID, and occasionally "C" or SOE'.

The information was filtered into handbooks which prioritised the regions and areas of focus for the unit as it went ahead of an advancing force. 30AU had personnel deployed with the ISTD to assist with the choreography of a lot of this work. Admiral Godfrey was an advocate of the ISTD output and he attributed much of the success

B Troop in Littlehampton. Photograph taken at Littlehampton in May 1944 before Operation Overlord

of 30AU to the intelligence provided by the teams in Oxford. For major objectives like Cherbourg or Paris, the ISTD produced comprehensive target dossiers covering the known targets of any importance in the cities, linked in with SIS and the French Resistance.

Volunteers for the unit were given general commando skills and weapons training but also more advanced military skills such as demolitions, counter-demolitions, parachute training, search and entry techniques including lock picking and safecracking. Many of the early recruits to the unit were policemen, who came in useful for their skills in interrogation and prisoner handling. Prior to June 1944 the unit had swelled to nearly 300 men. This was a reflection of increasing demands on the unit with military intelligence shifting steadily towards much larger-scale acquisition of German scientific and technical secrets. The Third Reich's hunger to develop the V1 and V2 missiles and potential atomic weapons had increased the tempo of what 30AU had become.

The unit's main strategy was to deploy ahead of advancing forces to act as the vanguard to gather intelligence from the retreating German forces in terms of documents, prisoners, cipher codes and radio equipment.

The Operation Torch landings in North Africa saw No. 33 Section deploy and have some good success when they captured the Italian Commission's building. The team had been supplied with ISTD pictures, maps and models showing the terrain of the landing site in Algiers, where the Axis HQ was situated and what they might find there. Over the course of the operation the section managed to find an intact Enigma machine and over 2 tonnes of valuable documents. The Enigma machine was flown back to NID in London and then onwards to the Intelligence Service Knox (ISK) section at Bletchley Park. It was during the Tunisia campaign and the advance on Tunis that 30AU perfected some of its tactics which would later be employed in Overlord.

With the build up to Overlord and the requirements for a vanguard intelligence collection unit to deploy forward in Normandy, Fleming recalled No. 33 and 36 Sections to Britain from the Mediterranean where some of the personnel had built up a reputation. Fleming famously told Granville, 'Forget anything that happened in the Med. You can't behave like Red Indians any more. You have to learn to be a respected and disciplined unit.' At the end of 1943, 30 Commando returned to the UK to reorganise and refit themselves for their participation in Overlord.

From 1 May 1944, 30AU came under the overall command of Admiral Sir Bertram Ramsay, the then Allied Naval Commander-in-Chief Expeditionary Force (ANCXF), based at Southwick House near Portsmouth. From that date all operational orders for the unit were issued by the Assistant Chief of Staff (ACOS) to ANCXF. From its outset the 30AU was commanded by Lieutenant Colonel Arthur Woolley who had been formerly the Commanding Officer of 47 Royal Marines Commando.

Special passes were given to 30AU officers prior to D-Day which gave authority 'By Command of General Eisenhower', and emphasising, 'The bearer of this card will not be interfered with in the performance of his duty by the Military Police or by other Military Organisations.'

B Troop marine Dennis Solly was drafted into the unit from the wider Royal Marines in early 1944. He recalls '… it was small, specialised and cloaked in secrecy. A band of colourful, and in some cases eccentric characters were given intensive commando

30 Assault Unit
Commandos
on Staghound
armoured vehicle

training before being dispatched on their often highly dangerous missions'. When the unit moved to its Littlehampton home, the conditions for the men were found to be quite respectable, '… the superb comfort of civilian billets in Littlehampton, a great contrast to living under canvas, in military barracks or Nissen huts. I shared my room with two other chaps and we then had someone to make our beds and keep the place tidy. All our washing was done for us obviating the rotten feeling after doing heavy washing. Littlehampton was quite a little seaside town with varied amusements to meet one's taste.

> 'The unit consisted of the Royal Navy, Royal Marines, Army and Royal Air Force, A, B, X and HQ troops. X troops carried out their parachute training up at Ringway near Manchester, and all troops were trained at Gliders on an airfield on Salisbury Plain. Commando training and D-Day landing craft training took place at the Commando basic training centre, Achnacarry at the foot of Ben Nevis, cliff climbing and abseiling over on the rugged Welsh coast.'

On 31 December 1943, a meeting was held at Combined Operations Headquarters (COHQ) to discuss 30AU. The minutes of this meeting highlighted the 'future Naval, military and Air requirements of No. 30 Commando'. As described, the functions of No. 30 Commando laid down in CCO's letter CR 10513/43 dated 1 November were:

(i)   The seizing of special intelligence data during the course of an operation.
(ii)   Before and during the first assault, to operate against enemy head-quarters in order to obtain ciphers, equipment, instruments, papers or any other intelligence data of value.
(iii)   To undertake under-water swimming operations to obtain equipment, ciphers and intelligence data from sunken vessels.

After discussion, it was agreed that function (iii) could not appropriately be included in an Intelligence Assault Unit's commitments, and that it should be deleted from the definition of the Unit's functions, which would be described as follows:

> 'To capture and immediately dispatch to appropriate authorities high-grade Intelligence Material.'

The Basic Intelligence Training requirements for the unit would include:

- the recognition of enemy documents and equipment
- the searching of premises and recovery of material from salvage
- safe-breaking, lock-picking and the entering of guarded premises
- the recognition of persons from photographs, the care of prisoners and the searching of persons
- photography and the interpretation of air photos
- conduct as prisoners of war and behaviour under interrogation.

More specialist intelligence training was also conducted and this took the form of:

- recognition of enemy underwater weapons
- enemy electronics, especially W/T, RADAR, infrared and thermal detecting devices
- elementary nuclear physics as applied to atom bombs
- power engineering, especially advanced steam plants and gas turbines
- map sketching, topography and hydrography.

One of the main remits for 30AU was to capture German and Italian cipher material for Bletchley Park, 'including specimens of the wheels used on the Enigma ciphering machine, particulars of the daily settings for wheels and plugs, codebooks and all documents relating to signals and communications'.

Around October 1943 a directive was passed in the Mediterranean theatre outlining that all captured cipher documents, signals documents and cipher equipment were to be directed to the Army Group HQ where arrangements would be coordinated to get the material dispatched immediately to GC&CS Bletchley Park. SHAEF Command wanted this to be replicated for the forthcoming offensive in Europe and as a result issued Intelligence Directive No. 8 on 7 May 1944, which listed a series of regulations for the handling of captured documents and signals/cipher equipment. This was subsequently followed up by more detailed instructions from 21st Army Group and headquarters ETOUSA to make sure the best use was made of these items in the field, and then a process was followed to dispatch them back as quickly as possible to Bletchley, the War Office and the ETOUSA Headquarters in London.

Bletchley Park set up its own room to liaise directly with 30AU, under Commander Bacon RNVR. It was vital that security was restricted to only named individuals. The majority of the unit had no idea about Bletchley Park, or its vital code work. Officers and men were not allowed to visit, have any knowledge of the work of Bletchley or, indeed, the methods or machinery being used. As operations and planning for the invasion of Europe began, 30AU recruited a large number of new officers and men.

They were all briefed on SIGINT, and the Enigma machine. It was also at this time that SIGINT requirements were put into the 30AU Black List for intelligence gathering, which was administered by Lieutenant Glanville in the NID. Security precautions were paramount for the unit and in order to preserve the work for the SIGINT community, 30AU followed a protocol:

a) No officer or OR of an IAU should be indoctrinated, although they could be briefed in the general appearance of the documents and equipment required. It is essential, however, that no-one taking part in Commando raids or front-line operations should be allowed to know anything of British cryptographic methods or of the machines used.

b) No raid should be laid on for SIGINT purposes only. The scope of the objectives should always be sufficiently wide to presuppose normal operational objects.

c) All the personnel of the IAU should be thoroughly trained in conduct as prisoners of war and behaviour under interrogation.

The unit was involved with the meticulous planning of Overlord from January 1944. Most of the Naval Officers in the unit devoted the two months prior to D-Day to operational planning. This was to concentrate 'in part to an intensive study of the technical aspect of intelligence requirements'. Many of the stores and equipment had been resourced from the Americans. They had attached a liaison officer, Lieutenant J.G. Ballantyne USNR from Commander Naval Forces Europe (COMNAVEU) to the unit.

It was given two clear objectives for Operation Overlord: the German Naval Headquarters and the port area of Cherbourg and the Douvres-la-Déliverande RADAR station. 30AU agreed that there were sufficient targets in and around the Cherbourg area to justify mounting an intelligence-gathering operation but there was heavy criticism at the time in the selection of Douvres as a target, most notably by Lieutenant Glanville. There were concerns that it was not a legitimate naval objective, and as it was positioned over 3 miles inland, the German military personnel at the site would have sufficient time to destroy all their documents and equipment before being captured. Alongside the ISTD model making work, Lieutenant Colonel Woolley commissioned SHAEF to produce some high-quality models for the two key objectives, Douvres and Cherbourg. These were used as the basis for planning the operations rather than those produced by the ISTD due to their 'superior finish and quality'. The reality, like is often the case in many military operations, that they provided an inaccurate picture of what was on the ground. 'They proved eventually to be an idealised and wholly inaccurate travesty of the objectives and in the case of Douvres nearly caused a disaster. It appears that the individuals concerned in producing the models were members of a Real Estate Corporation in the US whose natural inclination was to idealise the character of the land with which they were concerned.'

One of the X Troop team that had the RADAR installation as an objective was Sergeant Bob Burchell. He explained how the operation unfurled: 'we were given a last-minute briefing, using a model of the RADAR station we were supposed to capture after landing on Nan Red Juno Beach in the early hours of D-Day. During and after the briefing everything appeared so simple, but the finer Intelligence Reports relative to enemy defence positions and "Minen" fields were overlooked, as we were to find later. We went aboard the parent ship at Southampton and found we were closeted with the Canadians (Regiment Chaudierre and the North Shore Regiment). Not very good cruising weather and with D-Day delayed there we were, stuck below decks for twenty-four hours.'

Activities by 30AU in France shortly after D-Day indicated the value of the collaboration with Bletchley Park. A set of Germany Navy Enigma wheels was found at a Brittany RADAR station. At the U-Boat HQ in Paris numerous valuable cipher documents were found and on the operation in Douvres some German Airforce Enigma wheels were found with an associated cipher pad.

It was often a race. 30AU was very much part of the lead force into a Normandy town, and they needed to ascertain the targets of interest, such as the German Army HQ building in the town, where valuable intelligence might be gathered. The Germans would often have enough time to destroy what documents and cipher equipment they had, to prevent them falling into the hands of the Allies.

'W/T and ciphering rooms were found to be located on the third floor of the villa … the Germans had obviously been at great pains to destroy everything of intelligence value. Two ciphering machines had been completely wrecked, and it is only possible to state that the scramblers in use had been "B" and "R" so presumably the ciphering done here, at any rate latterly, was only of the second order of secrecy. A meticulous search, however, brought to light a number of documents of (Bletchley Park) BP interest including eventually in a cavity behind a panel, three small sacks of documents which had been shredded but not cross shredded. These were sent to the UK. Presumably the high-grade machines used by the (*Oberkommando des Heeres*) (OKH (West) had been removed by the Naval authorities at the time of their withdrawal some four days previously.…'

Royal Marine Patsy Cullen was a typical 30AU recruit. A Swansea lad, he had been brought up labouring on building sites in an around the town until he joined the

Royal Marines in July 1941. His father had served in the Royal Navy in World War I and he was keen to follow him into the Senior Service. After numerous stints in Africa and the Mediterranean with the Royal Marines, he was posted to the 30AU as a driver. This area of the south coast was deserted, as the area had been cleared in the run-up to D-Day, and many of the villages were standing empty. The troops destined for Normandy took the opportunity to use these villages to sharpen their infantry urban warfare tactics.

> 'All we did was escort the people who knew about intelligence. We were in little teams, with a driver, the intelligence officer sitting alongside him, a Corporal or a Sergeant, and the intelligence officer's batman. The officer was always Royal Navy, not the Royal Marines. He was a specialist in something … he was always in charge. They were a superstitious lot of bastards.'

The Commandos were billeted around the town, often in local houses. The training was comprehensive during the spring of 1944. The unit had assault courses, fitness and weapons training, escape and evasion, river crossings of the Arun, and speed marches out beyond Arundel and Amberley. Some of the 30AU personnel had to go on specialist training courses like the Parachute training course at Ringway, or explosives, safe-cracking, booby traps and mines courses at HMS *Volcano* in Cumberland.

The teams were to be going ashore in new American Willy's jeeps and attached trailers, and the Marines needed training in driving them. 'We spent a lot of time with the vehicles, learning how to reverse with the trailers. In the trailer was a motorbike, folded up in a big canvas bag. We had to learn how to take that out and fix it all up and keep it going because that was the officer's to cover his arse. If we were in the shit he got away in that and we protected him.'

The officers were the most valuable commodity in the four-man jeep teams. These Royal Navy officers had been specially selected for the unit and had the requisite background and training in intelligence gathering and were often recognised experts in one field or another, such as communications, gunnery, torpedoes or explosives. Cullen recalled: 'The officer was the priority, we had to get him to the target and you've got to get him out.' Other members of the team had been trained to dismantle booby traps, which they knew they would have to face on the streets and countryside of Normandy. The 30AU commandos had many opportunities to write home, even after arriving in Normandy. Marine Donald King was a prolific writer of letters to his family in Newton Mearns just outside Glasgow. There is one such letter, dated 15 June 1944:

> 'My Dearest Mother, do hope that you are all well and have received my two

previous letters posted a few days ago. As you will no doubt guess, I am now serving in France. Somehow it doesn't seem like it as the countryside and climate in the North is very similar to Southern England … you would be thrilled to hear of the news of the invasion…. I know you will be worrying about my safety and always will imagine that I'm in danger. But luck has been with me ever since I joined up and there is no reason for it changing now. The past week has been full of excitement and I think every one of us is relieved to know that we landed safely. My heart was certainly in my mouth when we landed on the beach, the noise of battle being so terrific. But you quickly get used to noise out here (you've just got to). I suppose that the invasion will be the main topic of conversation at home. We waited a long time for it to happen, didn't we? I'm glad to be taking part in it as I feel that our fight to free the enslaved people of Europe is very similar to the Crusades of olden days….'

Preparations for Overlord were completed by 25 May and the various 30AU detachments entered the closed concentration areas in readiness to embark. On 4 June 1944 the unit left Littlehampton for operations on the continent, leaving behind a small rear party. The Commanding Officer was Lieutenant Colonel A.R. Woolley RM. He resided on the first floor of the HQ building in Littlehampton.

'Shortly before D-Day security was stepped up with an armed guard posted on the CO's office both inside and out … the reason for this extra show of strength was the delivery of a large wooden crate, taken into the office and securely fastened to the centre of the floor. The mystery was lifted the day we received our briefing on the unit's first major target in France. The box contained a sand-tray model of Cherbourg, our job would be to capture the Villa Meurice, the German Naval HQ and the tunnels which were cut in the hillside below it and to gather what intelligence they contained.'

The 30AU teams were put in a landing craft that held eight teams, four jeep and trailer teams to the port and starboard in each line. The landing craft was a high-sided boat and the commandos saw nothing but sky for the whole of D-Day, until the ramps went down, which was a welcome relief from the seasickness. They went ashore with the first troops and headed towards the port of Cherbourg. The jeeps were followed up by Bedford 3-ton trucks, which were to be used to ferry captured prisoners and equipment back to Britain.

On D-Day, 30 Assault Unit split themselves across Juno Beach (Woolforce) and Utah Beach (Pikeforce). Pikeforce encompassed 'X' Troop with Captain Pike RM, Captain

Hargreaves-Heap and Lieutenant Glanville landing with the assault wave on D-Day near the town of St Aubyn-sur-Mer, and then accompanying the Canadian Infantry inland to capture the Douvres RADAR station.

On their assault on the German RADAR station at Douvres-la-Délivrande, they failed to control the facility but over time they worked their way to Cherbourg and on to Villa Maurice in Octaville where they found 'masses of material as well as an excellent wine cellar'. The teams spent over two days in this underground complex searching desks, lockers, safes and thousands of files and documents. This was the only time when a significant portion of 30AU operated together. From Cherbourg they worked in smaller parties of up to ten men roving the British and American sectors, gathering whatever secret material they could find and returning it to London.

Another team under Lieutenant Commander Postlethwaite and Lieutenant Hugill landed at Arromanches at H+4 on D-Day to search the local RADAR station, and then join Commander Curtis (Curtforce) to attack targets in the Ouistreham area. Curtforce included the Headquarters staff of the 30AU Naval wing who had landed at Port-en-Bessin, searching the lighthouse, harbour vessels and look-out station and then proceeding to Ouistreham. Curtforce was also charged with creating a Unit Headquarters for the British area at Douvres.

Woolforce, under the command of Lieutenant Colonel Woolley, landed near the Normandy town of Sainte-Mère- Église on the Cotentin Peninsula and was to follow the US Task Force as it made its way to Cherbourg to undertake missions against a number of naval targets in and around the town.

Not all the intelligence briefings before the Normandy beach assaults were useful

Advance party of 30 Assault Unit welcomed in the main square of Granville (first allied troops to arrive), 31 July 1944 (© ADM 202/599)

30 Assault Unit
TAC HQ in Rue
de la Falaise,
Granville, 2
August 1944,
showing jeep
and trailer set up
(©ADM 202/599)

to the deployed 30AU marines. A report on the Pikeforce activity on and after D-Day
by the second-in-command of the RM wing of 30AU, Major Evans RM, stated that
'reports on the defences both at Tailleville and at the RADAR station were remarkably
inaccurate'. Even the finely detailed models were under scrutiny 'the models gave a
very false impression and as to contours bore little resemblance to the actual ground.'

Much of the intelligence used by 30AU for their objectives in France had been built
up by liaison with intelligence departments across the country and choreographed by
the Admiralty. Only the officer in each team was privy to this information.

'When we were approaching a target, all the information about that town –
where the Chief of Police lived, where the Lord Mayor lived, all sorts of people
like that. We got this information from the Admiralty. We wouldn't get it, it
would be the officer. He'd know everything about the town. One of the targets
might be a factory and what they were producing. We also had safe blowers with
us, who could wrap cords around trees. Our principal job was driving – to get
us there and to get us back.'

30 Assault Unit was established from the ideas furnished from a successful German
intelligence unit. 30AU was to subsequently be copied by a unit established by the
Americans in the summer of 1944. This became known as TICOM (Target Intelligence

Instructions regarding War Diaries and Intelligence Summaries are contained in F.S. Regs., Vol. I. Monthly War Diaries will be enclosed in A.F. C.2119. If this is not available, and for Intelligence Summaries, the cover will be prepared in manuscript.

Month and Year June 1944.

WAR DIARY
or
INTELLIGENCE SUMMARY
(Delete heading not required).

Army Form C. 2118.
Unit 30 A.U.
Commanding Officer Lt Col A.R. Woolley

Place	Date	Hour	Summary of Events and Information	References to Appendices
Littlehampton	4.	1145	"Woolforce" left Littlehampton for concentration area.	
Southampton	8.		Embarked at Southampton.	
	10	1700	Landed at Ste. Marie du Mont.	
	10	2300	Sustained 20 casualties through enemy bombing. (Two (2) killed)	
	11		Location changed to Ste. Mere Eglise.	
	14		Moved to Benzeville en Plain. Patrols were sent out to Azeville & Emondville. Position of "Pikeforce" established at Douvres.	
	15		Patrol sent out to St. Marcouf.	
	17 17/18		Report on activities of 'Pikeforce' Examination was carried out of three "Crossbow" sites at La Haye-du-Puits. 6 E/5 203994, 146988, 176995.	see Appx. I.
	19.		"A" Troop left for Crossbow site W. of Valognes.	
	20		'B' & 'X' Troops plus operational H.Q. moved Quettetot.	
	21		'B' Troop relieved 'A' Troop on "Crossbow" site. Half "B" Troop returned to unit.	
	22		'A','B','X' Tps. & operational HQ joined 9th Div 47 Reg U.S. Army N.E. of Teurtheville-Hague.	
	25		Advanced to Octeville & returned to Teurtheville-Hague area for night Suffered casualties - 2 killed 2 wounded.	

ADM 202/308
XC4262
COPYRIGHT - NOT TO BE REPRODUCED PHOTOGRAPHICALLY WITHOUT PERMISSION

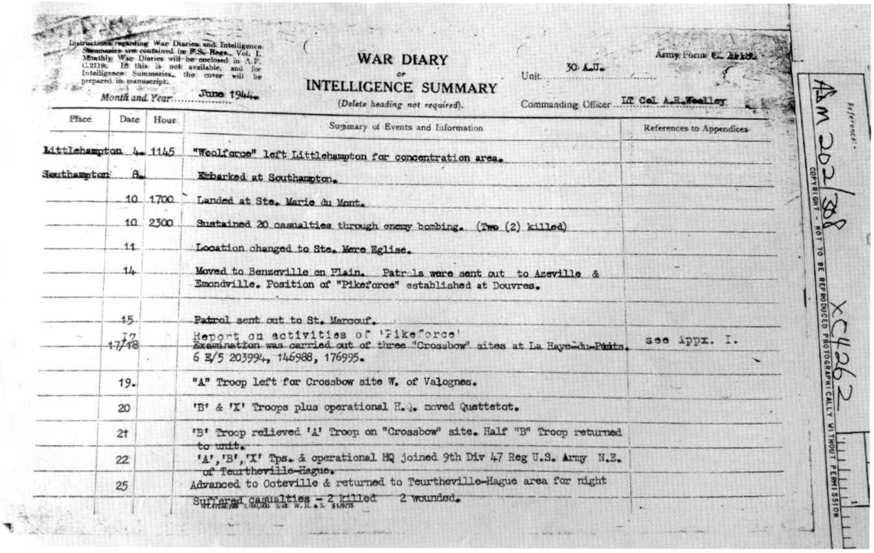

30 Assault Unit Intelligence summary from June 1944 by Lieutenant Colonel Woolley (© ADM 202/308)

Committee), which was initially intended to be a covert airborne unit to seize German signal intelligence targets identified through POW interrogations at CSDIC facilities and from ULTRA material.

The compilation of the Black List proved of immense value to 30AU and Naval Intelligence for Normandy. A further edition of the Black List was prepared in July 1944 (although it was never formally published). Some of the new editions included information from the US Navy Department through COMNAVEU and a broadened list of locations extracted from analysis of the vast amount of German documents captured during the early phases of the Normandy campaign.

The work of the 30 Assault Unit had proved its worth long before D-Day. Having eyes and ears on the ground, and specialist intelligence gatherers would help fight the covert war against the Germans. With the weight of the Allied invasion forces, and an initially uncoordinated German defence, it led 30AU to reap the rewards for a greater good – the intelligence community back in Britain. What these commandos found in each Normandy town and village from a retreating German army would help us to win the war.

(From the file ADM 223/500 held at TNA)

D.D.N.I
D.N.I
F

PROPOSAL FOR NAVAL INTELLIGENCE COMMANDO UNIT

One of the most outstanding innovations in German Intelligence is the creation by the German N.I.D. of Special Intelligence 'Commandos'.

These 'Commandos' accompany the forward troops when a port or naval installation is being attacked and, if the attack is successful, their duty is to capture documents, cyphers, etc. before these can be destroyed by the defenders.

They have various other intelligence duties, which are described in the attached memorandum.

I submit that we would do well to consider organising such a 'Commando' within the N.I.D., for use when we reassume the offensive on the Continent, in Norway or elsewhere. The unit would be modelled on the same lines as its German counterpart and would be placed under the command of C.C.O. perhaps a month before a specific objective is attacked.

Its duties would be to find out all N.I.D. Sections' requirements from the port attacked, e.g. cyphers, specimens of material (including enemy oil fuel and food, for instance) charts, enemy fleet orders, mines, R.D.F. gear, photographs, etc, etc obtain all intelligence available as to where in the particular port these things would be found.train with the raiding force proceed with 2nd or 3rd wave of attack into the port, and make straight for the various buildings, etc, where the booty is expected to be found, capture it and return.

Operation 'SLEDGEHAMMER' is a typical example of an objective which might yield valuable fruit if tackled by such a unit.

Propose:

I should submit the plan in greater detail with suggestions for organisation and personnel. The principle be worked out in collaboration with C.C.O

(signed) F

N.I.D (17)
20.3.42

CHAPTER EIGHT
LISTENERS

'It is contended that very few Armies went into battle better informed of their enemy ...'

Report by Brigadier E.T. Williams, Field Marshal Montgomery's Chief Intelligence Officer, on the British use of Signals Intelligence, October 1945

～～

World War II was defined by Signals Intelligence (SIGINT) more than any other form of intelligence, and for the Allied planners for Overlord it was to become the premier source. The ability to intercept, decrypt and locate enemy radio communications would provide insight into German intentions, something that other sources, like aerial imagery, could not produce.

SIGINT is the interception of enemy radio and electronic communications to gather intelligence regarding their capabilities and intent. The basis of all SIGINT is the partnership of three – intercept, traffic analysis and cryptanalysis – all working seamlessly together. During the war, each of the Armed Services developed their own independent signals interception capabilities in Britain. These were collectively known as the 'Y Service' and were the wireless interception arm of the GC&CS at Bletchley Park. Colloquially they were referred to as the War Office Y Group or WOYG. Their role was to intercept and analyse enemy radio signals, sending any encoded traffic to Bletchley for decryption. The service was a network of fixed stations, mobile sites and Direction Finding (D/F) sites dotted around the country and in a number of countries overseas.

The Royal Navy/Admiralty had key sites like Scarborough and Flowerdown; the RAF had sites such as Waddington, then Cheadle, and the Army had Chatham. Non-Services organisations also played a part in the effort – for example, the Metropolitan Police Service opened an intercept station at Denmark Hill in London in order to collect the few private diplomatic and commercial radio links that were transmitting. By the end of the war there were around 160 strategic intercept stations in Britain, with a similar number of smaller D/F sites. These were all overseen by five different authorities: the three Armed Services, GC&CS and the Radio Security Services (RSS).

The RSS was independent of the Y Service and was originally established by the War Office but it was transferred to SIS command from 1942. It ran a large nationwide network of Voluntary Interceptors (VI) to do work in their homes, originally against

German *Abwher* wireless operators. Most of the *Abwehr* agents operating in Britain in the early years of the war were known to MI5 and the police, as one of the *Abwehr* instructors was an MI6 agent. The Police Special Branch units, working closely with MI5, undertook a joint operation rounding up over 1,000 potential spies, and restricting the movements of over 6,000 additional foreign workers. This broad security purge effectively destroyed any effective German intelligence networks operating within Britain.

The process of radio intercept would start with operators (who would have been trained in Morse) searching for German communications of interest. Anything valuable would have been recorded in a running log, recording the time of intercept, frequency, any information between call signs, the signal strength of the transmission and any D/F fixes which would have been collected from separate D/F intercept sites. The collected signals and logs were the raw SIGINT product. Following this, Traffic Analysis (T/A) would be undertaken to research the German communication networks to establish call signs, pattern of life and any locational information about the collected transmissions. If enciphered material was intercepted, it would be forwarded to Bletchley Park for cryptanalysis. Some basic cryptanalysis could be done at the Y Service stations using techniques like hand copying and typically it was only the higher-grade material which would be forwarded through to GC&CS.

The work that was undertaken in Bletchley Park's Hut 3 may well have changed the course of the war, driven by the sterling leadership of Squadron Leader Eric Jones. But the majority of work undertaken at GC&CS on the high-echelon German Army and Air Force signals was by Hut 6 and the SIXTA (Traffic Analysis) personnel. By September 1944, Hut 6 had 560 personnel and SIXTA 348 on their books, making up a considerable portion of the Bletchley workforce.

In November 1940, with the war in Europe taking hold, MI8a was reorganised to focus on operational radio exploitation and given responsibility for the Y Service, basing itself in 2 Caxton Street, London. Interception had originally been coordinated by MI1b and subsequently transferred across to MI8 at the beginning of the war. MI1b lost its crypto work to the newly formed team at Bletchley under GC&CS, but the organisation would maintain the following main tasks:

– wireless intercept and its coordination
– dissemination of decoded traffic
– supply of suitably trained personnel and intercept equipment.

From February 1940, the Y Services introduced an official training formation referred to as the Special Operator Training Battalion (SOTB) based at the barracks in the quiet market town of Trowbridge. Its intent was to produce 100 W/T operators every month from their sixteen-week long training programme, which was later extended to twenty weeks. After *Luftwaffe* bombing, the training was moved to the Isle of Man.

Their intensive training covered the teaching of Morse (to thirty words/minute level), maintaining their radio sets, doing rudimentary D/F alongside the usual military training. They would also learn the 'Q-codes', which is a group of three-letter international standardised signals to convey instructions or conditions to the receiver station. QRM, for example, means interference, QSA is the signal strength. There were three grades to Morse speeds:

B3 – eighteen words/minute
B2 – twenty-five words/minute
B1 – thirty words/minute

Each grade would incur an increase in pay for one of the newly qualified Special Wireless Operators (SWOPS) who had graduated from the SOTB.

The Y Service recruited a lot of Auxiliary Territorial Service (ATS) women for the course, but in the initial SOTB courses there was concern about the throughput of new operators. The ATS element of the WOYG became so dominant during the war that they were responsible for 75 per cent of the wartime intercept.

The most important of all the WOYG stations was Beaumanor, a strategic fixed intercept station in an 800-acre estate near the village of Woodhouse in Leicestershire. It was chosen as a WOYG site as it was central in the country, rural and had good tree cover from *Luftwaffe* reconnaissance aircraft. The first batch of female ATS SWOPS arrived at Beaumanor in February 1942, and brought a significant culture change to the organisation, being put alongside their experienced male Radio Operator colleagues. A bespoke ATS training course was developed at Fearon Hall in Loughborough, where operators were taught German W/T procedures, how their networks functioned and how the WOYG intercepted them.

Beaumanor had four separate set rooms, each housing forty positions manned by thirty-six operators with an additional four sets for search work. There was also an adjoining teleprinter room where a runner would receive and transmit messages to and from Bletchley Park. By the early part of 1944, as requirements for signals intelligence were reaching a peak for Overlord, the site had a total of 196 sets operational. There were also teams that undertook Traffic Analysis (T/A) and detailed records were kept of German radio frequencies and call signs used. In total, there were nearly 1,300 W/T operators at Beaumanor. The T/A section at Beaumanor was often referred to as Compilation and Records Room (CRR), and it was to play a critical role in keeping the site efficient and organised. The combination of the Beaumanor T/A section and Hut 6 at Bletchley Park were key to the success of the exploitation of German military radio traffic – they had identified the networks, organisational command and control structures, geographic locations and movements. The coordination between the WOYG and Bletchley was vital. In July 1940, Bletchley created the Intercept Control, more affectionately known as 'Coleman's Section', which became the intelligence control hub for the Y stations and developed a robust prioritisation system to make sure they were concentrating on only the most vital tasks:

A – First class priority (using first class operators – double banked)
B – Good coverage (not necessarily double banked)
C – Covered by an average operator
D – Hold while active
E – Take a sample
F – unwanted

High Frequency Direction Finding (HFDF) was an important aid to the WOYG, to geographically locate a radio signal by taking a sequence of bearings from fixed or mobile sites in different parts of the country. This knowledge helped complement the T/A and other signal analysis. If operators could pinpoint where the transmissions were coming from they could better understand who they were. These HFDF stations comprised six locations – Montrose, Moulton, Thurso, Sutton Valence, Chacewater and Perton. They also could use three Medium Frequency D/F sites at Thurso, Chacewater and Croft Spa. Each of these sites were linked through a landline back to Beaumanor and had a Morse key so they could communicate with the WOYG operators. Once a D/F fix was attained on a signal in France, it was passed to Bletchley. By D-Day, D/F fixes were being requested every few minutes from the WOYG stations.

When operating the sets, the SWOPS key asset was target knowledge, experience that could never be taught in a classroom. The Germans utilised a complex radio network for their military and intelligence services which was run by their General Headquarters (GHQ) controlling eight armies and four Panzer groups. The longer an operator experienced working on a particular German network, the more they could pick up on styles and rhythms from the operators. At the early stages of the war the Germans were quite open in broadcasting call signs but they evolved to not using any at all. They would play loud music in the background or use speech at high speed to throw any interceptors off the scent, or even change frequency mid-message.

From 1942 the teams at Beaumanor were asked to cover radio traffic from the German police groups, and Bletchley sent a representative up to assist the WOYG in

Beaumanor, external view of SIGINT collection antenna and huts during World War II (© Crown Copyright, by kind permission of Director GCHQ)

developing the target. They were also to work against the *Organisation Todt*, the German civil engineering company that was doing the construction work in Normandy on Hitler's Atlantic Wall defences.

An outstation to Beaumanor was built at Kerley Downs, near Bishops Waltham in Hampshire and it came online in April 1944 to collect low power Medium Frequency (MF) German communications in France. It was staffed by around 120 General Post Office (GPO) personnel and was integral in following German army divisions around Cherbourg in the initial days of the Overlord campaign. On D-Day itself, the site collected one of the first radio intercepts of the operation which read 'Gliders landing in Caen…. Help…. Help…. Help….'

In February 1944, the Germans ran a number of significant military exercises across Belgium and France, operating over seventy-five separate radio frequencies which were intercepted at Beaumanor. The subsequent T/A done on these frequencies was to greatly assist the teams a few months later when the invasion of Europe began.

D-Day and the subsequent invasion caused the rapid decline in the use of landlines by the German military, and the campaign pushed them onto the radio networks. A low frequency so-called German NETZ network was established on 6 June 1944, whereby each station has an allocated call sign and set of frequencies assigned. Although the WOYG could intercept and identify this traffic, interception was largely undertaken at this stage of the campaign by the mobile forward field intercept units. These 'Tactical Y Groups' deployed into Normandy operated out of 10-ton trucks and followed the Allied advance across France. They were responsible for the collection, decoding, analysing and reporting of tactical German radio traffic and to relay the subsequent SIGINT back to their Army Group HQ as quickly as possible. They were also fitted with a rudimentary D/F capability so could provide location fixes on their target signals. The intelligence officers deployed to these teams were trained at Beaumanor on an eight- to ten-week course. A pre-requisite was they had to be competent German speakers, as it was expected that they would be responsible for some POW interrogations. The course covered the interpretation of wireless intercept and basic codebreaking.

Another significant organisation that was involved in signals interception and analysis was the Radio Security Service (RSS). It was originally established in September 1939 with the responsibility for the detection and monitoring of illicit wireless communications in Britain that may be transmitted by German *Abwehr* agents.

The RSS functions were:

1. The discovery and identification of all clandestine transmissions of all types in all areas, entailing general search of all frequencies for all types of signals.
2. The monitoring of all clandestine networks discovered to be active.
3. The location of clandestine transmitters by fixed and mobile D/F units in the UK, the Colonies and protectorates and territories occupied by the British and Allied armies.
4. The monitoring of all authorised British channels of communications as the agent of the Inter-Service Signals Security Committee.
5. The discovery of free frequencies for use by British and Allied secret communications networks.
6. The control and supervision of the clandestine and secret W/T networks of the Allies in Great Britain.

At its peak, the RSS had an organisation resourced to undertake the vast array of

SIGINT tasks that were levied on it from Bletchley Park and elsewhere. This included:

91 officers
1,945 other ranks
2 ATS officers
70 ATS ORs
115 civilians

Added together with the 1,215 assigned Voluntary Interceptors (VIs), the total manifest for RSS at its height was 3,438 staff. These VIs were the core of the RSS and their skills as amateur radio enthusiasts who could monitor the airwaves were a key asset to British Intelligence and were a vital cog in the work before D-Day. The interceptors would have two key tasks:

1. *General Search* – scanning an allotted radio frequency band. Over time they would get to know who was operating on these frequencies. The VI would have to log everything they would hear on the frequencies.
2. *Allocated Signals* – the VI would listen at a particular time to a frequency which would be monitored as routine.

The RSS logs were sent to a covert address, referred to as 'Box 25', which was a covername for the RSS HQ at Arkley Court in Barnet, north London, before a full-time listening station was established at Hanslope Park from June 1941 under the leadership of Captain Prickett. It was at Arkley that a team called the Collation and Discrimination Department would sift through the logs, extracting all the information they could out of the interceptor's log sheets to discern patterns and frequencies of interest. Any decoding that was needed would be sent through to Bletchley Park. Arkley would become the experts in *Abwehr* traffic and from 1941 was placed under the control of Section V of SIS.

RSS had access to a nationwide efficient Direction Finding (D/F) network to locate and triangulate suspect radio signals. Knowing where these signals were being transmitted from would be of value to ascertain whether it was the *Abwehr, Gestapo* or *Sicherheitsdienst (SD)*, as they would use different radio and cipher systems. During the course of the war, Bletchley Park was to decipher 268,000 RSS messages they had collected. The RSS were responsible for the identification and subsequent capture of five of the twenty-three German *Abwehr* agents who had been sent to Britain in 1941. At their peak, eighteen VHF stations were operating in the UK. VHF was also collected on RN ships – fifty of which were outfitted with VHF sets for the Normandy landings.

Five mobile Naval Y stations were sent to the Normandy beachhead after D-Day.

Guy Waters was reading Modern Languages at the University of Cambridge, and was studying in Florence, Italy when the war broke out. He returned to Britain and his university don recruited him into Bletchley Park where he served between 1940 and 1941, working on the decoding and exploitation of low-grade German bomber traffic. Waters was transferred from Bletchley to RAF Cheadle.

'Every nation at war knows that every other nation is intercepting its traffic, and it knows if its sending out easy traffic to intercept or not. It may not know the degree to which the analysis of this traffic is being carried out and operationally used. But it knows full well there is an enemy Y Service in any war. It is always difficult for anybody who is transmitting to realise how much can be picked up by just a little squeak and you'd know what it means, by analysis through card-indexing every damn thing you can find about the traffic. It is rather extraordinary to be in a state where you may know where he is going to move next.... Reconnaissance was important throughout the entire war. The Germans would send out reconnaissance aircraft who then radio'd back their weather results.'

The RAF Y Service comprised two main intercept sites: Chicksands, which was used for ground communications intercept; and Cheadle, for air-ground communications intercept. Enciphered material would go to the German Air Section (AI4f) at Bletchley and the SIGINT-ULTRA deciphered traffic would end up at the Air Ministry in London (AI4). This intelligence would be disseminated to around forty recipients across the Air Ministry, War Office, Admiralty, RAF/USAAF commands and groups.

By 1944 the RAF had a good understanding of the German Air Force (GAF) order of battle and allocated frequencies. The dominance of Allied aircraft over the Luftwaffe in northern France would provide dividends for the intercept community. The strategy for the Allies was to specifically target landline networks and exchanges in France in the days before D-Day, which would push the Germans more on to the wireless networks. Another priority task was detecting any GAF reconnaissance flights transiting the southern coast of England where huge amounts of personnel and military equipment were being coalesced for Overlord. Cheadle and Kingsdown were critical to this and provided early indication to Fighter Command.

At Cheadle the radio intercept material was collected, decoded and sent on to the Air Ministry. By May 1944 the site also had nine teleprinter links with the Block F Air Section at Bletchley Park. Cheadle was run with shifts or watches which maintained a 24/7 signals intercept capability against the Germans. Each watch would have around fifteen to twenty staff and as they worked their Luftwaffe targets they would get to

Y stations	Sets	D/F stations	VHF Coastal stations
CUPAR	10	CUPAR	SHERINGHAM
PORTRUSH	1	PORTRUSH	TRIMINGHAM
SHETLANDS	2	SHETLANDS	WINTERTON
SCARBOROUGH	120	ANSTRUTHER	SOUTHWOLD
CHICKSANDS	10	BOWER	FELIXSTOWE
FLOWERDOWN	32 German Naval 17 Japanese Naval 6 Spanish/Portuguese Naval	SCARBOROUGH KILMINNING OBAN NORWICH FORD END	ALDEBURGH SCARBOROUGH (WITHERNSEA) FAYRENESS ABBOTSCLIFF
SUTTON VALENCE	1	PEMBROKE	VENTNOR PORTLAND
PEMBROKE	1	LAND'S END	LYME REGIS
NAVAL SECTION		SUTTON VALENCE	TORQUAY
GC&CS	7	PERRAN LYDD CRAWLEY CHILBOTTAN GOONHAVEN	LOOE COVERACK

know their transmission patterns and habits. Prior to Overlord, Cheadle was tasked with getting German Airforce (GAF) intelligence for any mine-laying operations in the Channel, which would hinder a naval taskforce transiting to Normandy.

Much of the material the Y Service collected would end up as ULTRA intelligence, through the production line of Bletchley Park's teleprinter lines. The majority of operators had no idea what Bletchley Park was or how their encoded intercept traffic was being processed and analysed. But from Waters' posting there he was fully conscious of it, 'the interplay between ULTRA and low-grade intercept was extremely important. One of the difficulties in using ULTRA was the enemy might find out that you'd obviously known something which you could only know about through high-grade ... so you had to be terribly careful to make it quite apparent that you were deriving intelligence from wide sources, and that any of these sources might come up with the information. One of the sources was air reconnaissance, and we frequently did an air reconnaissance ... simply because we knew from ULTRA that something was going on but we wanted an excuse to know it.'

Waters was subsequently deployed with SHAEF Advance Forces HQ into Normandy with General Hoyt Vandenburg attached to the 11th US Airforce. At HQ they had direct access to both low and high-grade signals intelligence. 'I spotted that the German fighter force in Normandy were so stretched that you could calculate in just a few minutes take off and time of landing. So you knew when they'd be on the ground defenceless ... they would get up at dawn, they would then go fighting until their petrol ran out ... they would then come down and land. From high-grade we knew what air bases there were. So we were able to combine the low-grade information as to their times of take-off and landing and the deduction that we could apply what airfields they were using from ULTRA. The 9th Airforce was asked to attack those particular bases at those particular times ... to me it was the most dramatic, hands-on exploitation of low-grade plus high-grade that I recall.'

Flowerdown was the second most significant intercept station in Britain, with over ninety positions by 1945.

The HRO receivers were first manufactured in the USA from 1935 and were adopted for widescale use in World War II. They were used widely by the British Y Service intercept stations who preferred its good sensitivity and selectivity in terms of scanning the radio waves.

At the end of the war there were around 160 strategic intercept stations operating in Britain, alongside a similar number of D/F stations which were considerably smaller in scale. The intercept stations run run by five different authorities – the three Services, GC&CS and the RSS. However, all five partners were effectively coordinated by GC&CS who also received all their intercept reporting and results.

By 1940, RAF Chicksands had become the largest Signals Intelligence collection site in the UK for the RAF (by 1945 it had around 240 intercept positions). Its main role in the national collection effort was to concentrate efforts against the German Air Force Enigma traffic. Before D-day, in May 1944 the station had two direct teleprinter links with Bletchley Park's Air Section.

The German Y Service was a very professional and competent unit and mirrored

RAF Cheadle
set room during
World War II (©
Crown Copyright,
by kind permission
of Director GCHQ)

the British Military Y Service in many respects. A German fixed Y station dealt exclusively with the interception of strategic Army and Air Force traffic as well as international diplomatic traffic. In the field, the German Y organisation consisted of a Y Company and a Divisional Intercept Platoon. The Y Company resided at a Corps or Army HQ level and was manned by Army Signals troops. They were organised into intercept sections with a D/F component. The Divisional Intercept Platoon had a number of W/T interception sections and a number of sections for landline intercept. The Platoon was staffed by Divisional Signals staff. During the early stages of the war, the British exhibited poor operational security on their W/T networks, so providing the German General Staff with some useful strategic and operational intelligence. German intelligence also had their own signals intercept capabilities. The *Sicherheitsdienst* (SD) had a W/T specialist, Dr Jozef Götz, based in Paris. In his early thirties he was originally posted to SD from the *Geheime Feld Polizei* (Field Security Police). In early 1944 he had had some successes in picking up SOE F Section W/T operators through their mistakes when broadcasting. He and his team were aware of the SOE agents use of the BBC news services and '*Messages personnels*' and how they were being used to covertly message Resistance teams in northern France. Götz caught the stream of covert BBC messages on the night of 5 June 1944, no fewer than fifteen messages he personally recognised as being related to the forthcoming Allied

RAF Cheadle
Direction Finding
equipment, World
War II (© Crown
Copyright, by
kind permission of
Director GCHQ)

invasion. He immediately informed his superiors at the SD Headquarters building in
Avenue Foch, which relayed the information urgently to Berlin via Teleprinter. All
the German Army Commands were alerted to the messages and the potential Allied
plans. 15th Army Command, holding the Atlantic Wall from Calais-Boulogne did
promulgate the message of a pending invasion and were put on high alert. Fortunately
for the Allies, the 7th Army Command, which ran the Normandy coast in the Baie de
la Seine, ignored the message. This was to have a hugely significant ramification for
the outcome of the next day.

Similarly to the establishment of the RSS, the Germans also recruited radio amateurs
who were members of the *Deutscher Amateur Sende und Empfangs Verein* (DASV) into
the German *Abwehr*. The Germans had a very effective military SIGINT capability
spread across a number of military units, which, at the height of the war totalled some
12,000 signal troops. German commanders were better informed about their enemy
and his intentions than in any previous war.

Lance Corporal Heinz Herbst joined the Army in early 1941 in Dresden and started
his service with an intelligence unit for basic training. He then moved to the German
Army Intelligence school in Halle for a ten-week specialist training in all aspect of
intelligence gathering. Once proficient and promoted to the rank of a Private, he was
moved to Frankfurt, where a long-range reconnaissance/intelligence-gathering unit

was being constructed – H(orch) Company 613.

'I left the Army as a lance corporal, never an officer, I was not a good soldier, none of it really mattered to me.

'In the army, every unit has a particular call sign, from the divisions right down to the individual companies. We monitored every frequency so painstakingly that we were able to detect the signs for each unit and establish where each one was by the way each call sign was directed. In that way we were able to discover not only that individual units had been transferred but where they had gone. In this way we were doing a bit of long-range reconnaissance.

'The English were rather slacker and less disciplined than we were. At Christmas, for example, they did not bother to transmit in code or in ciphers as they did for the rest of the time and so we heard them transmitting "Goodbye" and "Happy Christmas". In the methodology of transmission, the operator's ear was so well schooled that he could recognise the style of his counterpart even when it was coming from some other location. There were even recognisable characteristics in Morse code that we could detect. One operator might linger on a "dash" or falter with a "dot" and those of us who listened on the frequency would be able to recognise the operator.'

In 1942 Herbst was transferred to St Malo, and in 1943 was deployed to Vitre, near Rennes.

'We were transferred away from the water because we had very valuable and important equipment and had it been damaged (in an air raid) we would have been without eyes. To all intents and purposes, we were the eyes of the army – espionage in England was no longer very viable at that stage.

'Then one began to suspect that there would be an invasion on the Channel coast, around Calais largely because the distance at that point on the coast was very short, I mean, they could probably have fired shots at us with long-range weaponry, it was so close. The English deceived us. Again and again, we heard on the airwaves, they seemed to be giving orders to start extensive troop movements towards the environs of Dover. We heard the English orders to move and American ones, because by then, the Americans were involved. I have to admit it was very skilled, because it caused us to think that that was where the invasion would come from. This was very obvious as far as the military forces were concerned, because it meant only a two-hour crossing or so, instead of a journey lasting three times that, as it finally turned out.'

In the spring of 1944, the German signal teams noticed a shift in American and British divisions that had been previously monitored in southern Italy or in the wider Mediterranean theatre, and they were suddenly being picked up in the British Isles. It was estimated that 95 per cent of the units that were landed in Normandy during Overlord had been monitored and identified in the British Isles through this interception effort. From this regular intelligence, the German High Command could calculate the strength of the Allied forces. Intercepted radio traffic during the landing exercises on the south coast of England also provided them with a rich picture of the projected invasion procedure, but not of the time or venue of the landing.

Herbst stated, 'we were therefore aware of a great massing of troops in the Dover area but we also questioned the fact that they should be planning to invade there where the Atlantic Wall was much stronger than along the Normandy coast. Then we confirmed it to ourselves by saying that their air force would handle that. The result of this suspicion was that we were moved from Vitré where we re-built the equipment and carried on listening to the airwaves.

'We heard, for example, when reinforcements were called in and we heard when ammunition transport was ordered up and where it was sent to, or tank movements. It was all coded in letters and numbers and these messages were sent to the de-coders, who got to work on it. We did round the clock duty – six hours on and then 12 hours liberty and then six hours duty again and occasionally, you got 24 hours free….it was very tense, exhausting for those who were on listening duties – there were times when for hours they heard absolutely nothing.'

Prior to the invasion there was a period of dedicated radio silence, which baffled the German signals intelligence teams operating in northern France. The Allied air campaign prior to the landings also disrupted the German command net, which would have reduced the speed at which intelligence results could be transmitted between the military commands. General Jodl, the German Chief of Armed Forces Operations Staff, as well as the Führer, routinely displayed a lack of confidence in signals intelligence. But short-range communications intercept was to provide such a huge amount of intelligence on the Allied offensive that any attack of greater than a divisional strength could be assessed to occur up to five days in advance. The Germans had compromised the American cipher device used in the field, and intelligence could be extracted from

HRO Receiver
(© Crown
Copyright, by
kind permission of
Director GCHQ)

HRO Receiver
– inside top
(© Crown
Copyright, by
kind permission
of Director
GCHQ)

the cipher over a delay of two to four days but as more and more enciphered traffic was collected the German cipher teams could extract intelligence from the American enciphered traffic in only a few hours. The US military units typically displayed less radio discipline than their British counterparts, so subsequently were a better source of intelligence. They also used quite primitive cipher systems below divisional level, many of which had been captured by the Germans in previous campaigns so it would only take around ten messages for the traffic to be decrypted. In the initial assault phases of Overlord, both American and British units would broadcast directly in the clear with little regard for the possibility of interception and exploitation. But it was the Canadians who were to provide the least intelligence from their radio traffic.

Even the Free French Army had their radio traffic intercepted before and after D-Day. They were employing a cipher system, but it had not been upgraded since 1940 and the Germans found it easy to exploit. The combined Naval cipher No. 3 (which was used by both the British Royal Navy and the US Navy) could be exploited every time it was collected between 1941 and 1943, which was to give the German the advantage on the Atlantic convoy operations during the early years of the war.

The Germans had six cryptologic organisations operational, four military and two civilian, during the war with a total complement of approximately 30,000 personnel. The four military branches were:

1. Army High Command Signal Intelligence agency (*Oberkommando des Heeres, General der Nachrichten Aufklaerung* or OKH/GdNA) – enemy Army traffic.
2. Navy High Command Signal Intelligence agency (*Oberkommando der Kriegsmarine, 4 Seekriegsleitung III* or OKN/4SKL III) – enemy Naval traffic.
3. Air Force High Command Signal Intelligence agency (*Oberkommando der Luftwaffe, Luftnachrichten Abteilung 350* or OKL/LN Abt 350) – enemy Air Force traffic.
4. Supreme Command Armed Forces Signal Intelligence agency (*Oberkommando der Wehrmacht, Chiffrierabteilung* or OKW/Chi) – enemy, neutral or friendly diplomatic traffic, commercial traffic and news broadcasts.

The two German civilian organisations were:

1. Foreign Office Cryptanalytic Section (*Personal Z Sonderdienst* or Pers Z S) – diplomatic traffic, enemy, neutral or friendly.
2. Goering's Research Bureau (*Reichsluftfahrtministerium Forschungsamt* or FA) – a Nazi Party agency dealing with diplomatic traffic, broadcast and telephone monitoring, including the BBC.

The OKL/LN Abt 350 had success in intercepting order of battle information from Allied air force radio activity around D-Day through dedicated traffic analysis and monitoring of radio-telephone and air-borne RADAR signals. The Navy SIGINT agency had very good knowledge at the start of the war on the Royal Navy organisation and disposition of the fleet through decrypting British Naval code No. 2. Another success was the breaking of British Naval code No. 4, which allowed the German *Kriegsmarine* to have full knowledge of Operation Stratford, the proposed British and French Norway expedition, which led to the subsequent German invasion of Norway.

During the first half of 1944, the German SIGINT organisations were producing some 3,000 significant decodes per month which were reported to Hitler, Generalfeldmarschall Keitel (the German Chief of the Armed Forces) and from Keitel to General Jodl (the Chief of the Armed Forces Operations Staff).

Decisions made in OKW/Chi that would turn the tide of the war and allow the Allied SIGINT effort at Bletchley Park and Vint Hill Farms to make the huge strides forward in breaking the German encrypted signal traffic, which would shape the outcome of Overlord. It was OKW/Chi that had responsibility for cryptanalysis and the deciphering of enemy communications and it was this organisation that insisted on the continued use of the plugboard Enigma and the SZ42 Lorenz cipher machines in their most insecure forms. The agency refused the introduction of the T52d teleprinter machines, some of the most secure cipher machines of their time. It left the gates open for Allied intelligence.

Herbst goes on to say:

'...this was particularly the case just before the invasion, we went for days without hearing a thing but we always had to listen. It was so dead just before the invasion that at times we thought the war was over. Of course this turned

German soldiers listening to a radio service (© Bundesarchiv Bild 146-1975-047-03)

out to be deliberate radio silence on the part of the Allies and there were those amongst us who said that such a deep silence undoubtedly presaged enormous events.

'Most of the material the English broadcast was the real thing, only we could not respond to it as an army because we were too weak. We had no air force to speak of, the few flyers we had were standing around uselessly – they had no fuel. We listened constantly to how the English Army was being strengthened by troops from America, we heard it constantly from 1942 onwards.

'Again and again, new units appeared, we had more and more call signs to deal with and we were bewildered by the numbers of troops that were being massed. Where was it all going to lead to, we asked ourselves.

'In our unit, because we had the possibility of listening in to what the English were broadcasting, we were getting quite a different picture (of the situation). Since 1933, we had not read any foreign newspapers, we only got what was printed here (in Germany) and what Goebbels wanted us to read. Suddenly, for the first time, not only were we hearing the transmissions but we listened to the BBC. When things were announced, we had to decide, now is this the truth we are hearing or propaganda.

'In Lambassade, where we were stationed at the time of the invasion, I was working at the HQ along with the company commander and the adjutant. They lived in one house and we wireless people lived in another and our teleprinter was in the company HQ and from here we sent the news to Fontainebleau or OB West. Now, our men were picking up the Allied advance on their sets – they were landing here, there and everywhere. On the wall, we had a large map on which we marked the progress of the enemy with tiny flags and coloured thread. On night duty, I was getting the information through and was sticking the flags on the map according to the results we had heard. Next morning, a sergeant came into the office and saw that I had marked St Lo and he said "who marked St Lo? Are you crazy? You'll be court martialled!" They simply didn't want to see the truth. The OKW (Supreme Command in the West) had not yet announced St Lo and so as far as they were concerned, St Lo had not yet fallen. He wanted to teach me my own job. "Don't you understand, these are all enemy broadcasts you are listening to, not our transmissions and you are supposed to act according to our broadcasts, not the enemy's."

'Next night, of course, it was announced that St Lo had indeed fallen. This illustrates what I mean when I say, one simply did not want to see much of what was contained in the transmissions and we, of course, were not allowed to talk about what we heard.

'On the night of the invasion, our unit picked up the three-line poem by the French poet. One of our despatch riders, with a pillion passenger was instantly sent to the OB, the army command to deliver the message. They arrived in the middle of the night, rang the Adjutant's bell, went in and announced that the three lines of the poem had been transmitted and here they were. The adjutant put the piece of paper in an "in-tray" to be dealt with the next morning.

'If they acted on it immediately, well … it was well-known that the second half of the poem was a signal for things to start happening – we had already picked that up in the course of listening to Allied transmissions, though we did not know it was to herald the actual invasion.

'If the bloke hadn't put it aside so carelessly, but had told someone in authority, they might at least have been able to alert the defences on the coast and we would have been more prepared than we were.

'I was on duty that night passing on the decoded and translated transcripts to OB West. For about three days before, there had been dead silence on the airwaves. We had already wondered why this should be as such radio silence was unusual, particularly as the troop movements that we had picked up prior to that had been massive, as well as embarkations. We heard not a thing. That silence was only broken after the first landings and we began to listen in again. After a time, we were able to track down those units whose call signs we recognised from earlier "eavesdropping".

'I was on duty on the night of June 6 and next morning, at about four or five o'clock, the news came through that there had been an invasion. It was still dark when the phone call came with the news and at first we thought it might be diversionary tactics to draw the troops away from Calais (towards Normandy) and then actually land around Calais. That the invasion should occur with such massive numbers was never imagined, nor had we been able to pick up on that from listening in to broadcasts.

'I was not cross that we hadn't been able to discover the extent of the invasion through our work, I simply never thought about it. All I thought about was getting to grips with the new situation. In military life, if something has happened, then it is over. After all, we were young.

'I was very busy during the day. Previously, things had been dead and now it was starting again. We had no sleep the night before and now we had to start tracking movements again. Also, as we did not know what was going to happen, we had to be ready for action, machine guns at the ready in case paratroops landed. We snatched a couple of hours sleep whenever we could. When night fell, we went out with our machine guns almost for the first time outside our precinct, walking the bounds, looking for any paratroopers who might have landed or airborne troops. But there was nothing in the area.

'And how we listened to English music! And what is more, we listened to it in the presence of officers, even though it was strictly forbidden. But you see, we had to monitor the BBC broadcasts and they played music. We assumed that they might interrupt the music to make significant announcements, so we had to listen to the music. In that respect, I think we were a rather informal unit.

'During the night of the invasion, we suffered a couple of air raids – what struck me that the English knew something important was located at Lambassade but nothing serious enough to say we were damaged, most of the stuff fell in the surrounding woods.

'The Army command could only establish what troop movements were carried out on the island (of GB) through the monitoring of the transmissions by units like ours, it was the only way. So we found ourselves playing quite an important part in the conduct of the war. General Unruh on one of his manpower gathering trips, looking for spare fodder for the Russian front, drew a blank when he reached our unit. Our work was considered to be too vital for the teams to be broken up – the Supreme Command needed us.

'When the invasion began, so did the monitoring start up again early in the morning, about 4 or 5 and we picked this up from their broadcasts that they had landed and where they were. We were also able to follow their movements once they had landed and the location finders could pick out exactly where they were on land or water. But by then, it was no longer possible to take counter measures. It was already history by then.

'They couldn't have won the war with our unit anyway. The people in it were much too intelligent, they could think for themselves and through their activities listening to the enemy, they were in possession of news, of information which they would not under normal circumstances have ever heard and the effect of that was to sharpen their senses even further. Knowing what we knew, it made us realise what madness it all was. But we did not oppose because if one had given in to the desire to oppose (the prevalent ruling beliefs) we would have ended up in Russia. So we thought, well better here than frostbite in Russia. The most we could do was discuss it endlessly amongst ourselves but there was never any question of a palace revolution here – we were, after all, the tiniest cog in the mechanism.

'It was like a thriller, following the movements of the various English Regiments. You could locate them on the map and then hear from the transmissions that they had been transferred down there, another … the individual units were very well known to us, as were the divisions and battalions, we knew each and everyone of them and wherever they moved, we were on to them, it was like a puzzle. You pushed around the bits of information and thought, well there must be some purpose to this. Sometimes there were movements that were intended to deceive us. You would notice that a regiment was ordered to a particular place and then suddenly it would appear somewhere else entirely and then you realised what had happened. Then they would change the call sign but from the style of transmission of the individual operator, you would recognise the unit again and so you would monitor it very closely and eventually discover that it was indeed the unit you suspected. And so you got to know the individual radio operators and we referred to them by the nicknames we had given them. This sort of life, well, it seemed to have little to do with war in our sense.'

The work of the RSS was invaluable to the task of breaking the Enigma ciphers in Hut 6 at Bletchley Park. It opened up some new insights into the inner workings of the German *Abwehr*. It has been estimated that over 268,000 messages from the RSS were decrypted at Bletchley.

The value and precedence that the British Y Service brought to the Overlord campaign has almost been lost to the shadow of Bletchley Park and the work of the infamous cryptographers like Alan Turing and Gordon Welchman. The size and scale has been forgotten – indeed the Y Service had 500 sets covering German Enigma traffic alone. Over 50,000 people were involved in SIGINT during World War II, including the Y Service, RSS and GC&CS. Without the incredible work of the Y Service collecting and analysing the German radio traffic, it is hard to know how Bletchley would have evolved against the German ciphers. For D-Day ULTRA was to provide Allied HQ with a complete German order of battle and, critically, knowledge on the locations of the German Armoured divisions. From 6 June 1944 onwards, the Y Service and ULTRA material was to provide a huge amount of timely intelligence, some German signals being intercepted, processed, analysed and reported to deployed commanders within hours. After the war, the Joint Intelligence Committee (JIC) was to report that SIGINT was 'by far and away the most valuable of all intelligence sources.'

Charter for Army SIGINT Forces in Overlord

SHAEF/ISC/20 Intelligence Directive No. 15 27th April 1944

I Signal Intelligence Section G-2

1. The Chief of the Signal Intelligence Section, G-2 Division, SHAEF, is advisor to the Supreme Commander, through AC of S, G-2, on all military Signal Intelligence matters affecting SHAEF and the forces under its command. He is responsible for:

   (a) Coordinating the activities of the Military Signal Intelligence organisations with the forces under command of SHAEF.

   (b) Policy direction of the work of Signal Intelligence Units and personnel in the United Kingdom under War Office and ETOUSA control respectively, engaged on medium and low-grade enemy Army traffic passing in the SHAEF theatre of operations in order to ensure:

       (i) The production of intelligence for SHAEF and the forces under its command.

       (ii) The provision of technical information for, and technical assistance to, the military Signal Intelligence organisations with the forces under command of SHAEF.

   (c) Ensuring that demands on ETOUSA and War Office for the provision of trained military Signal Intelligence Units and personnel to work with the forces under command of SHAEF are coordinated.

II British Forces

2. The operational and technical control of British Signal Intelligence Units allocated to 21 Army Group (except units specified at 3. Below) is exercised by BGS(I) 21 Army Group through his I(S) staff in accordance with War Office Directive 32/Wireless 717 of 26 May 1943.

3. British Signal Intelligence units to carry out on behalf of the United Kingdom British Signal Intelligence organisation may be placed under command of 21 Army Group. Any such units will receive technical direction from the United Kingdom through BGS(I) 21 Army Group.

4. Signal Intelligence Section, G-2 Division, SHAEF, will deal direct with GSI(S) 21 Army Group on any policy questions which may arise affecting the allotment, operation and control of British Signal Intelligence Units.

III US Forces

5. Signal Intelligence and Signal Radio Intelligence organisations of the US Army will be in accordance with existing War Department tables of organisation and equipment.

6. Operational control of US Signal Intelligence and Signal Radio Intelligence units with First US Army Group will be exercised by the Headquarters to which the units are assigned.

7. The Signal Officer, FUSAG, through the SIS Detachment, FUSAG, will exercise technical direction of the Signal Intelligence and Signal Radio Intelligence units within First US Army Group.

8. The Chief Signal Officer, ETOUSA, through his Signal Intelligence Service, will exercise general technical direction of Americas Signal Intelligence activities in the SHAEF Theatre of Operations, in accordance with War Department and SHAEF Directives. This will include:

   (a) Implementation of general policies established by the War Department and SHAEF in connection with US Signal Intelligence activities in the theatre.

   (b) Exercise, through Signal Intelligence channels, of technical direction to military US Signal Intelligence units with the forces under command of SHAEF, in order to ensure the following:

       (i) Uniformity of training and operating procedures

       (ii) Rapid dissemination of technical direction

       (iii) Mutual technical assistance between Ground Force units, between Air Force units, and between Air and Ground units of the US Army

       (iv) Enforcement of security regulations pertaining to US Signal Intelligence operations.

By Command of General Eisenhower

WB Smith – Lt Gen US Army Chief of Staff

Main World War II intercept stations

Organisation of Radio Intelligence Units under OB West

(A) At The Start of the Allied Invasion of France, June 1944

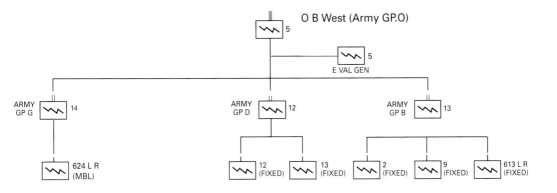

(B) After 1 January 1945

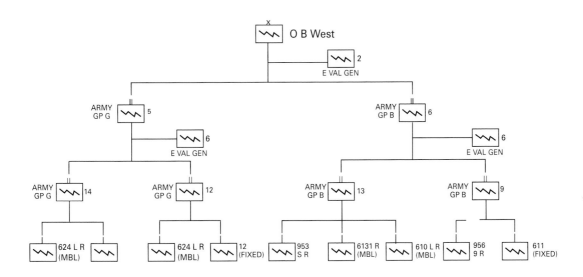

CHAPTER NINE
RHUBARB

'Photographic Reconnaissance prior to D-Day was always very accurate and was throughout of vital importance ...'

Commander Allied Air Forces for D-Day, Air Chief Marshal Sir Trafford Leigh Mallory

～

'This war will be won on the playing fields of Malvern.'

Albert Percival Rowe, Head of the TRE

～

Intelligence is of little use unless it leads to action. For the Allies to mount a successful amphibious operation into northern France they would have to understand the German RADAR network operating along the Atlantic Wall. RADAR had become a significant battlefield of World War II. Both the Germans and British were competing with innovative RADAR design and technology, and groups of scientists on both sides were fighting for a strategic advantage with their military customers during the blitz. Dr Reginald Victor Jones, attached to the Air Staff, was one of our key RADAR scientists of the time. He had studied physics at Balliol College, University of Oxford, specialising in infra-red rays. He was subsequently enrolled as the Scientific Officer to the Royal Aircraft Establishment, Farnborough, which was part of the Air Ministry in 1936, followed by a stint at the Admiralty in 1938–9.

Jones had earned a reputation within the Airforce due to his arguments that the *Luftwaffe* had developed a series of radio navigational beams so their night bombers could navigate in on British city targets. He helped the RAF develop a jamming capability for this system. By 1941 the British Airforce reciprocated by driving the war into the heart of Germany, which consequently forced the Germans to rapidly develop their defensive RADAR capabilities. It was Jones who developed a new branch of Allied intelligence, that of *scientific* Intelligence in the early part of the war. He outlined that this 'is to obtain early warning of the adoption of new weapons and methods by potential or actual enemies'.

For over two and half years, the Radio and RADAR section at the Central Interpretation Unit (CIU) had been researching the German RADAR systems, which

Giant Würzburg
RADAR at
Arromanches (©
ADM202/599)

presented a formidable defensive shield. The Allies determined that one of the key preparations for Overlord was the destruction and denial of the German RADAR systems around the Normandy area – an area stretching for over 450 miles between the French-Belgian border to Cap Fréhel in Brittany. On this area of coastline alone, there were nearly one hundred German RADAR stations, many of which had a number of peripheral installations. Each installation would have to be denied if the security and success of Overlord was to be achieved.

Along the whole stretch of the French coastline the Germans had constructed a sequence of RADAR stations, which all came under the jurisdiction of the *Luftwaffe*. The most common installation was the Würzburg array, which was designed and manufactured by Telefunken and the Zeppelin company. The Würzburg was for air raid warning, fighter guidance and to assist anti-aircraft batteries in reaching their targets more accurately. Würzburg arrays could ascertain the height and map the position of an aircraft. The second most common RADAR was the Freya, designed and made by GEMA. It was used for the detection of aircraft or ships up to a range of 200 km. It could only detect a two-dimensional range and bearing but not, significantly, the height of the aircraft, which was required if the aircraft were to be intercepted.

Normandy was particularly well served with numerous RADAR stations. The coastline between Cherbourg and Le Havre alone had fourteen Würzburg and two Freya arrays, alongside one identification RADAR, five long range coastal and seven mid-range coastal RADARs. Many of these RADAR installations had a defensive anti-aircraft battery positioned near to the site owing to their vulnerability to attack.

The Allied invasion force needed to get Photographic Interpretation (PI) on all these facilities as it was essential that they were bombed to allow aerial supremacy during the invasion. It was a critical pre- Overlord objective and a specific team (G Section) under RAF Squadron Leader Claude Wavell was established at Medmenham to specialise in RADAR and radio/wireless from 1941. Some of the earliest research undertaken by the section was to locate a source of 80 cm RADAR transmissions emanating from the Boulogne/Cap Blanc Nez area. Staff struggled to locate any transmitters initially but it was due to them being too small to be seen on the small-scale photographic images available at that time. As the techniques evolved with PI, it assisted in the discovery of what, nearly a year later, proved to be the Bruneval parabaloid RADAR equipment, which became the object of one of the most famous and successful raids of the war.

The section officially formed in November 1941 under direction from ADI Photography and it was tasked with exclusively working on W/T and RADAR. It was to be responsible for 'the collection of information for intelligence purposes of the signals organisation in enemy and enemy occupied territory and for handling all information dealing with the enemy's RADAR, navigational beam, wireless, point-to-point stations and land line organisation'.

With the new section forming, new procedures and working practices were developed at Medmenham to cope with an anticipated deluge of tasks. A new universal reference numbering system was brought in so information could be sourced, located and produced quickly. A large amount of mapping had to be acquired and a new card index system brought in. The modelling section assisted G Section in building scale models of various installations to assist with military briefings and operational planning. A recording mechanism was established for intelligence that had come in from other sources, for example ground reports, POW interrogations from the Prisoner of War Interrogation Section (PWIS) or the Combined Services Detailed Interrogation Centre (CSDIC), or signals intelligence.

G Section produced 253 reports (referred to affectionately as 'Rhubarb Operations, Appendix XII') on every RADAR, radio or wireless telegraphic device along 450 miles of coastline and reaching inland up to 20 miles. The reports totalled in excess of 80,000 pages on intelligence delivered several weeks before the due date. Wavell's team identified a hundred RADAR installations and in May 1944 the decision was taken to destroy the majority of them. Rockets fired by a Typhoon ground attack plane had successfully destroyed a RADAR installation near Ostende. A major operation, which began on 22 May 1944 to destroy as many RADAR stations as possible, used a similar method to the Ostende experiment, this time involving Typhoon and Spitfire aircraft. All of the stations, bar two, were destroyed. These were in the Pas-de-Calais area and were left alone for strategic reasons in order to assist with the Bodyguard deception plan.

As Wavell's G Section history, written in 1945 dictates: 'On 20th May 1944, a radical alteration of all procedure in the Unit was introduced to deal with the plotting of the very large numbers of sorties that were arriving and were expected. The interpretation personnel of the Unit were organised into teams which were to be called upon in numerical order to plot the sorties arriving, and on the following day, the 21st May, the first plotting teams went into action....

'For at least a fortnight before D-Day RADAR sites were continually attacked from the air with bombs, rockets and cannon and machine gun fire, and the Section was required to issue a Damage Assessment report on the results within twenty-four hours from photographs taken immediately following the attacks. This was done, although considerable difficulty in obtaining immediate prints was experienced, despite the special liaison which had been set up with the photographing reconnaissance units. Nevertheless, in a number of instances the Reports issued by the Section reached their destination before the 1st and 2nd Phase Reports issued by forward unit.'

Types of report	Number of Recipients
Reports on enemy wireless installations	19
Reports on enemy RADAR installations	2
Reports on enemy RADAR installations damaged by air attack	20
RHUBARB Appendices – Enemy RADAR, etc installations	47
Reports on Special Stations and installations	6
Total distribution of Reports	94

RAF Medmenham G Section reporting recipients

As the German development of RADAR systems continued at pace in the early 1940s, so did the appetite for intelligence exploiting this new technology.

A key intelligence requirement, from when it was introduced in the summer of 1940, was to find out what the Freya system looked like, and how it would perform against Allied aircraft and ships. Only so much could be obtained from photo-reconnaissance imagery and from the intercepted and interpreted signals from the RADAR transmissions. Some of the Enigma intercepted traffic suggested Freya and Würzburg RADAR equipment was being sent to Romania for coastal protection purposes by the Germans. CIU photographic interpreter Claude Wavell and Geoffrey Tuttle, the Commanding Officer of the Photographic Reconnaissance Unit (PRU) at RAF Benson led investigations into the Freya sites dotted around the coastline of northern France, and by the middle of 1941 the Allies had fair intelligence on the Freya stations providing a defensive shield along the French coastline.

Much of the intelligence on German Würzburg RADAR systems was gleaned from one of the most successful and famous of all combined operations raids of the war. This took place on the Bruneval RADAR site in northern France on the night of 27 February 1942. It had first been identified through the work of Wavell's team in the autumn of 1941 on the rugged chalk coastline of the Cap d'Antifer, about 20 km north of Le Havre.

G Section's work with the Telecommunications Research Establishment (TRE) generated the idea that a full-scale raid on the facility could provide some intelligence dividends. The idea got bandied around by the Air Staff and Combined Operations Headquarters (COHQ). Significant knowledge of the German defences in the area had to be established before a raid could be mounted and this fell to the French Resistance. The network responsible was led by Gilbert Renault (aka Colonel Rémy) and he had tasked two of his men, Charles Chauvenau and Roger Dumont, with assessing the German army disposition around the RADAR station and nearby villa.

This work helped the creation of a scale model by the team at the CIU in Medmenham to assist the operational planning. The raid was to demand an extremely accurate and realistic three-dimensional mock-up of the area.

Dr Reginald Victor Jones from the Air Ministry's Intelligence Branch was responsible for the training and briefing of the RAF engineer who would be responsible for the dismantling of the RADAR array under the cover of the Paratroopers. Jones was inextricably linked to SIS at this stage but had previously specialised in infra-red detection techniques at the Clarendon Laboratory at the University of Oxford. The intelligence work on the site was aided by the work of one Spitfire PR Mark IV pilot who took one of the most iconic images of World War II. On a visit to the CIU, Squadron Leader Tony Hill learnt of Dr Jones's interest in an object near the village of Bruneval.

On 5 December 1941, Hill took off to fly a sortie over the villa and RADAR array, after a failed first attempt to photograph the Würzburg. He had returned the next day and through some skilled flying at low level, and under fire, he managed to get some excellent low-level oblique photographs of the 'bowl-fire' array which after

Classic Sqn Ldr Tony Hill low-level oblique photograph of the Bruneval Würzburg RADAR installation (© IWM London Photo Archives – ref D12870)

subsequent PI measurements was determined to be a Würzburg array. This was no easy task, the Spitfire oblique camera was mounted below the aircraft, and arranged to point to the left of the fuselage. To capture an image such as Hill achieved he needed to fly low and on a right-tilt of the target.

The raid, codenamed Operation Biting, was the first battle honour of the newly formed Parachute Regiment. Commanded by Major Frost, the 120 strong force from C Company of the 2nd Parachute Battalion were dropped from 12 Whitley aircraft about 1½ miles from the intended Drop Zone (DZ). The teams were divided into three units, the first was under the command of Lieutenant John Ross and Lieutenant Euen Charteris who were responsible for the capture of the beach which would be used to extract the raiding force. The second unit, lead by Frost, was to attack the villa and Würzburg site, and the third team was to be held in reserve under the command of Lieutenant John Timothy.

They assaulted the RADAR station and within ten minutes RAF Flight-Sergeant CWH Cox, the RADAR expert who had accompanied the force, had dismantled the most important components of the array. This included the receiver (and its associated amplifier), the modulator for timing control, transmitter and antenna element. The only thing left behind was the cathode ray display equipment. Cox was an unlikely candidate for the task as he had never been on a ship or a plane before this operation.

Small model of the Bruneval RADAR station in northern France (© IWM London Photo Archives – ref D7821)

One of the myths that emerged after the raid was that if Cox was to fall into German hands during the raid his new-found paratrooper colleagues were to execute him, due to the knowledge of British RADAR developments he had in his head.

The Germans were not to know, but just offshore on one of the RN support vessels for the raid was Don Priest, a RADAR engineer from TRE. He was there to supervise the dismantling of the Würzburg array by Flight-Sergeant Cox, but from a safe distance. He carried with him a RADAR receiver system to monitor the Würzburg transmission frequencies, which would turn out to be a valuable source of intelligence on the array's output, alongside with the physical equipment that was returned.

The paratroopers extracted successfully via a join RN/RM commando force that had landed on the beach at the base of the cliff. Two men were killed and six were missing after the extraction by landing craft but the raiders managed to bring back two German prisoners, one of whom was the Würzburg operator at the site. Dr Jones and his TRE team spent an afternoon quizzing the *Luftwaffe* Würzburg operator after the raid. It was established that the Freya and Würzburg arrays at Bruneval worked in synchrony. The Freya would warn the Würzburg via telephone to switch on and focus on a particular line bearing.

By early March 1942 the components had made their way to the Air Ministry for initial investigations before being moved to TRE at Swanage for more detailed analysis. Intelligence gleaned from something as simple as the visible serial numbers on the components established that the Germans were producing one hundred Würzburg arrays a month. The intelligence also assisted in the development of Fighter Direction

Badly damaged coastwatcher RADAR array, Fermanville, pictured 30 June 1944 by 30 Assault Unit (© ADM 202/599)

Tenders (FDT), naval vessels that were used during Neptune to provide RADAR and communications cover off the Normandy coastline during the early stages of the invasion. Three FDTs were introduced for the Normandy landings and the protection of the beachhead, which provided immediate tactical intelligence for the RAF fighter command aircraft.

The intelligence also enabled Allied scientists to develop the 'Window', an effective RADAR counter measure technique (the Americans called it 'chaff') involving dropping strips of aluminium foil at the requisite altitude to deceive enemy RADAR operators. This technique was to prove invaluable in the hours before the invasion forces hit the shores of Normandy. But most importantly of all, the analysis on the Bruneval equipment allowed TRE to develop an effective jamming capability, which was employed successfully during the Overlord campaign.

TRE were also a vital cog in the push to exploit the Tunny system of the German High Command. They deployed Dr Charles Wynn-Williams, a circuit expert on RADAR, to assist Alan Turing and William Tutte in the development of a new solution for digital circuitry with electronic valves which had the ability to switch a thousand times the speed of a relay switch. The construction of the 'Heath Robinson' machine at Bletchley Park was the brainchild of Tommy Flowers, with the assistance of Wynn-Williams. This machine could run teleprinter tapes at over 1,000 characters a second. It was to lead to the development of Colossus, which would have such a marked effect for Bletchley on the provision of ULTRA intelligence for Overlord.

1943 saw a rapid increase in the routine tasking on G Section. At this stage of

Wassermann tower
RADAR array
at Fermanville,
pictured by 30
June 1944 by 30
Assault Unit (©
ADM 202/599)

the war the Germans were developing new types of RADAR and modifying their existing equipment and installations. The team discovered an experimental facility at Kothen and the large factories at Siemens and Telefunken in Berlin, producing RADAR equipment which had emphasised to Allied intelligence how much the Germans were utilising this technology to aid their defences along the Atlantic Wall.

There was a huge increase in ground information on RADAR and W/T coming to the section during 1943, estimated to be in the region of half of all the intelligence coming into Medmenham at the time. This information was passed to the specialists in the section often for critical comment – the number of comments added to reports per week averaged around forty, but in the five months preceeding April 1944 comments were issued on 901 reports which covered over 1,800 RADAR and W/T installations.

As the defences hardened and the density and scope of the German RADAR network along the French coastline began to take shape during 1944, some changes took place within G Section. On 20 May 1944, the unit overhauled its procedures to deal with the large-scale plotting which became necessary due to the volume of work that was hitting the section. They were pulled off the call-out list, allowing them to focus on the necessary research into the expanding German RADAR network. In the critical month for D-Day, June 1944, the section identified fifty-three new installations. The section was deluged with requests for target material on all the known RADAR sites in northern France in preparation for the Overlord assault.

The work of Dr Reginald Jones in understanding and interpreting German RADAR systems was to rapidly escalate the development by the Allies in effective counter-measures and deception techniques as were employed in the hours before D-Day. Jones had displayed the value of scientific intelligence as a discipline and shaped the future. This science discipline as an arm of intelligence was going to be here to stay and it is now a routine component of all Defence Intelligence structures around the world.

The creation of G Section at Medmenham, under Claude Wavell, was a game-changing moment for the work and the value of the output from Medmenham. The ramifications were vast for the outcome for the safety of the invasion fleet and aircraft in the initial phases of Overlord, but it went much beyond that. The Section had managed to identify the whole of the German RADAR network and navigational beam systems employed throughout Europe. Its scientific approach was exemplary and it had allowed an almost complete understanding of how Germany was employing its RADAR systems against the Allies. Ably abetted by daring raids on key installations and scientific advice from the likes of TRE, the section helped set the groundwork for Eisenhower's plan.

CHAPTER TEN
JELLYFISH

'No single operation of the Second World War was so dependent on Bletchley as the Normandy landings. Indeed without the work which was done here there is no way the landings could have gone ahead let alone succeeded.'

Sir Martin Gilbert, official biographer to Winston Churchill

The scale and complexity of the intelligence collection effort for Overlord is most appropriately displayed by the work undertaken at Bletchley Park. What happened at Bletchley in the early 1940s was a tremendous merger of mathematical brilliance, electrical engineering expertise and unrivalled cryptography. This was not fully admitted until the publication of *The Ultra Secret* by F.W. Winterbotham in 1974, when the story became public knowledge.

One word synonymous with Bletchley is ULTRA, which was the covername for the intelligence product derived from the decryption of enemy ciphers. The campaign in Normandy was won by the breadth and depth of ULTRA's reach. Churchill was obsessed with intelligence work and had a deep fascination with ULTRA decrypts. It was under his direction that Whitehall departments began to incorporate intelligence into wartime operations and strategic thinking.

The Mansion,
Bletchley Park
(© author)

At its roots, the story of breaking codes at Bletchley precedes World War II. During the Spanish Civil War, deployed German forces had started to use the Enigma electro-mechanical rotor cipher machine for the relay of encrypted and decrypted secret messages to and from Germany. Dilly Knox, a brilliant mathematician and cryptologist, was tasked with deciphering the Enigma system during the civil war, and by April 1937 managed to break the machine code, but the addition of a plugboard used by the *Wehrmacht* Enigma operators proved a more difficult nut to crack. In 1939, Knox was joined in his endeavours by Alan Turing, a King's College Cambridge fellow.

A sequence of meetings in early 1939 with the French *Deuxième Bureau* and Polish codebreaking organisation *Bureau Szyfrow*, who had managed to decipher the Enigma machine, gave the British team a leap forward in their work to counter the device. A few months earlier, the Poles had managed to build an electro-mechanical analytic processing machine called the *Bomba kryptologiczna* to successfully decipher the coded traffic. All this work was scuppered in December 1938 when the Germans introduced two additional rotors to their Enigma machines. The Poles needed to catch up again, which led to the three-way meetings with the French and British teams. It was to be a combined effort. The Poles, who respected the history of British code-breaking going back to World War I, would greatly assist in the effort against Enigma. The Polish team at *Bureau Szyfrow* was led by Colonel Stefan Mayer who stated, 'as the danger of war became tangibly near we decided to share our achievements regarding Enigma, even not yet complete, with the French and British sides, in the hope that working in three groups would facilitate and accelerate the final conquest of Enigma'.

The Polish *Bomba* exploited weaknesses in operating procedures by the German Enigma operators. However, during the course of 1939 these began to be tightened up, denying the Polish teams their valuable decryption and subsequent intelligence. A few months after arriving at Bletchley Park, Turing started to design his own decryption machine based around the Polish one. However, conceptually they were very different. Turing did not want to exploit the human operator errors, but wanted go after the 'crib', which is the presence of text which typifies a certain section of an encrypted message.

The original designs for the British electro-mechanical *Bombe* machine were collaboratively put together by Alan Turing from Hut 8 at Bletchley, Gordon Welchman from Hut 6 and Harold 'Doc' Keen, the Chief Engineer for the British Tabulating Machine (BTM) Company in Letchworth, Hertfordshire.

The BTM Company had experience in high-level machinery design and manufacture, producing Hollerith recording equipment and other data processing machines. Doc Keen was the energy behind the company and had over sixty patents to his name. He had joined the company in 1912 aged just eighteen and moved with it to the new Letchworth premises in 1921. The building of the *Bombes* (under the project 6/6502 codenamed Cantab) was to be his most significant project. He had acquired the 'Doc' nickname due to the medical bag he carried with him wherever he went. At the height of its manufacture, over 200 people were working on the assembly lines to produce the heavy *Bombe* machines which weighed over a tonne.

The *Bombes* were made from a bronze metal frame, manufactured at a Government training centre in Pixmore Avenue, Letchworth and were brought across to the BTM site in Icknield Way. Each frame housed thirty rotating drums to mimic the actions of the wheels of ten Enigma machines. The wiring for each *Bombe*, which totalled over 4 miles long, was undertaken by the women workers at the factory. The first *Bombe* was completed within three months and installed in Bletchley's Hut 1 on 18 March 1940 and named *Victory*. Gordon Welchman further modified the initial *Bombe* design to encompass a diagonal board, which led the second *Bombe*, called Agnes, to be installed on 8 August 1940.

Over 210 *Bombes* were built during the war, and to avoid German bombing they were deployed to a number of sites, not solely Bletchley Park. A total of five *Bombe* outstations were established, at Eastcote, Adstock, Wavendon, Stanmore and Gayhurst. They were delivered to the outstations in utmost secrecy, often being delivered by a single driver in a lorry covered with a tarpaulin to avoid suspicion. In the initial months of use, servicemen were employed as *Bombe* operators, but as male service personnel were at a premium, the *Bombes* became operated by WRNS from March 1941. By the end of the war, there were over 2,000 *Bombe* operators, the majority of them from the WRNS.

The senior officers at Bletchley Park had struggled to find the raw recruits necessary for the work at the site, to resource the Hut sections. Colonel John Tiltman, one of the most outstanding cryptologists of his generation, was tasked with establishing a training school for cryptanalysts, to give the raw recruits a basic understanding of the methods being used at Bletchley. Initially set up in Buckingham, the Inter-Services Special Intelligence School, as it became known, soon moved to Ardour House in Bedford, where it quickly became affectionately known as the 'Spy School'. Many of the WRNS deployed to work on the *Bombes* were trained at Ardour House and billeted around the Bedford area.

Word had gone out to suitably cleared personnel in Military Intelligence circles that the race was on to break the Enigma code. The Allies needed to get their hands on actual Enigma machines, especially that of the German navy or *Kriegsmarine* sets, as they had, at this stage, been unbreakable. The first German U-Boat to be seized during World War II, *U110*, was captured on 9 May 1941 off Iceland by the British Third Escort Group operating in the area. The U-boat had been spotted shortly after it had sunk two merchant vessels and accidentally left its periscope up, to be spotted by HMS *Aubretia*, one of the convoy's escorts. U110's Enigma machine was delivered by HMS *Bulldog* to Scapa Flow six days later, and it quickly was transported to the teams at Bletchley Park and was being exploited by the end of the month. This contributed to intelligence leading to the sinking of German naval vessels in both the North and South Atlantic. To preserve the Enigma secrecy, *U110* was scuttled and its crew interned in Iceland until the end of the war. Maps and charts taken from the U-boat allowed Allied intelligence to plot the German minefields, which was to assist the future raids on the French coast between 1942 and 1944.

At a small Metropolitan Police unit collection site at Denmark Hill in early 1940, a stream of unidentified German non-Morse signals was picked up. The unintelligible traffic, which was enciphered teleprinter code, was analysed here with assistance from the GPO interception site in St Albans. What they were picking up was an experimental *Wehrmacht* link using a *Schlüsselzusatz* Lorenz SZ40 cipher machine between Vienna and Athens. The Lorenz machines worked off twelve separate rotor wheels, ten to encode the message and two drive wheels. The intercepted messages were converted to letters and sent to Colonel Tiltman at Bletchley. Tiltman sought the expertise of a young Cambridge graduate, Bill Tutte, to establish how the Lorenz cipher machine might operate. Over the course of the next two months, Tutte dissected the Lorenz traffic and worked out how the machine may work, without even seeing the device.

The *Bombe* production line at the British Tabulating Machine (BTM) Company in Letchworth (© Crown Copyright, by kind permission of Director GCHQ)

The *Bombe*
production line
at the British
Tabulating
Machine (BTM)
Company in
Letchworth (©
Crown Copyright,
by kind
permission of
Director GCHQ)

It must be remembered that ULTRA intelligence did not just encompass decrypted Enigma traffic, but also traffic from the higher grade *Geheimschreiber* and *Schlüsselzusatz* cipher machines. These relied on the Baudot Murray system, the machines punched a series of holes in reeled tape, the sets of five holes in different configurations would ultimately represent a letter from the alphabet. It was the broken-out intelligence from this traffic, known collectively as FISH, which provided Allied Commanders with the key strategic insight into German operational planning in Normandy before and after D-Day. These were not tactical signals being carried from low-level units like the Enigma traffic, these were transmissions from the German High Command and occasionally from Hitler himself.

Tunny was the designation given to traffic emanating from the *Heer* (German Army), Sturgeon to the *Luftwaffe* (German Airforce) traffic and Tharsher for the traffic emanating from a German Army military district, which was unbroken.

Collection on the Tunny traffic began in earnest from early 1942 from a newly created site on the North Downs at Knockholt, staffed by Auxiliary Territorial Service (ATS) operators. Most of the work against the Tunny material during 1942 had to be done by hand and the site at Knockholt was purpose-built to deal with vast increase in teleprinter intercept. As preparations were to begin for Overlord, the site was to

A *Bombe* nearing completion at the British Tabulating Machine (BTM) Company in Letchworth (© Crown Copyright, by kind permission of Director GCHQ)

become strategically very important, acting as the main Y station responsible for collecting German radio teleprinter traffic. The facility at the site of Ivy Farm was located at Knockholt Pound on the North Downs just outside Sevenoaks in Kent. The 160-acre site was the home of Government Communications Wireless Station (GCWS), which was co-located with the Foreign Office Research and Development Establishment (FORDE). FORDE was created to develop the German teleprinter intercept in conjunction with Bletchley. The site was run by Harold Kenworthy, the previous commander of the Metropolitan Police SIGINT facility at Denmark Hill before the start of the war.

The site expanded in July 1942, with the purchase of more land, bringing the total area to 160 acres. The site was to grow in importance with the access the Allies had onto the FISH network, and its staffing grew to a headcount of 815 by May 1945. Knockholt was to produce more intercepted messages than could be decrypted at Bletchley. By May 1945, Knockholt had intercepted 167,727 messages – just over 27,000 were sent onwards to Bletchley, of which less than half were successfully deciphered. Knockholt was a critical enabler for breaking into the most sophisticated of the German strategic cipher systems.

A mathematician called Max Newman wanted to apply some of Alan Turing's principles to build a machine to find the wheel patterns of the Lorenz. Newman was given the support to set up a research team, develop the designs and build with the Telecommunications Research Establishment in Malvern. By May 1943 these collective ideas spawned the creation of the prototype 'Robinson', which could compare teleprinter tapes with the enciphered text with tape where the wheel patterns were known to look for statistical anomalies for the settings of the Lorenz wheels. This was the first major breakthrough against the Tunny traffic, although the Robinson prototype was having teething problems.

Turing drafted in a well-respected telephone engineer from Dollis Hill, called Tommy Flowers, who changed the way the Tunny traffic was to be analysed. Flowers, the son of a bricklayer from East Ham in the east end of London, had always had a talent for mechanics. From his education at a local technical college he had subsequently applied for a job as a trainee telephone engineer. Telephones were at this stage under the control of the Post Office, and Flowers quickly started to excel in his career and moved to the forefront of the research and development in telephone exchanges.

Flowers was keen to use valves and ring circuits instead of relays in the new machine and over the course of the next ten months, Flowers and his research team at GPO Dollis Hill built the prototype machine, which they called Colossus. This 1,500-valved machine could not decrypt the message itself, it could only identify the positions of the rotor wheels. The funding and materials for the Colossus development had all come from the GPO.

Operating at speeds of 5,000 characters per second, it transformed the way the Tunny traffic could be decrypted. It was delivered to Bletchley Park on 18 January 1944, but it was not until Saturday 5 February 1944 that the Colossus got the opportunity to attack its first German message. The Bletchley hierarchy was immediately impressed with the doubling of the Tunny output and ordered more Colossi. By March they had ordered four, by April they wanted twelve. Flowers and his Dollis Hill team were put under significant pressure to deliver the machines as quickly as possible and, in the run-up to June 1944, cracking the strategic messages emanating from the German High Command and from Hitler himself became hugely important to the Allies' intelligence effort.

The much faster Colossus II was installed in Bletchley on 4 May 1944. The intent was to test it on site rather than at Dollis Hill, to save precious time. It was operational by 1 June and it helped augment the first Colossus which had given unbridled access into German preparations in Normandy, and also showed that the deception plans under Operation Fortitude had been absorbed by the German leadership. It has been estimated that the Bletchley research team working with Colossus could break around 90 per cent of all the traffic given to them, including messages from Hitler. From when the ULTRA product from Hut 3 began to be delivered to Eisenhower's HQ in January 1944 until the end of the war, it has been estimated that over 25,000 ULTRA messages reached his HQ and the Western Commands.

The following is an excerpt from an account by Tommy Flowers describing the value of Lorenz decrypts for D-Day:

'On 5 June, Eisenhower was in conference with his staff when a courier arrived from Bletchley Park and handed him a piece of paper to read. Hitler had sent Generalfeldmarschall Rommel battle orders by radio transmission which Bletchley Park had decoded with the aid of the new Colossus. Hitler had told Rommel that the invasion of Normandy was imminent, but that it was a feint to draw troops away from the channel ports, against which the real invasion would be launched later. Rommel was not to move any troops. He was to await the real invasion, which could be expected five days after the Normandy landing. This was what Eisenhower read from the paper. He then knew that he could start the invasion of Normandy assured of five days without determined opposition – enough time to build up his forces even with indifferent weather. But he could not tell his assembled officers what he had just read. He just handed the paper back to the courier and said, "We go tomorrow." And on the morrow, 6 June, they went.'

Tunny Machine at TNOMC Bletchley Park (© author)

General Montgomery's key Intelligence Officer at the time of Overlord, Bill Williams, stated that 'few armies ever went to battle better informed of their enemy. ULTRA played a positive part in the formulation of the plan of invasion in that late reports of changed enemy dispositions in the Cotentin Peninsula enabled us to re-allot the dropping zones of the American airborne troops: one of the most contributive elements in the overall scheme. Intelligence officers at BP were briefed before D-Day and thereafter we made it our business in Normandy to send a daily Intelligence summary from 21st Army Group saying what we thought was happening in front of us and in general attempting in a

Knockholt – Ivy Farm (© Crown Copyright, by kind permission of Director GCHQ)

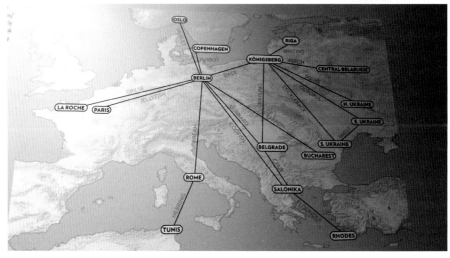

Lorenz SZ40/42 German network with associated BP codenames (© Bletchley Park)

friendly and unofficial fashion to keep the Park aware of what we were trying to do. The whole series of signals was conversational. One felt one was talking to friends and from that feeling of gratitude, which we hoped was reflected in the casually worded terms sent to the Park, emerged at least from the point of view of one consumer, a belief that because of them he was getting a better service. The people at the other end knew what he wanted and there seemed to be no hesitation in the answer.'

One of the final steps in intelligence coordination involving Bletchley Park occurred just a few days before the invasion took place in Normandy. Brigadier Edgar 'Bill' Williams, Montgomery's Chief Intelligence Officer and Hut 3 arranged a visit to discuss

Multichannel printer deluxe at Knockholt (© Crown Copyright, by kind permission of Director GCHQ)

the Overlord plans in detail with the relevant Hut sections and explain his requirements at each stage of the invasion. Selected intelligence officers from the Air, Military and Naval sections scoured over the Normandy maps, laying out the Overlord objectives for each day of the operation. To many, this was the first exposure they had had to the needs of senior Intelligence staff operating in theatre with a commander in charge of a sizeable military formation. Planning at Bletchley for Overlord had to ensure that signals intelligence could be immediately conveyed to the military units engaged in the combat zones in northern France and during the initial stages of the assault phase to the Fighter Direction Tender (FDT) and HQ ships operating directly off the coast of Normandy.

This was successfully achieved by the development of an intelligence broadcast system which was piped from Kingsdown (the Carpenter broadcast) and Cheadle (the Walrus broadcast). The Walrus material included cryptanalytical data which would enable deployed field units to decrypt their own traffic. This would interweave the skills and experience of the Y Service and the deployed field teams and give them the autonomy to decrypt their own traffic, giving them a vital role in their command structures to disseminate timely signals intelligence.

Some of the last minute information from the Tunny system was crucial in establishing the final safe drop zones for the Allied paratroopers. By June 1944, the Tunny system was a dispersed and widespread radio network with regard to the German High Command. There were twenty-six different links known to the British at this stage, each with its own name. The Berlin-Rome link was Bream, Berlin-Copenhagen Turbot and the most valuable link for German strategic intelligence prior to D-Day, the Berlin

The Colossus machine at TNMOC Bletchley Park, original design by Tommy Flowers from the GPO Dollis Hill (© author)

Colossus 6, used to decrypt the vital FISH traffic before D-Day (© Crown Copyright, by kind permission of Director GCHQ)

to Paris link, known as Jellyfish. The FISH traffic contained the most intimate secrets of the German High Command. The deciphering of the traffic between Berlin and Generalfeldmarschall Gerd von Rundstedt, the German Commander-in-Chief West at his headquarters in St Germain near Paris, was probably its biggest success. It yielded information on the German forces' disposition in northern France, most significantly the Panzer divisions, many weeks before Overlord was mounted. Intercept from the Commander of the Panzer divisions, General Heinz Guderian, provided knowledge of the complete order of battle of the divisions. In May 1944, von Rundstedt moved two divisions to where the US Airborne forces were due to land and ULTRA revealed these plans, making Allied planners change the drop zones to be nearer to the US designated beaches of Utah and Omaha.

Much of the work of the Bletchley Park GC&CS staff was focused on breaking the German Enigma code. This original commercial device for encrypting and decrypting classified messages was successfully broken into when the machine had three rotors. When the company developed a four-wheel rotor device and the switch over on 1 February 1942, it put SIGINT in the dark at Bletchley.

Hut 3 was the hub for reporting on the German Air Force and Army Enigma communications, which would have been deciphered by Hut 6. Bletchley at this time was strewn with temporary wooden huts and an array of brick buildings to accommodate the thousands of staff. The site huts and blocks all had distinct roles:

Hut 1 – built in 1939, it originally housed the wireless station but became the main administrative hut for transport, typing and the maintenance crews for the *Bombes* (the first BP installed Bombe 'Victory' was housed in Hut 1)

Hut 2 – recreational hut

Hut 3 – intelligence reporting section (translation/analysis of German Army and Air Force decrypts)

Hut 4 – Naval Intelligence (analysis of Enigma and Hagelin decrypts)

Hut 5 – military intelligence (Italian, Spanish and Portuguese ciphers, German Police codes)

Hut 6 – cryptanalysis of German Army and Air Force Enigma

Hut 7 – cryptanalysis of Japanese intelligence and naval codes

Hut 8 – cryptanalysis of Naval Enigma

Hut 9 – ISOS (Intelligence Section Oliver Strachey)

Hut 10 – Secret Intelligence Service (SIS/MI6) codes, Air and Meteorological sections

Hut 11 – *Bombe* building

Hut 14 – communications centre

Hut 15 – SIXTA

Hut 16 – ISK (Intelligence Service Knox – Abwehr ciphers)

Hut 18 – ISOS (Intelligence Section Oliver Strachey)

The brick block buildings were organised in the following way:

Block A – Naval Intelligence
Block B – Japanese codebreaking and Italian Air/Naval
Block C – stored punch card index
Block D – Enigma work (an extension of Huts 3, 6 and 8)
Block E – Typex and incoming/outgoing radio transmissions
Block F – Newmanry and Testery, Japanese Military Air section
Block G – traffic analysis and deception operations
Block H – Lorenz and COLOSSUS

Of all the Bletchley sections, it was the Naval Section that was typically the best informed, largely due to the enlightened policy of the Naval Intelligence Division (NID). The Naval Section was formally known as NID12 and had direct contact with the Operational Intelligence Centre (OIC) at the Admiralty in London, which acted as the intelligence hub for the Royal Navy.

In May 1944 there was a significant visit to Bletchley Park by a senior officer from the 21st Army Group's Intelligence staff to brief selected staff on the Normandy landings and the outline plan for Overlord. Sections understood how they would contribute to the invasion and help them prepare for the expected huge increase in signals traffic. Most of the work done for Overlord at Bletchley was undertaken in Block D, which had been constructed between 1942 and 1943.

Traffic analysis was a key part of the work at Bletchley in 1944 to understand the

Captured German Teleprinter sets from Fort D'Octeville, seized by 30 Assault Unit, 27 June 1944 (© ADM202/599)

organisational structure of the military units in France. Much of this work was developed by building network diagrams showing the different radio stations on the network. Daily information was compiled into a weekly summary report on the networks in question and they were passed through to the SIXTA fusion room and then onto a group managed by Major Morrison. This group had developed an indexing system and diagrammatically displayed the networks on their hut wall, which became affectionately known as the 'Morrison wall'. This showed the location of the German transmitters, how they communicated between each other and the types of traffic they sent.

The Europe-wide Lorenz SZ40/42 network comprised twenty-six different links by June 1944. The hubs of the network were centralised fixed exchanges. The Western part of the network was linked to the hub in Strausberg outside Berlin and Eastern Europe to a hub in Konigsberg. At the external edges of the network the radio transmissions were coordinated at mobile units, which comprised two separate wagons. One of these carried the Lorenz cipher machines (including teleprinter equipment, cipher attachments for the transmission and receiving of encrypted messages) and the other wagon contained the radio equipment. It was only the radio transmitted Lorenz traffic that could be collected and deciphered. Lorenz could also be used on a landline, which the British could not intercept. During Overlord, many telephone exchanges and teleprinter networks were targeted to force the Germans back on to radio. As a

Receiver Control Bay at Knockholt (© Crown Copyright, by kind permission of Director GCHQ)

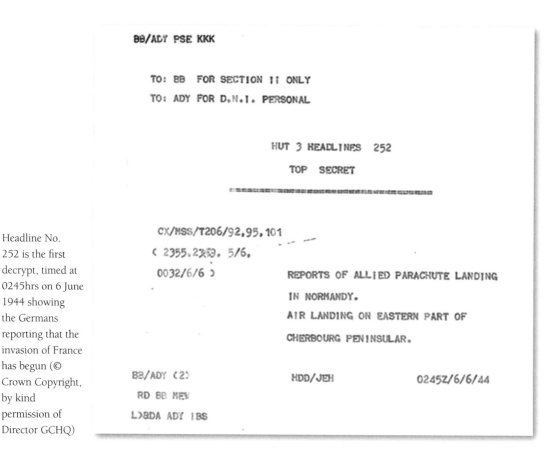

BB/ADY PSE KKK

TO: BB FOR SECTION II ONLY

TO: ADY FOR D.N.I. PERSONAL

HUT 3 HEADLINES 252

TOP SECRET

CX/MSS/T206/92,95,101

(2355,2369, 5/6,

0032/6/6) REPORTS OF ALLIED PARACHUTE LANDING

IN NORMANDY.

AIR LANDING ON EASTERN PART OF

CHERBOURG PENINSULAR.

BB/ADY (2) HDD/JEH 0245Z/6/6/44

RD BB MEV

L)8DA ADY IBS

Headline No. 252 is the first decrypt, timed at 0245hrs on 6 June 1944 showing the Germans reporting that the invasion of France has begun (© Crown Copyright, by kind permission of Director GCHQ)

result, after D-Day there was a significant increase in the amount of Lorenz traffic being intercepted and deciphered at Bletchley.

The value of the decrypted signals could only be measured in the way it was disseminated to the operational commands. This was achieved through Bletchley's partner agency, MI6, under the direction of RAF Group Captain Frederick William Winterbotham. Major military commands would have Special Liaison Units (SLU) attached to them on Special Communications Unit (SCU) links, to provide SIGINT to Bletchley, with secret encryption supplied through Typex. These SLU teams were headed-up by a British Army officer who was referred to as a Special Liaison Officer who had the responsibility for passing the ULTRA intelligence to the cleared senior officers within the military command attached to the SLU. The SLU then acquired its ULTRA intelligence, whether a fixed or mobile unit, through radio communications. Each SLU had a Special Communications Unit or SCU who were responsible for the radio links. The units were all recruited, trained and deployed under the SIS Section VIII based in the Buckinghamshire village of Whaddon. Windy Ridge in the village was the site of the radio transmitter which broadcast ULTRA summaries from Bletchley Park, via a dedicated landline, to the destination SLU in military command HQ dotted all over the world. Much of this deciphered material was sanitised in the text using phrases such as 'reliable information indicates …' to disguise the fact that this intelligence was gained from signals intercept. The traffic was encrypted using the Typex cryptographic equipment supplied by the RAF and augmented by One-Time Pads printed in Oxford. The work at Whaddon and Windy Ridge by SIS Section VIII was a vital cog in the Bletchley machine.

As the naval phase, Operation Neptune, got underway with the invasion forces on 6 June, the SLU/SCU teams were confined to the Command ship which would circulate the intelligence to other headquarters until their forward units got ashore. Once a bridgehead had been secured on the Normandy coast, the SHAEF Advanced and Read commands had a direct encrypted teleprinter line from Hut 3 at Bletchley Park. To keep abreast of this huge increase in volumes, GC&CS adopted a new and more robust prioritisation and summarisation process.

The SLU and SCU teams within SHAEF had responsibility for the security and handling of product emanating from Bletchley. Interestingly, the British and Canadian command merged BP SIGINT with other sources of intelligence, unlike the US Command which kept the Bletchley product independent. As Dan Bussey, an SLU intelligence officer attached to Allied Commanders in June 1944 stated with regard to ULTRA, 'the most important thing ULTRA had to tell us was the complete German order of battle. We would know their divisions by number. We would know where they were … this gave us the kind of information which is absolutely indispensable.'

The development of the British *Bombe* by Turing, Welchman and Keen was the primary means to exploit the German Enigma traffic, which constituted a massive contribution to the war. One certainty is that the ULTRA signals traffic from decrypted German messages played a huge role in the success of Overlord. They provided routine but critical intelligence on the size, locations and strength of the German defensive units in Normandy. One fundamental ULTRA access was the breaking of the Enigma key used by the *Luftwaffe*. This traffic could also expose detailed intelligence into the German Army divisions, as they would have embedded *Luftwaffe* liaison officers.

Without its timely and reliable intelligence informing operational commanders through the SLU teams up to and after D-Day, the Allies may well have seen a very different outcome. The clicking of the Colossus thyratron rings built and conceived by a few great minds transformed the way signals intelligence was collected, interpreted and disseminated. Unknowingly, Tommy Flowers and his team had built the world's first digital computer. The scale of the effort was almost incomprehensible. During the height of the Normandy campaign, Bletchley Park was deciphering over 18,000

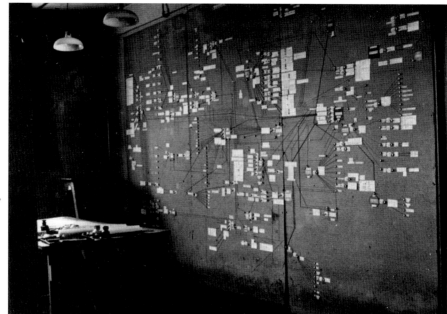

The 'Morrison wall'
showing detail
of German W/T
Morse networks
(© Crown
Copyright, by
kind permission of
Director GCHQ)

The 'Morrison wall'
showing detail
of German W/T
Morse networks
(© Crown
Copyright, by
kind permission of
Director GCHQ)

messages a day. This was an immeasurable achievement, which was one of the greatest intelligence success stories for Overlord. As General Dwight Eisenhower said in a message to staff at Bletchley shortly after the Normandy operation, 'the intelligence which has emanated from you before and during the campaign has been of priceless value to me…. It has saved thousands of British and American lives and, in no small way, contributed to the speed with which the enemy was routed and eventually forced to surrender.'

The success of the Jellyfish decryption and work at Bletchley had a marked effect on the outcome of Overlord. But it resonated after the landings in Normandy. Around 60 per cent of the German cipher tables could be identified as being previously used in other theatres from the work that had been done before D-Day. This allowed the field SIGINT teams that were to deploy with the various Army Groups going into northern France after D-Day an ability to function from the start, in a very different way from that which had been experienced in previous offensives like Operation Torch.

The work at Bletchley in the run-up to D-Day was critical to exploit the strategic planning of the German hierarchy. In a question of scale, in the anticipation of the Allied invasion of Europe in June 1944, the number of staff at Bletchley Park swelled to over 7,000. It has been speculated that the work that was done on the German Enigma messages during the war may have shortened the war by a few years. It may well have shortened the war but Bletchley only read about 15 per cent of the total Enigma messages. This was certainly enough to make ULTRA an instrument of advantage for the Allies, particularly for the Allied planners for D-Day.

Organisation of sections and staff in Hut 6 at GC&CS Bletchley Park at its peak in 1944 (from History of SIGINT in World War II, p. 830, diagram 1)

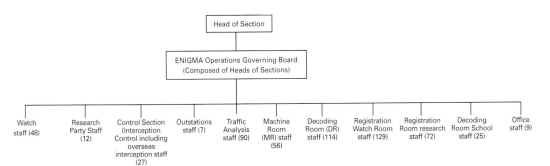

Hut 6 – Staff Deployment 1944 (peak)

The German FISH Army Radio network
(November 1942–July 1944) (reproduced from *British Intelligence in the Second World War: Its influence on Strategy & Operations*, Volume III Part I by F.H. Hinsley – Appendix 2 Geheimschreiber (FISH), p. 482)

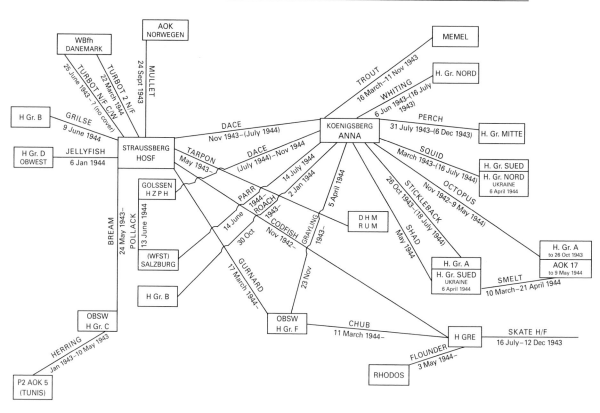

CHAPTER ELEVEN
MAGIC

'Our main basis of information regarding Hitler's intentions in Europe was obtained from Baron Oshima's messages from Berlin.'

General George C. Marshal, letter dated September 1944

❦

In the early 1930s, as the British began to understand the Enigma machine, an initiative to create a British version was commenced by Wing Commander Alan Lywood, and by 1934 the first prototype was produced in conjunction with Creed & Co. manufacturers. This was so similar to Enigma it was originally dubbed the RAF Enigma with Type X attachments. The first production variant of the Typex machine, as it became known as, was delivered to the RAF in 1937 and used throughout World War II. As the machine could work like Enigma, the staff at Bletchley used the Typex machines to discover the settings on Enigma traffic. It was suspected the Germans

3rd Officer Eillen Wood operating a Typex Mark II crytograph machine, which encoded and decoded messages (© IWM London Photographic Archives – reference A23510)

captured at least two Typex machines during the war, including one seized at Dunkirk, but they could never break the Typex cipher.

The exploitation of the Enigma and Lorenz cipher machines was a hugely significant step for the Allied war effort, but it did not always go the way of the codebreakers. Throughout the war, Germany had developed its ability to encipher communications traffic. The skill, dedication and expertise of Bletchley Park and associated establishments managed to break into some of the most complex cipher material ever known. But towards the end of the war, Germany developed its last World War II cipher machine, the SG-41, and brought over 500 of them into service from 1944. This machine operated on a pinwheel rather than the rotor system of the Enigma and Lorenz machines. The SG-41 was intended to replace the Enigma and did manage to defeat the Bletchley codebreaking teams.

It was Admiral Wilhelm Canaris, the Head of the *Abwehr*, who had suspected the Enigma cipher had been broken by the Allies. He had commissioned the development of the SG-41 but it was never a popular cipher machine, as it was much more complicated to set up and operate in comparison to the Enigma and its mechanical reliability was questionable.

The SG-41 cipher machine (© Crown Copyright, by kind permission of Director GCHQ)

One of the greatest intelligence insights into the German military strategy in Normandy came from a quite unlikely source: Japanese Diplomats. The Japanese were using numerous codes to encrypt their messages during the war, the highest security code being referred to by Allied intelligence as the 'Purple' cipher, due to the colour of the folders that the decrypted intelligence was distributed in. They started using this new harder-to-crack cipher on 20 February 1939. It was an upgrade to the previous cipher system, called 'Red', which had been broken since 1936. This purple machine was much more complex that the red cipher machines previously used by the Japanese.

Similar in design to the German Enigma, the Japanese had developed what they called the *97-shiki O-bun In-ji-ki* or the Alphabetical Typewriter 97. The number 97 represented the Japanese calendar year of 2597, or in Western parlance 1937. They more simplistically referred to it as the machine, an electro-mechanical rotor cipher machine, which rotated by stepping switches rather than the keys that Enigma had. It had a similar four-rotor configuration to the Enigma. The exploitation of the cipher was aided when the Japanese ran both the red and purple cipher machines in tandem on the same diplomatic circuit for a few months. The first few words of each message would become a cryptologic clue or 'crib'.

One of the main problems for the US agencies was that they had struggled to gain access to an actual device. A US Signals Intelligence Service (SIS) team based in the Munitions Building in Washington, led by the legendary cryptologist William Friedman, built a functional replica, which helped them break the cipher codes in August 1940. Friedman had been the Chief Cryptanalyst of the US War Department since the 1930s and was charged with pioneering much of the US Army codebreaking work. The Munitions Building had a close neighbour in the Navy Building on the Mall. It housed the US Navy's radio intelligence department, which had been developing radio fingerprinting, Direction-Funding (D/F), traffic analysis and cryptanalysis since the 1930s. The 700-strong unit referred to itself as OP-20-G, an acronym describing its home as the Office of the Chief of Naval Operations, 20 for the 20th Division of the Office of Naval Communications, and the G reflected the Communications Security Section. It was to work closely with Friedman's team on the exploitation of the Japanese ciphers.

The man responsible for building the replica equipment was Leo Rosen, an Army officer who had been educated at the Massachusetts Institute of Technology (MIT) who, taking parts from an electrical supply company, built the 'six buster'. A lot of the main work against the device was undertaken by other members of Friedman's team – Frank Rowlett, Albert Small, Samuel Snyder and Genevieve Grotjan. The six buster became more formerly known as the 'Purple Analog'.

Ironically, the cryptology teams in Washington were given many of the answers to decoding the cipher by the Japanese! They were aided in their efforts against the Purple cipher through a commercial treaty that was being negotiated at the time between the Japanese government and the US State Department. During these negotiations the Japanese were transmitting long, detailed messages back to Tokyo using the cipher and many of these contained long sequences of English text. On receipt of the treaty documents, it allowed the Friedman team to exploit substantial sections of the enciphered message with little effort. It took over eighteen months to break the Purple cipher. The intelligence from this unusual access was referred to as 'Magic', so named as Friedman liked to refer to his fellow cryptanalysts as magicians.

This was an unprecedented engineering and mathematical achievement, which mirrored some of the accomplishments at Bletchley Park. Friedman himself went on to have a significant role in the development of post-war cryptology. Both Arlington Hall and Bletchley Park were instrumental in decrypting the Purple traffic. Working off the back of a US Army agreement in August 1940, the approved exchange of cryptologic information began with the Government Code & Cipher School (GC&CS) at Bletchley Park. A few weeks later the US Army and Navy signed an agreement on the joint exploitation of the Japanese Purple cipher machine, and one of the Purple Analog machines made its way across the Atlantic. By early 1941, the dissemination of Magic intelligence was so highly restricted that it was limited to just ten people in the USA: the President; the Chiefs of the Intelligence Agencies; Chiefs of Staff; the Secretaries of War, Navy and State; the Chief of Naval Operations; and the Chiefs of the War Plans divisions for the services.

The importance of signals intelligence to the US military and intelligence community evolved over the course of World War II, and by June 1942 the US Army managed to acquire Arlington Hall station for the development of the work of the SIS. This was shortly to follow in October 1942, when the US Army acquired Vint Hill Farms, which was to be instrumental in breaking the Purple cipher traffic.

Lieutenant General Hiroshi Oshima was a Japanese diplomat and Imperial Army General assigned to Berlin as the Japanese Ambassador, who became a close confidante of Hitler, even during the rise of the Nazi Party during the 1930s. He was described as 'a typically courteous, polite Japanese officer of undoubted intelligence and considerable personality of a gregarious nature and enjoys society; discreet at all times'.

He had previously been posted to Germany as the Military Attaché in 1934 and knew the country and its circle of power well. During his time in Germany he was quickly promoted from the rank of Colonel to Lieutenant General. The British Military Attaché to Berlin, in a report to MI3 in October 1938 noted that 'unlike many of his countrymen

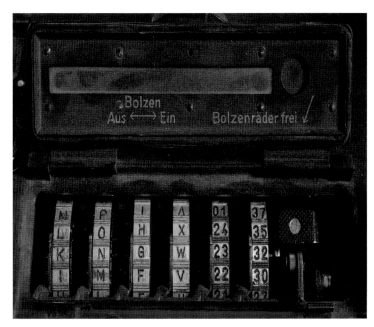

The SG-41 cipher machine (© Crown Copyright, by kind permission of Director GCHQ)

The SG-41 cipher machine (© Crown Copyright, by kind permission of Director GCHQ)

General Oshima talking to General Muff of the German infantry at a ceremonial reception on 15 June 1941 in the foyer of the Opera House in Hanover (ref TNA WO208/4703)

he is a gregarious creature and enjoys society. This is probably mainly due to the fact that he drinks like a fish. He is very rarely sober in the evening and the more he drinks the more he talks. On the other hand his discretion seems to increase under the influence of alcohol, and I have often seen him surrounded by a circle of his colleagues, all hoping that he will produce some pearl of information, and all invariably disappointed at getting absolutely no return for their outlay on Kirsch, which is his favourite tipple.'

He was a regular user of the Purple cipher machine and routinely transmitted detailed reports back to his superiors in Tokyo. In 1944 alone he sent over 600 detailed reports back to Japan. Many of these sensitive diplomatic cables were read by Allied intelligence long before they were read in Tokyo. Lieutenant General George Marshal referred to Oshima as 'our main basis of information regarding Hitler's intentions in Europe'.

On the morning of 10 November 1943, Oshima sent an enciphered message to the Minister of Foreign Affairs in Tokyo, which was to have reverberations across both sides of the Atlantic with the Overlord planners. Signals interception teams with the 2nd Signal Service Battalion at Vint Hill Farms collected fragments of the message and over the course of the next few days it was combined with other messages collected at Vint Hill and Bletchley to reveal one of the greatest intelligence coups of the war. Between 24 October and 3 November 1943, Oshima had been on a tour of the Normandy defences with a Japanese delegation including secretaries Uchida and Ushiba and accompanied by Lieutenant General Nishi. They travelled from Berlin, via Paris, arriving on the morning of 26 October 1943 in Brest on the western coast of France. They inspected the coastal defences around Lorient on 27 October, staying in La Baule-Escoublac that night. On 28 October they went on to inspect the fortifications around St Nazaire before moving to Nantes for the night and onwards to Paris for 29 October. In Paris they were hosted by Generalfeldmarschall von Rundstedt for an informal luncheon and had detailed discussions afterwards with Rundstedt's Chief of Staff who talked through the military defences with them in the region.

Oshima was able to get a significant understanding of the disposition and command of the German forces in the region: 'Field Marshal Rundstedt in Paris has a double role to fill. As Commander-in-Chief, Army Group D (Heeresgruppe D) he controls the Netherlands Defence Army (Air Chief Marshal Christiansen), the Fifteenth Army (General Salmuth), the Seventh Army (General Dollman), the First Army (General Blaskowitz) and the Nineteenth Army (General Sodenstern). At the same time, as Supreme Commander of the Armies in the West (Militaeroberbefehshaber West) … the forces which the chiefs of the Military Administration in Belgium and France (respectively General Falkenhausen and General Stulpnagel) have under their charge, the Third Air Fleet (Marshal Sperrle) and the Naval Group West (Marinegruppe West), (Admiral Kuranke).' He would also get a good feeling about the morale of the German troops manning the Atlantic Wall: 'what I most rejoiced at during my inspection was the excellence of the morale of the fighting men of the German Army and the strictness of their military discipline … this spirit prevails down to the very last individual soldier'.

He outlined that the German Army maintained a force of around 1.4 million men under the command of the *Oberbefehlshaber West*, which included Naval and Air Force personnel. Oshima detailed the German strategy behind the strengthening of the key French coastal ports. 'In areas centred on the principal harbours and Naval bases (these, in the area which I inspected, were Brest, Lorient, St Nazaire, Rochelle and Bordeaux) works have been specially strengthened and fortified zones have been established with the necessary equipment to meet attack by land, sea and air. Each of these zones has a *Kommandeur der Verteidigungszone* (the equivalent of a fortress commander) who exercises unified control over the land, sea and air forces in his area.'

Oshima was to meet Joachim von Ribbentrop, the German Foreign Minister, on a number of occasions which allowed him to better understand the German objective in France, 'in regard to a second front, Germany considered this a possibility and although the point at which it would be opened was uncertain, the most likely area seemed to be Belgium and the narrow waters between England and France'. Oshima was to give some insight into the thoughts the Germans had on the invasion of Europe and hinted that they were concerned about Normandy, 'the difficult landing on the Anglo-French narrow waters would not be attempted at the outset, but by operating in the Normandy Peninsula or the Brittany Peninsula, the promise to the USSR would be fulfilled'.

Oshima gave away to Allied intelligence what the command responsibility was within the Normandy units: 'An Army Group Commander, in addition to commanding his own Army Group, exercises control over the Naval forces in respect of operations at sea and air forces, the forces of the Military Administration and the *Organisation*

Todt his defence zone, not only in the actual conduct of operations but in the various arrangements for defence. Unit commanders below the rank of Divisional Commander have power of command only in operational matters which concern their units.

> 'Fortress commanders have command of all three arms of the fighting forces within their respective fortified zones. Although they are independently responsible for the defence of these zones they are in each case under the command of the divisional commander for the area concerned. The divisional commander, on his part, has at his disposal not only the fortress garrison but all the other defence troops and reserves, and he is the officer actually appointed to the charge of defending the defence zone assigned to him.'

Oshima transmitted a lengthy sixteen-page report back to Tokyo with the details of the fortifications, the German troop dispositions and insights into the German defensive strategy on this section of the Atlantic Wall. Oshima postulated that General Friedrich Dollman's Seventh Army in Normandy only consisted of eight under-strength divisions. 'The German fortifications on the French coast are all very close to the beach, and it is clear that Germany plans to smash enemy landing positions as far as possible at the water's edge. On the other hand, however, the forts centring round Naval bases, including even the small Resistance nests (*Widerstandesnest*), are protected on the landward side, while even the smallest fortifications have been made sufficiently independent to enable them to fight alone for a considerable period. The provision in the centre of a large mobile reserve force is the same from the Army Group (*Herresgruppe*) down to the detachment charged with the permanent defence of the coastal area, so that even were the enemy to effect a partial landing, it would be proposed to smash them by flank fire from the Resistance nest close at hand and also by a sortie by the movable force. This must be called an original idea on Germany's part for defence in the West.

> 'The whole coast which Germany desires to defend is of course extremely extensive, and in present circumstances in particular, when the air force has to acknowledge inferiority, if the enemy were to assemble powerful air forces and carry out landing operations regardless of sacrifices, it is natural to expect that it would not necessarily be possible to obstruct their landing over the whole line.'

The level of detail in this report was staggering. Oshima would elaborate on each German division's strength, organisation and location. He even reported detail on the tank ditches along the defences, which were 'built in a triangular cross section with a span across the top of 5 metres and a depth of 3.5 metres'. Much of the intelligence was acted on prior to the invasion – such as the layout of gun turrets along the shoreline, and how the Germans might defend against an amphibious landing 'were (the Allies) successful in a partial landing … lateral shell fire from the neighbouring posts and the appearance of mobile forces would annihilate them'. He had even made observations of the small arms and artillery, 'in the areas I inspected it is probable that coastal heavy guns between 34 centimetres and 17 centimetres in calibre are used, but 15 and 12 centimetre are also used. There are 12, 10.5 and 8 centimetre anti-aircraft guns and I noticed that there were in service a large number of anti-tank guns of various calibres, and among the small arms, a large number of captured weapons (French, Belgian, Czech and Russian).'

The workers used in the construction by the Organisation Todt (OT) were often non-Germans, and Oshima eluded to this, as well as the fact that the Germans were aware that secret information about the building and design of the Atlantic Wall fortifications was getting out to the Allies, 'apart from a small number of Germans, the workers used by OT have been mostly foreign, chiefly French, secret information about the fortifications leaks out to the enemy, as even the Germans realise'.

The knitting together of the messages was painstaking – they were being transmitted in sections, many of which were deliberately placed out of sequence. It was not until 9 December 1943 that the completed deciphered message could be disseminated. Sam Snyder, one of the decoding unit working to exploit this traffic stated, 'American leaders often had the opportunity to read the intercepts only two hours after they were sent.' The transmission of the messages between Berlin and Tokyo were often delayed due to technical problems: 'We gave them good clean copies with no more than a word or two missing sometimes.'

The Oshima messages were augmented by two messages sent from the Berlin Embassy, which Bletchley Park had collected and deciphered, from Admiral Itō Seiichi, the Japanese Military Attaché. He had undertaken his own tour of the Normandy defensive positions at the end of 1943, culminating in a lengthy thirty-two-page summary report back to Tokyo. The report was deciphered in Hut F over a six-month period by the Japanese Military section at Bletchley Park, and issued shortly before D-Day. Seiichi was using a Coral machine cipher, which had been broken through a joint UK/US initiative in which Hugh Alexander played a leading role. Alexander was head of Hut 8 at Bletchley Park and had been instrumental in

Colonel Itō Seiichi

breaking the German Naval Enigma code. The Coral cipher itself had been exploited through the work pioneered by Colonel John Tiltman.

The Oshima intercepts and those of the Japanese Military Attaché in Berlin were particularly enlightening for the D-Day preparations, as they gave the Allies confidence that the 'Bodyguard' deception plans which had been put in place had been taken as fact by the Germans and their preparations for an Allied invasion were focused in the wrong part of France. A key section of the message read: 'the Germans plan to smash any attempt to land as close to the edge of the water as possible.... The Straits area (Calais, or Strait of Dover) is given first place in the German Army's fortification scheme and troop dispositions, and Normandy and the Brittany peninsula come next in importance.' This was not just from the German officers in the region, but direct from the Führer himself. They had unwittingly provided significant intelligence on German defensive dispositions and strategies in Normandy.

The Allies were not the only players in the cryptanalysis game. It was a game of cat and mouse during the war. German cryptanalysis teams were able to acquire key strategic intelligence on the British 8th Army as they had broken the diplomatic codes being used by the American Military Attaché based in Cairo. He was routinely informing Washington of British military plans and dispositions.

Oshima was to return to inspect the Normandy defences in April 1944, under the invitation of Generalfeldmarschall von Rundstedt. During this tour von Rundstedt was to convey to Oshima that the Allies were building large concrete structures on the south coast of England and German intelligence had assessed them to be anti-aircraft gun platforms. At this time no thought had been given to the fact that they may be portable harbours, the cornerstone of what Allied commanders would need to rely on to sustain a Normandy bridgehead after the initial assault.

Oshima's visit to the Normandy defences during late 1943 was not the only intelligence dividend for the Allies planning for Overlord. Captured documents are a critical source of intelligence in any theatre of war, and on both sides. Shortly after D-Day the Germans found a briefcase on a dead American officer on a boat washed ashore. It contained detailed plans and operational orders for the two major American Vth and VIIth Corps commands. But the Germans could not act on the information with the lack of air superiority and wide battlefront it was trying to sustain.

The Combined Intelligence Section (CIS) was brought under the Chief of Staff of the Supreme Allied Commander (COSSAC) control from the spring of 1943 and intelligence from seized documentation would work its way back to this section. They were to 'collect from the three Services and other Government Departments and Agencies the type of information required for the planning of the invasion and prepare the intelligence data in a form suitable for operational planning'. The CIS was transformed from September 1943 into the Theatre Intelligence Section (TIS) and was transferred to SHAEF control from January 1944.

Captured Italian documents during 1943 described a similar visit to Oshima's. An Italian mission inspected the German coastal defences of the French coast in March 1943 and the resulting captured report was considered 'reliable and accurate'.

The Italian delegation included Captain di Vascello Santi Bondi of the Admiralty, Lieutenant Colonel Modesto Pascio of the Italian Engineers (General Staff), Lieutenant Colonel Gioele Feresin from the Berlin Embassy and Lieutenant Luigi de Manincor from the Italian Naval School at Gaeta. They were accompanied throughout the tour by senior German officers from the relevant areas and Lieutenant Commander von Crosith of the German Admiralty attached to Gruppe West. The visit toured the ports of Ostend, Zeebrugge, Calais and Gravelines, and numerous artillery batteries and according to the document the badly organised visit 'had laid greater stress on the tourist value rather than on the military side'.

This part of the French coastline had been heavily fortified since the failed Dieppe raid, and had been a model for how the German High Command wanted to build 'Festung Europa' or Fortress Europe. The transmitted report was to read, 'it can certainly be stated that any attempt to land from the sea would not only cost the enemy incalculable losses but would also have extremely limited chances of success as there is not only one single metre of coastline suitable for landing which is not covered by mighty cement fortifications, sited in depth according to the terrain, with protected flanks … bristling with arms of all types and sizes, capable of putting up a defence against attacks from all sides, fully completed by offensive and defensive obstacles of all kinds; and capable of resisting up to 15 days without help from outside.'

Information like this for the Overlord planners would have made unpalatable reading. But they knew Normandy was the soft underbelly of the French coastal defences. The nature of the report eluded to some of the defensive systems that might well be integrated into the Normandy defences:

(a) The siting of weapons (medium, light guns and equipment) must be as far forward towards the sea as possible, so that the greatest density of frontal and enfilading fire can be brought to bear at the moment which is most critical for the attackers, ie. at the instant of landing.

(b) The major danger to a defensive plan lies in air attacks, consequently men and equipment must be protected as much as possible from such an attack, hence the mighty works which are proof against even the very heaviest bombs.

(c) Defensive weapons must cover an area of 360°. If it is not possible to protect an equipment on account of its particular characteristics, the personnel must be able to take cover from sea or air bombardment in critical moments until they are called upon to face the landing itself.

(d) The enemy should not be able to get through the coastal defences; nevertheless having accepted that some infiltration might take place, the various fortifications, even if isolated, should be in a position to resist until the arrival of the mobile reserves quartered 30/50 kilometres in the rear.

The report goes on to highlight the command structures in the German military dispositions on the coast and how authority is transferred between commands during an invasion. During such an invasion the command of the defences would pass to the Supreme-Commander-in-Chief of the three Services. Where command would become difficult to manage would be due to the Naval Commander-in-Chief having the authority for deploying surface or underwater naval weapons or defending the vessels coming out of a defended port: '... this transfer of authority from the Navy to the Army in the delicate phase of the initial stages of an invasion might cause difficulties'. It was noted by the Italian delegation how well the three independent services worked together on the defences: 'collaboration between the 3 services is perfect and that the respective Commanders-in-Chief are continually in contact with one another ...'

One intelligence requirement for Allied planners was to understand how the Germans would employ their artillery in their coastal batteries. It would be necessary to know what deficiencies, if any, there were in the artillery at the batteries and how they would be used in the event of an Allied invasion. The Italian delegation report kindly laid out how the Germans proposed to do exactly that.

'Heavy batteries are only sited near naval bases or to cover the essential shipping routes; medium and light guns are sited along stretches of shore of lesser importance or are concentrated near the ports ... heavy coastal artillery is always flanked by two, or whenever possible, more batteries of dual purpose medium or light guns, which are used for AA defence, or against landings or attacks from the rear and also to fire starshell. These batteries are so sited as to be able to shoot down to a minimum range of 400 metres ... by day the destructive fire of the Batteries is distributed generally over the various targets; concentrated fire is not ordered to the coastal Batteries except by night and then only under conditions when Radar cannot select individual targets.

'The possibility of engaging ships by spotting their gun-flashes has not been considered ... no special arrangements are provided for spotting and controlling fire when the Batteries are firing on the same target; for normal gunnery spotting, spotters are sited away from the batteries and are equipped with rangefinders.'

The report even covers how the batteries would mark their targets and how they could communicate with each other along the chain of defensive positions, '... pre-determined data for the various well-defined targets which are marked on 1/25,000 maps held by each Battery ... they are connected by telephone and teleprinter with the High Commands of the Navy and Army, by telephone to the commands of the dependent Battery groups, ports and to the central RADAR and area warning system'.

The Germans were adept at camouflage for these key strategic positions: 'great care is given to the camouflage of weapons and fortifications (even the works which have been constructed so that they are proof against the heaviest bombs are camouflaged in detail ... normally the layout of the camouflage is such that it rotates with the equipment, differs with each weapon and is so constructed that it will not be damaged when the equipment fires. The four turrets of the Grosser Kurfurst for example are camouflaged to simulate farm houses or trees with quantities of leaves or are covered with metallic nets thickly entwined with imitation shrubs in conformity with the surrounding vegetation. Great use is made of camouflage nets (especially metallic ones even for concealing the communication trenches between the guns and the pillboxes containing close-range land and AA weapons. There has been great development in the construction of dummy gun positions for all sizes of guns.' This emphasises why the Allies would mount sustained coastal and beach reconnaissance missions by highly trained commando units between 1942–4 and why they would be so vital to the intelligence collection effort for Normandy. Aerial reconnaissance would not provide all the answers.

The report details the measures that have been taken by the German military to defend against potential Commando raids and insertions against the batteries on this part of the coast. 'There are at present no special weapons or preparations (infra-red ray network, nets of special types, depth charges, equipment for detaching limpet mines etc). The defences against such attacks rests solely on a high state of watchfulness; on the surface, apart from the personnel manning the weapons on the moles, there are also armed patrol vessels equipped with hydrophones: underwater there are nets carrying listening devices. No special obstructions were seen.' It was the German Army that provided personnel for the defensive batteries against any potential land attack. Sentries were posted in large numbers, especially at night – often a distance of only 20 m apart.

The batteries were heavily defended for any potential land insertion, 'according to the importance of the batteries and their vulnerability to land attack, so they are given a varying number of small reinforced concrete pillboxes equipped with flame-throwers, automatic weapons (the Grosser Kurfurst Battery as 14) and anti-tank guns (up to 75mm)'. Many of the batteries were vast in scale employing huge quantities of both equipment and personnel. The Lindemann battery employed over 1,000 workmen from the *Organisation Todt*, many of whom would have been prisoners of war.

TIS reports were often annotated with a commentary at the end to assess the intelligence and what was contained in the actual report. A key point TIS raised was that 'the German defensive positions on the coast are a line of strongpoints covering the beaches and exits from the beaches. The strongpoints are organised for all-round defence but are NOT sited in depth and are NOT always mutually supporting.'

What was clear from the Italian visit was that on this stretch of French coastline and undoubtedly also on the Normandy coastline there was no real strength in depth. To the rear of these fortifications were reserves, divisional and GHQ batteries, and local defences set up on bridges, road junctions and within villages. None of these were devised to be mutually supporting. They were regarded as a coastal crust rather than a defensive line and something that Allied planners could seek to exploit. If they could punch a hole and gain a foothold on the beachhead, they were in with a chance of opening up the fabled second front. From one captured document and the intercept of a Japanese diplomat, Allied intelligence had potentially found the weak spot in Hitler's Atlantic Wall.

CHAPTER TWELVE
LONDON CALLING

Signals intelligence was of enormous significance to the intelligence insights that it provided for planning for Overlord. But there was another sizeable but less publicised source of intelligence from the airwaves that was instrumental for the outcome for D-Day – the BBC. As a public broadcaster it was constrained by policy, but Britain was at war and the intelligence community were to exploit the medium to its fullest extent.

The tall, grey-haired and rather suave-looking Commander Rodney Slessor took over the Admiralty Photographic Library (NID11) in the basement of the Bodleian Library in Oxford. The fledgling library began in 1940 when Frederick Wells, effectively the second-in-command of the ISTD, first started collecting topographical photographs. It was to work closely with the ISTD at Manchester College and the developing 'Contact Register' which was being compiled in London and Oxford.

Lord Louis Mountbatten, as the Chief of Combined Operation had stated to the head of the ISTD, Colonel Sam Bassett RM, that he wanted as much information as possible about the small beaches of Europe for the commando raids he was starting to plan. The idea was hatched between Bassett, Wells and Slessor, and approved by the

91 ARROMANCHES. — La grande cale par temps calme

Pre-war postcard of Arromanches from the BBC appeal in 1942 (@ Portsmouth History Centre)

58 COURSEULLES

Un aspect de la Plage

Pre-war postcard of the beach at Courseulles (which was to be Juno Beach during D-Day) from the BBC appeal in 1942 (@ Portsmouth History Centre)

Director of Naval Intelligence, Admiral Godfrey, to use the BBC for public appeals. On questioning the BBC managers about the use of its radio airtime for these speculative broadcasts, Bassett tried to ascertain what the response might be, 'it depends on what day the broadcast's made and at what time … on our last appeal of this kind – an appeal to people to send foreign phone directories and guide books to the Ministry of Economic Warfare – there were about ten thousand replies!'

Bassett was to task Rodney Slessor with creating the now famous BBC broadcast – a radio request for the British public to send in all their holiday photographs. The broadcast got scheduled on a Sunday night, just after the nine o'clock news. The BBC had arranged for a commercial firm to deal with the queries. Bassett received a frantic phone call first thing on the Monday morning from the BBC stating Broadcasting House had been inundated in the morning post with nearly 30,000 letters.

The unit became overwhelmed with the weight of the response. It has been estimated that over ten million individual photographs came from 60,000 replies. These were stored and reviewed on the ground floor of the New Bodleian Library and it was a painstaking process, involving nearly sixty different processes. It would require significant numbers of staff to man the tables of the Bodleian Library to sift through the photographs. Bill Donovan, the head of the Office of Strategic Services (OSS), saw the value in what the ISTD had achieved through the BBC and promised fifty US Servicewomen to be flown in from Washington to assist with the task.

These pictures were used to build up the intelligence picture of key countries and regions of the world where operational planners would find the insight of value. It

TRANSCRIBED FROM A TELEDIPHONE RECORDING

THURSDAY 25th MAY 1944 – BBC Radio Broadcast by W.R. Slessor

'*Copies of photographs taken by civilians in peace-time have proved of great value in preparing operational plans during war. The Admiralty Photographic Library, which is the main supply centre of ground photographs for the British Forces, is now in urgent need of more photographs of Japanese-occupied territory.*

Two years ago we asked you for photographs of foreign countries. 70,000 people offered us over 9 million photographs.

Your photographs have been and are being of tremendous use. Thousands of them were used in the invasion of North Africa and Sicily, and at this moment many thousands more are being used in the successful operations in Italy. All over the world small parties of raiders and parachutists are continually carrying out immensely valuable small-scale operations, often relying on information from your photographs. During the past year we have been working around the clock and have already produced two million prints for use in operations for the liberation of Europe. Every month we make over half a million more.

Thanks largely to you, force commanders will lead their men into the greatest enterprise of war in our history with all the knowledge that ground photographs can give to make the operation a success.

That first appeal was a shot in the dark, but it scored a bull; so I'm sure that we can count on your help again. Please do not send us your actual photographs – just write and tell us what photographs you can lend us ... we shall then call in your photographs, copy those we need, and return your collection intact. We only borrow photographs – we don't want to keep them. Will you please send your offer, as before to "Photographs", Admiralty, London.'

was the largest single library of topographical photographs in the country and could produce over 300,000 copies every month to operational commands.

Pam Braham, a WRNS, joined the ISTD in 1942. She started work initially in the New Bodleian Library in their photographic department. She recalled: 'the BBC broadcast a programme requesting people to send in their holiday snaps. These arrived in shoals and our job was to check out where they were if there was no destination given. They came in from all over Europe and you got to know certain destinations very well so we were able to add details from other sources ... these photographs were all filed in boxes and then personnel who were interested in a certain area or place would come in and hopefully find the destination they were looking for and all information that could help them with their particular job. Needless to say we never knew anything of what they were looking for. Our job was to inform on the backs of the copies of the photographs as much relevant information as we could – i.e. Time of day when it was taken – rocky coast, very high cliffs behind the coast, sand dunes along the coast, big harbour....'

TRANSCRIBED FROM A TELEDIPHONE RECORDING

Monday 26th July 1943 6pm – BBC Radio Broadcast by W.R. Slessor

'Many listeners will remember that in May of last year we broadcast an appeal for holiday photographs made on behalf of the Admiralty. About five million photographs were offered. A great many of them have played their part in recent operations. Here is an explanation, recorded by the original broadcaster. He is a member of the Naval Staff.

I am speaking to you again to express the thanks of the Admiralty for this great effort and I think the best way to convince you of our appreciation is to tell you something of the use that has been made of your contributions. Your private snapshots have been, are, and will continue to be on active service of the highest importance in the operations of all the services, land, sea and air, from the smallest raid to the biggest invasion.

We will begin with North Africa. This campaign was planned very soon after our appeal. A squad of examiners read the sixty-thousand letters concerned and picked out as many offers covering these areas as was possible in the time. From these photographs we acquired a vast amount of material which added enormously to the value of the plans. In particular, the first problem in planning this gigantic undertaking, the biggest amphibian operation in history, was to discover on what beaches troops and tanks could be landed. It was not enough merely to know that a fine, sandy beach existed – it had to be known whether that beach was of firm sand or whether it was rocky, and more important than all, whether the slope of the beach was such that the landing of craft which carried the troops and tanks could come close enough inshore to get them quickly on to dry land. To estimate the slope of a beach is no easy matter. But get a family photograph, showing the baby paddling at the water's edge, Mother up to her waist with an anxious eye on the child and Father way out, as usual, in deep water up to the neck, then you have a pretty good idea of the gradient of that part of the beach.

It was this kind of intimate snapshot which helped the planners decide, not only what beaches could be used, but equally important, what beaches could not be used.

And now Sicily. How many of you have been to Taormina and stayed at the Hotel San Domenico? Many of you at any rate sent in photographs showing this hotel, little realising that it would one day be the Axis headquarters for the defence of Sicily.

Or take another instance; Sicily is a mountainous island with very few areas of level ground where gliders can land without crashing, or parachutists come to earth without breaking their legs. Again, these parachutists were able to land, who helped so much in the capture of our first port in Sicily.

Wherever possible, of course, photographs taken from the ground are examined with photographs taken from the air. Each is complementary to the other, and each indispensable in the planning of operations of war. Together, they help to construct the total picture of the theatre of total war.

In conclusion, may I say something to those who have offered us photographs which have not yet been called in. We engaged a large staff for this work and trained them. Even then we were faced with two alternatives, either to call in all photographs and select from them at high speed, or to call them in piecemeal, at a rate permitting of that minute study which is essential for their safe use in operations affecting vitally the lives of men and the resources of shipping and armaments. You will readily understand that we chose the latter method unhesitatingly, though fully realising that that meant that some willing contributors would be kept waiting for their offers to be accepted. Let me assure you these photographs will be called in, and at an increasing rate as we acquire and train more staff.'

BBC TELEDIPHONE RECORDING – NEWS TALK TRANSCRIPT BY A MEMBER OF OUR NAVAL STAFF

Sunday 17th May 1942 1pm – BBC Radio Broadcast by W.R. Slessor

'I am going to tell you about a very important, and a very interesting, aspect of our raids on enemy-occupied territory which have been made recently by our combined forces. There's quite a long list of these, and the list is continually growing. You naturally know that these raids are planned in advance with the utmost care, but I wonder if you realise what a vital part is played in them by photographs?

Take Bruneval, for instance, where the big German radio-location centre was destroyed. I can tell you for the first time of one simple little incident which contributed greatly to that success. When every possible source of information about that area had been thoroughly combed for details, we still lacked an actual picture of those few hundred yards of France to complete our knowledge, and it's in this connection that you can see how this talk affects you personally. Quite by chance, it transpired, that one of the staff officers working on the plan had spent a holiday in the Bruneval neighbourhood just before the war; he hurried off to his house, where he found his photograph album stored away in a trunk. He looked through it, and there sure enough were photographs taken on his holiday, showing in minute detail the exact spot involved. It was five of those photographs put together that formed the last link in the whole plan.

So you see, private photographs helped to ensure the successful operation at Bruneval. Photographs taken in the carefree pre-war days, without any thought of their later value. Now there are thousands of such photographs in the country. I ask you to lend these photographs to the Admiralty – photographs taken when you went abroad on business or for holidays; not only old photographs that you would otherwise give to the salvage, but more still your most treasured collections. We want to examine them, and to copy those that interest us. We shall look after your property most carefully, and return it to you intact when we have finished with it.

Not long ago, the Minister of Economic Warfare appealed to you for old guide-books and foreign directories, and so on, and your response was most generous. The Ministry passed much of this material to us; and we were very glad to have it. But it is photographs we want now – photographs of every single country in the world, except Great Britain itself. Needless to say, we already possess a vast collection of photographs – but even the Admiralty cannot have a photograph of every port and dock, and every inch of coastline, and more than that, every road, railway, bridge and factory in the world. Yet that is what we want. Inland area as well as coastline. All three Services use our files, for many and various purposes, and you who are listening to me now may possess one photograph which, though unimportant to you, may provide a vital missing part of the whole picture, and perhaps the means of saving lives.

There was a photograph sent to us the other day; it was one of a large collection of private holiday snapshots taken solely for personal interest. This particular one showed a beach scene, including a side view of a road leading down to the beach. Near the bottom of the road were two men beside a large car. You might not think that interesting to us – but it was, extremely ... it was a foreign beach – never mind where – and we already had photographs of it; although some of them showed the road ... was taken at an angle showing how wide that road was ... it could have been a footpath, for all we *could tell. Well this ... showed that the road had a good surface.*

In other words, it was wide and strong enough for a landing party to drive their tanks up it from the beach, and it was the only way to do so. We'd been searching for that information for weeks.

Well you see, I've told you the kind of information we want you to give us; possibly some of you possess a photograph which properly used could be a more deadly weapon than ten torpedoes or twenty tanks. So now please look out all your snapshots and postcards taken abroad – it doesn't matter where they were taken, from Boulogne to Fiji, from Amsterdam to Madagascar, inland or on the coast; we want them all. Your snap may seem just Mother in sunglasses on the beach to you – but experts may see a lot more than that. Just write and tell us what you've got. Don't send the photographs yet. Simply write and describe them to us. Send your letter to the following address. It's very simple:

Photographs, Admiralty, London ... I'll repeat that: Photographs, Admiralty, London'

By early 1944 the SOE and Resistance groups operating in occupied France were primed to take action against specified targets under direction from covert radio broadcasts from the BBC. The targets were comprehensive, and included telecommunications facilities, arms/fuel dumps, railway infrastructure and interfering with the French road network to prevent German troop movements.

The concept of using covert messages in mainstream radio broadcasts was the brainchild of Georges Bégué, the first SOE agent to be parachuted into France. German intelligence began monitoring and jamming his radio broadcasts and were getting very good at Direction Finding (D/F) the signals he was emitting. He made the suggestion

BBC
Phonograph
cylinders (from
BBC website)

to his SOE headquarters in Baker Street that the BBC Foreign Service could be used to convey short covert messages as prearranged phrases. These '*messages personnels*' quickly took off as a means to communicate with deployed agents and they were used in every SOE country section. Baker Street gave these messages the ignominious title of 'Iodoforms'.

These operational messages were for confirming an operation was to take place, or for cancelling an operation. The text of the message was typically constructed by the free French forces and passed to the BBC by either the SOE or the SIS in time for the various stages of the operation, often conveyed by telephone. Even the Political Warfare Executive (PWE) was using the BBC to transmit coded messages overseas, on the discretion of the organisation's regional directors.

These French '*messages personnels*' were choreographed between the BBC and the SOE country section and were integral to the planning and sequencing of French Resistance and SOE sabotage efforts to sync with D-Day on 6 June 1944.

They were sent in their hundreds to alert the Resistance to the invasion and to stimulate specific actions. Messages were often transmitted back, at huge risk to the W/T operators, and these messages were received at the Poundon and Grendon base stations. One example would be the tasking of French agent Robert Benoist. If he was to hear the message on the BBC French Service '*C'était le sergent qui fumait sa pipe en pleine campagne*,' he was to alert his sabotage teams for an imminent invasion from the Allies. If he was to hear '*Il avait mal au coeur mais il continuait tout de même*', he was to initiate his teams that night.

As Operation Neptune materialised on the night of 5/6 June 1944, the BBC messages initiated the French Resistance and SOE teams to make over 950 sabotage missions across the French railway network, disrupting the flow of German personnel and equipment in potentially reinforcing the defence of the Normandy beaches.

It did not always go to plan, however. On 1 May 1944, one of the BBC transmissions sent out a number of warning messages which initiated Resistance teams to cut telephone wires and undertake road and railway sabotage missions, outlining that a major offensive was to occur within a fortnight. This was sent in error and long before an effective invasion force had been amassed in southern England.

To avoid security compromise, the Resistance groups could not be continually listening to their wireless sets in anticipation of tasking from the SOE and SIS. They were subsequently ordered to listen on the 1st, 2nd, 15th and 16th of every month for warning messages broadcast on the BBC. If they were to receive one of these *Warning Messages* they were to maintain a listening watch each night for direct tasking, what the SOE referred to as *Action Messages*. The total number of *Warning Messages* which would need to be broadcast if the SOE were to put all their D-Day plans into effect simultaneously was estimated to be around 315. SHAEF Headquarters wanted simultaneous action from all the Resistance networks across France to initiate chaos for the Germans on D-Day itself.

There were two essentially two categories of BBC covert messaging:

(1) Messages informing Resistance reception committees that an Allied air operation was to take place (these were typically broadcast daily through the BBC).

(2) Messages informing the entirety of the French Resistance networks – that certain action was to be taken in connection with military operations (these were the messages sent out around D-Day).

The timings for these specific broadcasts were set and followed the following pattern:

Timings	Content
1230 – 1300 GMT	First warning to reception committee that operation is to take place
1530 – 1600 GMT	Programme carries messages to certain reception committees who stated that conditions in their area allow them to receive first warning later than the 1230 broadcast. The 1530 broadcast therefore relieves the pressure on the 1230 broadcast to a certain extent
1730 – 1830 GMT	All messages sent on the above programmes have to be repeated on this programme, to confirm to the field that the operation is still mounted. This repetition is vital, in case the earlier broadcast was clearly received

These broadcasts and messages were often interwoven with dummy messages to throw any German Y Service interception teams off the trail. They were typically broadcast during the moon period, as the moon state affects the weather in the atmosphere, which subsequently alters the quality and transmissions of radio broadcasts each month.

It was clear that there would be a bottleneck of messages that would need to be transmitted for D-Day. There would be many thousands of members of various Resistance movements, so the supply of short-wave receivers was almost out of the question but the BBC could broadcast on medium-wave and there was a push to use the ASPIDISTRA transmitter at Crowborough, owned by the Political Warfare Executive (PWE).

Between November 1943 and January 1944 the covert BBC transmissions typically averaged between two-and-a-half to three minutes per news broadcast. By February 1944, the Allies were given a significant increase in aircraft to drop arms to the

French Resistance groups, principally the *Maquis* in the southeast of the country. This increased requirement resulted in a transition to four-and-a-half to five minutes of covert messages on each BBC broadcast. If there were periods of fine weather, this would increase the available aircraft drops, subsequently increasing the broadcast time on the BBC to seven minutes during each broadcast.

By March 1944, Allied aircraft were amassing a large number of sorties over France to resupply the Resistance networks. To coordinate these drops with the Resistance, the SOE required on average nine minutes per broadcast for their covert messages, which could increase to ten to twelve minutes if the weather conditions were favourable. This inevitably would also have to incorporate the SIS broadcast messages as well.

At the time there was much consternation between the SOE and the BBC on how much of the news programmes would be taken up by these rather random transmissions. These monotonous messages had to be verbalised correctly to prevent any poor pronounciations or mistakes. A memo at the time read, 'I rather think that this is getting beyond a joke. It seems that the general opinion is that any announcer, good, bad or indifferent, can stand up in front of the microphone for 30-40 minutes and read out without a break some 300-400 messages. It is an established fact that a really first-class announcer of the BBC have had enough after 20 minutes … the quality of the announcers required by us must be first rate. Any slip might prove disastrous to an operation. A suggestion to this problem is that we use announcers from the "stand-by" pool of the BBC reading for 10 minutes each. Under these conditions we would have first class readers, minimising the risk of "failing to get the message through clearly".'

Efforts were made to reduce the length of the broadcasts by the SOE, SIS and BBC ostensibly by keeping the messages as short as possible and using short-wave only for a proportion of the reception committees if they had short-wave battery receivers available. This would negate the BBC messages been broadcast on long-, medium- and short-waves. An SOE memo stated, 'it is possible that a few committees will be able to take their BBC messages on short-wave only in April and the number should increase in May. This will reduce the time we require on each medium-wave programme, which is at present the principal bottleneck, but we cannot count on any great improvement in the situation by this method until many more sets have been delivered and Reception Committees have completed trials and confirmed that the sets work reliably in the field.'

In August 1943, the SOE noted the lack of W/T operators in France and the lack of equipment available to the French Resistance networks to receive these BBC broadcasts. For Overlord something needed to be done. SOE levied a requirement to deliver large numbers of short-wave midget receiving sets. In August 1943, the

Graphic showing the BBC and SOE 'Conduct of Work' (from HS8/445)

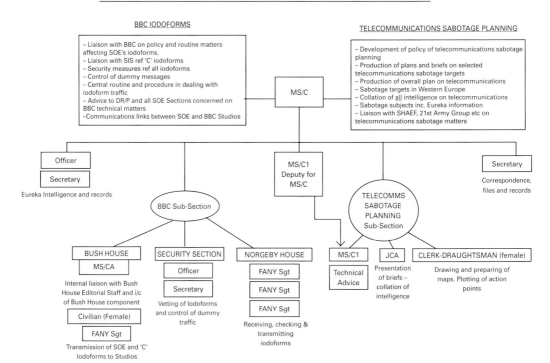

SOE intended to deliver forty sets, and by the end of 1943 have an additional one hundred sets in country. This was to be scaled-up for 1944 as a prelude to D-Day, with them delivering 500 sets to the Resistance networks. There was a mutual dependency between the SOE and the BBC on the conveyance of operational messages, but the SOE had to deliver the means by which these messages could be received. SOE was to write, 'this section has in the past had to rely largely and may in the future have to rely solely on the BBC for transmissions of operational messages. If we are unable to send these messages through lack of Midget sets, we shall be greatly handicapped in our work of exfiltrating agents from the field.'

An internal SOE memo dated 17 March 1944 showed the BBC editorial staff had taken the decision to restrict last-minute amendments by the SOE to any broadcasts, and they decreed a fifteen-minute curfew prior to the broadcast commencing as a cut-off for messages.

The deadline for radio transmissions were then set to be:
      1316hrs BST
      1615hrs BST

1815hrs BST

2100hrs BST

The memo stated that 'additional BBC messages less than 15 minutes before any programme starts creates a difficult problem for the BBC editors and language supervisors....'

The BBC could not just rely on the availability of short-wave radio sets; they also requested support for the use of medium-wave broadcasts to augment the transmissions on short-wave. A memo read, 'with regard to D-Day planning, we are probably justified in assuming that the delivery of short-wave receivers to the Field has by this time appreciably increased ... we must allow that among the vast number of individuals in the Field, whose activities are controlled by our Iodoforms, there will be undoubtedly some, and they may be key men, who will lack short-wave sets on D-Day. Since provision must be made in our planning for adverse conditions, we cannot dismiss their number as negligible. Therefore, we are compelled to claim a safeguard in the allotment of at least two medium-wave channels over and above the short-wave channels to be reserved for the broadcasting of our messages.'

On 10 September 1942, the following messages were broadcast from the BBC for three different organisations at the 1815hrs and 2015hrs time slots:

PWE: *'Joseph souhaite bonjour a sa petite Paulette et sa femme Marie. Bonne santé'*

SOE: *'Gil c'est votre chef'*

France Combattante (Passy): *'Christian envoie un ami prendre des nouvelles'*

One of the most significant *'messages personnels'* was the one broadcast five days before D-Day to convey when the Allied invasion of France would begin. It would consist of the first two lines of a Paul Verlaine poem called *'Chanson d'Automne'*:

Les sanglots longs des violins d'automne (the long sobs of autumn violins)

Bercent mon Coeur d'une langueur monotone (soothe my heart with dull languor)

The first line would be a warning to the French Resistance that the Allied landings would happen that week, the second that the assault would commence within forty-eight hours and a call to arms to get the Resistance units to carry out sabotage operations against the railway network, communications lines and roads. Operations were to commence at midnight of the day the second message was broadcast. These two messages became known as the 'Verlaine couplet' and German intelligence had gleaned some insight into its use and meaning.

An SOE F Section team led by François Garel, his wireless operator Marcel Rousset and courier Marcel Fox were apprehended by the Germans in the Le Mans area of France in 1943. Rousset agree to work with the German SD and was assigned a wireless specialist Josef Goetz. Rousset had to routinely transmit back to SOE communications HQ with a security check and he stated to Goetz he had to broadcast Butler's messages in English to London, and Fox's messages in French. In fact, the reverse was true and it tipped off the SOE that his team had been compromised.

Shortly after the transmission, Rousset managed to escape from German detention and failed to get through to SOE headquarters in London to inform them that his radio set was now under the control of the German SD wireless teams. Goetz was to use this set to interpret these covert BBC messages transmitted before D-Day, making him aware of the importance of the Verlaine couplet.

Much of the coordination of the BBC messaging fell to the SOE Liaison officer at Bush House, a Major Buxton. A special section of the SOE MS Directorate (MS/C) was made responsible for the relay of messages to the BBC for later transmission on their Foreign News Service, using a dedicated teleprinter-telephone service. It was to be the only link between the SOE and the BBC for coded messages. These messages were collated at the MS/C in Norgeby House using a standard pro-forma, although urgent messages could be relayed by phone or verbally.

A typical day of transmissions could be demonstrated on 4 February 1944. Seventy-one messages were broadcast on this day, on the 1930hrs and 2115hrs BBC News programme. These messages took eight-and-a-half minutes to broadcast in their entirety, absorbing much of the fifteen-minute long broadcast. The BBC were required to significantly increase their covert transmissions from February 1944 and were concerned that a 100 per cent increase in traffic by March 1944 would mean they

BBC Bush House radio transmissions (from BBC website)

Section	Number of daily broadcasts	Wavelength of messages	Type of message	Average number of messages	Form of message
French country section	Twice	All 3 wavebands	Recognition Ops 'on' timed target	20/30 per day	Phase 3-30 words
Fighting French	Three times	All 3 wavebands	Ops 'on'	25 per day	Phrase 3-8 words
MASSINGHAM relay	Twice	All 3 wavebands	Ops 'on' and 'off'	4 per day	Phrase 5-20 words

would have to extend the actual news programme out to around seventeen minutes. And even then, this was not taking into account additional messages that would be sent out on D-Day. MS/C was to write 'special facilities for transmission on D-Day must be arranged'.

In a letter to the Prime Minister entitled 'BBC messages to French Resistance Groups', the BBC outlined the value and problems associated with these covert broadcasts, 'because the normal channels of communication by W/T are not sufficiently rapid SOE's final messages to reception committees, advising them that weather conditions do or do not permit the execution of a pre-arranged dropping operation that night, have to be broadcast in code messages by the BBC in their ordinary continental programmes. The greatly increased deliveries of arms to France during February and March have on this account caused serious embarrassment to the Minister of Information. As many as 107 messages have had to be interpolated into his programmes on a single day, interrupting the programme for seven minutes on each occasion while these messages were being rattled off. I have been greatly indebted to the Minister of Information and the BBC for their cooperation in this matter, and with the excellent technique that they have evolved I hope to be able to get all the necessary messages through for the April moon period, as has been achieved in February and March. A difficulty has, however, arisen in connection with SOE's directives in connection with Overlord. For a period from a day or two before to a day or two after D-Day I shall have to ask for time on the BBC programmes to send out signals to over a thousand groups throughout France to attack their allotted targets. For this I should require a minimum of eight minutes (possibly rising to ten minutes).'

On the night of 5 June 1944, the BBC was to broadcast all the *'messages personnels'* in their entirety, a total of 325 messages to stimulate the French Resistance into action.

Sabotage operations were to begin hours before the actual Overlord assault forces started to land on the Normandy beaches, which was intended to divert attention away from the invasion. It would also scupper the ability of the German military to communicate and re-supply the Normandy defensive positions

The German Y Service did intercept these messages. The first line of the Verlaine couplet was intercepted on the 1st, 2nd and 3rd of June and the wireless teams intercepted the second line at 2115hrs on 5 June. It had been broadcast fifteen times that day. German intelligence in the region was to assess that this was all part of the Allies ruse to confuse the Germans.

But the unique nature of the transmission of the second line of the couplet was to initiate General Hans von Salmuth to alerting his 15th Army, which covered the Pas-de-Calais region. Significantly, no action was taken by the German 7th Army covering Normandy, even though von Rundstedt was made aware. The BBC had been transmitting these messages for weeks so it should be no surprise that German commanders like von Rundstedt were mindful to ignore them.

The BBC Monitoring Service began in 1939 under direction from the British War Office and Ministry of Information to access information on foreign media and propaganda during the war. It started life in a series of wooden huts in Wood Norton, Worcestershire, until the service outgrew the temporary site and by 1943 it had moved to Caversham Park in Reading, a mansion house that was being used as a hospital.

In the summer of 1940, the BBC Monitoring Service structure was made officially public. It had no direct engagement with the Press in Britain, but the material would

Monitoring Service Unit	Role/Remit
Engineering Measurement Room	Technical nerve centre of the Service
Main Listening Room	Voice broadcasts received here. Monitors listen on headphones, record and record timings
Morse and 'Watching' Listening Room	Monitors receive Morse signals, principally from news agencies, taking material down directly onto typewriters. Part of room is dedicated to keeping a watch on various groups of voice broadcasting stations
Hellschreiber Rooms	Foreign agency material is received on Hellschreiber teleprinters – the material being translated and selection made from it on the spot
Information Bureau	The above rooms submit material to the Information Bureau. Staff here select the material required for the Daily Digest or any urgent/ flash service. Staff here are the focus for all inquiries relating to monitored materials
Index Section	Attached to the Information Bureau. Index section indexes and files the Services output and for recording and inquiries purposes
Editorial Room **Publishing**	Here the material is sub-edited and prepared for the Daily Digest Material comes from editorial and is typed on stencils, duplicated and dispatched from this section

reach the press via the Ministry of Information. The Service was organised into a number of sub-units:

The Reception Unit was the listening arm of the Monitoring Service, which routinely collected radio traffic on 240 separate broadcasts in thirty-two different languages. The Information Bureau selected and teleprinted all urgent material as soon as it was transcribed from the Reception teams. The Editorial Unit was charged with the production of the *Daily Digest of World Broadcasts*.

The comprehensive *Daily Digest* publication would total in the region of 100,000 to 150,000 words and was dispatched by 1015hrs every morning by motorcycle couriers to Whitehall Departments. It was also distributed to the wider BBC and to the PWE. The Editorial Unit also published a *Daily Monitoring Report*, which gave a general synopsis of the monitored material and provided 'an objective analysis of the political trends in world broadcasting'. This was typically published for the War Cabinet staff. Urgent or flash information was transmitted via teleprinter to nineteen separate War, Government and BBC departments (typically in the region of 25-30,000 words transmitted a day via this means).

There was another unit in the Monitoring Service, known specifically as the Special Listening Section (SLS), which was responsible for checking programme schedules, searching for new stations, channels and transmissions. Prior to a country being invaded, the SLS would often spot the increase in material broadcast from the aggressor state. It would note emergency channels being established if an Axis Power was occupying a country. Once a country was liberated, it was the SLS who would monitor for new broadcast transmissions from the country.

The service played a significant role alongside the PWE in collecting propaganda traffic from the German propaganda machine led by Joseph Goebbels. The Germans used a kind of teleprinter referred to as as the *Hellschreiber* to broadcast and BBC Monitoring intercepted the traffic. German propaganda on France during 1944 would have been obtained from the Broadcasting Division and the Counterpropaganda and Enemy News Service of the Ministry of Information (MoI) who would have dealt with this type of content.

The German High Command, which passed its secret enciphered material over the airwaves using the Lorenz cipher machine, was also an active news broadcaster. This news from the Germans was actively reported on by the BBC Monitoring Service. They broadcast daily, typically at their 1400hrs, then 1500hrs slots after the German Home Service news. It was then repeated during the four remaining news bulletins of the day. Inevitably, the news policy of the German High Command was influenced by

Daily Digest dispatch riders for BBC (from BBC website)

propaganda and the simplicity with which wireless propaganda could be broadcast to the population.

By the end of the war, over 1,000 people worked at Caversham Park, providing the War Office and BBC journalists worldwide with regular and up-to-date news, propaganda and information from the Axis powers.

By March 1944, the BBC had become a vast news organisation with over 11,000 staff and became, through its understanding of enemy broadcasts, a hugely significant intelligence cog in the wheel of Overlord. As a producer of radio news and entertainment broadcasts it had never been associated with the covert work of the British Intelligence agencies during the preparation for D-Day.

The work it undertook in transmitting covert broadcasts for the SOE and French Resistance networks was vital to the outcome of the Normandy campaign. Similarly, the knowledge gleaned from the millions of photographs collected by the Admiralty Photographic Library because of the BBC appeal would lay firm foundations for the enhanced topographical intelligence on Normandy generated by the ISTD. The BBC had fundamentally woven itself into the Allied intelligence machinery and it was to help another critical component of Overlord – propaganda.

CHAPTER THIRTEEN
FOURTH ARM

'The success of propaganda is due to the continuity and consistency with which it is applied.'

Adolf Hitler, *Mein Kampf*

~~~

'The Supreme Allied Commander calls upon Political Warfare, the Fourth Arm in this combined operation, to reduce not only for our fighting men, but for the peoples of Europe the cost of ultimate victory.'

PWE Director of Plans, Special Directive on Operations against Western Europe issued by the PWE and OWI

~~~

The BBC radio broadcasts were a stalwart of truth and wartime news and had a huge audience beyond the shores of Britain. The people of Europe, and even Germany, looked to the BBC for honest and timely news on the war. It was by design a significant propaganda tool. In the early years of the war, ownership of the real propaganda effort became a turf war in a number of government departments, including the Foreign Office, the BBC, the Special Operations Executive (SOE), the Secret Intelligence Service (SIS), and the Ministries of Information and Economic Warfare.

In 1940, when Dr Hugh Dalton was appointed to run the SOE, he drafted a memo entitled 'The Fourth Arm', which exposed how propaganda within the organisation could be potentially employed during the war against the Germans:

'The Germans have shown that success in war can, to a large extent, be achieved by "Subversion", by which I mean not only propaganda but subversive activities in the widest sense. Before a shot is fired, before even war is declared, the ground has been so well prepared that [the] opposing nation, divided, discouraged and even to some extent, disarmed, is unable to offer the desperate and united response which alone can prevail against military resources at Germany's disposal. In other words subversion, I suggest, is an essential element in any large scale offensive action....'

By 1941, Churchill gave the authority for the creation of a new organisation to win the propaganda war against Nazi Germany. It was formally announced to the House of Commons on 11 September 1941. The SOE was split in August 1941 to augment

French propaganda poster, 'Honour and Country' (© IWM – PST3104)

some of the earlier propaganda operations which they had undertaken. Strategic propaganda directed against Germany was termed as 'Political Warfare'. This was formally defined as '… the marshalling and employment of propaganda coordinated in one plan with the Foreign Office, the Fighting Services and all other branches of the British war machine with the object of destroying the German war machine'. The organisation was to be led by Robert Bruce Lockhart, a former banker and diplomat.

This new world of propaganda was folded into what is called 'psychological operations', or PSYOPS for short. A specialist unit was established within SHAEF to generate some innovative PSYOPS ideas. The Psychological Warfare Division (PWD/ SHAEF) was to officially define this as 'the dissemination of propaganda designed to undermine the enemy's will to resist, demoralise his followers, and sustain the morale of our supporters'. PWD/SHAEF was the representation from the Supreme Commander Eisenhower and it was to form a partnership with the Office of War Information (OWI), representing the US State Department, and lastly the Political Intelligence Department (PID), which was the representative of the British Foreign Office. PID was the covername for the Political Warfare Executive (PWE). It was one of the early members of PWE staff, David Bowes-Lyon, who first coined the name.

The PWD was to operate under the direction of a US Brigadier General, and had four main branches:

1. Psychological warfare
2. Public relations
3. Censorship
4. Communications

PWD served a number of functions for SHAEF, predominantly the control and release of operational news, and the coordination and conduct of the distribution of propaganda. It would also have responsibility for the coordination of combat zone propaganda executed by the individual Army Groups and ensuring that propaganda conducted by civil agencies conformed with operational requirements of the Commander-in-Chief. It would provide operational and intelligence information necessary for the dissemination of propaganda by the civil agencies.

Brigadier Brooks was the head of the PWE Military Wing who sat on a number of Service Committees relating to covert intelligence. He worked closely alongside his deputy, Air Commodore Groves. The Wing was divided into four sections:

1. Leaflet coordination dissemination (under command of Captain Ryer)
2. MI19 (and other MI branch) Liaison (under command of Captain Steege)
3. German POW (under Cyrus Brooks)
4. Bomb damage assessment and leaflet content (under Captain Savage)

Psychological warfare units would concentrate efforts on overt propaganda methods to instil credibility into their messages. There were three distinct classes of propaganda:

1. White – whose source is clearly indicated and is regarded as overt. No disguising of source.
2. Black – a false source is given and covert in nature. Disguises its origins.
3. Grey – source is not revealed and applied covertly.

Much of the PWE output was 'White' propaganda, coordinating the production of leaflets for air-drops from aircraft or artillery shells, or coordinating BBC broadcasts to enemy countries involving news and music.

PWE staff underwent no formal training programme but some instruction in the propaganda arts was delivered initially by a team led by Major John Hackett. From late 1943, as the PWE began planning for D-Day, it established a formal training programme to create a cadre of 'Propaganda Intelligence Officers' who could deploy with the invasion forces or work covertly with the French Resistance.

As planning for D-Day ensued, the BBC, SOE and PWE became embroiled in bitter disagreements on the broadcasting of all forms of propaganda. The Musgrave section of the SOE was responsible for D-Day planning and was under the direction of Major Saunders and Captain Franklin Canfield, who had been drafted into the team from the OSS mission in London. They were to state that 'it is clearly essential that Broadcasts, black or white, before or after D-Day … shall NOT conflict with, but shall conform to, operational plans made by SOE for execution by Resistance Groups'.

The figurehead at the centre of the propaganda war was Sefton Delmer, who had been recruited into the PWE from the BBC because of his experiences working with the Nazi regime in the 1930s. Prior to any assault on French beaches, propaganda would have to be routinely dispersed against the German occupiers but also targeting the French population in northern France. Planes would need to saturate the Normandy villages and towns with propaganda leaflets. Radio broadcasts would need to transmit messages to furnish the Resistance uprising and dishearten the German defenders.

Sefton Delmer was born in Berlin, to an Australian academic father, in 1904 and had spent most of his early life in the German capital. He was a fluent German speaker and understood the mindset of the Germans – a critical component for effective propaganda. In the 1920s–30s, Delmer was the German correspondent for the *Daily Express*, at a time of the rise of the National Socialist party. He met Adolf Hitler several times during this period and whilst covering the Spanish Civil War for the newspaper was exposed to the propaganda techniques employed by Joseph Goebbels. He was recruited into the PWE in early 1941.

Over time, Delmer was to build an effective propaganda organisation with hundreds of staff drawn from the Ministry of Information, SOE and the BBC. It would have its own studios, intelligence departments and dedicated printing firms all geared to wage psychological warfare against a foe who were masters of the art.

Under his direction, the PWE set up a radio station operating in the Bedfordshire town of Milton Bryan, which would broadcast radio programmes to Germany, designed to convince the German public that it was been broadcast in Germany. These included programmes such as '*Atlantiksender* and *Gustav Siegfried Eins*', which incorporated genuine German music and commentary. The programmes were transmitted down the road from Milton Bryan, at the relay stations based in the villages of Potsgrove and Gawcott. These were just a few miles from the PWE headquarters at Woburn Abbey. The American OWI also created its own propaganda radio station in Britain, Radio ABSIE (American Broadcasting Station in Europe).

As the Overlord plans started to mature in late 1943, Delmer started broadcasting a new radio station called *Soldatensender Calais*, aimed at Hitler's vast Atlantic Wall. The Germans were made to believe it was being broadcast in northern France by the German forces. It was a huge success. After D-Day, the interrogation of POWs near the beachhead by CSDIC and PWIS staff found that nearly 50 per cent of German prisoners had heard *Soldatensender Calais* at least once on a radio in the week to 1 July 1944. German troops found the station entertaining and the music very current. They also found the news was more trustworthy than that broadcast by German radio. *Soldatensender Calais* was being used as part of the Bodyguard deception campaign, to add weight to the ruse that the beachhead for the Allied invasion of France was to be in the Pas-de-Calais region. Some of the Black radio broadcasts were targeted specifically at U-boat crews. Admiral Godfrey and Lieutenant Commander Fleming from the NID in the Admiralty directly helped the PWE to put these programmes together.

Prior to the PWE being created, its predecessor, the SO1 branch of the SOE had recruited a number of foreign nationals to record propaganda radio broadcasts. These teams of foreign nationals based in the Woburn area, each referred to as a Research Unit (RU), would record their broadcasts, lasting no more than twelve-and-a-half minutes, on to 16-inch glass discs for transmission from one of the main transmitter sites at Potsgrove or Gawcott. The first RUs began producing radio broadcasts in May 1940. The two main French stations were F1 (Radio *Inconnue*) and F2 (Radio *Travail*), which broadcast subversive programmes. The RU for F2 Radio *Travail* produced 551 programmes between November 1940 and May 1942. *Inconnue* operated from November 1940 until January 1944 and sustained the veil of cover that it was broadcasting from Paris. It also broadcast subversive programmes in an attempt to generate passive resistance in occupied France. Another station, *F3 La France Catholique,* operated up to May 1944, just before D-Day, and was run by the Free French broadcasting content with an aim to train the Resistance groups.

German propaganda, under the direction of Reich Minister of Propaganda, Joseph Goebbels, had a head start on the PWE. It ran a number of Black radio stations such as 'Workers' Challenge', a communist station, and the 'New British Broadcasting Station', which purported to be being run by an underground British fascist movement. They were being run by the *Büro Concordia* in Berlin, which was owned by Goebbels, with a number of British collaborators as staff, including the infamous William Joyce, more affectionately known as 'Lord Haw-Haw'.

Much of the Goebbel's propaganda effort had been discredited by the Allies. Twice his propaganda machine had promoted successful attacks on HMS *Varbel*, the then headquarters of the X-Craft midget submarines training. It was of course a fallacy, as *Varbel* was a shore establishment.

The PWE was also to produce the *Deutsche Kurzwellensender Atlantik* or *Atlantiksender* radio broadcasts which began in early 1943 and targeted the German U-boat crews with such topics as the names of German streets that had been bombed, stories of German soldiers deserting or even tales of sexual exploits of the wives left behind in Germany with foreign workers. The stories were interwoven with news and music. Delmer and his team got much of the information for these broadcasts from German newspapers, POW letters and interrogations, and from the NID. *Atlantiksender* was originally broadcast on short-wave frequencies, but to achieve maximum reach it needed to be transmitted on medium-wave.

In May 1941, Churchill authorised the PWE to invest in a 500kW medium-wave (MW) transmitter tower, called Aspidistra, which would be able to reach the whole of occupied Europe and potentially jam some of the significant radio broadcasts, such as the Nazi Party celebrations in Berlin broadcasting to the *Volkesempfangener* or German people's radio sets. It was realised the two short-wave (SW) transmitters at Potsgrove and Gawcott were not powerful enough. It would quickly become the most powerful MW transmitter in Europe at that time. The transmitter was purchased on 17 May 1941 from the American company Radio Corporation of America (RCA) as a 'radio counter-battery' aiming to subdue or jam German propaganda broadcasts.

Aspidistra was to cost the British government £111,801 4s 10d and was built outside Crowborough, in the Ashdown Forest, by Canadian Military Engineers who were awaiting orders for Operation Jubilee, the assault on Dieppe. It became operational in November 1942, just in time for the concerted PWE propaganda effort to support the Allied landings in North Africa (Operation Torch). The experience of using Aspidistra for propaganda purposes supporting an operational force would help the PWE to shape what was to come in 1944. As Delmer was to write, 'although we have had very satisfactory evidence of wide-spread listening among German troops ... a medium-wave broadcast would give us access to a much larger public in Germany itself than we can hope to contact with low powered short-wave transmitters.... We feel the time has come for the launching of more offensive political warfare against Germany, particularly of operations of internal agitation and confusion. B.B.C. broadcasts to Germany rightly confine themselves to straight news – mainly of military and strategic developments and comments thereon. They refrain from revolutionary agitation

PWE Overlord leaflet ZF.4 invasion warning (© Lee Richards, www. psywar.org)

MESSAGE URGENT

du Commandement Suprême

des Forces Expéditionnaires Alliées

AUX HABITANTS DE CETTE VILLE

Message urgent

du Commandement Suprême des
Forces Expéditionnaires Alliées
AUX HABITANTS DE CETTE VILLE

Afin que l'ennemi commun soit vaincu, les Armées de l'Air Alliées vont attaquer tous les centres de transports ainsi que toutes les voies et moyens de communications vitaux pour l'ennemi.

Des ordres à cet effet ont été donnés.

Vous qui lisez ce tract, vous vous trouvez dans ou près d'un centre essentiel à l'ennemi pour le mouvement de ses troupes et de son matériel. L'objectif vital près duquel vous vous trouvez va être attaqué incessamment.

Il faut sans délai vous éloigner, avec votre famille, pendant quelques jours, de la zone de danger où vous vous trouvez.

N'encombrez pas les routes. Dispersez-vous dans la campagne, autant que possible.

PARTEZ SUR LE CHAMP !
VOUS N'AVEZ PAS UNE MINUTE A PERDRE !

Z.F.4

ZF.4 leaflet reverse (© Lee Richards, www.psywar.org)

against the regime as such agitation coming from the openly enemy B.B.C. would be ineffective. They cannot embark on confusion operations. All this is the task of "black" and an amplification of our "black" channels to Germany is therefore necessary.'

At the end of 1943, Apidistra was used to good effect in disrupting German *Luftwaffe* operations. The PWE would record *Luftwaffe* ground control instructions during one night's operations, and the next night re-broadcast them to the night fighters, sending them off to target the wrong areas.

Milton Bryan was wired to the outside world through a number of high-grade lines which would link the studio to the two transmitter sites at Potsgrove and Gawcott, the huge MW transmitter site Aspidistra in Crowborough, Reuters, the BBC, the Press Association and the two main POW interrogation centres being overseen by CSDIC – Latimer House and Wilton House. It would form the basis of a multi-lateral flow of relevant information on enemy news, morale and intelligence. On 5 February 1943, Delmer took over responsibility for the Milton Bryan studio and brought in Air Commodore Lyster Blandy, who had earlier in the war set up A11(e), the Air Intelligence section charged with intercepting and analysing the German *Luftwaffe* wireless transmissions. Blandy's experience was to prove invaluable to Milton Bryan.

When Eisenhower was appointed Supreme Allied Commander, he appointed General Robert McClure as his head of the newly formed Psychological Warfare Division (PWD). As the SHAEF structures evolved, McClure attached Lieutenant Commander McLachlan from NID17Z to the Naval staff of Admiral Ramsay, the Supreme Naval Commander for Operation Neptune – the naval and amphibious phase of Overlord. McLachlan was experienced as he had been supporting Delmer on his PWE operations from January 1943. By March 1944 McLachlan was made responsible for coordinating all PWE Black and Grey propaganda operations within SHAEF.

Just four days before D-Day, Delmer was appointed Director of Political Warfare for Enemy and Satellite, which would give him the autonomy he required and the authority to broker resources for the PWE from PWD/SHAEF and OSS. He was gifted a top-floor office in BBC's Bush House, where he would have a flurry of secret meetings with members of the French Resistance based in London to help choreograph what was to be the biggest challenge for the PWE during World War II.

The PWE had its own intelligence section which would gather information of use to build content for their radio broadcasts, leaflets or *Nachrichten* newspapers. They would receive intelligence from the various Armed services intelligence directorates, the BBC Monitoring Service at Caversham, the interrogation centres being run by the CSDIC/PWIS and the RPS. This was complemented by the access PWE had to the German news releases as they happened. At the start of the war the Allies had requisitioned a *Hellschreiber* radio-operated teleprinter, which allowed direct access. The studio also received routine aerial photographs from the aerial reconnaissance hub at Danesfield House. Alongside debriefs from RAF aircrews, the information collated after a bombing raid by RAF bombers was powerful material for propaganda activities. Milton Bryan was to acquire a reputation for its intelligence analysis. It appointed Clifton Child as its main intelligence expert managing a team of female researchers.

In 1942, the Director-General wanted to reorganise PWE Intelligence, as material had first to arrive at Woburn, where it would be utilised by the RU teams. The BBC teams at Bush House were often left out of the loop, lacking the necessary intelligence picture to effectively plan their broadcasts. The Director-General appointed Lieutenant Colonel Eric Sachs to act as the Director of Political Warfare Intelligence (DPWI) based in Bush House. Sachs reviewed all the methods to disseminate intelligence across the PWE and recommended the establishment of a new role of Central Intelligence Officer (CIO) in each regional team. They were to act independently of any propaganda activity within their regions. In his review, Sachs also concluded that Brigadier Brooks should retain his function in collecting intelligence from the various service departments. By 1944 PWE had built up nearly half-a-million intelligence documents, and the German files were distributed into groups, four dealing with the population attitudes and three concerning the morale of German *Wehrmacht*. These document groups were subdivided into thirty-four further groups, providing a hugely comprehensive intelligence picture of the enemy vulnerabilities.

In late 1943 COSSAC invited a joint PWE/OWI plan for Overlord propaganda. Whatever plans they were to form, they had to mesh in well with the Supreme Commander's overall plan for Normandy. All political warfare activity was overseen by the Tripartite Committee, which involved senior representatives from the PWE, PWD/SHAEF and the US OWI. Prior to D-Day, this body was to become the policy-making authority for propaganda. Its first requirement was to oversee the leaflet planning for Overlord. There was a flow of intelligence from the Army Groups and Armies assigned for the operation directly back to SHAEF. POW interrogations, for example, would help derive content for leaflet and newspaper sheets, focusing on current trends of German military morale and psychology.

There were four areas of focus for the covert propaganda campaign for Overlord:

1. Daily newspaper (*Nachrichten für die Truppe* – or *News for the Troops*) printed for the German troops on the ground
2. Radio broadcasts of news and music (*Soldatensender Calais* and *Kurzwellensender Atlantik*) targeting the German Armed Forces

3. Subversive leaflets distributed by air and agents
4. Medium-wave broadcast of talks for the opposition movements

PWE leadership structure (c/o Ingram Murray)

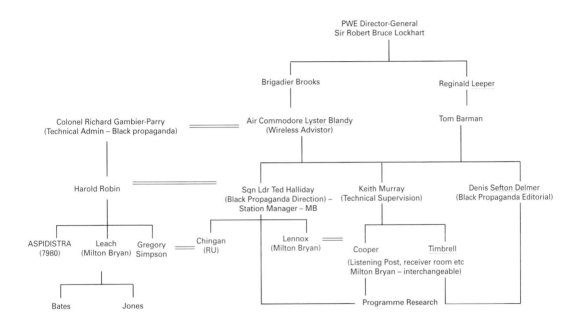

Leaflets were a critical part of the plan. It was an industrial operation printing leaflets at a scale required for occupied Europe and undertaken before D-Day by the civilian agencies. The techniques and methods for leaflet printing and distribution changed considerably up until 1944, and again after D-Day once the Allies had a foothold in France. It has been estimated that during the pre-D-Day period 2,750,000,000 leaflets were printed and distributed (2,151,000,000 by the RAF and 599,000,000 by the 8th Air Force). The US 8th Air Force began leaflet operations to support the RAF missions from August 1943.

Cheddington Airfield, near Leighton Buzzard, was assigned the name Station 113, after it was transferred to USAAF control in August 1943. It had a number of squadrons assigned to the airfield and had two primary missions before D-Day, the development of a number of leaflet drop operations, and RADAR/communications jamming operations to support the Neptune invasion force. One such squadron was the 406th Bomb Squadron of the USAAF which was regarded as a 'Night Leaflet

Nr. 51. Dienstag, 6. Juni 1944

NACHRICHTEN FÜR DIE TRUPPE

Atlantikwall an mehreren Stellen durchbrochen

Panzer tief ins Innere eingedrungen: harte Kämpfe gegen Fallschirmjäger

Nach letzten Meldungen ist der Atlantikwall an mehreren Stellen durchbrochen, nachdem anglo-amerikanische Panzerverbände heute früh, zwei Stunden nach Tagesanbruch, von der See her an der Kanalküste in Frankreich gelandet sind.

Heftige Kämpfe werden von der Seinemündung und der Normandie gemeldet.

Schon gestern abend waren starke Fallschirmjäger-Verbände und Luftlandetruppen mit eigener Artillerie und leichten Panzern, denen es gelang, einige Flugplätze der Luftwaffe überraschend zu besetzen, hinter dem Atlantikwall abgesetzt worden. An mehreren Stellen haben sie sich mit den Panzerverbänden vereinigt, die von der Küste aus vorstossen.

Vom Meer, aus der Luft und von der Landseite werden die Verteidiger in den Bunkern des Atlantikwalls angegriffen.

Schwere Schiffsartillerie englischer und amerikanischer Schlachtschiffe und Kreuzer decken die Stellungen ein. Auch die Hafenanlagen an der Küste werden beschossen. Als erste Hafenstadt kam Le Havre unter Feuer.

Im Hoch- und Tiefangriff werden die Befestigungsanlagen und Truppenbereitstellungen von der Normandie bis über Calais hinaus durch unübersehbare Bomberverbände angegriffen, die nach allen Seiten durch Jäger abgeschirmt sind. Gegen diese erdrückende Luftüberlegenheit sind die wenigen Jäger und Schlachtflugzeuge der Luftwaffe machtlos.

Im Rücken haben Fallschirmjäger und Luftlandetruppen die Verbindung mit den französischen Widerstandsgruppen aufgenommen.

Für die deutsche Führung ist die Lage noch unübersichtlich, da jede Luftaufklärung angesichts der erdrückenden Luftüberlegenheit der Anglo-Amerikaner unmöglich ist. Auch die Befehlsübermittlung nach verschiedenen Küstenabschnitten ist gestört.

Am gesamten Atlantikwall und im gesamten Befehlsbereich wurde gestern abend kurz vor Mitternacht Alarmstufe 3 gegeben, als die ersten Luftlandungen gemeldet wurden.

Die eigentliche Invasion begann aber erst nach Tagesanbruch.

Lange Reihen von Sturmbooten und Panzerlandeschiffen, geleitet von einer Unzahl von Zerstörern, Kanonenbooten und Geleitschiffen aller Art, näherten sich hinter einer Nebelwand unter dem Deckungsfeuer von Schlachtschiffen und Kreuzern der Küste.

Deutsche Schnellboote aus Cherbourg, Le Havre und Ymuiden wurden in heldenhafter Aufopferung gegen die alliierte Übermacht eingesetzt.

WAS BEREIT STEHT

5000 km Atlantikwall, vom Nordkap bis Bayonne, werden von 60 deutschen Divisionen gehalten.

Das sind 3/4 Millionen Mann, die über den ganzen besetzten Westen zerstreut sind, um gegen Angriffe aus verschiedenen Richtungen eingesetzt werden zu können.

Durchschnittlich 18 Flugzeuge kommen auf je eine deutsche Division im Westen. (Im Frankreichfeldzug hatten die deutschen Truppen noch je 80 Flugzeuge pro Division.) 160 Flugzeuge auf jede Division hatten die Anglo-Amerikaner jetzt vor Rom.

Im Westen rechnet man mit einer anglo-amerikanischen Luftüberlegenheit von 12:1.

Die Hauptlast der Abwehr zur See tragen die U-Boote. Sonst werden Nordsee, Kanal und Atlantik von rund 60 deutschen S-Booten, etwa ebensovielen Räumbooten und einigen Vorpostenboot-Flottillen verteidigt. Kein grösseres deutsches Kriegsschiff liegt westlich Kiel.

Italien-Rückzug in 2 Teile gespalten

Noch nie haben deutsche Soldaten das durchmachen müssen, was die Soldaten der Armee Kesselring heute auf ihrem Rückzug von Rom erleben.

Tausende von anglo-amerikanischen Bombern, Jägern und Schlachtflugzeugen stossen unablässig auf die einander gerissenen Kampfgruppen der Italien-Armee herab, decken sie mit ihren Bombenteppichen ein und beschiessen, was ihnen vor die Rohre kommt.

Zu Hunderten liegen die brennenden, zerschossenen und gebombten LKWs auf den Strassen. Dicht aufgefahrene Kolonnen, selbst 100 und mehr Kilometer hinter dem Kampfgebiet, werden von Raketen feuernden Jägern in Brand geschossen. Das flache Gelände der römischen Campagna bietet keine Deckung.

Der Zusammenbruch vor Rom hat die deutsche italienische Armee in zwei Teile gespalten, die jetzt ohne Verbindung miteinander zurückfallen.

Reste von vier Divisionen — der 3. Panzer-Grenadier-, der 4. Fallschirmjäger-, der 65. und 334. Infanterie-Division — ziehen sich, so gut sie können, entlang der Küste zurück. Die Anglo-Amerikaner folgen ihnen mit Panzern und schnellen Truppen.

Hilfe nicht zu erwarten

Ostwärts Rom fluten die Reste von neun deutschen Divisionen in die Berge. Die Rückzug nach Norden ist ihnen schon verlegt. Auch auf sie stossen die anglo-amerikanischen Kampfflugzeuge unablässig nieder. Aus dem Hinterhalt werden sie von Fallschirmjägern angegriffen.

Aber weder hier noch an der Küste war es bisher möglich, die zersprengten Kampfgruppen wieder zu einer Abwehrlinie zusammenzufügen oder die zusammengebrochene Befehls-Übermittlung wiederherzustellen. Die einzelnen Verbände sind ganz auf sich selbst gestellt. Regimenter und Divisionen sind kunterbunt durcheinander gewürfelt.

Letzte Vorbereitungen zur Sowjet-Offensive

Starke Truppen- und Material-Zusammenziehungen der Sowjets werden laufend von den Aufklärern an der Ostfront gemeldet und lassen darauf schliessen, dass die Sowjets die Vorbereitungen für ihre Sommer-Grossoffensive beschleunigen.

Auch deutscherseits werden die Vorbereitungen in Erwartung der Sowjetoffensive mit allen Kräften fortgeführt.

Besonders am Karpathenwall werden immer wieder OT-Einheiten und Bau-Bataillone bei der Anlage von Befestigungswerken eingesetzt.

Kampfhandlungen werden nur vom Raum nordwestlich Jassy in Rumänien gemeldet, wo deutsch-rumänische Truppen neue Vorstösse gegen die sowjetischen Stellungen unternahmen.

Zeitzler besichtigt Ostfront

Auf einer Besichtigungsreise an der Ostfront befindet sich zur Zeit der Chef des Generalstabes des Heeres, Generaloberst Zeitzler.

Zu den Einheiten, die Generaloberst Zeitzler im Osten besichtigt, gehören auch Verbände, die in letzter Zeit aus dem Bereich des OB-West an die Ostfront abkommandiert wurden, wie die SS-Panzer-Divisionen „Hohenstaufen" und „Frundsberg" und die 349. Infanterie-Division.

Squadron' and very much a covert arm of the US 8th Airforce. They operated the B-17 Flying Fortress and B-24 Liberator bombers for the task.

In the early hours of D-Day, the 406th dropped thousands of leaflets warning French civilians of the bombings to come. Different variants of leaflets were designed

Front page of Issue 51 of *Nachrichten für die Truppe*, dropped on German positions in Normandy on D-Day (© Lee Richards, www. psywar.org)

NACHRICHTEN FÜR DIE TRUPPE 6. JUNI 1944

Jäger werden nach Osten verlegt

6. Tag der Bomben-Pause

Die Bombenpause im Reichsgebiet dauerte auch gestern, am 6. Tage, an. Bei Nacht wurde lediglich die Stadt Köln von anglo-amerikanischen Schnellbombern angegriffen.

Mit starken Bomberverbänden mit Jägergeleit setzten die Alliierten bei Tag und bei Nacht die Offensive gegen deutsche Stellungen, Flugplätze, Ortungsstationen und Verbindungswege im Westen fort.

In den Morgenstunden wurden vor allem die Stellungen im Raum von Boulogne und Calais, sowie der Flugplatz Le Crotoy von Hunderten von Kampfflugzeugen mit Bomben belegt, nachdem die gleichen Ziele bereits in der vergangenen Nacht von starken Verbänden angegriffen wurden.

Die Angriffe der viermotorigen USA-Bomber nahmen dann in den Nachmittagsstunden zu. Jagdbomber auf, die Eisenbahnziele in Nordfrankreich und Belgien angriffen, vor allem bei Conflans, Tisors, Mezieres und Beauvais.

Wieder bekämpften Zerstörer-Flugzeuge auch deutsche Flakbatterien hinter dem Atlantikwall. Zahlreiche Angehörige der Flakbedienungen fielen den Tiefangriffen zum Opfer.

Dr. Goebbels und die Geigerin

Eine kostbare Stradivarius Geige hat Reichsminister Dr. Goebbels durch eine japanische Geigerin Nejiko Suwa zum Geschenk gemacht.

Die charmante junge Japanerin, die sich mit ihrer Kunst in das Herz des Reichspropagandaministers gespielt hat, gab mit der neuen Stradivarius einen Violinabend in Mozartsaal des Wiener Konzerthauses.

Reichsminister Dr. Goebbels, der dem Konzert nicht beiwohnen konnte, hatte die Ausschmückung des Künstlerzimmers mit Frühlingsblumen in den Lieblingsfarben der japanischen Künstlerin veranlasst.

Handel mit Nerventröster verboten

Der Handel mit „genanntem Mischtabak aus dem Balkan, den bulgarische und griechische Arbeiter ins Reich bringen, soll verboten werden.

Dieser Mischtabak besteht keineswegs bloss aus mazedonischen Tabaksorten, sondern auch aus Beimischungen von Hanf- und Stechapfelblättern, die dem Raucher ausser einem besonderen Genuss eine starke Nervenberuhigung vermitteln.

Die Preisüberwachungsstelle hat festgestellt, dass Tausende deutsche Rüstungsarbeiter, die auf den Geschmack dieses neuen Trösters gekommen sind, bedeutende Überpreise dafür zahlen, obwohl man Hanf- und Stechapfel in jedem Garten Deutschlands ziehen kann.

Fritz Sauckel:
Seine Stellung ist erschüttert

Sauckels Mitarbeiter abgesetzt

Die scharfe Kritik, die seit einiger Zeit an der Amtsführung des Generalbevollmächtigen für den Arbeitseinsatz, Gauleiter Sauckel, von Kreisen im Ministerium Speer geübt wird, hat jetzt zur Entlassung des ersten Mitarbeiters von Gauleiter Sauckel geführt.

Gauleiter ehrenhalber SS-Gruppenführer Prof. Rudolf Jung hat seinen Posten als Leiter der Reichsinspektion der Arbeitseinsatzverwaltung aufgeben müssen und hat den Posten als Vorsitzender und Geschäftsführer der Sparkasse Prag angetreten.

Professor Jung hat auch seine Villa in der Lessingstrasse 6 in Erfurt geräumt und sich im Protektorat niedergelassen.

Hauptwortführer der Sauckel-Gegner im Ministerium Speer ist Reichsarbeitsminister Ingenieur Gotthard Friedrich.

Nach Ansicht von Pg. Friedrich hat Gauleiter Sauckels unsystematische Massenmobilisierung von Frauen und Fremdarbeitern, statt zu einem Anstieg zu einem Absinken der europäischen Rüstungsproduktion geführt.

OKL erklärt: USA-Bomber in Russland sind keine neue Gefahr

Die Parteistellen in den Ostgauen sind angewiesen worden, beruhigend auf die Bevölkerung einzuwirken und zu erklären, dass die Landung der amerikanischen Luftflotte in Sowjet-Russland keine neue Gefahr vor Angriffen für die bisher bombensicheren Ostgebiete schaffen wird.

In einer amtlichen Erklärung heisst es:

„Die Zwischenlandung von USA-Flugzeugen, die aus dem südtalienischen Raum gestartet waren, auf sowjet-russischem Territorium hat im OKL keinerlei Aufsehen erregen können, da mit diesen Möglichkeiten seit geraumer Zeit gerechnet wurde.

Das vom Feind dabei verfolgte Ziel, die bisher bombensicheren Ostgaue des Reiches anzugreifen, ist mit derartigen Schwierigkeiten

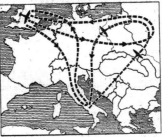

Dies sind die Flugstrecken, die die anglo-amerikanischen Bomber jetzt im Pendelverkehr benutzen können, um das Reich und die besetzten Gebiete zu bombardieren, nachdem in Russland von den Amerikanern Flugzeugstützpunkte geschaffen wurden.

verbunden, dass man kaum von mehr als Prestigeflügen sprechen kann und die Rückwirkung auf die deutsche Luftabwehr in keiner Weise zu erwarten."

Soweit die amtliche Erklärung.

Inzwischen haben mehrere Jagdgruppen im Westen Befehl erhalten sich fertig zu machen für die Verlegung nach dem Osten bezw. Südosten. Im OKL dauern die Beratungen an.

Neue Tarnungsmassnahme

Der Angreifer kann nämlich:
- ein viel grösseres Gebiet als bisher bestreichen
- aber hat er die Wahl zwischen drei verschiedenen Abflugzonen, entweder nach Gross-Britannien, Italien oder nach Russland zurück, während
- die Bomber aus dem Westen und dem Süden ihrerseits nach Russland weiterfliegen können.

Inzwischen haben die deutschen Flugzeugwerke, Treibstoffbetriebe, und Rüstungsbetriebe, die aus den bisher gefährdeten Teilen des Reichs in die bisher bombenfreien Ostgaue verlagert worden waren, neue Tarnungsvorschriften erhalten. In allen diesen Werken werden Luftschutzvollübungen stattfinden.

Wegen der neuen Bombengefahr aus dem Osten, haben die Kokereien in Oberschlesien jetzt Nacht keinen Koks mehr zu löschen, weil der Feuerschein der geöffneten Koksöfen den Fliegern als Wegweiser dienen könnte.

DIE LETZTEN 21 TAGE

17. Mai: Anglo-amerikanische, französische und polnische Truppen vergrössern den Einbruch zu beiden Seiten des Liri-Flusses.

18. Mai: Cassino in Italien von den Anglo-Amerikanern genommen.

19. Mai: 2000 anglo-amerikanische Kampfflugzeuge bomben Berlin und Braunschweig zweimal bei Tage.

20. Mai: 5000 anglo-amerikanische Bomber und Zerstörer greifen Eisenbahnanlagen und das Nachschub-System der Wehrmacht in Frankreich und Belgien an.

23. Mai: Anglo-Amerikaner beginnen am Landekopf von Nettuno neuen Grossangriff. Im OKW wird die Gesamtlage in Italien als zufriedenstellend bezeichnet.

24. Mai: Via Appia und die Eisenbahnlinie nach Rom von Anglo-Amerikanern durchschnitten.—Schwerer Tagesangriff auf Berlin.

25. Mai: Die anglo-amerikanischen Streitkräfte im Landekopf von Nettuno vereinigen sich mit den aus dem Süden vorstossenden Armeen.

28. Mai: Reichsminister Speer erklärt in einem Berliner Rüstungsbetrieb, dass vierzehn Zweige der deutschen Flugzeugindustrie zur Sicherstellung der Produktion nach dem Osten verlegt sind.

29. Mai: Grossbrände nach Luftangriffen in 10 Gauen des Reichs, von Pommern bis in die Donau-Alpengaue.

30. Mai: Seit Beginn der anglo-amerikanischen Offensive in Italien am 11. Mai hat die Armee Kesselring 15000 Mann an Gefangenen verloren.

1. Juni: Anglo-Amerikaner brechen in deutsche Riegelstellungen in den Albaner Bergen ein. Kriegsschiffe beschiessen den Vorfeld von Rom.

2. Juni: USA-Bomber landen auf eigenen Flugplätzen in Russland.

3. Juni: Anglo-Amerikaner nur noch 15 km. von Rom entfernt.

4. Juni: Die Anglo-Amerikaner ziehen in Rom ein. OKL erklärt: USA-Bomber in Russland sind keine neue Gefahr.

Zigaretten teurer

Die offiziellen Preise für Tabakwaren in Frankreich sind erhöht worden. „Tabac gris" kostet jetzt 14.— statt wie bisher 6.- Francs pro Paket und die „Gauloises bleues" jetzt 12, statt wie bisher 9- Francs.

Gotterdämmerung im Bier-Saal

Der Münchener Löwenbräukeller wird jetzt als Konzertsaal von den Münchener Philharmonikern benutzt, nachdem die Tonhalle und der Odeonsaal den anglo-amerikanischen Bomben zum Opfer gefallen sind.

An der Stelle, an der der Führer einst mit Hitler die erste nationalsozialistische Revolution einleitete, wird Wilhelm Furtwängler demnächst als Gast das Vorspiel zur „Gotterdämmerung" dirigieren.

Sportmeldungen

Um Goldene Räder

Das „Grosse Goldene Rad" über 50 km und das „Kleine Goldene Rad" über 30 km gewann der Kölner Jean Schorn. Die 30 km legte er in 25 Min. 41 Sekunden zurück und schlug den Luxemburger Kraus und den deutschen Meister Bautz.

Über 50 km siegte Schorn in 43 Min. 38,2 Sek. vor Scheller Bautz, Zerner und Kraus.

Walther Lehmann, Bochum holte sich das „Goldene Rad von Nürnberg" auf der Bahn im Reichelsdorfer Keller Lohmann schlug vor fast 10.000 Zuschauern Kilian und Lorenz. Vopen und Didier schieden vorzeitig aus.

Eine 229 km lange vierte Etappe beendete die belgische Radrundfahrt. Gesamtsieger ist Moerenhout mit 19 Stunden 40 Min. 51 Sekunden vor Sommers und Grysolle.

ihren alljährlichen Reichswettkampf führte die HJ durch, wobei es manche ansprechende Leistung gab sowohl im Dreikampf der Pimpfe und Jungmädel im 75 m-Lauf, Weitsprung und Schleuderballwurf, als auch bei den älteren Jungen und Mädchen im 100 m-Lauf, Weitsprung.

Deutschlands Kanumeister Hans Seiling, Brandenburg, wurde in Wien im Kajakeiner nur dritter hinter Unteroffizier Klepp und Leser.

Die Wasserkampfspiele der HJ wurden für den 17.-23. August ausgeschrieben. Sie umfassen Rudern, Kanusport und Segeln.

Der Staffellauf „Rund um Deutschland" wird am 10. Juni zum 20. mal veranstaltet.

Viermal siegte der deutsche Strassenmeister Harry Saager bei den Aschenbahnrennen in Spandau. Er holte sich das Hauptfahren, das Punktefahren und gewann das Fahren über 43,4 Sekunden auch die Zeitfahren.

Schliesslich gewann Saager mit Augsburg das Mannschaftsfahren über 50 km in 1 Stunde 19 min. 28 Sekunden.

---

according to the stage of the Overlord offensive. By the middle of 1944 around 80 per cent of the total British rotogravure printing capacity was being utilised for the propaganda effort, all coordinated by PWD/SHAEF. During the initial phase from 6 June–27 July, the leaflets conveyed the unmatchable weight of Allied armour and

Whitley Bomber dropping leaflets – 'Nickelling' sorties (© IWM London Photographic Archives ref C826)

weaponry and the weak German defences on the coastline of Normandy.

As Overlord ran its course, the use of propaganda leaflets became intricately intertwined with mainstream military operations. From D-Day onwards, some Army Groups and attached psychological warfare units operating in Normandy produced their own localised leaflets, but the Allies still heavily relied on the PWD/SHAEF leaflet production line and distribution from aircraft operating from the UK. PWD was to supply the bulk of the leaflets after D-Day, with advice being forthcoming from the civilian agencies.

A special section of psychological warfare was established within SHAEF to coordinate this activity with the other HQ staff sections. Within this small unit a Leaflet Section was created to oversee all leaflet production. It had its own editorial/writing team, packing, a transportation department and the ability to control a bomber squadron (known affectionately as the Special Leaflet Squadron) to distribute the final leaflets.

Major Robert Garey from 8th Air Force HQ and Frederick Payne from the PWE took the printing requirements to the various firms involved and ordered the plants to be sealed secure in the critical days before D-Day. Security was paramount. The Allied propaganda leaflets for the Overlord campaign all had a ZF prefix, and a total of twelve designs were used:

No.	Leaflet title	No. of Pages	Size	Producer
ZF.1	Les Armées Alliées Débarquent (Eisenhower proclamation)	2	21.5 x 26.5 cm	PWD/SHAEF
ZF.2	French transport workers	2		PWD/SHAEF
ZF.3	Proclamation. Citoyens Français (Eisenhower proclamation)	2	20.5 x 25 cm	PWD/SHAEF
ZF.4	Message Urgent du Commandement Suprême des Forces Expéditionnaires Alliées... (Warning message)	2	21.5 x 13.5 cm	PWD/SHAEF
ZF.5	Discours du General de Gaulle le 6 Juin 1944 (De Gaulle's statement)	2	20.5 x 25 cm	PWD/SHAEF
ZF.6	Message to people of Cherbourg	2		PWD/SHAEF
ZF.7	Transport workers leaflet	2		PWD/SHAEF
ZF.8	14 July 1944	2		PWD/SHAEF
ZF.9	Eisenhower declaration	2		PWD/SHAEF
ZF.10	People of combat zones	2		PWD/SHAEF
ZF.11	Aux habitants d'Alsace, de Lorraine et du Grand Duché de Luxembourg (To the people of Luxembourg)	2	21.5 x 26.5 cm	PWD/SHAEF
ZF.12	Français! Partiotes! (Forces, patriots)	2	13.5 x 21.5 cm	PWD/SHAEF

The leaflet carrying the Eisenhower proclamation (ZF.1) had a print run totalling 320,000 copies, which were placed in eight bombs for distribution in the afternoon of 6 June 1944 on the areas of France being bombed by the Allies.

ZF.4 was a generic warning leaflet, printed in French by the printers Odhams, Samuel Stephens and Waterlows. The translation of the French text read 'Urgent message from the Supreme Commander of the Allied Expeditionary Forces to the inhabitants of this town…. To win the battle against our common enemy, the Allied air forces will attack transportation centres and facilities of communication vital to the enemy … it is essential that you send your family and remove yourselves at once for some days out of the danger zone in which you live…. Keep off the highways; disperse in the open country. Start now. You have not a minute to lose.' The leaflet was dropped on 6 June 1944 on sixteen towns and villages in Normandy by the B-17 bombers of the 422nd Special Leaflet Squadron all painted in black. They were to be the first Allied bombers over France on D-Day.

PWE used commercial printers due to the volume and speed of turnaround that they were able to achieve. Their first print run totalled 9.6 million copies, to be followed by a second print run of 10 million, which were delivered to the depot on 4 and 5 June. To maintain secrecy at the printers, all the staff were locked inside the plant for five days.

ZF.2 was another warning leaflet about French transport, dropped in vast numbers on 6 June 1944. The leaflets were printed at three different firms – Odhams in Watford, Waterlows in Dunstable and Samuel Stephens. Around 1.6 million copies of ZF.2 were printed and dropped over eighteen villages in Normandy.

The *Nachrichten* operations began a month before D-Day and were coordinated by the PWD and a combined PID/OSS editorial team, all based in the pre-fabricated huts at the Milton Bryan facility. The two-sided, and later four-sided, newspaper was initially printed at the Marylands print facility near Woburn in a production run of 100,000 partitioned into ten leaflet bombs. It would provide a detailed and up-to-date account of events on the German home front and over the course of its production developed a reputation for reliability in its news. A continual narrative the editorial team repeated during the Normandy offensive in *Nachrichten* was that the German High Command only cared about the Russian front.

By D-Day one million copies of *Nachrichten für die Truppe* were being produced a day, packed into one hundred leaflet bombs. These were printed at the Luton News printers, Home Counties, on Alma Street, Luton alongside their regular printing of six local newspapers. It was a seven-day a week operation which had outgrown the facilities at Marylands. The workers at the printers arrived on D-Day at nd over the course of their shift they were to print-off the whole D-Day story by 1000hrs the same day which would make the content for the newspaper.

After D-Day other newspapers began to be printed. From August 1944 *Frontpost*, a white propaganda and semi-tactical newspaper started to be produced in France by the 12th Army Group every week. It, too, was distributed by aircraft.

Alongside the newspapers, the bombs were often filled with forged ration books and leave passes – which were often signed off with a forged signature of the officer responsible for the particular region where the drop was taking place. The demands on the paper industry in Britain at this stage of the war were acute. The propaganda printing effort would require in the region of 3,500 tonnes of paper to meet the demand for Overlord.

After the print-run was complete, the bundles were driven 2 miles down the road to Gibbs and Bamforth at Leagrave, where they were cut and packed, ready to be driven to the airfield by 1700hrs It was overseen by the PWD Leaflet Section who had a specialist military unit of over eighty men and twenty-five trucks for the leaflet distribution around the country to the various airfields. This was always coordinated by telephone and with the use of codewords for the date and time that the aircraft would depart from the airfield.

The following squadrons were at Cheddington airfield:

850th Bombardment Sqn: 11–27 May 1944 (B-24 Liberator)

858th Bombardment Sqn: 19 June–10 August 1944 (B-24 Liberator)

406th Bombardment Sqn: 5 August 1944–16 March 1945 (B-24 Liberator)

36th Bombardment Sqn: 15 August 1944–28 February 1945 (Boeing B-17 Flying Fortress, B-24 Liberator)

The PWD/SHAEF had its own dedicated Special Leaflet Squadron assigned to 8th Air Force, which could fly ten aircraft a night for the various operational tasks. This enabled the PWD to get leaflets to areas in France and the rest of occupied Europe at a time when it was deemed most critical to a military operation.

On D-Day itself, one million copies of Issue 51 of *Nachrichten für die Truppe* were dropped from eighty bombs over German troop positions in northern France by the 422nd Bomber Squadron. The publication covered a breach of the impregnable Atlantic Wall and detailed the ferocious battles involving armour and airborne troops.

The bulk distribution of thousands of propaganda leaflets was an onerous task. In the early stages of the war this was done by hand, through the flare chutes. The 8th USAAF distributed all their leaflets using a canister called the T-1 Leaflet Bomb or referred to affectionately as the Monroe bomb, as it was developed by a USAAF Captain James Monroe. This cylindrical paper container measured just 60 inches long and 18 inches in diameter, but it could contain as many as 80,000 leaflets. Ten of these Monroe bombs were fitted to each aircraft in a leaflet drop operation. Up to twelve bombs could be fitted in the adapted bomb bay of a B-24 aircraft of the PWD/SHAEF Special Leaflet Squadron.

The containers were fitted with a British 860A barometric fuse – which functioned at 2,000 ft in activating a primer cord which blew the container apart and caused a wide dispersal of the leaflets. The RAF initially resisted the use of the Monroe bomb, as the Commander-in-Chief of Bomber Command, Air Vice-Marshal Arthur 'Bomber' Harris did not want to reduce the bomb payload in the aircraft for distributing propaganda and they were not introduced into the RAF aircraft until later in 1944. The RAF Operational Training Units did distribute leaflets over France using small bomb containers, which were normally used for dropping incendiaries. If an aircraft was carrying a bomb load, it was common for the crews to distribute propaganda leaflets in spare spaces in the bomb bay. In that way leaflets were dropped when the bay doors were opened approaching the objective.

The use of these Monroe bombs simplified the distribution and avoided the previous wide distribution of leaflets over a huge area. At that time, leaflets were dropped at altitudes of around 20,000 ft where the B-24 and B-17 bombers normally operated. Leaflets dropped in northern France at this altitude were sometimes found as far afield as Italy.

The scale of leaflet production and dissemination for Overlord was staggering. In March 1944 it has been estimated that around 320,000,000 leaflets were printed, of which 265,000,000 were distributed by the RAF and USAAF. Over 90 per cent of all the leaflets air-dropped on occupied Europe were printed and designed in Britain and dispersed by bombers flying out of British airfields. It is extremely difficult to gauge the effect the Allied propaganda campaign had on Overlord. But various Leaflet Reaction reports produced by the 12th Army Group suggested the leaflet campaign in northern France had had a huge impact on the outcome of Overlord. 'It is impossible to determine the exact effectiveness of airdrops, but it is a fact that over 80% of all prisoners we have netted on the Brest Peninsula have come in with leaflets in their possession … when the final count came in for Le Havre, it showed 11,302 prisoners out of a 12,000 garrison. Analysis shows that over 75% had leaflets on them.'

But it was not just leaflets and newspapers that were utilised for propaganda purposes during Overlord. The BBC was to broadcast two special programmes announcing the invasion of Europe and scripting the Eisenhower proclamation. The PWE radio stations, *Soldatensender Calais* and *Atlantiksender*, had numerous propaganda themes for D-Day, including that the OKW plan for the Normandy defences was the deliberate sacrifice of the Coastal Division, and that there would be no reinforcements to bolster the Normandy forces. They also played on the inferior *Luftwaffe* strength in northern France and that the situation on the other European fronts was worsening. It was intended to demoralise an already shaken German military.

There were also small specialist teams with loudspeakers which had been formed weeks before D-Day itself. The 13th Amplifier Unit (AU) was mobilised on 14 April

1944, alongside four other specialist Amplifier Units, which were to work alongside the specialist Leaflet Units. Their objective was to provide mobile loudspeaker support to psychological war and civil affairs activities for Overlord. 13AU landed in France on 10 June 1944. A few days after landing, the unit was involved in supporting an infantry unit in the American 79th Division who requested the loudspeakers to broadcast to a German artillery unit dug in a wood. They were to broadcast the following brief message in German: 'Your position is hopeless. If you come over to us you, will be treated as honourable prisoners of war. If you insist on fighting this out, you will sacrifice your lives in vain. It is for you to decide whether you desire to see the Fatherland again or to be buried here in France. You have ten minutes in which to decide. Should you decide to come over, you will approach this van with your hands on your head and showing a white emblem.'

A few minutes later, 600 German soldiers emerged from their defensive positions and surrendered to the American officers. They were then marched off to the nearest CSDIC prisoner of war processing centre.

The PWE radio broadcasts and *Nachrichten* newspapers convinced many layers of German intelligence that the Allies had informers and spy networks from the German High Command downwards, which would tie up scarce resources in the Gestapo.

Graphic showing the reach of Aspidistra

Northern Zone – reached by BBC short-wave (SW) or ASPIDISTRA medium-wave (MW)

Southern Zone – reached by BBC short-wave (SW) only

USAAF personnel
packing PWD/
SHAEF leaflets
(© US Office of
War Information
– provided by Lee
Richards www.
psywar.org)

USAAF personnel
packing PWD/
SHAEF leaflets
(© US Office of
War Information
– provided by Lee
Richards www.
psywar.org)

Monroe bomb drop (© US Office of War Information – provided by Lee Richards www.psywar.org)

PWE Intelligence Directorate structure 1943

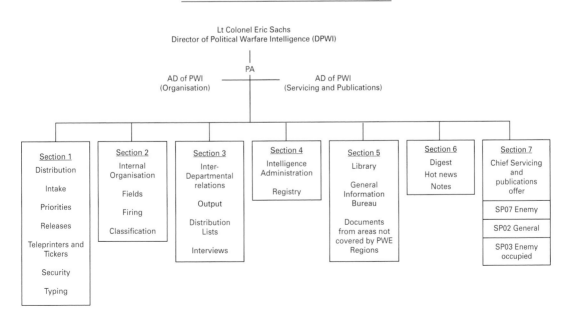

Lt Colonel Eric Sachs
Director of Political Warfare Intelligence (DPWI)

PA

AD of PWI (Organisation) — AD of PWI (Servicing and Publications)

Section 1	Section 2	Section 3	Section 4	Section 5	Section 6	Section 7
Distribution	Internal Organisation	Inter-Departmental relations	Intelligence Administration	Library	Digest Hot news Notes	Chief Servicing and publications offer
Intake	Fields	Output	Registry	General Information Bureau		SP07 Enemy
Priorities	Firing	Distribution Lists		Documents from areas not covered by PWE Regions		SP02 General
Releases	Classification	Interviews				SP03 Enemy occupied
Teleprinters and Tickers						
Security						
Typing						

The Aspidistra transmitter building at Crowborough during World War II (from © IWM Book 81-4080)

The Aspidistra transmitter control desk at Crowborough (from © IWM Book 81-4080)

The Aspidistra transmitter audio control console (from © IWM Book 81-4080)

CHAPTER FOURTEEN
DECEIT

*'The application of radio counter-measures immediately preceding the assault proved
to be extraordinarily successful ... these results may be summarised as follows; the
enemy did not obtain the early warning of our approach that his RADAR coverage
should have made possible; there is every reason to suppose that RADAR controlled
gunfire was interfered with; no fighter aircraft hindered our airborne operations; the
enemy was confused and his troop movements were delayed.'*

Sir Trafford Leigh Mallory, AEF Air Force Commander, official dispatch,
London Gazette, 2 January 1947

~~~

'... the truth is so precious that she always be attended by a bodyguard of lies'.

Winston Churchill at the Tehran Conference, November 1943

~~~

Deception is as old as war. It is also inextricably woven into the fabric of Intelligence
and is a critical component of the modern battlefield. Intelligence staff are ideally
placed to understand the enemy, their morale and mindset, and are critical to applying
deception techniques to enemy forces. Deception was intertwined with Overlord at
many different levels and was to play a significant role in its success. Dieppe had
taught Allied intelligence many lessons, and one area they needed to get right was
an effective and broad deception plan. The German intelligence services had almost
convinced themselves that any invasion of France would occur north of the River
Seine, most likely in the Pas-de-Calais region, with its proximity to Britain and deep
water ports like Boulogne and Calais. These would be critical to the logistical support
to an invasion force of this scale.

During the Allied landings on Sicily in 1943, deception operations were employed
successfully, and this was the model that the Allied planners on Overlord wanted to
repeat. Central to this plan would be the work to deceive the Germans of the pending
date and location of the Allied invasion.

When COSSAC (Chief of Staff to the Supreme Allied Commander) was created
in 1943 to oversee the planning for Overlord, it established its own deception
arm, referred to as the 'Committee for Special Means', often represented as 'Ops
B'. Underneath this committee was the London Controlling Section (LCS) and its

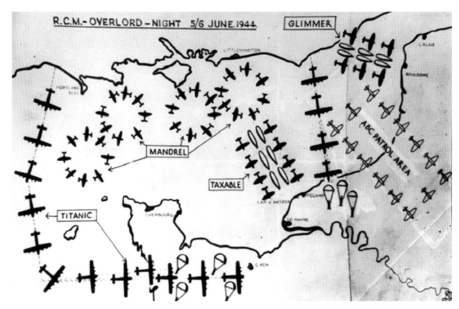

Graphic showing RADAR counter measure operations over northern France for Operation Overlord on the night of 5/6 June 1944 (DEFE 2/502)

American equivalent, the Joint Security Control (JSC), which would coordinate all deception activity across the military and civilian services.

The all-encompassing deception plan, Operation Bodyguard was born. The mosaic of deceit for D-Day would include creating false military units in southeast England with well-designed dummy rubber aircraft, landing craft and tanks, a sequence of air and sea operations to disrupt enemy RADAR, false lighting in key ports on the south coast, a barrage of wireless traffic and the creation of a network of double agents. It was a global project involving thousands of military and intelligence staff.

The plan was split into numerous operations, and the work covering the cross-Channel invasion would be known as Fortitude South. Colonel David Strangeways was one of the key architects of the plans, in his role at General Montgomery's Deception section. He worked with Major Roger Fleetwood-Hesketh, a SHAEF Intelligence officer was job it was to fuse deception ideas with military planning. Coordination of deception tasks between the intelligence agencies and military was organised through the London Controlling Section (LCS) under the command of Lieutenant Colonel Johnny Bevan. There were to be a number of areas of focus for the deception plan:

1. Wireless traffic
2. Lighting deception
3. Double agents

4. Controlled leaks of information
5. Physical deception – use of decoys and dummies
6. Planting high profile staff at areas in public eye

The deception measures developed by the LCS were appearing to be successful until April 1944 when the German military reinforcements, including three armoured Panzer tank divisions, moved into the Caen-Falaise region, which caused consternation in Allied intelligence. Further moves of infantry and armour occurred over the following weeks and it was suspected at the time that the Germans might be aware of Allied plans for Normandy. But the key decisions to retain the German 15th Army, with its fifteen Divisions, were left to the north of the Seine River.

A number of joint Navy and Royal Air Force deception operations were undertaken on the night of 5/6 June as a prelude to the Allied invasion and to further instil belief into the German forces that the attack would occur further up the coast. These operations all involved RADAR counter-measures and over a thousand aircraft were employed in these aerial bluffs. Allied bombers were also tasked with striking the ten most important batteries on the Normandy coastline, but this was merged with bombing operations further up the French coast, which was all part of the deceit.

Much of the Allied bombing campaign in the lead-up to D-Day aimed at targeting the German landlines, combined with similar operations undertaken by the French Resistance. This was orchestrated to disrupt the flow of German communications to and from Normandy, but it was also aimed to push the German military units onto the airwaves. The Allies could not intercept landline communications in occupied France, so this campaign aimed to push the military communications teams on to using their wireless sets, which could be subsequently intercepted.

It was not just the Allies that were getting in on the deception game. The German *Abwehr* had its own successful deception operation referred to affectionately as the *Englandspiel* or the 'English Game'. This was a counter-intelligence initiative by the Germans, using codes used by SOE agents who had been captured in the Netherlands to continue to get the Allies to provide information and supplies. It was to become the worst compromise for the SOE during the entire war.

195,000 tonnes of bombs were dropped by Allied aircraft between April and June 1944, two-thirds of which were outside the Normandy invasion area. For each aerial reconnaissance mission that was mounted by the RAF or USAAF over Normandy, at least two would be flown over the Pas-de-Calais region. It was all part of the deception plan under Bodyguard.

A complete phantom army was created under the command of Lieutenant General George Patton – fields were transformed into giant tank parks but filled with inflatable dummy tanks which would look real from the air. The bogus army was known as the First United States Army Group (FUSAG), comprising a number of real Army units – that were to be used later in the Normandy campaign – mixed with some dummy Army units. Communications around this fictitious army were broadcast as though it was a real structure so the Germans could intercept. The Germans appreciated the military guile and skills of Patton and refused to believe that the Allies would leave him out of any D-Day plans which helped to sell the ruse. Even after the Allied landings, the Germans continued to believe that Patton and this FUSAG would be part of the main invasion to target the Pas-de-Calais region, where the German Fifteenth Army was defending.

Sixteen Avro Lancasters from the infamous 'Dambusters' 617 Squadron were deployed as part of Operation Taxable to drop tonnes of chaff (or thin strips of aluminium foil) through their aircraft bomb chutes to disrupt the enemy RADAR. Taxable was to drop a chaff window from around 3,000 ft which would mimic a convoy covering an area of 14 by 16 miles off the coast between the French towns of Le Havre and Fécamp-d'Antifer. The flight choreography for this number of Lancasters needed meticulous planning and a high standard of precision flying. The leg to France was to take exactly two minutes and thirty seconds and the return leg two minutes and ten seconds, which was done to make sure the RADAR signature moved through the air at the correct speed of 7 knots.

Avro Lancaster B Mark I dropping 'Window' aluminium foil strips (© IWM London Photographic archives – reference CL1405)

John 'Dinger' Bell joined up aged eighteen, in 1941, as RAF aircrew and trained in Rhodesia as an observer, as being 6 ft 4 in tall he was deemed to be 'too long in the leg' for anything else! He was subsequently posted on to the Wellingtons in an Operational Training Unit (OTU) at RAF Cottesmore for three months' intensive training in navigation and bombing. In the observer role, he would be the bomb aimer. The squadron was commanded on the mission by Group Captain Leonard Cheshire.

Operation Taxable was complemented by a number of other deception operations on the same night, again employing similar techniques of RADAR counter-measures. Operation Mandrel took place on a wide expanse of coastline between Portland Bill and Littlehampton. Sixteen Stirling bombers from No. 199 Squadron and a number of B24 Liberators from the US Air Force undertook circular flights, setting up a RADAR jamming screen with Mandrel Early Warning (EW) jammers. These could effectively jam both the Freya and Würzburg RADARs on the French coast.

Another operation in play on the same night was Glimmer, which aimed to simulate an invasion fleet heading out from Kent in the direction of the Pas-de-Calais, towards the town of Boulogne. This involved six Royal Navy motor launches alongside six Stirling bombers from No. 218 Squadron who dropped chaff similar to the Taxable crews. Both Glimmer and Taxable were mounted about three hours before that of the actual assault on the Normandy beaches. Special wireless scripts were written to be used aboard these specialised Naval Harbour Defence Motor Launch (HDML) vessels. The Naval telegraphists aboard had rehearsed these scripts and made sure the transmissions, which were likely to be intercepted, were as convincing and as authentic as they could make them. They even broadcast samples of interference and static so certain call signs could not get through. Prior to deploying on the Taxable and Glimmer, the telegraphists had been made familiar with the TW12 and the Army type 22 transmitters, which they would use to broadcast the bogus radio transmissions. They had been briefed that they were producing spoof traffic and that the information was classified as 'Secret'.

Far out in the western Channel, the Allies also mounted Operation Titanic, a dummy parachute raid incorporating an assembled force totalling forty aircraft, including Stirling bombers, alongside Halifaxs and Hudson aircraft. Dummy parachutists were dropped near Dieppe and Caen.

John Bell's Lancaster, the Casey A, was affectionately adorned with some detailed World War II nose art – a picture of Thumper the rabbit from *Bambi*. After his training was completed by June 1943, he was posted to Woodhall Spa and on to his first operational squadron, 619 Squadron, a little over two years after he had signed up. Over the six months he was with 619 Squadron, he flew a number of Bomber

Command missions over Germany. By December 1943 Wing Commander Leonard Cheshire accepted that the whole of the squadron personnel be transferred across to 617 squadron billeted down the road. At the time they were not aware of the preparations for D-Day. Between January and April 1944 the squadron was tasked with bombing operations over France targeting munitions factories, aero-engine plants and other significant infrastructure targets. During the whole of May 1944 the squadron undertook detailed navigation exercises over the Humber estuary and into the North Sea. This was preparation for what was to come.

On the afternoon of 5 June 1944, the original date for D-Day, the squadron crews were called to a briefing room at Woodhall Spa to be told about Taxable. Unusually each Lancaster was to carry two crews, with twelve men in each plane. The Lancasters were to fly in two lines, with eight planes in each just 2 miles apart. They were to fly a series of loops at 3,000 ft and at a speed of just 180 miles an hour in the direction of Le Havre and fly for one minute and thirty seconds, before turning to port and running back to England. It was John Bell's role to drop the chaff from the bomb chute at the appropriate signal from the navigator. The chaff bundles were dropped at intervals of a few seconds, with the chaff decreasing in size from the French coast. It may have been just two hours of operational flying over the Channel, but it was to have a huge effect on the response of the German military defences in Normandy. Many of the shore batteries along this stretch of coast were taken by the deception and fired waves of artillery rounds into the approaching armada that did not exist.

One last deception plan, Operation Moonshine, was markedly different from the other combined RAF and Naval operations that night. This involved a small flotilla of twelve Royal Navy launches which were to work in synchrony with Operation Glimmer. The flotilla, with an accompanying group of four rescue launches, were to tow twenty-eight RADAR reflective barrage balloons, called 'Filberts' to just 10 miles off the French coast. Each balloon carried a transponder which could return and multiply a German RADAR pulse to resemble a large formation of planes or the equivalent RADAR return of a 10,000 ton ship. The balloons, which were tied to floats, also carried loudspeakers which played recordings simulating a vessel dropping its anchor. This was all done to deceive the enemy into thinking the invasion was beginning, and in fact it was, but many miles south on the coast of Normandy.

Alongside this aerial effort to deceive, months before D-Day British intelligence hatched a plan to order in huge quantities the Michelin Map 51 of the Pas-de-Calais area to further verify the ruse to German intelligence that Normandy was not the area of France in which the Allies were interested. They were ordered in significant numbers as far afield as Istanbul, Bern and Lisbon. When a bulk purchase of Map 51 was made by someone in Geneva, the Head of the *Fremde Heere West* (FHW) was informed.

For many months prior to D-Day, a network of double agents had been recruited and matured under the authority and direction of the Double Cross (XX) committee led by the University of Oxford don John Masterman. The Committee, which sat weekly at 58 St James's Street, London, included officers from MI5, MI6, the Directors for Intelligence at the Army, RAF and Navy, and Home Forces and Home Defence. The spies were an eclectic bunch of personalities and nationalities but they harboured a common goal, to deceive the Germans under the plans laid out under Operation Bodyguard. The network included the following agents:

- *Dušen 'Duško' Popov* (MI5 codename Tricycle or Skoot)
- *Lily Sergeyev* (MI5 codename Treasure)
- *Elvira de al Fuente Chaudoir* (MI5 codename Bronx or Cyril)
- *Roman Czerniawski* (MI5 codename Brutus, Armand or Walenty)
- *Juan Pujol García* (MI5 codename Garbo or Bovril).

Juan Pujol García, Agent Garbo and Araceli Gonzalez de Pujol, García's wife

The case officer for Brutus in Paris, Colonel Oscar Reile, had become an expert in understanding how the BBC was being used covertly to relay messages to the French Resistance and special forces troops on the ground in France. The day before D-Day, fourteen such messages were broadcast by the BBC, and Reile's work in interpreting these caused the 15th Army in the Calais region to raise its state of alert. Fortunately for the Allies, the 7th Army in Normandy ignored the messages.

Shortly before D-Day, Tricycle – or Dušen Popov – made a tour of Kent and the south coast to further the deception around the build-up of forces in southern England to attack the area around Calais. He produced a stream of reporting that the Allies were preparing a vast naval force but tried to draw the Germans off the scent by playing down the immediacy. The Allies were 'preparing and improving cook houses, wash houses, tented camps and landing grounds … in spite of intensive preparations there are no signs that invasion is imminent'.

In February 1944, Tricycle submitted a list of fictitious FUSAG units to one of his *Abwehr* handlers in Lisbon. He continued to furnish his contacts throughout the spring of 1944 with false data and FUSAG units operating on the south coast, preparing for the invasion of France.

The most significant of the double agents was the MI5-run Garbo, ironically a native Spaniard who was a former businessman and chicken farmer. Experiencing the Spanish Civil War first hand, he hated Nazism and Communism. As the war ran its course in Europe, he approached MI6 in Madrid but was not accepted and by 1941 he volunteered his services to the *Abwehr*, via a man called Wilhelm Leissner. After initial training he was deployed to London but he actually moved to Lisbon where he began sending a series of bogus intelligence reports about Britain. From 1942 Bletchley Park, through its associated RSS teams at Hanslope Park, had been intercepting signals carrying spurious intelligence on a Madrid to Berlin link from an *Abwehr* agent supposedly in Britain. Bletchley had been able to decrypt the *Abwehr* Enigma cipher from 1941 and read the messages. The intercept from Garbo was referring to a fictitious large convoy transiting from Liverpool to Malta, encouraging the German Navy to interdict it.

Eventually the signals were traced to a Lisbon-based operative. He was recruited and was smuggled out of Portugal, arriving in England in April 1942. He was put up by MI5 with his wife, Araceli Gonzalez de Pujol, and infant son in a house on Crespigny Road, north London. He was being run by a thirty-four-year-old MI5 case officer and half-Spanish artist called Tomas Harris. Between them they created a fictional network of up to twenty-seven agents, dotted around England and overseas, who were creating intelligence on military dispositions in the build-up to the invasion. Garbo was the only real agent amongst them. They were as imaginative as a Gibraltarian NAAFI waiter from Chislehurst (codename Chamillus), an ex-sailor from Swansea (Dagobert) to a Venezuelan student in Glasgow (Benedict). Garbo even convinced the *Abwehr* he had an agent operating in the Headquarters of the Supreme Allied Commander, South-East Asia (SACSEA) in Peradenyia, in what is now Sri Lanka.

Garbo had convinced the Germans to pay him the equivalent of £20,000 to finance his network, which was to produce a stream of intelligence on any entirely fictional army group. Pujol would take the Underground into central London every day to meet his handler, Harris, at their Jermyn Street offices to develop their sub-agent network and scripted messages that would be sent on to the *Abwehr*. The intelligence was low grade but it confirmed to the *Abwehr* and ultimately the German High Command that the invasion would come much further north, in the Pas-de-Calais.

By 1943, Garbo's wife Araceli was becoming tired of her life in England and her husband's work. She longed so much to return to Spain that she threatened to expose his work as an agent. She had even attempted suicide. Garbo and his MI5 handler concocted an elaborate hoax of its own to attempt to turn her around. They created a

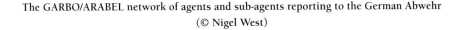

The GARBO/ARABEL network of agents and sub-agents reporting to the German Abwehr
(© Nigel West)

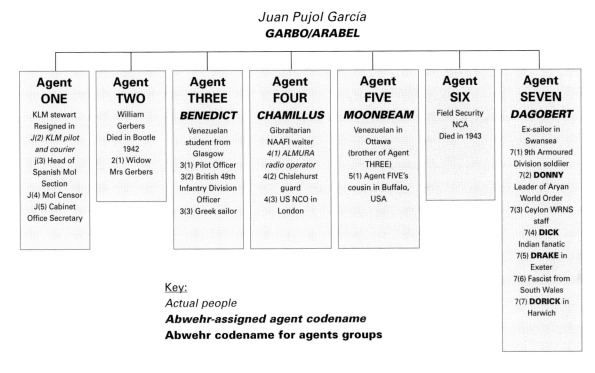

Juan Pujol García
GARBO/ARABEL

Agent ONE	Agent TWO	Agent THREE	Agent FOUR	Agent FIVE	Agent SIX	Agent SEVEN
		BENEDICT	***CHAMILLUS***	***MOONBEAM***		***DAGOBERT***
KLM stewart Resigned in *J(2) KLM pilot and courier* j(3) Head of Spanish MoI Section J(4) MoI Censor J(5) Cabinet Office Secretary	William Gerbers Died in Bootle 1942 2(1) Widow Mrs Gerbers	Venezuelan student from Glasgow 3(1) Pilot Officer 3(2) British 49th Infantry Division Officer 3(3) Greek sailor	Gibraltarian NAAFI waiter *4(1) ALMURA radio operator* 4(2) Chislehurst guard 4(3) US NCO in London	Venezuelan in Ottawa (brother of Agent THREE) 5(1) Agent FIVE's cousin in Buffalo, USA	Field Security NCA Died in 1943	Ex-sailor in Swansea 7(1) 9th Armoured Division soldiier 7(2) **DONNY** Leader of Aryan World Order 7(3) Ceylon WRNS staff 7(4) **DICK** Indian fanatic 7(5) **DRAKE** in Exeter 7(6) Fascist from South Wales 7(7) **DORICK** in Harwich

Key:
Actual people
Abwehr-assigned agent codename
Abwehr codename for agents groups

story around Garbo being arrested and subsequently imprisoned at Latchmere House (Camp 020) and brought her, blindfolded, to him. She was to sign a sworn statement that she would never tell the Germans her husband was been run as a double agent. Harris was later to write that 'the extraordinary ingenuity with which he has conceived and carried through this plan has perhaps saved a situation which might otherwise have been intolerable'.

Over the course of the next three years, Garbo and Harris were to inundate the German *Abwehr* with over 1,200 wireless reports and 315 letters which had been written in secret ink, with accompanying cover letters. Each of the letters averaged over 2,000 words. Over 500 of the wireless reports were transmitted between January 1944 and D-Day alone. Harris had concerns that the Germans may be suspicious when just one agent was producing such a quantity of intelligence.

These packages were transferred via a KLM airline courier using a diplomatic bag to *Abwehr* cover addresses in Portugal and Spain, through his controller 'Felipe'. Replies were picked up from a bank safe-deposit box in Lisbon. This was all overseen by MI6 on the ground in Lisbon. Later on in the war the network relied on radio and Morse transmissions using an *Abwehr*-supplied code and a left wing group of sympathisers who had a radio ham as a member.

Just three hours after the invasion commenced on D-Day, Garbo reporting to his handlers suggested that this was the first the *Abwehr* knew of the invasion, further solidifying his authenticity. On 9 June 1944, after a meeting that Garbo had with some of his sub-agent network, he decreed that the Normandy invasion as a deception for the real thing which was to take place in the Pas-de-Calais. The German High Command, and even Hitler himself, believed the reporting which led them to keep twelve German armoured divisions positioned for over 120 days around Calais.

Hitler's main intelligence officer, whom he trusted implicitly, was Colonel Alexis von Röenne, the Head of the *Fremde Heere West* (FHW), who was responsible for intelligence emanating from Britain. He was another anti-Nazi sympathiser and an acquaintance of Admiral Wilhelm Canaris, the head of the *Abwehr*. From 1943 he had continually overestimated and in cases deliberately inflated the order of battle for the Allies. According to aerial reconnaissance from the *Luftwaffe*, radio/signals intelligence and agent reporting it was estimated the Allies had around thirty-five divisions in Britain. Von Röenne took the number and doubled it. The inflated detail in his report to the High Command outlined eighty-nine divisions operating in Britain. It convinced Hitler that FUSAG existed. His reporting from the double-cross agents in Britain faithfully passed upwards to Hitler and his Generals helped feed the seeds of doubt that Normandy was the objective.

In all the deception planning that was undertaken before D-Day, at no point was GC&CS involved, but its role as the principal source of information on the extent to which the Bodyguard deception plans had been taken in by the Germans was vital. The Radio Security Service (RSS) and Bletchley had worked for years against the German *Abwehr* and knew in detail the information it received and to whom it was reported in the command chain. The Enigma collect from Hut 3 would show how the *Abwehr* had passed this material to the commands, reflecting the results and misguided interpretation.

The wider Y Service collection effort around Britain would also contribute in the understanding of how the deceit had embedded in the German military. The Enigma traffic from their counterparts, the German Y Service, helped the Allies appreciate how the information on the deception operations was being taken by senior officers.

The Allies had agreed to pioneer the idea of lighting deception to fool the Germans about the build-up of forces on the coast of England prior to D-Day. At a meeting of senior officers from COSSAC, the AEAF, 21st Army Group and the Air Ministry in January 1944 a plan was hatched to provide deceptive lighting at a number of major ports on the south coast of England. These included Portland, Southampton, Gosport and Falmouth. The 'object of deceptive lighting is to apportion the enemy over a long period to the presence of vehicles at hards at night … when the Expeditionary Force begins embarkation prior to D-Day, the illumination of ports and hards will not occur for the first time … deceptive lighting be operated periodically … coinciding with periods of wireless silence and large scale exercises, during the months of February, March and April'.

These so called 'hards' were concrete promontories that jutted out into the sea to allow for easier embarkation and disembarkation on to landing craft. It was the Air Ministry that would provide the resources to equip at least 50 per cent of all hards with deceptive lighting, potentially increasing to 75 per cent as the weeks moved on towards June 1944. To prevent these hards being attacked, especially if they were located near large towns, the lighting would be moved to a distance of 1½ miles from the location of the hards. It was decided that in the area between Deal and Ramsgate the deceptive lighting would be employed at, or in the immediate vicinity of, the hards.

Alongside this lighting deception, wireless radio traffic could be used as part of the Fortitude plans. The aim of radio deception was to persuade the German Y Service interception teams to draw conclusions from the Allied wireless traffic. It was critical that the wireless deception be worked in full knowledge of the Neptune operational activity.

The wireless deception operations were coordinated from the autumn of 1943 by the Signals Security Committee of COSSAC, which was subservient to the Combined Signals Board. It was this Committee that developed the schedules for periods of wireless silence, normal activity through to periods of intense wireless bursts to deceive the Germans of heightened military activity as a prelude to invasion. Pre-prepared and scripted military radio traffic was broadcast in the clear, which the Allies knew would be easily intercepted and read by the German intelligence teams in northern France. These signals would be complemented by Direction Finding (D/F) capabilities – getting geolocation fixes of the wireless transmissions in England. These scripts or stories were a fundamental part of the plan to deceive the enemy. If the story was not coherent or operationally sound, then the deception plan would be compromised. It was a difficult game to play.

The key to wireless deception operations was in the preparation of traffic. A huge amount of effort went into this for Neptune. There were various stages to this preparation:

a) Army and Navy Deception personnel meet.
b) An appropriate exercise area is chosen where the 'Navy' can in fact put the 'Army' ashore and the latter can deploy.

c) The Army gives an outline of the 'battle' it intends to fight (representative of the 'G' Staff is essential on the Army side). This eliminates the possibility of the traffic of the two Services presenting different stories; for example, if the Army intends to show troops landing on Green Beach with little opposition, it would be inappropriate for the Naval signals to report heavy losses on that beach.

d) The 'Loading Table' (a precise statement of the Army elements carried in each craft) is then worked out. The landing craft required to lift the troops and vehicles are then formed into convenient 'groups' and a 'Landing Table' worked out to ensure that these groups beach in accordance with the tactical requirements of the Army. COMPLETE AGREEMENT AND UNDERSTANDING BETWEEN THE TWO SERVICES ON THESE TABLES ARE ESSENTIAL if the bogus exercise is to appear real.

e) H Hour is fixed according to tides and to operational requirements such as the story it is desired to tell the enemy as to our choice of a real H Hour.

f) Navigational details (shoals, obstructions, etc) of the exercise area are noted for appropriate reference in the Naval signals.

g) A rough chart is drawn on a blackboard, showing agreed beach and Sector limits, waiting positions, swept channels, etc.

h) Signals are then written in the light of previous experience of actual amphibious exercises with details supplied. This is done for all waves – within one Assault Force alone there are about 15 of these, not including external waves. The correct codes are, of course, employed. In this connection the appropriate time lag between the time of origin and time of despatch must be made. It will take a signal longer to pass through the message handling organisation of an LCH, for example, than through that of an ML.

i) As the signal writing continues, tactical developments are added to the blackboard with the times of origin of the signals announcing them. For example, the Beach Signal Station on BAKER GREEN may inform the D/SOAG that LCTs are unable to kedge off. This will be noted, with time, on the board and, until that part of the beach is reported to be clear, groups should be diverted or warned.

j) After the assault, the Force is reformed into return groups and the exercise 'rounded off' with, if possible, 'berthing signals' being arranged on the appropriate Port Waves.

Much of the fake wireless transmissions were created by Mobile Wireless Deception Units which were placed under the ANCXF (Allied Naval Commander-in-Chief Expeditionary Force) orders during the planning and execution of the Fortitude plan.

Many of the telegraphists that were drafted into the deception units had come originally from the Assault Force resources. Without them, the deception plan supporting the Neptune invasion would never have been a success.

Fortitude was split into two operations. Fortitude North would concentrate on deception operations against Norway, and Fortitude South would focus on the Pas-de-Calais region of France. The earliest phase of the Neptune deception occurred through April–May 1944 as part of Fortitude North, in an attempt to induce the Germans to retaining a significant military presence in Norway, pulling away potential resources from defending France. The Allies created two fake Assault Forces (Forces V and W) using mock radio networks between associated command ships and vessels in the Clyde area, alongside an invented army contingent of 52nd and 55th Divisions. The scripts and schedules for the thousands of radio transmissions would work through a comprehensive story mimicking the assembly, training and deployment of a significant Assault Force. Much of this was broadcast in plain language or using low-grade cipher so the Allies would know the Germans could intercept and decipher the traffic.

Fortitude South was aimed at creating a diversionary effect for the German military in northern France, aiming at drawing their attention to an Allied assault on the Pas-de-Calais region rather than Normandy. It commenced before Neptune and was to persist after the Neptune assault on Normandy. A fictitious force (Force F) was created, operating in between Harwich and Yarmouth, and using scripted wireless transmissions it portrayed the build up of a significant assault force ready to head across the Channel from Kent.

The Naval wireless traffic for the two bogus forces (V and W) operating in the Clyde was produced by two of the Mobile Deception Units, which were aided by the transmitters from the Naval ships and from the aircraft deployed to the area. The mock operational traffic was designed to convey three main things:

1. A general increase in activity in the Clyde area.
2. The presence of three important units which were in some way distinct from other ships at Greenock, as shown by their appearance on separate frequencies of their own.
3. The occurrence of important movements and exercises, when the service traffic to and from these ships was materially increased.

Wireless silence was going to be critical in the hours before D-Day, and in order to emphasise the periods of wireless silence, a number of periods of intense wireless activity were to be observed by military formations and establishments. The periods of wireless silence were to occur on the following dates:

29–30 December
20–22 January
25–26 February
8–11 March
20 April
12–14 May
1–2 June
7–10 July
20–29 August
8 September

It was proposed that wireless activity would occur for at least eight hours each day. A standalone British wireless deception unit was formed and trained by 1 March 1944, which was to broadcast wireless transmissions to simulate at least a military division strength unit and be placed under the command of 21st Army Group. The British unit was formed to ostensibly cover the move of the Rosyth force to the south coast and to augment the wireless facilities of the notional assault and follow-up forces in the southeast. In Chatham a fake combined headquarters was to be created by 21st Army Group using bogus wireless traffic to mimic the size and scale of a headquarters.

A supplementary US radio deception battalion was established in March 1944 to simulate the transmissions of a Corps of two Divisions. The Allied planners organised for the military Y Service and SIS sections under Army Group control to intercept the deception wireless activity to ascertain its effectiveness in the reaction it may cause to a German interception team. The team at Chatham was to connect with two additional bogus units – the 3rd US Army in Chelmsford and the 1st Canadian Army based out of Leatherhead.

The following formations in First and 21st Army Group were tasked with observing periods of wireless silence:

a) Formations and units under control of ETOUSA
b) GHQ, Home Forces, and field formations under command. Command, District, sub-district and garrison headquarters
c) War Office reserve formations
d) Units under Chief of Combined Operations

The plan was to stage a series of diversionary operations in the Pas-de-Calais region, starting two weeks before D-Day, and it was to work in synchrony with the air plan, whose main objective was to reduce the threat from the *Luftwaffe*. The diversion aim

REPORT: OPERATION NEPTUNE – RADIO DECEPTION (REF: CLH/a.160/44)

APPENDIX 'B'
'FORTITUDE NORTH – THE THREAT AGAINST SCANDINAVIA'

REF: CLH/A.162/44

Dated: 19th July 1944

1. The SHAEF cover plan for Operation NEPTUNE required (among other things) that a military threat should be established against SCANDINAVIA with a target date for NEPTUNE D-Day minus 30. This was designed to persuade the enemy to retain troops in NORWAY. It is understood to have succeeded further than this in that he actually reinforced them. The creation and maintenance of the forces necessary for this had largely to depend on 'spoof' Navy and Army Wireless Traffic.

2. The creation of the forces, both Naval and Military, was in itself a more or less straightforward task. The presentation of these forces sufficiently trained together in amphibious assault to constitute a threat by the time allowed was, however, considerably more difficult.

3. The requirement was for two Divisions to be amphibiously trained with two Naval Assault Forces. At the time in question (Spring 1944) the NEPTUNE Assault Forces were training hard and as a result of this only one reasonable area was left in which to place the notional Forces, namely the CLYDE. Here there were Military reasons for no more than a Division to exercise at a time. Following on the principle that a practical timing must be followed in presenting a story of amphibious training it was to be concluded that two Assault Forces could not be fully trained in the time allowed (it is understood also that Army wireless resources did not permit notional assault training for more than one Division in any case).

4. It was agreed, therefore, that:

   (i) One Division should train with one Assault Force for an amphibious assault 'one Brigade up' on a fjord coast In Northern Norway, and
   (ii) Another Division should be prepared with its associated Naval lift for an invasion against a very lightly defended part of Southern Norway.

5. On this basis the bogus Assault Force 'V' was created by wireless and carried out the necessary assault training with 52 Division. For the relatively unopposed landing the bogus Force 'W' was created by wireless and carried out embarkation and disembarkation exercises with 58 Division.

6. Detailed stories were then prepared to determine the programme the Naval traffic should follow. These were, in fact, carried out as follows:

STORY TOLD BY WIRELESS TRAFFIC IN THE CLYDE AREA APRIL/MAY 1944

SUMMARY

(i) In the month of April two separate and mutually distinctive Naval forces ('V' and 'W') assembled in the Clyde area. Each of these consisted of 1 Headquarters Ship and the Naval lift for one Division (with which they eventually became associated) and were heard to be working up with Escort and Fleet Carriers

(ii) One of these Forces ('V') was ready to sail by 15th May; the other ('W') by 1st May. Both continued to be heard, however – 'V' until 19th and 'W' until 21st May. Then, at the beginning of July, it was evident that at least one Headquarters Ship and some craft (SOAGs) were making last-minute preparations in the same area.

was to contain the German ground and air forces, for as long as possible, away from the Normandy assault area, most notably the area around Caen. It also had a secondary aim, to keep the Germans guessing on the date and time of the actual assault.

Force F was bolstered by the use of transmitters at Chatham, Dover and Cleethorpes, along with integrating with headquarters and ships harboured in Rosyth during wireless exercises. Many of the units used the 'Exercise Call Sign Book', which would allow all the radio teams to use the same call signs within the different assault forces. Signals exercises (which would normally precede any amphibious operation) went ahead by wireless on 1 June and these bogus exercises were repeated at Divisional level up until D-1.

Bogus amphibious exercises were created and interplayed with bogus wireless traffic. The Cent exercise was focused on headquarters communications, and Dollar which concentrated on a Brigade level Amphibious exercise on 16 and 25 April 1944 in the Studland area. All the vessels that were involved in this exercise were moved to Studland Bay, along with the Mobile W/T Deception Unit. This would help satisfy any potential enemy wireless D/F. The deployed teams also were provided with reach back from a Brigade HQ in Poole to a Divisional HQ in the East of England by the No. 5 (Army) Wireless Group.

SHAEF had to continually adjust the wireless scheduling in the run-up to June 1944 to make sure the deception plan was working. By March 1944, SHAEF stated that the '21st Army Group are arranging to continue the wireless activity associated with the training of airborne forces up to and including D-Day with the object of not disclosing the fact that these forces are preparing to take part in Neptune.'

One of the American units assigned to undertake bogus wireless transmissions, the 3103rd Signal Service Battalion, created seventeen separate radio teams spread around thirteen locations in southeast England and began transmitting on 20 April 1944. These British and American signals units were experienced in what normal unit level radio transmissions would look like on the airwaves and it took little ingenuity to mimic it. But the bulk of the wireless deception transmissions did not begin broadcasting until 26 April. It was an audacious plan: the creation of mock radio networks between fictitious headquarters to fake battalions and units scattered around southern England.

There were three main objectives to the wireless deception:

1) Achieve a measure of surprise by eliminating an 'enforced' wireless silence in the event of a postponement of D-Day
2) Cover the final moves of Assault Corps
3) Overcome the obvious disadvantages of a prolonged wireless silence in the

event of a postponement of D-Day

DURING TRAINING:
– Disguising the nature, size and organisation of assault forces
– Obscuring details of capabilities and equipment of the two services during assault training
– Accustoming personnel to intentional interferences and interpolation of bogus messages

STRATEGIC COVER
– Indicating Norway as the objective
– Indicating the PAS-DE-CALAIS area as the objective

TACTICAL COVER – EXERCISE FABIUS AND AFTERWARDS
– Hiding the date and objective of NEPTUNE
– Diversions prior to H Hour
– Diversions after H Hour

Exercise Fabius was the rehearsal for Neptune. The principal wireless deception requirement levied on FABIUS was:

(a) During the Exercise –
    (i)   Obscure the magnitude and inter-relation of the Forces exercising
    (ii)   Underplay the importance of the Portsmouth area and obscure the fact that this was not the focus of the exercise
    (iii) Make it appear that Fabius was not the last of the pre-assault exercises

(b) After the Exercise –
    (i)   Remove emphasis from the Portsmouth area. This was done by 'planting' it in the east (Chatham, Harwich and Dover)
    (ii)   Hide the fact that certain characteristic types of ship (LSH) were carrying out extended H/F exercises of a peculiar character in the Portsmouth area
    (iii) Cover the period or wireless silence that resulted from the amphibious forces waterproofing and loading immediately before D-Day
    (iv) Continue this cover to obscure the sailing into the Assault
    (v)   Remove any possibility of D-Day being compromised in advance by any peculiar wireless signalling.

REPORT: OPERATION NEPTUNE – RADIO DECEPTION (REF: CLH/A.160/44)

TOP SECRET

APPENDIX 'C'

'FORTITUDE SOUTH – THE THREAT AGAINST THE PAS-DE-CALAIS'

REF: CLH/A.163/44

Dated: 31st July 1944

1. It was the intention of the SHAEF overall cover plan for NEPTUNE that, as the amount of activity associated with preparations for the operation in the South increased, the enemy should be induced to anticipate the main attack in the area of PAS DE CALAIS and Eastward of there in order that resources should not be made available to reinforce NORMANDY. The execution of this plan (FORTITUDE SOUTH I) was entrusted to HQ. 21 Army Group and ANCXF. It was launched before NEPTUNE and its intention persists after the Assault, which the enemy was persuaded to regard as a large diversionary operation.

2. The establishment of this particular threat by bogus wireless activity was always a precarious matter, especially at first (April 1944). There were four main reasons for this, if the assumption is accepted that an assault can never be considered imminent, no matter how highly trained the Army element is, until that element has exercised with the craft that will lift it. Those four reasons were as follows:

    (i) The East Coast is notoriously unsuitable for amphibious assault training

    (ii) Enemy air reconnaissance could easily expose the bogus nature of any 'spoof' wireless arranged unless visual evidence to support it were forthcoming

    (iii) The time allowed for 'creating' and working up a Naval Assault Force to lift the Army elements was insufficient

    (iv) There was every likelihood of the Army elements that constituted the threat from East Anglia during April or May being removed to add to the Forces available for NEPTUNE.

3. The only way of dealing with the situation immediately (April) was to provide notional amphibious training for at least one Brigade of the troops assembled in the East.

During the previous Italian campaign, the Allies' deception efforts had identified that there was a particular interest from the enemy's wireless teams in locating the FOB (Forward Officers, Bombardment) teams, which often were some of the first units ashore during an amphibious operation. An FOB acts as a spotter for the Allied Naval ships to direct Naval gunfire on to enemy defences, and as such their activity was often the source of keen interest to enemy wireless teams. The enemy would D/F these teams through their distinctive wireless procedures and mortar them. For this purpose, during Neptune, a special call sign system was worked out so they would blend in more with the Army teams ashore.

Naval wireless traffic typically was transmitted by a number of methods, each with its own characteristic messages:

- Point to point services between headquarters usually ashore
- Broadcasts from shore to ship normally serving specific areas
- Direct services from shore to ship requiring the ship to answer (rare in wartime and normally restricted to harbour areas)
- Ship/shore waves, used relatively infrequently in wartime on account of the dangers of D/F, and as a rule for the passing of strictly urgent operational traffic.

During Neptune, three new broadcast services were to be made available during the operation to serve the ships and authorities afloat. These were used during the Fabius exercises and also kept open for a whole month before D-Day and used to broadcast dummy traffic. One Royal Navy officer and one rating were occupied on this task for sixteen hours each day.

During the full-scale rehearsal for Neptune, a full month before D-Day, security on the Allied wireless transmissions was paramount. It was essential that wireless deception should play its part.

Trust lies at the very heart of the relationship between an intelligence officer and his agent. The reports fed back to Germany that came from double agents been run by British Intelligence and the XX Committee would have a significant impact on how the Allied deception plan was to be taken in by the OKW (*Oberkommando der Wehrmacht*) and by Hitler himself. The role these double agents played whilst operating in Britain were critical to the outcome of Overlord.

The Allied deception plan was developed to confuse the German High Command, who had been taken in by the ruse. The vital reconnaissance undertaken of the Normandy beaches and defensive fortifications were only a minor scale – there was more reconnaissance being undertaken by the Allies in areas where they were not intending the invasion to occur than where it was actually going to take place. It had fooled Generalfeldmarschall Rundstedt and Rommel into believing the Pas-de-Calais was to be the Allies point of entry into Europe.

CHAPTER FIFTEEN
DICING

*'The military organisation with the best aerial reconnaissance will win the next war
...'*

General Werner von Fritsch, German High Command, 1938

*One of the most impressive advances made in the Air Forces operating overseas is the
great improvement in our photographic reconnaissance and tactical reconnaissance
work. During my stay in England, the ground officers went out of their way to state
that the Photo Reconnaissance unit work done in support of the ground assault and
in preparation for the invasion was outstanding as a contribution to the success of the
enterprise.'*

US Assistant Secretary of War Robert Lovett, 4 July 1944

Even before the outbreak of World War II, aerial reconnaissance was becoming a valuable tool for gathering intelligence. It had progressed a great deal since the early years of military aerial photography in the Boer War. Over the course of the war its contribution to the war intelligence machinery cannot be underestimated, especially for the valued work that was done up to the execution of Operation Overlord. It was written by General Lee Chennault that 80 per cent of all intelligence in World War II came from aerial reconnaissance photographs.

The mainstay of all photographic reconnaissance and interpretation was undertaken from 1941 at RAF Medmenham, based at Danesfield House, a beautiful stately home set in 65 acres of land on the banks of the Thames, just outside Marlow in Buckinghamshire. It had quickly outgrown its previous location in Wembley, which had suffered from German bombing during the Blitz. RAF staff used the clocktower side of the house, with its ornate Grand Banqueting Hall, as the Officers' Mess. Churchill affectionately referred to the site as the 'chalk house with the tudor chimneys'.

The unit at Medmenham was referred to as the Allied Central Intelligence Unit (ACIU) and was controlled by the ACAS (I) Assistant Chief of the Air Staff (Intelligence) at the Air Ministry. It came under the umbrella of MI4, but this was very much a paper link.

The unit grew rapidly at Medmenham between 1941 and 1943 and became involved in the planning stages of every major military operation that was undertaken and the scale of the operation became apparent towards the end of the war. The daily throughput included 60,000 prints and 25,000 negatives from a variety of locations supporting the aerial reconnaissance effort. The significance of the site and the intelligence role it played was staggering. By the close of the war it has been estimated the Medmenham photo library held in the region of five million prints which had helped in the creation of over 40,000 official imagery reports. In terms of scale, the Overlord operation alone accrued over half-a-million hours of Photographic Interpretation (PI) time.

Much of the lead-up to D-Day hinged on vast numbers of sorties being flown by Allied Spitfires and Mosquitoes to gain intelligence on the beach defences, obstacles and terrain. The Allied Expeditionary Air Force (AEAF) mounted nearly 5,000 low-level aerial reconnaissance sorties over the heavily defended areas of the Normandy coast between 1 April and 5 June 1944. Prior to D-Day a reconnaissance wing was formed at RAF Northolt and was operated in direct support of the Allied forces in northern Europe.

World War II photographic interpretation was done using a three-phase system.

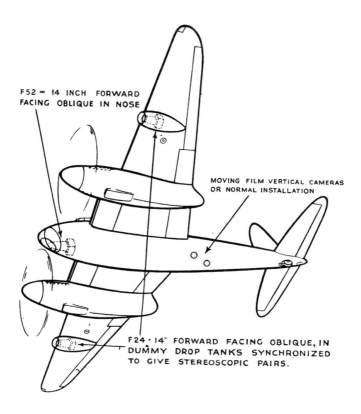

F52 = 14 INCH FORWARD FACING OBLIQUE IN NOSE

MOVING FILM VERTICAL CAMERAS OR NORMAL INSTALLATION

F24 - 14" FORWARD FACING OBLIQUE, IN DUMMY DROP TANKS SYNCHRONIZED TO GIVE STEREOSCOPIC PAIRS.

Mosquito aircraft and its camera locations (© Medmenham Collection)

The first phase interpretation was always undertaken by a specialist PI Section locally at the airfield, before the film was dispatched, often by car, to the ACIU at Danesfield House for printing and second and third phase interpretation. The second phase interpretation was undertaken within 24 hours of the film processing being done at the Photographic Interpretation Unit (PIU) at Wembley, or latterly at Medmenham. Second phase was very much a summarisation of the intelligence derived from the aerial photography.

The third phase was when the ACIU drew in deep specialists who acted as the hinge between the customer for the intelligence and their requirements and the analysis of the photographic intelligence. The units were split into railways, telecommunications, shipping, etc. They even had the country's leading expert on U-Boats. It was these specialists who provided the expert analysis and interpretation that was to be so valued by the D-Day planners.

CIU report output during the course of World War II – from first to third phase analysis

Year	1940	1941	1942	1943	1944	1945–VE day
First to third phase CIU Reports issued	864	3,157	5,437	7,001	16,254	5,772

Mosquito Mk 34 PR aircraft (© Medmenham Collection)

The third phase sections were organised as follows:

A section – Navy/Shipping

B section – Army (referred to as the Army Photographic Intelligence Section or APIS)

C section – German airfields

D section – heavy industry in German occupied Europe

E section – enemy camouflage

G section – RADAR, radio/wireless

K section – Battle Damage Assessment (BDA)

L section – aircraft

N section – night photography (purposed during night bombing raids)

Q section – decoy hunting

R section – railways/transport infrastructure

T section – target folder preparation (for RAF Bomber crews)

V section – model-making

W section – photogrammetric (process of measuring size and scale of specific objects in aerial photographs)

Z section – second phase unit (including some specialist analytic teams)

The main reconnaissance camera in use by the RAF prior to D-Day was the F24. It had been designed as far back as 1925 but it had not come into full operational use until 1935, initially with the RAF Lysander aircraft of Army Co-operation Command,

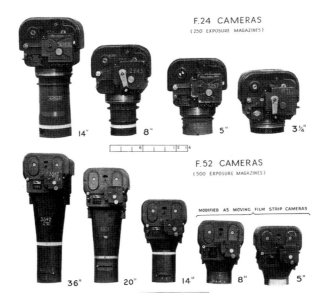

F24 and F52 cameras (© Medmenham Collection)

and Blenheims. They were designed and manufactured predominantly by Williamson but their main factories in north London were repeatedly bombed by the *Luftwaffe*, so alternative manufacturers were sourced with W. Vinten Ltd and Houghton-Butcher, both of whom made large numbers of the F24 camera.

In the mid-1940s both the Spitfire and Mosquito aircraft were fitted for aerial reconnaissance and used the F24 until this was subsumed by the more advanced Williamson F52, which was retained in service until the Cold War. The Mosquito, the fastest plane of its type at the time, was preferred by senior officers because it had a longer range, enabling it to penetrate much further into occupied Europe. The pilots preferred the more manoeuvrable Spitfire, with its rapid rate of climb, allowing them to shake off enemy fighter aircraft.

The preparation and maintenance of the cameras fell to the Trade Group 14 personnel in the RAF, and they were installed by air camera fitters. There were normally two cameras (sometimes three, dependent on the mission) fitted in the Spitfire in the wings or behind where pilot sat in the fuselage. They were controlled by the pilot using a small control box, replacing the gunsight of a normal, non-Reconnaissance Spitfire. The negatives produced by the F24 camera measured 7 x 8.5 in, which caused processing and logistical storage issues further down the line.

Germany had its own aerial reconnaissance effort with adapted planes like the Junkers Ju 88. By the middle of 1943 the *Luftwaffe* had over 700 aircraft fitted for short- and long-range reconnaissance missions. Strategic intelligence was derived from aerial photographs assessed by the *Luftwaffe* General Staffs 5th (Intelligence) Branch Main Photo, which operated out of the old Prussian Legislature in Berlin. It is often written about the failure of *Luftwaffe* reconnaissance to detect the Overlord preparations in southern England. It is certainly true. In May 1944, the *Kriegsmarine* reported that 'especially on account of the lack of constant comprehensive air reconnaissance, the (enemy's) main transport effort in one sector or another of the Channel coast is not ascertainable'.

Aerial reconnaissance sorties over German held territory such as Normandy carried huge risks, especially as none of the reconnaissance aircraft were armed. It fell to the pilot's pure skill in flying to avoid enemy fighter engagements.

The graphic below highlights how the plane cameras worked with a 60 per cent overlap to allow for stereo image interpretation later. The aircraft flew at 30,000 ft at a minimum speed of 350 knots. Some of the images captured of the Normandy beach obstacles were taken at a dangerously low altitude (or *zero elevation*) of around 50 ft at a speed of 300 knots with a technique known as a 'dicing sortie'. Flying at such minimal altitude was fraught with risk and many pilots were killed. Their ideal was to operate no closer than 2,000 yards offshore, as this was the range of the German anti-aircraft batteries on the coast. It was these valuable images which were used to stitch together mosaics of photographs of the beaches and their defences from the view of a naval vessel. These mosaics were printed in their thousands to provide the real-time orientation that the crew of a landing craft would need in the vital early hours of D-Day. The quality of the photographic panoramic prints even impressed Eisenhower. He ordered forty sets of the prints, which in reality required the reproduction of over 40,000 prints at a time when paper and photographic materials were in short supply.

Number of original photographic mosaics produced by CIU Photographic Section at Medmenham during World War II

Year	1940	1941	1942	1943	1944	1945–VE day	Total
CIU Photographic Section – mosaics constructed	–	117	1,076	1,251	1,855	1,190	5,489

Prints from Medmenham were taken to Hughenden Manor, only a few miles down the road in High Wycombe. Over one hundred Air Ministry staff here created targeting maps in secret from the prints provided by Medmenham PI.

RAF Mount Farm, outside Oxford on the site of what is now Berinsfield, played a crucial part in the intelligence collection effort in the run-up to D-Day in June 1944. It was originally a satellite station of RAF Benson but over time had fulfilled a function as headquarters of the RAF Photographic Reconnaissance Squadron and the United States Air Force Photo Reconnaissance and Mapping Squadron. The predominant airframe in use at Mount Farm was the P-38, which was especially good at low-level sorties.

As Benson and Mount Farm began to professionalise its aerial reconnaissance in the early 1940s, the move to Danesfield House and the concept of centralising all the key sections and functions together under one organisational structure – that of the Central Interpretation Unit (CIU) – took hold. It was subordinate to the RAF Directorate of Intelligence, which had the intent of coordinating all PI/PR requirements from the various military commands and government agencies/departments that used the CIU imagery intelligence.

The highly valued PI staff were sought after to work as embedded staff in other military establishments. There were key crossovers with units such as the Inter-Services Topographical Department (ISTD) operating out of Manchester College, Oxford. The recognition of the importance of topographical intelligence for military

Churchill's 'Chalk House' or Danesfield House/RAF Medmenham, showing Nissen huts in 1941 (© Medmenham Collection)

Clocktower of Danesfield House today (© author)

commanders after the debacle of the 1940 Narvik landings in Norway showed how intertwined the ISTD and CIU needed to be. Liaison staff were deployed between the units. A CIU RAF officer, Flight Lieutenant John Hope-Simpson was sent to Oxford, as was one of his Army PI colleagues from Medmenham, Lieutenant Fred Mason.

Lieutenant Mason was born in May 1915 in Derbyshire and went on to Nottingham University in the 1930s to study French and Latin. After gaining a teaching diploma, he taught French and Music at Fakenham Grammar School in Norfolk. As war broke out, his uncle had read a notice in the *Daily Telegraph* requesting applications for 'work of national importance'. Fred applied, was interviewed and subsequently accepted. After four months of basic training at Brock Barracks in Reading, some short follow-on training then took place at the Intelligence Corps Other Ranks Depot at King Alfred's College, Winchester. He was then posted to 1 Division Field Security section in Norfolk.

The grand lounge of Danesfield House today, which served as the Officers' Mess of RAF Medmenham (© author)

A while later Mason became interested in a new Army PI course which had started at the School of Military Intelligence in Matlock, on which he enrolled. By October 1943 Mason was posted to the basement of Danesfield House, the then home of the CIU. He was set to work in F Section, the Communications and Transportation Section, as he had had a major interest in railways throughout his life.

In February 1944, Mason was given a Direct Commission to Lieutenant and a few weeks later found himself being posted to the ISTD at Manchester College, Oxford. He was drafted in to assist with the work on the French coastal and railway topography before D-Day, an essential logistical asset when the Allied forces stepped ashore on the beaches on Normandy a few weeks later. Much of this topographical work was being informed from CIU aerial photography but also from the holiday pictures sent in by the British public via a BBC appeal.

The training of PI analysts started with a two-week basic course, run at Medmenham (then later at RAF Nuneham Park nearby) from the autumn on 1940 onwards by Pilot Officer Alfred Stephenson.

Part of the basics was an introduction to the use of 3D stereoscopic viewers, which allowed PI analysts which two photographs out of alignment to be viewed in 3D. This was all achieved by the work of the Spitfire and Mosquito pilots taking film exposures at an interval, which under calculation allowed for a 60 per cent overlap.

In the immediate weeks running up to D-Day, up to eighty aerial sorties were being flown over Normandy each day by Allied reconnaissance aircraft. The processing and logistics effort required to analyse, process and disseminate the images from these flights involved a huge amount of time and manpower. At its height there were more than 3,500 staff working at Danesfield House.

Since 1941 photographic reconnaissance was the responsibility of just one squadron, No. 140 Squadron, assigned to GHQ Home Forces and AC Command. The demands on the unit from Overlord would far outweigh their resources, so it was decided that a photographic reconnaissance Wing would be formed under the 21st Army Group Headquarters and 2nd TAF. 140 Squadron utilised the PR version of the Spitfire Mk V but the new Wing aimed to convert its 16 squadron to fly the Mustang, and eventually re-equip to the more modern Spitfire Mk XI as these came online. This new Wing was commanded by Group Captain Lousada, who had been in charge of 34 Wing. Some of the work undertaken by the wing was critical in the reconnaissance of the Normandy coastline.

Lousada was to state, 'the first operational Mosquito was collected from Benson on November 5th and Richard Bowen flew it in exceedingly dirty weather on November 11th on a dice of some supposed rocks off the coast near Port en Bessin, the existence of which we succeeded in proving to the Navy by means of his photographs and which later played a vital part in the Invasion of France as the "Calvados Reef".

'Mosquitos and Spitfires continued to be allotted and, by February, 16 Sqn were almost fully equipped and 140 were now taking an active part again in daylight operations in Mosquitos. The weather improved and tasks became more and more numerous so that, on Feb 24th, we were able to fly 31 sorties of which 29 were successful and produced 7,451 negatives and 23,466 prints.

'At this period 140 were given an interesting and important new task … 91 small areas in Normandy were to be covered, using survey cameras, in order to select sites on which the future airfields of 2nd Tactical Air Force and the United States Army Air Forces were to be built when the ground had been captured. This involved flying over the targets at about 9000 feet, so the Mosquitos were flown across the Channel at 25000 feet and dived down from that height onto their target. This was felt to be a hazardous undertaking in the unarmed and highly vulnerable Mosquito as many PW190's and ME109's were based in the target area, but the task was completed in less than two months in spite of very poor weather.

'From February onwards events began to move rapidly and pressure of work had increased. Coastal defences, beaches and ports were covered more frequently: the sea-bed off Normandy was photographed: vast mosaics of Normandy and the Pas-de-Calais were completed: bomb damage, railways, marshalling yards, bridges, airfields, V-1 sites, entrances to underground HQ's and dumps … RADAR installations were all covered. Overlord put significant pressures on the ACIU, so vital was the product of aerial reconnaissance to the operational planners.'

'On 29 May, Air Marshal Coningham addressed the Wing on the tasks that lay in front of us and it was by this time obvious to everyone that D Day was only a week or two ahead. The coastal strip, 2 ½ miles wide and stretching from Blankenberghe to Avranches, which used to be covered once in every three months, was by this time required every three days, and certain beaches were being flown with a special moving film camera at 6,000 feet so as to get large scale photographs of the obstacles which the Huns had erected in the sea to prevent landing craft from reaching the shore. They were seen to have mines attached to the tops of the stakes.'

One particular insight into aerial reconnaissance comes from the work of 34 Wing RAF. Over 500 officers served in the wing during its existence.

From the reconnaissance flights, each roll of film (which could contain up to 500 exposures) would be couriered via Dispatch Rider to Medmenham. The original prints would be submitted into the Photographic Library, which at the height of the war was receiving in the region of one million prints a month. It has been stated that by the end of the war the Medmenham Library had around eight million photographs from over 80,000 sorties. It was industrial in scale.

The negatives were stored in the film library. These sets of negatives could be recalled to provide additional prints at any time using a Williamson Multiprinter installed for that very purpose. At a full run, this printer could print up to a 1,000 photographic prints per hour.

In May 1942 an APIS section of ten Medmenham staff was deployed to Norfolk House in St James's Square under the command of Major George Yool who reported to the Chief of Staff of the Supreme Allied Commander (COSSAC). They were tasked with identifying potential landing sites between Holland and the Spanish border. The unit was to test itself first in the raid on Dieppe on 19 August 1942. The failure of the Dieppe raid was partly due to the poor intelligence gleaned from aerial reconnaissance. It had not been good enough. The team had failed to identify some key defensive batteries around the town. The invasion of North Africa, under Operation Torch, in November 1942 was to be the next test. One of the APIS team, Colonel Tom Churchill, had boldly even briefed the Commando Brigade spearhead of the landing force, under Brigadier Laycock. He said shortly after Torch, 'having air photographs of a strip of coast we were about to attack explained to us by Tom Churchill was the most interesting of all my experiences. His interpretation of air photographs proved accurate to a degree which I could not have believed possible.'

This direct liaison with military commanders started a trend which was to see APIS analysts deploy in small teams into the field. Utilising a caravan or small truck, they would be embedded as part of the military command but could provide the PI expertise to assist with intelligence assessments.

Terrain models have been used for centuries by the military to support their operational planning. As the concept of Combined Operations took hold for all three services and Allied commando units began to undertake raids on the French coast, the requirement for model-making increased dramatically. They were used to cascade information and plans from officers down to their men so they could comprehend the strategic requirements and the topography facing them on the ground. The intelligence gleaned from the plethora of aerial imagery from reconnaissance flights would greatly assist the model-makers. Model-making became one of the aspects of the successful intelligence work undertaken at RAF Medmenham, some of which were reproductions of the D-Day landing beaches and made from a rubber composite formed in a plaster cast mould. The detail on these was exceptional and being made of rubber they were intended to be used and rolled-up by commanders on the beach.

The work of Medmenham's V – or model – Section began developing Overlord model requirements from as early as the summer of 1943 and used the basement of Danesfield House for its work. The problem was that they had to satisfy a broad spectrum – from the highest strategic command groups at SHAEF down through the operational and tactical layers to producing waterproof rubberised models that could be rolled up and taken ashore from the landing craft by troop commanders.

These detailed terrain models were typically constructed using information gleaned from aerial reconnaissance photographs and built using two main methods:

1. *Egg-crate* – the basis for this method is the use of vertical sets of cardboard but to the profiles established from maps and aerial imagery. Typically quicker to construct than photo-skinned models but generally had less detail.

2. *Photo-skinned* – using contoured maps, the model-makers construct contour
   shapes from hardwood sheets smoothed over by chisels and saws and given a
   smoother surface by using Watertex (a mixture of wood pull, glue and Plaster of
   Paris) interweaved with aerial photographs of areas represented by the model.

During the planning months before the Normandy landings, echelons of the 21st Army
Group were requesting 1:1,000 and 1:500 large-scale models. It has been estimated
that over 700 egg-crate models were built for the American, British and Canadian
Corps and Divisions falling under the command of 21st Army Group during this
planning phase before June 1944.

Total CIU models produced during World War II

Year	1940	1941	1942	1943	1944	1945–VE day	Total
Models Produced	35	134	205	487	407	82	1,350

Larger models for strategic command level briefing purposes were produced at a scale
of about 1:5000 and were about 16 ft square. They were extremely detailed, showing
the beach defences and fortifications, rivers, forests and villages in the hinterland.
Sixty-three of these original models were constructed by joint British and American
model-makers, each with three copies made.

Not all model-making for D-Day was centred on Danesfield House. The Cotswold
town of Tetbury became the adopted home of the American 654th Engineer
Topographical Battalion under its Commanding Officer, Lieutenant Colonel Charles
Ruzek. Over 300 American personnel were billeted in the town and they played a key
role in the success of the invasion. They were ostensibly a mobile engineer unit which
had a mobile printing capability at scale. According to the unit's war records, they
produced over eight million maps during the European campaign.

The Battalion consisted of three different companies:

A Company – based in/around Tetbury (including the old Malt House), which was
responsible for turning aerial reconnaissance photographs into maps. The Company
consisted of Draughtsmen, Photographic Interpreters and Artillery specialists.

Photographic
Interpreters
in the
Malthouse,
Tetbury
(© Merlin
Fraser)

B Company – based at the Chavenage House outside Tetbury, which was responsible for printing the maps.

HQ Company – centred around the Malt House in the middle of Tetbury which the 654th took over from December 1943 to June 1944 before they deployed to France.

The Malt House was chosen because it was off the beaten track and easily guarded. On the top floor the unit constructed a 3D sophisticated terrain model of Omaha Beach using Plaster of Paris and *papier maché*. It was built by a team of sculptors, stage designers and architects who reconstructed it from aerial photographs and other intelligence.

The middle floor of the Malt House was occupied by the Photographic Interpreters, where photo-mosaic products were made, as well as the creation of photographic maps for mass printing.

They were subsumed under General Omar Bradley's 1st Army Group and had deployed personnel based in Bristol. The First Army Group requested that its G2 (Air) branch form a new unit – called the Aerial Photographic Interpretation Department (APID).

Back at Norfolk House, once the green light had been given from the Quadrant conference in Quebec in August 1943 for the Overlord plan, the APIS team set to work to map out the prospective beaches for the amphibious invasion of Europe. Their focus was the beaches and immediate hinterland, and to develop a broad understanding of the German defensive positions and fortifications. It was this knowledge that the Allies relied on to break through the beachhead on 6 June 1944.

Aerial reconnaissance served the tactics for Overlord. It was to disclose the enemy dispositions and concentrations, and to monitor the defensive fortifications along the Atlantic Wall. Commanders valued and trusted the photograph, and the skills and experience of the Medmenham PI. The vast and comprehensive intelligence collection effort at Medmenham had responded to the ask upon it and generated significant quantities of high quality imagery of the Normandy coastline to where it was needed most, to the vanguard of the invasion force.

Number of CIU combined RAF/USAAF sorties during World War II, showing a clear spike towards the invasion of Europe in 1944*

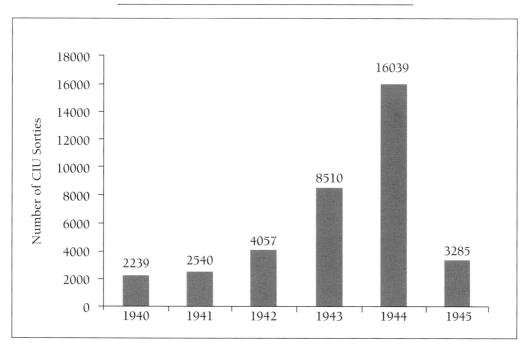

(* this includes data from RAF PR, Bomber and Coastal Commands, TAF, USAAF PR, Bomber TAF and other miscellaneous missions)

Number of CIU prints per year from aerial reconnaissance missions during World War II*

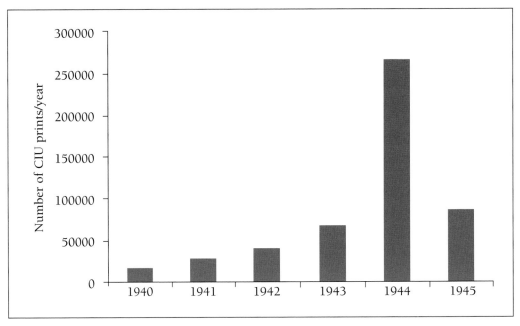

(* this includes data from RAF PR, Bomber and Coastal Commands, TAF, USAAF PR, Bomber TAF and other miscellaneous missions)

Photographic Recconnaissance organisation in the UK – Photographic requirements

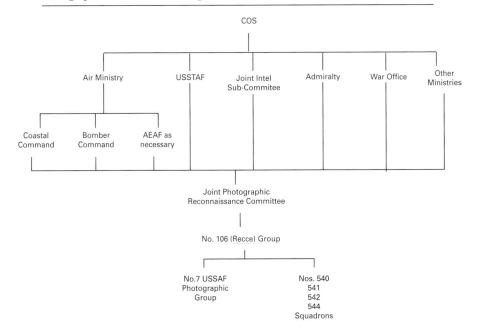

Aerial reconnaissance photograph of Port-en-Bessin coastline, taken by 34 Wing (© 34 Wing an Unofficial Account – Portsmouth History Centre)

2nd TAF, F24 aerial cameras being checked before being fitted to Mustangs of No. 35 (Recce) Wing RAF at Gatwick (© IWM London Photographic Archives – reference CH13455)

Photograph of the Omaha Beach model built by the US 654th Engineer Topographic Battalion in the Malthouse, Tetbury w(© Merlin Fraser)

271

COPY   RESTRICTED

                                  Supreme Headquarters,
                                  Allied Expeditionary Force,
                                      Office of the Supreme Commander.

                                  14th June, 1944

Dear Sir Archibald,

    On behalf of the troops who have had occasion to use relief models
in connection with operations now in progress, I desire to express my
sincere appreciation for the whole-hearted co-operation and diligence
with which the demands of this headquarters for various relief models
have been met.

    During the past five months there have been transmitted to you
numerous requirements for relief models which considered collectively
represent a construction programme of great magnitude.   These
requirements have been met in accordance with exacting time schedules
in spite of the difficulties occasioned by unavoidable alterations in
the programme and readjustment of priorities.

    I should be please to have you convey to the members of your Staff
concerned and to the combined British and Americal Model Making Section
my commendation for a task well done.   It is appreciated that they
must have been called upon to work long hours and still maintain high
standards and accuracy and workmanship.   May they feel that theirs is
a real contribution to our ultimate victory.

                         Sincerely,

                         Sgd.   DWIGHT D. EISENHOWER

The Right Honourable Sir Archibald Sinclair, Pt.K.T., C.M.G., M.P.
Secretary of State for Air,
Air Ministry,
Whitehall,
LONDON, S.W.1.

Letter from General Eisenhower to the ACIU in June 1944, thanking staff for their model-making expertise
(© Medmenham collection)

Overhead view of topographical model of German gun battery at Merville
(© IWM London Photographic Archives – reference HU100233)

CHAPTER SIXTEEN
CONTACT REGISTER

'Intelligence planning and procurement must, without question, come before operational planning.'

Admiral John Godfrey, Director of Naval Intelligence

Admiral John Godfrey (© IWM London Photographic archives – reference A20777)

Sometimes the best ideas are born out of failure. The German invasion of Norway in April 1940 had displayed how poorly prepared Allied forces were. RAF Bomber Command pilots flying on missions to attack Norwegian airfields shortly after the invasion were using Baedeker's tourist guidebooks from as far back as 1912 to assist with navigation. At the time, the Royal Navy and Army had different intelligence units that were completely independent of each other. Norway had exposed some deplorable gaps in topographical knowledge.

Hidden away in rooms adjoining the marble-floored corridors of the historic colleges of Oxford and Cambridge were one of World War II's biggest secrets – a clandestine unit which had a massive impact from the higher echelons of SHAEF right down to the tactical level on the beaches with individual fighting sections where men would be risking their lives.

Topographical and geological intelligence started to take hold in the early stages of the war and with its global reach the Admiralty was best placed to deliver a solution. This led to the formation of the Naval Intelligence Department (NID6) in May 1940. Months before, the Director of Naval Intelligence (DNI), Admiral John Godfrey, was concerned over the lack of topographical intelligence being generated within NID and he wanted the equivalent of NID32, established during World War I for that very purpose.

Although it was still effectively overseen by the Admiralty, the need for an unified approach to gathering topographical intelligence beyond the shoreline was understood.

This early thinking by the Admiralty evolved into a tri-service organisation during the move from London to Oxford in October 1940, with the new name of the Inter-Services Topographical Department (ISTD). The ISTD was not formerly established until a JIC paper published on 24 October 1941. Admiral Godfrey visited both the Universities of Oxford and Cambridge to draw up plans for a collaborative approach to establishing the ISTD. It would pool military engineers, geologists, model-makers with university geographers, and other specialists to be based at the School of Geography in Oxford and at the Scott Polar Research Institute (SPRI) in Lensfield Road, Cambridge.

The ISTD was to play a critical but often overlooked role through World War II, but it was a key factor in the planning and intelligence insight for D-Day. The ISTD and its timely and thorough topographical intelligence quickly became the backbone for all military operations. A few months later, the Joint Intelligence Committee (JIC) followed suit and established its own Topographical Section to supply the Joint Planning Staff and Director of Combined Operations with a series of Inter-Service Information Series (ISIS) reports to senior intelligence officers, planners and operational commanders.

A few years later, as the ISTD had matured and the value of topographical intelligence was appreciated across all the service commands, the ISTD provided

Harris Manchester College, University of Oxford, from Mansfield Road (© HMC)

275

excellent intelligence for the Royal Navy torpedo aircraft attacks on the German battle cruiser *Tirpitz* in September 1942 and later in 1944.

Born in Handsworth, Birmingham in 1888, Admiral John Godfrey had previously served during World War I in the Dardanelles aboard HMS *Euryalus* as Navigation Officer and had seen for himself at Gallipoli how poorly prepared the invasion force was in understanding the terrain. After the war he served at the Royal Navy Staff College as Deputy Director. At the outbreak of World War II he became the Director of Naval Intelligence (DNI) between 1939 and 1942. It is widely believed that Ian Fleming based his character 'M' on Admiral Godfrey. It has been said of Godfrey that his idea of establishing the ISTD was 'conceived, nurtured and brought to maturity, in the face of initial apathy in other departments, almost entirely as a result of Godfrey's vision, drive and enthusiasm'.

Over time, Godfrey's thoughts matured on the void the Allies had in mapping and topographical intelligence. The Overlord forces needed a good understanding on the terrain, geology, facilities and transportation infrastructures that could support that force once ashore. In 1940 some new service sections were established: the Operations Planning Staff and the Joint Planning Staff. These new bodies furthered the demand and appetite for a combined services topographical department to pool the knowledge from specialists throughout the forces and wider academia. Bolstered by the Prime Minister's own directive after the debacle of the Norwegian campaign, the DNI gave it the go-ahead.

The ISTD was structured around two centres of excellence. The first was the University of Oxford under Professor Kenneth Mason, the first Professor of Geography at the School of Geography on Mansfield Road, opposite Manchester College. Professor Mason had been appointed as Chair of Geography at Oxford in 1932 but prior to this he had been trained at the Royal Military Academy in Woolwich and had served in the Middle East and France during World War I, so he understood the needs and wants of the military machine well.

The second was at the University of Cambridge under Clifford Darby, who was fortunately one of the leading geographers of his time on his knowledge of Europe, which would prove to be very valuable. Darby recruited and ran a team of around twenty-five geographers and over the period between 1941 and 1945, thirty intelligence volumes were produced combining rich geographic text, maps, photographs and statistical appendices. The volume on France ran into four separate volumes with over 1,000 pages. After the war, Darby was presented with an OBE for his services to the ISTD.

One of the most legendary Royal Marines of the twentieth century became the figurehead of the ISTD in its early years of development. The friendly and effervescent

Colonel Sam Bassett had risen from the rank of private when he joined the service in 1907 and served through both World Wars, with a career that finally totalled fifty-three years. Like Godfrey, he was posted to the RN Staff College in the 1920s, the first low-ranking Royal Marine to receive such an appointment.

One of Colonel Bassett's roles laid the bedrock for what he was to evolve at Oxford. He was posted to Capetown in 1926 as a Staff Officer (Intelligence) and at this time was heavily involved in undertaking solo reconnaissance of docks and harbours for future war planning. He saw the immediate scope in developing good mapping, models and topographical intelligence for important strategic locations and targets. In January 1930, he was transferred to the UK into the Admiralty's Naval Intelligence Department (NID). He was passionate about the value of topographical intelligence, 'Topography … means drawing up a detailed picture of any area, city, town, manor, parish … and everything that exists in that area must be recorded, natural or artificial. From a military point of view, this means knowing a great deal more than the fact that a beach exists somewhere. We've got to find out the nature of the approaches to that beach so that we can land on it; what the beach itself consists of – what kind of mud, sand, pebbles compose it – how troops can be moved inland after a landing. Then we have to know all about what is beyond that beach – the roads, railways, ports, harbours, cities, towns.'

This was never more apparent than for a large-scale amphibious landing, which is the most difficult of all military operations to orchestrate. The reliance of naval commanders on naval charts for such operations could only be detrimental. As Bassett once stated, 'they simply tell ships how to stay off beaches'.

NID 6 spawned the ISTD in March 1940 with just one civilian member of staff, the University College Classics don Freddie Wells, who was renowned for his meticulous attention to detail. Wells was to become the main editor for the ISTD publications and it was under his tutelage that the product from the teams were of such a high standard and well finished. Wells and the effervescent Bassett struck a good mix, and they were subsequently joined by a surveyor from the Admiralty Hydrography team who had recently returned from Singapore. The team started life on the Edgware Road until a move was instigated to the School of Geography in Oxford. A significant number of staff had departed academic life and joined up, so there were a number of vacant rooms. Wells and Bassett commandeered two rooms for themselves and placed their two typists into the Anthropological Library. Their first task was to produce an intelligence brochure on the Atlantic Islands, the Cape Verdes, Azores and Canaries.

Over time personnel were assigned to the unit from all over the country and the wider Allied contingent, including staff from Norway, USA and the Netherlands. With the numbers swelling, more accommodation was needed and Bassett lobbied the

University registrar, Sir Douglas Veale, to serve a Notice to Requisition on the principal of Manchester College, which lay directly opposite the School of Geography. The intelligence requirements levied on ISTD before and after the 6 June 1944 invasion were stipulated as: 'Geological work with 21 Army Group. Including pre-D Day planning and post-D day planning and operations done by SO [Staff Officer] Geology to CE (Chief Engineer) 21 Army Group (Lieutenant Colonel King followed by Major Shotton) and from January 1945 also by DADW (Deputy Assistant Director, Works), Major Ponsford. Assistance from time to time from ISTD (Inter-Services Topographical Department).'

Pre D-Day

1. Detailed study of nature of invasion beaches
2. Study of sand-bank changes on a British beach, as a guide to similar changes on the invasion beaches
3. Selection of a British beach simulating the invasion bridgehead
4. Co-operation in vehicle trials and bombing results on the British counterpart beaches
5. Detailed study of the Loire and Seine rivers, with a view to assault crossings
6. Selection of an English river comparable to the Seine, and tests of amphibious vehicles on its banks
7. Provision of information on the submarine geology of invasion ports
8. Selection of parts of British coast for training commando parties in assault of French coast
9. Preparation of water supply prospect maps for NW France (1:50,000 and 1:250,000 scale)
10. Study of the reaction of common French and Belgian road metals upon mine detectors
11. Collaboration with MEW (Military Engineers Works) on quarry resources, NW France
12. Forecast of soil characteristics of projected airfield sites
13. General co-operation with ISTD (Inter-Services Topographical Department) and TIS (Theatre Intelligence Section) on terrain appreciation
14. Advice on bomb weights and fusing

Post D-Day

1. Continuation of water prospect maps, Belgium, NW France and W Germany
2. Control of boring work RE (Royal Engineer) Boring Platoons

3. Co-operation with CRE (Commander Royal Engineers) (Quarrying Groups) and SHAEF (Supreme Headquarters Allied Expeditionary Force) on road stone resources

4. Preparation of soil maps for DCE (Deputy Chief Engineer) Airfields, and soil forecasts and developments for selected sites

5. Preparation of soil maps (Holland and Germany) with particular reference to operational vehicle movement

6. Collection of vehicle movement data (in co-operation with ORS) to provide a check upon correctness of 'trafficability' forecasts

7. Detailed study of the shores of S. Develand and Walcheren previous to the assault thereon

8. Detailed study of the shores and approaches of the Fresian Islands, preparatory to proposed assault

9. Study of the River Rhine in detail, with a view to assault crossings and bridge building

10. Selection of training area on River Meuse, with conditions as near as possible to those which would hold on the Rhine assault crossings

11. Study of soil in relation to frost and thaw deterioration of roads

12. Opinion, when required, on nature of foundations

The newly formed 30 Assault Unit, eager to get involved with the Overlord operation had quickly realised the importance of what was going on at Manchester College. Two of its Marines, Lance Corporal Bert Morgan and Corporal Bon Royle were posted there to develop the targets that 30AU would strike in Normandy. Years later, Admiral Godfrey attributed the success of 30 Assault Unit in no small part to them making use of a wide variety of Naval intelligence resources, most notably the ISTD.

At its height, the ISTD was comprised of a number of separate sections:

Section A was the Geological Section drawn largely from the Royal Engineers. As a founder member of the section, Major John Leonard Farrington RE commanded the section from August 1944 to June 1946.

Section B was the Norwegian section and had a number of Norwegian exiles in its ranks, and also some US Army personnel. It was overseen by Commander Clowser RNVR.

Section C was focused on France and was responsible for all the work on Normandy/Overlord.

US Army soldier Hedin Bronner at work in the Section B hut (© Harris Manchester College)

Section B group photograph, with Lieutenant Commander Clowser RNVR in the front row (© Harris Manchester College)

Section E was run by Major Gerald Andrews RM who had been seriously wounded by German 88 gunfire in the spring of 1940, whilst re-embarking the French Foreign Legion at Narvik in Norway. E Section was the Economics section and reported on resources. Major Andrews was also responsible for the requirements of SOE.

The ISTD was also believed to have a Section D, Section F and Section K. Furthermore, it also had a dedicated 'railway' section and a typing pool. As the ISTD work started to evolve, a centralised Admiralty Photographic Library (which became known as NID11) was established at the New Bodleian Library in Oxford to house the ever-expanding library of ground photographs and a Contacts Register was set up there to list the names of all persons, British, Colonial or refugee, who could provide some expert insight or knowledge of a country. This register begun originally by NID6 in January 1941 under Lieutenant Robert Harling RNVR but it was to grow rapidly and by the spring of 1941 an ex-Paleobotanist from the British Museum, Mr F.M.

Major Sydney J. Freedberg, US Army, Section E, was a Professor of Art History at Harvard University and Wellesley College (© Harris Manchester College)

Members of the ISTD Geological Section 1945

Wonnacott started directing the Contact Register alongside Lieutenant Commander Anthony Hippisley-Coxe RNVR, a trained architect. Aligned with this in NID was a unit that was set up to directly assist the ISTD, known as the Contacts Section or NID21 based in London. Godfrey had long insisted that there would be an expert or specialist somewhere in the British Isles on every conceivable subject and topic, which could be vital to the intelligence community. Harling introduced the concept to the Americans who had been disorganised in this field due to the number of competing agencies and departments.

NID21 was to have access to the Home Office's Refugee Department and the Royal Patriotic School (RPS) in Wandsworth to interrogate immigration records, yielding names for people residing in Britain that could be added to the register and be subsequently approached by the NID for specific information. The liaison with RPS was to be the responsibility of Lieutenant Patrick Reilly RNVR. This work with the Home Office was to generate over 4,000 names and details for the register which would assist Allied intelligence with detailed topographical intelligence. This would include information in coastal defensive positions and shipping movements off the Normandy coast. They interviewed Royal Mail captains who had good knowledge of the French coastline. The Register had even helped to track down a man in a café in Glasgow who had a wealth of knowledge of the marshland around Cherbourg.

In Oxford, NID21 had ten rooms booked out every day until 4.00 pm at the Wilberforce Hotel, which were used to interview potential sources of intelligence. This was in conjunction with the ISTD at Manchester College and MI5 down the road at Blenheim Palace, who would arrange suitable security vetting. The individuals on the register would have been interviewed by a mix of geologists, hydrographers, economists and a variety of other specialists. By the end of the war, this Contacts Register was to have over 70,000 entries. It was a phenomenal undertaking and was to provide serious dividends in the pursuit of detailed topographical intelligence for northern France.

The ISTD worked very closely with the Ministry of Economic Warfare (MEW) and the Central Interpretation Unit (CIU) in the preparation of a product that became known as the Inter-Services Information Series (ISIS) reports. These comprehensive studies formed the core tenet of joint military planning.

A key source of information for the unit came directly from the French Resistance. Smuggled plans acquired through a variety of means outlined German minefields and defensive positions along the coast, military dispositions around the country and the RADAR stations which would need to be targeted before any invasion force came close to the French coast.

Working closely with the local Oxford University Press (OUP), the unit had established how to print and bind the intelligence volumes which would satisfy the requirements not only of the fighting units on the frontline, but also the needs of the technical and scientific staff assigned to the planning boards of any modern operation of war. The oversight of all ISTD printing fell to Margaret Godfrey, the wife of Admiral John Godfrey, the then Director of Naval Intelligence at the Admiralty. A couple of times a week she would corral the orders for maps, reports and intelligence handbooks to the OUP, then based on Walton Street. This industrial-scale operation was overseen at the OUP by the Assistant Printer to the University, Charles Batey. It has been estimated that the OUP printed over 170 million maps alone for the ISTD during its time in Oxford.

Godfrey's flame-haired wife Margaret was an integral part of the ISTD from its outset. She had left an Economics degree at the prestigious women-only Newnham College at the University of Cambridge to marry the then Captain Godfrey RN in 1921. Before entering the DNI and ISTD world, Margaret had worked at Bletchley Park and was well used to working under a cloak of secrecy. When she came to work with the ISTD, she took on more and more responsibility with the OUP and managed the printing of all mapping, illustrations and photographic plates for the whole department. When Admiral Godfrey was posted to India to take command of the Royal Indian Navy in 1943, her loss to the ISTD was felt enormously. It had to create a whole department to fill the void.

The ISTD grew to around 700 staff at Manchester College. The HQ had been relocated from the West London Victorian prison Wormwood Scrubs because of the Blitz in September 1940. Indeed, many of the Blenheim MI5 staff were being billeted in university buildings in the city.

The ISTD was instrumental in providing photographic booklets involving panoramic beach imagery showing the Normandy beaches that had been taken from Spitfires and other aircraft flying at 'zero elevation' at great risk to the pilots. These booklets were used by landing craft and naval coxswains to steer the vessels to the right locations on the French coast.

Many of the French maps in use in the early 1940s had been printed in the nineteenth century and were hopelessly dated. They were at a scale of 1:80,000 and were also in black and white, so of limited value operationally, especially with the lack of relief or contour lines. The ISTD had to provide maps on an unprecedented scale. By the middle of 1941 it had twenty-one draughtsmen and women working tirelessly to produce maps. The ISTD also took over the Ashmolean Library to accommodate the numerous draughtsmen and map-makers.

The Directorate of Military Intelligence (DMI) alone wanted a set of 1:50,000 maps from Cherbourg to Ostend, and for a depth of 10 miles inland. It requested

Manchester College, Oxford, courtyard and Lawns (© Harris Manchester College)

the maps be illustrated with details of the beach defences, airfields, ammunition and fuel dumps, and Wireless Telegraphy (W/T) transmitters and stations. Over 4,000 Naval ships and thousands of smaller vessels would need to be supplied with maps, photographic silhouettes and chartlets produced and distributed by the ISTD and NID. The Normandy maps were controlled and printed by the Geographical Section of the General Staff (GSGS).

Between 1941 and 1946 a series of comprehensive Geography handbooks – referred to as the *Naval Intelligence Division Geographical Handbook Series* – were produced by the academic teams at Oxford and Cambridge. They totalled thirty-one separate titles of fifty-eight volumes, making them the largest piece of geographical research ever published. The Preface of these publications was left to Admiral Godfrey to write, 'The purpose of these Handbooks was to supply by scientific research and skilled arrangement, material for the discussion of naval, military and political problems, as distinct from the examination of the problems themselves.'

For Overlord, the most significant NID Geographical Handbook was the *France – Geographical Handbook Series Volume I – IV*, published by NID in June 1942. The volumes' contents were *Physical Geography* (published in June 1942), *History and Administration* (published September 1942), *Economic Geography* (published October

1942) and *Ports and Communications* (published in October 1942). The volumes had been prepared for NID at the ISTD Cambridge sub-centre by the Director, J.M. Wordie, with the General Editor being Dr H.C. Darby.

It was not until 1944 that US personnel joined the unit. The first batch to join were put into Section A. Life at the college was good for those who had witnessed the other side of the war. As Norwegian exile Eleonore Fredrikke Knudtzon said: 'Oxford was a beautiful, quiet and lovely town. There was very little traffic and no air raids.... Some of us would lunch together ... it seemed to always be Welsh Rarebit and tea. There was not much to choose from. I had a happy life in Oxford during World War II and I remember those years with sentimental pleasure. I will never forget the very first day I walked through the large entrance doors into Manchester College. In a small, dark office I met up with a Norwegian Naval Officer who introduced me to what I would be doing. I would work in Section B, and before I could do anything else I had to sign the Official Secrets Act and was then issued an ID card. Outside the door leading into the garden two wardens stood guard checking everybody's ID cards. They also brought us our mail which always arrived in boxes.'

Security was tight at the college and inter-section contact was firmly restricted. As Eleanor states: 'Section B never visited the other departments or Nissen huts in the College. We met the others in the garden when we had a break, and became good friends, but we never talked "shop".... I worked in Section B which was a hut, a so-called Nissen Hut, and was one of two huts put up on the College lawn. The other hut was Section A which was so secret we were not allowed to enter or indeed know what they were doing.'

Many of the SOE operations to land agents ashore on the north French coastline were preceded with intelligence from the ISTD at Oxford. This intelligence was often delivered at short notice but was invaluable to successful and safe infiltration and subsequent extraction of agents.

Another Oxford college played a significant role in the war and D-Day. As Bletchley began to expand rapidly, a small section of thirty staff from the Broadway building in London formed the 'Code Construction Section' in August 1939 and established themselves at Mansfield College with the task of preparation and production of signals publications, codebooks and sheets, using the OUP for its printing requirements. The printers were also being used to produce geographic handbooks and guides to a variety of theatres of war for the ISTD at Manchester College, and a collection of studies for inter-services intelligence, what was the Theatre Intelligence Section (TIS).

The section, which came under the control of the Foreign Office for security reasons, was led by Commander Edward Hok RN. Its postal address was: Room 47b at the Foreign Office. The OUP referred to its customer simply as the 'Foreign Office

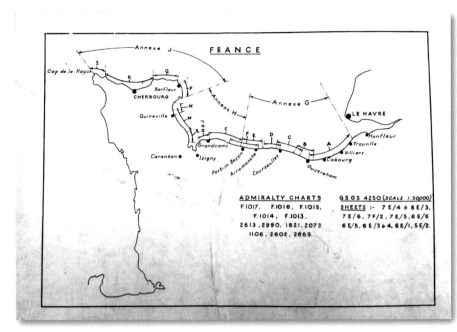

ISTD Booklets
for covering the
coastlines of
Normandy and
Brittany

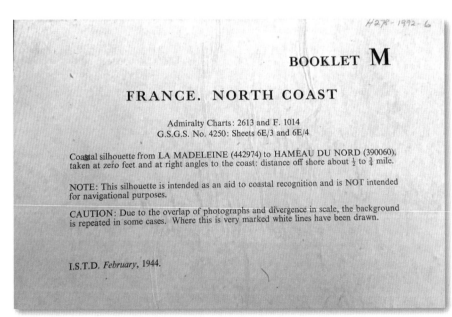

ISTD *Booklet*
M – Covering
La Madeleine
to Hameau du
Nord

section'. Over time, the Mansfield College section grew to nearly 300 staff and was accommodated as at Manchester College in temporary wooden huts in the college grounds and quadrangle. It had a close working relationship with GC&CS at Bletchley, and Brigadier Tiltman in his role as Chief Cryptographer was routinely consulted on the security of UK codes and ciphers. But the section administration was overseen by Commander Travis at Bletchley Park.

Secrecy was never a problem at the OUP. It was used to printing four to five million examination papers a year without any leaks. For many years the OUP produced examination papers for the Universities and Examination bodies of Britain, India and some of the colonies. The boss at the OUP, John Johnson, is alleged to have slept with the most sensitive documents they were asked to produce hidden under his bed in the office. 'For reasons of security I myself have not left this building since the eve of the outbreak of war, sleeping here, eating here and working here…. I have been tied to the wheels of warfare for so many years and have confined myself within these walls so steadfastly.' Johnson was very proud of his firm and of the role it played in the war effort. 'The greatest security in the Press is our tradition,' he was to write. 'I have the greatest of all possible satisfactions in feeling that the work goes on and is work of intimate national interest for the war effort.'

John Johnson was invited to be the Printer for the University in 1925 after working for Lord Cromer in the administration of Egypt and was tasked with reorganising production, re-grouping and re-staffing what was then the largest printworks in the country. It was also to bring in the trade unions. By the autumn of 1938 the spectre of war loomed, and Johnson prepared the OUP. 'I foresaw that the confidential training of this Press could play its own part in warfare if it were to come.' It was to cease all University printing and this was outsourced to printers all over the country. The OUP turned its hand to a huge production effort for the Mansfield section, which was to be its primary customer and the ISTD. Its work was to become one of the most vital cogs in a vast Allied war machine. As a reflection of this, hidden away in his desk drawers Johnson had stored away a personal letter of thanks from General Eisenhower after the opening of the campaign in North Africa.

In 1942, the 'Foreign Office Section' dealt with 37,000 different editions or issues producing over five million copies. The OUP was to scale-up production year on year throughout the war. In 1943 production increased to 80,000 different editions and delivered more than fifteen million copies. This was in comparison, for example, to 1938, when the OUP printed just 254 editions.

Johnson was always complementary of his Foreign Office colleagues and had immense respect for the way Hok ran such an efficient satellite of Bletchley. 'The huge increases in output of the Foreign Office Section in 1943 over 1942 has been made possible by the consummate skill of Commander Hok in interlocking with his producers and in getting the best out of all of us … in the punctilious execution of his duties and in his devoted disinterestedness I can say that I have never known Hok's superior. These sort of men just happen once in a generation whether they win recognition or not.' Johnson could probably see a lot of his own personality and characteristics in Hok, '… a first rate organising genius, has a good inventive and practical brain, just lives his job and doesn't care a damn for anything else'.

Hok was to devise a new method of preparing codebooks which permitted their reproduction by the lithographic process. By 1944 Hok was asked to return to his Royal Navy service but declined the move and his chance of promotion by remaining at Mansfield College where he had worked since 1938.

At its height the OUP had a staff totalling 800, all of whom had to sign the Official Secrets Act. They would collectively work an additional ten hours of overtime each week, bringing a total of fifty-five hours per week under union regulations. The facilities in Walton Street, Oxford became a secure area or 'Protected Place' under the Defence of the Realm Act, which gave them the protection of secrecy. Physical protection of the site included an air raid siren in the Secretary's Tower, sandbags on the roof and the buildings were never left unguarded. Each night twenty hand-picked volunteers were on duty within the gates ready for any call. Two of these were night watchman who constantly patrolled the perimeters. Another two were armed Home Guard soldiers who slept each night within the safe room containing all the printed code sheets and books. They were literally locked in overnight with their beds and a telephone.

The OUP was the pioneer of microfilm in Britain at the time, and the ISTD was to rely on it greatly for this microfilm service, often from samples collected by the

Photograph of Colonel Sam Bassett RM (© IWM London Photographic archives – reference A34311)

French Resistance, including the critically important films collected of the Normandy defences along Hitler's Atlantic Wall. Around March 1942, Johnson and Colonel Sam Bassett from the ISTD were working together to reproduce photographs from the NID Photographic Library. This was to rely on reproduction techniques using microfilm, which was then subsequently enlarged or reduced. Johnson was also to use Bassett's colleague Rodney Slessor to liaise with the microfile camera company in America.

This vast quantity of cipher sheets and codebooks fed the demand of a voracious Allied force now preparing for the biggest invasion of the war. They would be distributed down to some of the smallest fighting units in all of the services and many of the soldiers, sailors and airmen would have gone into battle on 6 June 1944 accompanied by a product of the Oxford University Press.

By the start of June 1944, each defensive battery in Normandy would have its own ISTD folder which would include its latitude and longitude, calibre/ammunition, arc or field of fire, number of available guns and their ranges and siting. It was not since the Dardanelles landings during the Gallipoli campaign in World War I that the British military had faced such a complex combined operation against a heavily defended shoreline at an enormous scale.

CHAPTER SEVENTEEN

SAND

'The cool and calculated bravery required to make this sustained and impudent reconnaissance under the very noses of the enemy and in the extremely unnatural conditions of life in X20 is quite outstanding.'

Admiral Sir Charles Little, Commander-in-Chief Portsmouth, February 1944 writing of Operation Postage Able in January 1944

~~~

The earth sciences of Geology and Geography are two subjects which seem a world apart from the secret and covert world of intelligence. Combined, this topographical knowledge was critical to the success of large-scale amphibious invasion, not just in the understanding of the beach and cliffs but also the hinterland, and how an invading force could logistically sustain a bridgehead. Aerial reconnaissance and intelligence collected from the French Resistance was invaluable in understanding the beaches. But there was no other way to establish the gradients, slopes, composition or, indeed, load-bearing capacity of a beach, or if the beaches were mined without putting men ashore. This critical work needed to be done, and from the sea.

Reconnaissance of the Normandy beaches was a British responsibility and during 1943 COSSAC was under some considerable pressure by the Combined Chiefs of Staff in Washington to get an estimate of the trackway required for the invasion vehicles. This was to meet their production timelines if Overlord was to occur in the summer of 1944.

Few accounts of D-Day mention the exploratory geology work that was undertaken to support the intelligence and planning efforts of the SHAEF and COSSAC staff. It was the British military geologists – such as Major William King from the Royal Engineers – that appraised the Normandy beach geology, leading to them being used as the landing point for the Overlord invasion. King was the most senior of the geologists assigned to the military during World War II and in civilian life he was a Professor of Geology at the University of London.

The geological research and planning for Overlord was very much a British affair and commenced nearly a year prior to D-Day. King had had previous experience in military geology during both World Wars which had led to his appointment as Geological Advisor to the Chief Engineer of 21st Army Group as it prepared for the Allied landings of June 1944.

The senior military geologists were to work alongside an Inter-Service Topographical Department (ISTD) Geological Section who proposed further effort in the creation of a soil unit comprising two geologists and two soil scientists. In October 1943, King left the Army to take up the appointment of the Professor of Geology at the University of Cambridge. His role was handed over to Captain Fred Shotton, who had been recalled to the UK from active service in North Africa. He would join the 21st Army Group team led by the physicist and scientific advisor to Combined Operations, Professor John Bernal. There was limited interaction between 21st Army Group Royal Engineers and those geologists residing in Oxford as part of the ISTD. This was largely due to the tight-knit secrecy around Overlord.

The Geological tasks that were put on the team were to include, '... library and photographic study of the cliffs of the proposed invasion areas; the provision of information on the foundations of enemy defences for their effective bombing; the preparation of water intelligence maps; information on sources of road metal, sand and gravel, and on the submarine geology of ports; and the detailed study of certain rivers with a view to assault crossings.' But clearly the most important aspect of the pre-Overlord research was the study of the beaches.

The massive amount of military vehicles that would have to pass across the landing beaches on D-Day and the following days and weeks would produce considerable strain on the surface of any beach, and intelligence needed to be collected on the geology and topography of each of the five invasion beaches. It would involve many different aspects – academic research, aerial reconnaissance using the assets and expertise from RAF Medmenham, and actual beach analysis by putting specialist troops like the COPP (Combined Operations Pilotage Parties) swimmer/diver teams ashore to collect sand samples. Aerial reconnaissance imagery did exist for the beaches but these would not convey the height of the beach obstacles, the weight-bearing capacity of the beaches nor whether the beaches would actually be mined, which would seriously impede an amphibious landing.

The COPP teams were based at Hayling Island Sailing Club on an isolated spit of land not far from Chichester harbour. The COPP comprised a small unit of special service volunteers who had been highly trained in beach reconnaissance under the leadership of Lieutenant Commander Nigel Clogstoun-Willmott RNVR as its Commanding Officer. If Clogstoun-Willmott was away on operations, Ralph Stanbury would step in as Acting Depot CO. Training at Hayling Island and Scotland would take three to four months. Each COPP team would typically comprise:

1 Lieutenant Commander (Navigator or Hydrographer) – in command
1 Lieutenant RNR or RNVR, Assistant

1 Captain Royal Engineers, Commando Special Boat Section (SBS) – Second-in-
,he warle, ted as D/F in the Acronyms and Abbreviations section. so, the closing
inverted comma in the previous para should be dcommand

1 Lieutenant RNVR, Maintenance and Intelligence

2 Seamen ratings (up to Petty Officer) Leadsmen, coxswains or paddlers

1 Seamen rating –Maintenance or as a reserve (to above)

1 Electrical mechanic/maintenance Petty Officer

1 Corporal or Sergeant SBS Commando – paddler guard

1 Draughtsmen Royal Engineers (Commando SBS)

1 Writer RN

Rare photograph of Lieutenant Commander Nigel Clogstoun-Willmott RNVR (© D-Day Museum/Andrew Whitmarsh)

Like many of the small covert units established during World War II, it was to have a significant contribution in this context for the outcome of Overlord. It owed its existence to the belief and drive of one man: Clogstoun-Willmott. He knew that a poorly prepared invasion would falter on any coast without adequate intelligence of the beach and hinterland. Assault forces could not rely on aerial photographs and charts alone. There was no substitute for putting a man ashore to gauge the hardness of the sand and whether it could support the weight of heavily armoured vehicles.

Clogstoun-Willmott was one of the first to learn of the Overlord plans, as far back as August 1943. 'They didn't know what the beaches were like. They might be rock shelves … or they might be a false beach, a bar on which the landing craft would debeach and out would come the tanks get deeper instead of shallower as they went in and they would all drown. So it was important … that's how it all started.'

Nigel Clogstoun-Willmott was the father of the whole beach reconnaissance organisation both in the Eastern Mediterranean and for Operation Torch, the North Africa landings. As commander of COPP he was responsible directly to Chief Combined Operations. The COPP teams started training with the X-Craft midget submarines as fully qualified submarine crew from 1 November 1943. The X-Craft were ideally suited to the role, and Clogstoun-Wilmott provided detailed specifications of how they could be used for delivering COPP diver/swimmer teams for the beach reconnaissance missions of Normandy.

Admiral Sir Max Horton instigated the development and trials on the X-Craft at the Admiralty, using HMS *Dolphin* as the main submarine base and the three submarine builders who had been requisitioned to assist with the build across multiple sites. Little was Horton to know what a vital role they would play in the critical reconnaissance of the beaches prior to the landings. Acting as way markers on the day itself was a fitting tribute to their work in the months prior.

The first X-Craft brought into operational service was the X3 launched on 15 March 1942, and over the first two years of their deployments it transpired they were ideal for such a clandestine operation with the profile of their superstructure so small that enemy RADAR would find it near impossible to detect them.

They were to need at least two months to become proficient X-Craft crew members at their training base at HMS *Varbel* on Loch Striven on the western coast of Scotland, alongside their normal duties of maintaining their own physical fitness and training techniques for beach reconnaissance. The Scottish phase of the training would also include tricks on sentry evasion, silent killing and the more humdrum aspects of the Overlord work in studying aerial reconnaissance imagery from Medmenham of the Normandy coast, getting lectures on the topographical features that they might encounter and MI9 lectures on enemy morale and psychology.

Clogstoun-Willmott was to state, 'Operating mainly with midget subs, and sometimes with native craft, or occasionally fast launches – whichever happened to be appropriate, but mainly midget submarines and working out of them by canoe and swimming. It soon became apparent to me, because at that time, I had spent quite a long time in subs, that it wouldn't be at all popular in the submarine command, to have to go in close to the Normandy beaches because they were fairly shallow and you could hardly submerge there, something always sticks out. So I knew there were these midget submarines and so I said to someone at SHAEF HQ – by that time we had all transferred to Norfolk House, where I had a number of colleagues and friends, who were planning people, mostly navigators or hydrographers. "I don't think we can do this with major subs … we'll need something else, possibly midget subs." Which raised a completely new set of problems because I didn't know much about them, how far inshore they could go, how long they could remain submerged. Eventually, it was decided that we had better take over, or partially take over some midget subs and do the job from there.'

The X-Craft were being built at three British precision engineering firms which had been tasked with the construction of a fleet of midget submarines: Marshall's in Gainsborough, Thomas Broadbent's in Huddersfield and Markham's in Chesterfield. Working in close collaboration, the firms' engineers and workers were subject to the Official Secrets Act, their very construction on the engineering yards being segregated off. The craft had been designed and built with a degree of urgency, as the Admiralty was keen to launch an attack on the German flagship, the *Tirpitz*.

The 52-ft long submarines were fitted out with diesel propulsion engines (similar in design to those used on the London buses), which were used when they were on the surface, and an electric drive motor for use when submersed. The submarines were designed to be towed long distances – as they were for the attack on the *Tirpitz* – by a conventional sub, or by a surface vessel as was the case for D-Day and the beach reconnaissances beforehand.

The COPP leadership would have to select two or three teams to do this beach reconnaissance work. Each COPP team was around nineteen in number and was led by a naval navigator, generally a Lieutenant, sometimes by a hydrographer or 'droggies' as they used to call them. Second in charge was a sapper captain, usually from the Special Boat Section (SBS). The plan to use X-Craft to deliver a COPP team to the Seine Bay beaches was vetoed by Admiral Sir Charles Little, the Commander-in-Chief Portsmouth. There was concern the submarines might become stranded on the Calvados Reef, so the first reconnaissances that were achieved used fast LCP(L) landing craft. Due to the topography of the western fringes of the Seine Bay and the distances involved for the craft transits, the teams would have to use the X-Craft instead.

Clogstoun-Willmott was front and centre of the planning. 'They asked me what could be done on the beaches ... they refined it to about three or four specific things and said "well, if you can get any more, we'd be glad to have it". Eventually, when the time of being able to do this – which was going to be in mid-winter because if the invasion was going to be in June, they would need knowledge of what they could alter and plan six months in advance. As the time grew nearer, the thing they were most worried about were these dark areas in some of the beaches, which were said to be peat, into which vehicles could sink. They had gone right back into pre-Norman and even Roman history ... the Romans had dug up peat from these very places and if these dark areas were peat, it would be too bad and they would have to think up some means of getting vehicles and tanks over that.'

The X-Craft crew had been trained on the west of Scotland where much of the covert reconnaissance teams were trained for Overlord and other Allied operations as part of the 12th Flotilla. They were based out of the Kyles of Bute Hydropathic Hotel at Port Bannatyne (HMS *Varbel*) where over 300 personnel were based at the height of the war as part of the Royal Navy's 12th Flotilla. *Varbel* had been a propaganda target of Dr Joseph Goebbels, the Reich Minister and lead propagandist for the Nazi regime. He had allegedly 'sunk' HMS *Varbel* twice, even though it was a shore establishment and unlikely to be torpedoed!

The training routines included entering the submarine, flooding up and down the Wet and Dry (W&D) compartment where the COPP divers would enter and exit the

DEFE2 1059
SBU DO387/C/43   MOST SECRET   4 NOV 1943

FROM: OIC COPP DEPOT. c/o GPO HAYLING ISLAND
DATE: 27 Oct 43 No. 23/4
To: Capt SBU
Copy to OC (COHQ) Ref: ISRB s DMN/5829 of 1st Oct 1943

    SUBJECT RECONNAISSANCE SUBMARINE

1. Opportunity was taken four weeks ago at the request of Colonel Neville RM of COHQ, to visit ISRB to view the Welfreighter and various other products.
2. The Welfreighter was found quite unsuitable for normal recce work, but the actual requirements for a CO Recce Submarine were discussed. These are not fulfilled by the X-Craft which will be a difficult craft to work with, from the point of view of exhaustion and various other reasons.
3. It was thought it might be necessary to design a modified Submarine or X-Craft or Welfreighter (say) type for recce purposes. For this reason the requirements have been put on record and are forwarded herewith (Enclosure No.1). They have with the exception of No.17 and No.18 been discussed with ISRB. No.17 and 18 were thought of since the meeting there.
4. ISRB state that the Admiralty Small Craft Committee are the deciding authority to whom such requirements are normally forwarded for preliminary consideration.

                                          (Signed) N. Clogstoun-Wilmott
                                                Lieutenant Commander

Enclosure No.1
Outline requirements for a COPP submarine
Enclosure No. 1 to COPP Depot s No. 23/4 dated 27 October 1943
                MOST SECRET

OUTLINE REQUIREMENTS FOR COPP SUBMARINE
1. 1000 miles endurance, more if possible. Speed? Engines?
2. Good accommodation for 5 men, suits etc. Human endurance at least 10 days, 14 days if required, cooking etc
3. Room for 3 Canoes Mark III (free-flooding with Kingstons in each compartment if necessary) must be protected by casing from sea
4. Good seawater seaworthiness
5. Low silhouette, no high conning tower
6. Able to dive for whole of daylight with a good margin of safety. Protosorb etc
    6a. Battery charging if necessary
7. Suggest round section hull with free-flooding flair etc.
8. Navigational and survey fittings as for X-Craft (list attached – Appendix 1)
9. Accessibility of diesel motors and batteries for maintenance
10. Simple as possible to operate, dive etc (part of crew will be RE)
11. Non-magnetic material in way of compass is required. At least one magnetic compass is essential
12. Browns or Sperry gyroscope compass and Submarine pressure type repeater required in conning tower
13. Good astern power
14. Draught as shallow as possible
15. Craft must be towable
16. Craft must be capable of being hoisted
17. W & D (Wet & Dry) Compartment in conning tower compartment for going on deck in swell (as for X-Craft principle)
18. Remote control of steering and motors from conning tower

craft, and carrying out shoreline reconnaissance using the periscope. Getting in and out of the submarine was an art form in itself for the diver teams, with the hatch openings being just 2 ft in diameter. Each member of the crew had to be able to do everyone else's job in case it was required. The air was often foul inside, particularly on long stints submerged. The carbon dioxide gas produced by the crew was absorbed by Protosorb canisters embedded in the ventilation trunking.

As the development of RADAR by the Germans gathered apace during the early 1940s, there was concern by the Royal Navy that these midget submarines might be prone to be detected close to shore, whilst surfaced. During their design, a low profile was factored in to give the vessels a low silhouette, making them ideal for beach reconnaissance.

The training was arduous and broken down into three phases. The Initial Training Exercise (ITX) involved running dives, dry manoeuvre training in still water and again with a significant tidal stream running, and manoeuvring with defective instruments. Following this would be the ANX (Advanced Navigation Exercise), where the crews were tested in busy shipping lanes, and the final Advanced Penetration Exercise (APX). This phase concentrated on manoeuvring the submarines through narrow entrances to lochs and returning out the same way, working with the currents and with more advanced techniques of dealing with instrument breakdowns.

By Christmas 1943, under pressure from the Allied command to move forward with the Normandy beach reconnaissance, COPP1 was instructed to finish its training with the X-Craft. The COPP teams and X-Craft were moved by specially adapted railcars down to Fort Blockhouse, at the western entrance to Portsmouth harbour to commence preparations for Overlord.

The two X-Craft that were used to carry out the reconnaissance of the Normandy beaches were fitted with directional hydrophones to monitor the movements of German craft in the water. These sonic devices were mounted on the housing of the night periscope. Alongside these, the midget submarines were also fitted with a recording device which could allow for capturing permanent records of any measurements taken, which would be of use to the Overlord planners. Both of these craft were painted a yellow ochre, stone and Hooker's green colour to minimise the potential of aerial observation by German spotter planes. The paint that was used on the hull was a specialist anti-magnetic paint to prevent contact with any magnetic nets in the area.

Under direction from the scientific advisor to Combined Operations HQ, Professor John Bernal, the COPP teams trialled their equipment at night on Brancaster Beach in north Norfolk, with backing from the Prime Minister's Chief Scientific Advisor Professor Frederick Lindemann. They were brought to the beach using Landing Craft Tank (LCT), which had sailed from King's Lynn. The COPP swimmers managed to get ashore, took sand samples, avoided the sentries on the beach and extracted to the LCT under the cover of darkness without being spotted. The two COPP swimmers were Major Logan Scott-Bowden from the Royal Engineers and Sergeant Bruce Ogden-Smith from the SBS. It was to be the first real test of a partnership that was to be vital to the outcome of the Normandy beach reconnaissance over the coming months.

Shotton would scour hundreds of aerial photographs taken by low-flying Spitfires and Mosquito aircraft to estimate the weight-bearing capacity of the sand in various sectors of each beach from the depth of wheel marks left by German carts transporting defensive equipment. Shotton even managed to get on aerial reconnaissance flights himself, sitting in the co-pilot seat, to witness firsthand the geology of the beaches.

Specialist research was also undertaken in the laboratory on beach processes, overseen by a Royal Engineers officer Brigadier Ralph Alger Bagnold, who also happened to be the founder and first commander of the Long Range Desert Group (LRDG) in North Africa. He was a veteran of World War I with the Royal Engineers, and a specialist in sand transport by wind. He had left the military in 1935 to research the physics of sand movement at Imperial College London but rejoined at the outbreak of World War II.

One of the COPP swimmer/diver teams that went ashore was Sergeant Bruce Ogden-Smith and Major General Logan Scott-Bowden, who reconnoitored Gold Beach. 'I served in Special Forces in the Norwegian campaign, and for that reason Nigel (Willmott-Brown) was pleased to accept me as his senior soldier and member of the number one reconnaissance team.

'We were sent over on New Year's Eve to examine an isolated metre square block of peat which was there on the beach and the probability was the peat would be clay fairly near the surface which would be highly dangerous to an invading force and

Major Logan Scott-Bowden (© COPP Heroes)

Sergeant Bruce Ogden-Smith (© COPP Heroes)

so we made our way back. The Germans were having a New Year's Eve party and they were an hour ahead in time on us and we could hear they were very well on so we didn't think we'd have any trouble, and so we carried out our examination and set about getting out through the breakers but the wind had blown us off course and we had some difficulty getting out but we did eventually break through. Bruce Ogden-Smith started yelling and he was slightly behind me, I swam back to him and he was shouting "Happy New Year!" and I wished him a Happy New Year too!

'We then swam out and shone our directional torches towards where we hoped our recovery boat would be and it was a little while before it fetched up, but suddenly it was there. We were hauled in, first in the recovery boat and then the motor torpedo boat which took us over, we were hauled into that and set off for home.'

Each time the swimmer went ashore they were heavily laden with an array of equipment, including sounding lead, auger, trowel, compass, shingle bag, beach gradient reel, stakes, condoms for collecting sand samples, bandolier, underwater writing pad and pencil, torch, .45 pistol and the all-important brandy flask.

The most difficult of the five beaches to assault would be Omaha Beach, which would be the task of the American 1st and 29th Infantry Divisions. In late January 1944 a COPP team was deployed to repeat the beach reconnaissance and surveys that had been undertaken at the other beaches. Bradley had made a specific request to see if the Omaha Beach topology could stand up to tanks.

Scott-Bowden was to state, 'General Bradley, who was commander-in-chief of all the American invasion forces, having heard we had examined the British beach he wanted Omaha Beach, as it became to be known as, to be examined too. By this time our midget submarines had come down from Loch Striven to the inner harbour at Fort Blockhouse. We went over in one of those, being towed out a third of the way by an armed trawler and then we were on our own. We went on overnight, arriving just after dawn, to find a French fishing fleet outside Omaha Beach with their nets out. Ken Hudspeth, who was the Australian in command of our boat decided we could get through underneath the nets, but of course a German soldier was in the bow of the boat with his greatcoat on and collar turned up and smoking a Bavarian pipe. We didn't want to be seen by him but we avoided that alright. We were then able to go about our main reconnaissance of Omaha Beach which took us another three days.

'We spent the best part of five days in the midget submarine. They were very smelly to say the least because we couldn't dispose of any gash. So when we came in to Gosport, to the inner harbour, when we opened up with the slightly onshore blowing breeze, the reception committee took a very smart step backwards.'

Made by Broadbent in 1943, HMS *Exemplar*, or X20 as it was more commonly known, had been towed on to target by an armed trawler. The midget submarine was commanded by Lieutenant Ken Hudspeth RANVR.

A day after Scott-Bowden returned to England he was sent to London. He was summoned to SHAEF Headquarters at Norfolk House in St James's Square to address a group of senior officers to establish the ground truth on what his reconnaissance mission had found. He faced five British and five American Admirals, as well as Major Generals Bedell Smith and Bull who were to command the US Armies and the British Major Generals Brownjohn and Inglis.

Also present was Lieutenant General Omar Bradley. After delivering his detailed summary, Scott-Bowden on his departure stated to General Bradley: 'I hope you don't mind my saying it, but this beach is a very formidable proposition indeed and there are bound to be tremendous casualties.' Bradley responded to Scott-Bowden with, 'I know, my boy, I know ...'

Operation Postage Able was the covername for a series of beach reconnaissance missions between 17 and 23 January 1944 by X-Craft and COPP swimmers, led by the indomitable Lieutenant Commander Nigel Clogstoun-Willmott RNVR. The operation was under the command of the Commander-in-Chief at Portsmouth who was to say of the operation: 'The cool and calculated bravery required to make this sustained and impudent reconnaissance under the very noses of the enemy and in the extremely unnatural conditions of life in X20 is quite outstanding.' Alongside Clogstoun-Willmott, who was in general command of the expedition, the team also comprised Lieutenant Ken Hudspeth RANVR who would act as the Commanding Officer for X20, Sub. Lieutenant Bruce Enzer as First Lieutenant and the two COPP1 divers, Major-General Scott-Bowden and Sergeant Ogden-Smith.

Like the procedure which was to follow in June 1944 with the X-Craft and COPP diver teams to waymark the invasion force, X20 was towed by a trawler to a point in mid-Channel by HMS *Darthema*. After the Normandy reconnaissance, X20 was to return to St Catherine's Point to rendezvous with the trawler and return to harbour. The mission was to undertake a reconnaissance of the beaches in the American sector of the Overlord area, such as the Colleville, Les Moulins (St Laurent) and Vierville beaches. The methods of daylight periscope reconnaissance had been pioneered during the training off the coast of Kintyre.

During the operation Major General Logan Scott-Bowden was the eyes and ears

1. Robin Harbud inside X-Craft midget submarine (© IWM Photographic Archives)

2. X25 CO at X-Craft speaking tube (© IWM London Photographic archives Ref A22905)

3. X-Craft underway (© IWM London Photographic archives Ref A21698)

4. Inside X-Craft (© IWM London Photographic archives Ref D 62203)

5. Profile of an X-Craft

behind a huge Overlord intelligence machine that would absorb everything he would witness on the beach. 'We could see the soldiers at work and everything, underneath a camouflage netting, and we were able to confirm what type of emplacements some of them were, whether they were likely to have 88 millimetre guns.... This all helped the interpreters, who were at 21st Army Group. Sleep was at a minimum. But then we were very fit ... and then the following, the third night, we swam ashore again.'

Born on 21 February 1920 and part of COPP1, but originally from the Royal Engineers, Scott-Bowden joined the army at the Royal Military Academy Woolwich in 1938 before war broke out and was commissioned on 3 July 1939. He volunteered to join the COPP unit on 28 May 1943.

'I had served in Special Forces in the 2nd Independent Company in Norway in 1940, and Major Stopple, as he then was, and I had to leave them in October 1940, on promotion going back to Territorial Division of which I'd served previously.'

He had been stuck in the UK for most of the war and was volunteering for 'anything that came along'. He joined as a Senior Officer, responsible for recruitment and training at the unit. 'In order to do that I had to go through the mill myself, and the training was really intensive and extensive, in that one had to learn a lot of naval techniques, and navigation courses.... I also went through the basic Commando course at Achnacarry.'

COPP began training for operations around September 1943. Scott-Bowden was there from the outset. 'We knew that reconnaissances were getting to be necessary on the Normandy beaches, over and above hydrographical reconnaissance, which were already being done and all the air photographic surveys that were being done and being utilised to try to work out the pilotage problem, which in the plateau, the Calvados area, was really extensive.' The teams at the time were not privy to the location being Normandy but they appreciated that this was the beginning of the campaign to open up a second front.

'Our standard technique, for which we trained, using two-man canoes from submarines, couldn't be utilised in the Channel because of the development of RADAR, and any submarine that surfaced in the Channel in proximity to the French coast would be DF'd immediately. So we had to start thinking of something else.'

Their equipment list was extensive: 'one had to have a buoyant swimsuit ... a weapon, a pistol and dagger. I preferred an automatic despite the fact that it needed extensive cleaning when you came back in. And we needed augurs to take samples as necessary from the beach. We needed wrist compasses, watches, torches, and all the essential things which one needed to get oneself on schedule to do a reconnaissance and get back out to the recovery vessel….' They would collect individual sand samples in condoms, which had been pre-prepared by WRNS staff using broom handles for practice.

The diving suits were old-fashioned and one of the COPP team, Galway, arranged for C.B. Gorman to make a specially designed suit

'I never cared for swimming very much, and one didn't have to be a good swimmer in the conventional sense, because you needed to swim in these swimsuits on your back, so that if there were stars and so on, you could keep direction, you could pilot yourself in the right direction, turning over occasionally to have a look at the shoreline if it was at all visible … we swam every day and night. Clogstoun-Willmott was a hard task master, he had us out in the water at dawn every single day, including the north end of Oxton when there was skim of ice on the water.

'Training went extremely well. We trained, initially, in the original X-craft … X-2 or X-4, and they were somewhat leaky, and they weren't quite as sophisticated as the X-20 series, which we actually operated in.

'… there was great concernment about the beach-bearing capacity of the beaches, particularly on the British side, because there's been considerable erosion over a period of 2,000 years of the coastline, and original port on the plateau of Calvados, the Roman port, was 2 kilometres out from the shoreline today, and in that area, it was known that there were extensive peat reserves. Professor Bernal, who was the Chief Scientific Officer to Chief Combined Operations, read up the geological history of the Normandy beaches, in five languages. He had the books all over his desk I remember, including Latin.

'I was reasonably apprehensive. It was not a very pleasant night. The wind was rising, it was blowing up the Channel. I don't know what the wind force was officially, but I think it was 3 to 4 and rising. And as we went in to our absolute astonishment, the light house, which stands back from the beach up on a bit of high ground behind Luc-sur-Mer was operating, and then it started drizzling and raining a bit … that was perhaps advantageous, but being exposed every so often from the beam of a light from the lighthouse on a beach where you feel extraordinarily naked anyway, even when it's pretty dark, well, it's not a good prospect. Somewhat apprehensive, yes …'

Hydrographical reconnaissance could only go in so far to a beach, and in this case didn't do the top end of the beach and beach defences and didn't get down to the beach weight bearing capacity problem.

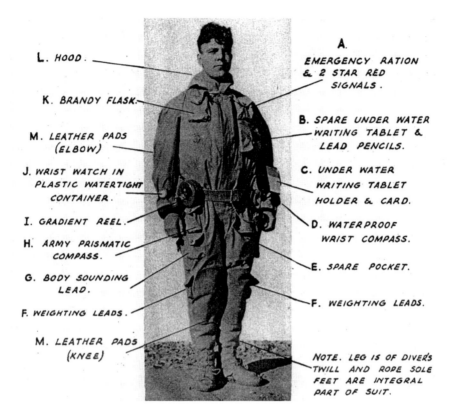

L. HOOD.

K. BRANDY FLASK.

M. LEATHER PADS (ELBOW)

J. WRIST WATCH IN PLASTIC WATERTIGHT CONTAINER.

I. GRADIENT REEL.

H. ARMY PRISMATIC COMPASS.

G. BODY SOUNDING LEAD.

F. WEIGHTING LEADS.

M. LEATHER PADS (KNEE)

A. EMERGENCY RATION & 2 STAR RED SIGNALS.

B. SPARE UNDER WATER WRITING TABLET & LEAD PENCILS.

C. UNDER WATER WRITING TABLET HOLDER & CARD.

D. WATERPROOF WRIST COMPASS.

E. SPARE POCKET.

F. WEIGHTING LEADS.

NOTE. LEG IS OF DIVERS TWILL AND ROPE SOLE FEET ARE INTEGRAL PART OF SUIT.

COPP swimsuit

'We transferred quite a way offshore, because the MTB had to carry on as if it was doing a normal patrol … and then we went in this craft, some two miles offshore … outside the breakers to make sure that the craft didn't broach to or anything. I and Bruce Ogden-Smith went into the water and left it.'

The COPP team would have swum in from a few hundred yards on the rising tide, about an hour before midnight. This night had been chosen as it was thought the defenders might be too busy celebrating to note any suspicious activity on the beach. Scott-Bowden made landfall about three-quarters of a mile from where they should have been, due to the tides.

'We were aiming for a point about a kilometre to the west of Luc-sur-Mer, but the set, which is the current which runs along a beach at certain stages of the tide, will probably run the other way when the tide's going out. It was very strong, and we actually were taken right eastwards to a point opposite Luc-sur-Mer, the village which is expanded nowadays, but it was fairly small then, and

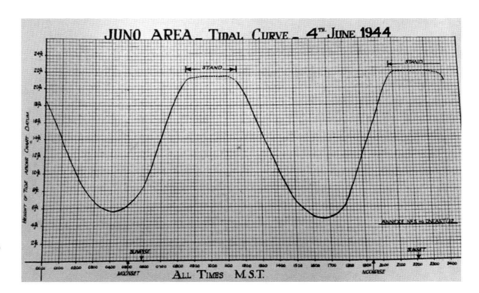

Tidal curve graph at Juno Beach pre-D-Day

so we then had to make our way back up to the area where we were going to do a detailed beach survey in a W-shape, and take samples, and put them into twelve inch bandoliers, 12-inch tubes which we had a dozen each on our backs, numbered tubes with a phosphorescent number on the top. As best we could but noting directly where on our underwater writing tablets which we wore on our arms, approximately where each sample had been taken from.

'… we trained so much and under so many varying conditions in the recovery business that one's confidence was good, but the anxiety was there, and if that were to occur, then we had wire clippers … we were to get ourselves through the wire … and get as far inland as possible. The Resistance were alerted that there would be people to be picked up, and that they were to look out for us. We also carried photographs and so on, and they would provide the necessary papers for us.'

The COPP teams wore rank badges on the cuffs of their diving suits. They had been aware of what had happened to Blondie Hasler's people after the famous Cockleshell heroes raid on St Nazaire, who had been shot on Hitler's orders. Scott-Bowden met one of the teams who had done these trips and had thought he had actually done a Normandy beach reconnaissance! He had clearly been elsewhere – it was all part of the deception plan being coordinated through Operation Bodyguard.

'We crawled for a while, and then we walked, and crawled … and we went flat before this beam came passed. Damned lighthouse, we flattened ourselves every time when we knew – we timed it, when it was coming.

'We thought we could hear some carousing going on in Luc-sur-Mer as we were going past her. And so they were, obviously celebrating. It was wet and windy, and we didn't think they'd be all that alert. We made sure we kept below the high-water marks, so that our tracks could be obscured by the rising tide that was still coming in.

'We also came across an outcrop of peat, which was suspected from air photographs, and so we confirmed that there is peat there. People were interrogated about beaches, the full length of the coast from the Pyrenees to Denmark, who'd sent in photographs which they were asked to do, and they all were concentrated in a place in Oxford, with an intelligence unit there we visited from time to time. We weren't surprised by this peat, but beneath it, of course there might be clay somewhere. But by and large, we knew that the area we did was going to turn out all right from the point of view of bearing capacity.

'We were each carrying a bandolier with a dozen tubes, but we didn't fill that amount … we've each got, I think, about eight.

'… the breakers were quite heavy, and we were positively bogged and tattered up with the bandolier and all our other kit and we had a go at getting out and were flung back … we sat as far out in the water as we could, there were smaller waves coming over us, and watched the rhythms of these breakers until such time as we could time it, the difficulty being when you get out of your depth … we got separated a bit, and we swam like hell to make sure we weren't going to be pitched back in again.

'We got to a point where we started flashing out torches, and of course you've always got to be careful that in quite a rough sea that you don't get slung around and flash in the wrong direction … and after what seemed rather a long time, we saw the craft coming in to pick us up, but it wasn't long, really.

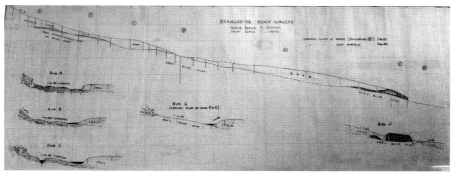

Results from Brancaster Beach surveys, January 1944 (© Shotton Archive)

'… Nigel thought we'd been rather quick, but with this increasing bad weather, and in view of the difficulties we'd had getting out, I think we timed it about right … we weren't exhausted, because we were very fit. We then went in that craft and had to rendezvous with the MTB, that was the next operation … and we set off for home … the MTB then decided that we had no chance of getting back to Gosport, and so we ran for Newhaven, and landed there. We had quite a bit to do, to write it up, and the following day I took samples to Combined Operations Headquarters where the experts were to analyse these … they didn't want the lot, but he took the ones from known points from each of us.'

About three days later Scott-Bowden opened one of the tube samples that COHQ had not been interested in, and when he got the sample out, it had discoloured to a jet-black colour. Panicked by that and wondering what had caused the reaction, he called through to Bernal's office and in guarded language got to speak to his assistant. He explained what he had found and responded 'Well, no … don't worry about that, it's a perfectly normal organic reaction when you stuff it in one of those tubes.'

The next time the teams went in was on Monday 22 January, in a boat commanded by Ken Hudspeth from the Royal Australian Navy. He had famously worked with George Armor on the *Tirpitz* operation. The X-Craft midget submarines were towed into position by armed trawlers. X20 was towed in by HMS *Darthema* commanded by Lieutenant Commander Brunning and escorted by a couple of Motor Launches (ML) which had been equipped with special radio navigational equipment for the operation. The operation was to follow a 2-mile wide corridor to its objective beach, made vacant of any Allied aircraft or shipping on night patrols. The vessels got to their rendezvous point off the Normandy coast by 0400hrs, at about the position of a German minefield. The *Darthema* was a deep draft ship so it could not transit the minefield, unlike the shallow drafted X-Craft which could take the risk. The tow connection was troublesome, costing the crews nearly an hour to uncouple before X20 moved off to the coast where it would remain for a week. The *Darthema* and its escort vessels would return to England.

'The anxiety was the same as before, but we strongly suspected that if we found everything alright that this was going to be the American sector, which at that time was confined to Omaha Beach. And then, of course, this sector was extended by Field Marshal Montgomery to take in Utah as well.

'We developed a technique of bottoming at periscope height, and taking a bearing on two narrow shore objects, and then taking bearings of what we could see on the periscope. Often we could see things which weren't visible from air photographs, even an aircraft flying at 50 ft above the water couldn't see underneath camouflage … we were looking from a worm's eye view, and we were able to see an awful lot … for Omaha Beach we were able to prepare an extensive panorama, confirming air photographic interpretations of a majority of the defences….

'We crossed over, I think on a Monday. We were towed out so far by … a converted trawler not halfway across the Channel but something like that which saved fuel, and we made better speed, and we slipped and submerged. We had to be on the surface for a while to put on a charge, recharge the batteries, and then we went in the following morning … we actually had to be careful because there were naval mine fields laid across the Cherbourg peninsula and across to Le Havre, which the Navy was secretly keeping swept channels through for operations such as the hydrographical operations that had been carried out … we approached from the West and to our considerable surprise we found a fleet of small fishing trawlers, fishing, more or less opposite the cliffs leading out of Pointe du Hoc. Nigel spotted a soldier in the bow of one of them, and gave the periscope to me to see if I could get any identification … I was able to see this fellow quite distinctly, with his collar up and his rifle slung over his shoulder, and even the shape of the curved pipe he was smoking, he was smoking one of those curved German cherrywood pipes, and very complacent. It was a pleasant morning … and we actually, to avoid the nets, passed right under their trawler. We got close to the shore and then were able to do considerable visual reconnaissance during that day. Then, as soon as it got dark, which it did fairly early in January, of course, the first thing we had to do was get out and put on a charge, which takes some time. It means you switch on the diesel motor and charge the batteries. And during that time, we had to then change into our swimsuits, which we did above the battery compartment … from the top of the battery compartment to hull was 2 ft 10 in. And so one at a time, we were able to creep in there, get our swimsuits on, and you had to be quite a contortionist to do that.

'… we again had to take samples. They weren't too worried about taking too many samples. They reckoned that if we judged with our augers, we could get down 18 inches with our augers, that we could test the firmness of the beaches adequately and we did the left-hand sector first, on the first night, and that operation went right according to plan, and we were able to take our time. And recovery, when we swam out, was quite straightforward. There was a slight sea riding, but nothing much to worry about.'

After about an hour and half on the beach collecting samples, taking measurements and assessing the defences, the COPP team had to swim about 300-400 yards to get to the recovery submarine. They reached the submarine successfully and repeated the operation the next night for the right-hand sector of the beach.

'... we did daytime reconnaissance, which was very interesting on Omaha Beach, because of the extent of the fortifications and concrete work was simply enormous'.

The team saw a lot of activity on the shore, with any number of soldiers preparing the defences.

'I was easily able even with the periscope to identify they were using two-wheeled carts. The cart excavated stuff away up an incline and deposited it somewhere over the top of the ridge behind Omaha Beach, and I was able to identify that it had two horses to a cart.

'... the sea was unexpectedly calm, and that was one condition one doesn't like, because you feel an extremely naked object in a calm sea, rather like a lake. And we were very careful about how we came in, and we came in facing forward, easing our way in with the tide, and then we were spotted by an alert sentry who had shone his high-powered torch directly ... we'd stay very still and gradually eased our way back out ... we were opposite the little village of I think Vierville, which is the right hand village of Omaha Beach, more or less opposite it, and then we eased our way back out and swam to the eastward, and then went in at a quiet place, well, a place where there were less buildings. We got up the back of the beach there and had a look at the round stones at the back of the beach. Bruce Ogden-Smith brought one back ... we had little bags to put those in, and I actually lost mine. I don't know what happened to it and was very alarmed. By this time, of course, they had not put the obstacles on the foreshore ... they were working from the Pas-de-Calais westward ... on what they thought were the higher priority beaches, and as time went by, we were able to see from the air photographs later on, how things were being developed.

'We'd got any amount of training, with our own chaps acting as sentries. We trained, we'd done a special rehearsal on the Brancaster beaches a bit before Christmas. And Professor Bernal, being very sceptical ... had reckoned that it would be extremely difficult to do an accurate reconnaissance and get away with it from the sentry point of view, so we arranged to do this at the Brancaster beaches, which are geologically very similar to the Calvados beaches in the British sector.

'I think we had considerable influence in getting permission for the reconnaissance to take place, because it had been ruled by Winston Churchill, through the Chiefs of Staff, that no reconnaissance would take place without his specific authorisation. And it was deemed a British responsibility, which slightly knocked the Americans, but they did not have the professionalism for this type of reconnaissance which Nigel had developed since 1942 when he first reconnoitered Rhodes.

'We went in the following morning to have a final look…. I think they spotted the periscope, because we then did get some firing … we could hear the shells exploding above us in the sea, and we only took a peep or two after that as we went to ensure our navigation was alright as we eased our way back out and set off for home.'

The thin periscope, about the thickness of a man's thumb was only raised between 6 inches and a 1 ft above the waterline, and only raised at short intervals typically less than a minute to avoid being observed. The X-Craft would be sighted during the periods of beach observation with the periscope as close as 400 yards but more typically much further away.

The intelligence the crews had collected during the Postage Able mission was passed onto COPPs and Allied planners. Of the beaches the team was to establish the following facts for Allied intelligence:

(a) Bearing capacity of the beaches inspected was adequate for all classes of vehicles

(b) Character of the beaches in this sector was uniform

(c) The surface was hard well-compacted sand. Samples were obtained

(d) Runnels exist; near low water mark they are sufficiently deep to cause 'drowning' of vehicles

(e) Shingle exists at the back of the beach. It is very large (diameter 6" approx), lies at a slope of 1/8 to an average height of 6 ft. A sample was obtained. It is a natural anti-tank and anti-wheeled vehicle obstacle. Where there is a sea wall, there is less shingle.

(f) Vierville sea wall is NOT being extended. It is a complete anti-tank obstacle.

The Postage Able team had provided invaluable first-hand detailed intelligence for the landing beaches, something that could not be replicated by other intelligence sources. It was a remarkable operation fulfilled by a remarkable group of men. In this report on the operation, Clogstoun-Willmott was to comment, 'all personnel remained reasonably fit during the operation (Benzedrine and Hyosein, as prescribed helped in some cases) … a fine spirit prevailed throughout amongst all hands, and in spite of the foul air, super-slum conditions and distasteful sewage system, a strain on the temper, no person was heard to pass strictures upon the habits or antecedents of any other…. Lieutenant Hudspeth's grasp of submarine technicalities, coolness and dexterity in handling the craft submerged was of the highest order, and Sub Lieutenant Enzer's skill and continual cheerful hard work must have been greatly responsible for the success of the expedition in that no major breakdowns and few minor ones occurred…. Major General Scott-Bowden's and his Sergeant Assistant's fine performance scarcely requires comment from me.'

It had been such a successful operation that it was not necessary to repeat it before D-Day. What had been proved was the versatility of the X-Craft midget submarines for this type of reconnaissance work. As was described aptly in the Postage Able official post-operation report, 'the x-craft has proved its suitability for these reconnaissances and appears in most cases to be preferable to the LCP(L) for this purpose … LCP(L) are more suitable for certain short reconnaissances in fair weather'.

During the final stages of planning for Overlord, concern arose about the impact that severe aerial and naval bombardment would have on the landing beaches in Normandy. The fear was that tanks, Bren carriers and other armoured vehicles coming ashore might be scuppered by the array of bomb craters left behind from the bombardment, or indeed whether the sand could support the weight of the tanks anyway. Allied Expeditionary Air Forces (AEAF) decided trials needed to be undertaken at beaches in England that mimicked the geology of the Normandy beaches. Beaches on the north Norfolk coastline were selected in January 1944 for the trials – Brancaster, Hunstanton and Thornham beaches, and the work was coordinated through the AEAFs chief bomb damage expert, Solly Zuckerman, and involved the geology experts at the ISTD in Oxford and COHQ.

Marauder and Mitchell bombers dropped 100 lb, 500 lb and 1000 lb bombs and the newly developed Typhoon fighter bombers fired their rockets directly on to designated areas of the beach. The scientists also wanted to gauge from these trials whether aerial reconnaissance alone could be used to assess, through analysis of bomb craters, whether a beach could repair itself sufficiently over time with a tidal sea, and what significant composition of sand and clay the beach had. This would provide a good awareness of whether the beach could sustain heavy armoured vehicles. Craters in areas of beach with little clay could fill within two days, and it was found 'that the suggestion of using craters to distinguish between beaches with clay and sand foundations is feasible …'

Photographic interpretation and expert analysis was provided to the trials by

21 Army Group and TIS, COSSAC alongside the CIU at RAF Medmenham. In all, some ten to twelve sorties were flown over the cratered beaches. One of the trial's conclusions by the Road Research Laboratory staff was 'areas unsuitable for traffic occurred where an insufficient thickness of sand rested on top of a soft wet clay. The varying stability of various parts of the beach was due to:

1) Varying thickness of sand
2) Differences in moisture content (and softness) of the clay.'

The investigations which were reported back to the War Office in December 1943 suggested that 'further full-scale tests are required to permit the critical sand thickness to give stability for various classes of vehicles to be correlated against the soil-moisture properties of the underlaying clay'. From this research, it was concluded that estimates of sand stability could be gleaned from just a small 60 gram sample taken from future beaches.

Four days after the COPP teams had finished their beach reconnaissance missions they were invited to 21st Army Group headquarters. At this stage, the scientists and intelligence staff had analysed every word in Major Scott-Bowden's operational report and had assessed that the Normandy beaches would offer no major topographical obstacles to a landing force. The sand was hard and compact enough to hold tanks and armoured vehicles. The gradients at the right tide were suitable.

Bomb crater from trials at Brancaster Beach, north Norfolk (© Shotton Archive)

Bomb craters
from trials at
Brancaster Beach,
north Norfolk

Each of the beach obstacles encountered during the COPP and Commando reconnaissances were rebuilt at the Combined Operations Experimental Establishments (COXE), where specialist teams like the Landing Craft Obstacle Clearance Unit (LCOCU) divers would rehearse methods to destroy them.

The intelligence staff had commissioned a number of sand-tray models of the beaches to be constructed for the headquarters. As the assembled staff drew Scott-Bowden and Clogstoun-Willmott's attention to them and peppered them with questions of their experiences during the reconnaissance missions, one thing was clear: the beaches had been selected well.

The successful planning and implementation of the Operation Overlord planning was undoubtedly shaped by many factors, but not least the geological research and intelligence-gathering missions that were undertaken months before D-Day, which helped contribute to the preparation of the detailed mapping and models used by the assault troops. It was also instrumental in better understanding the nature of sustaining a sizeable invasion force, with analysis of potential airfield sites, water sources and the seabed to guide the laying of the PLUTO (Pipeline Under The Ocean) fuel supply lines from the south coast.

CHAPTER EIGHTEEN

SURVEY

'I am impressed by the results that have been achieved and request that you will convey to these officers and to their crews my congratulations on the hard work they have done in training and preparing for the operations and on the resolution and skill with which their tasks were carried out in the face of considerable difficulty and hazard. On these operations depends to a very great extent the final success of Operation Overlord and I can assure you that the necessity for each one of them is carefully weighed before instructions are issued for them to be carried out.'

Admiral Ramsay in a letter of appreciation for the hydrographic survey operations, January 1944

~~~

It was Captain James Cook who introduced hydrography to the Royal Navy. It was his maritime experience and guidance which set the standards required. It is a fundamental component of the initial planning phases for all amphibious operations. The disastrous Dieppe Raid of August 1942, which resulted in a robust Allied force scuppered on the beach with over 3,000 dead, injured or captured servicemen, without any objective being reached, was a turning point in the war. It convinced Allied planners that any frontal assault on a defended port on the Atlantic Wall would fail. The raid also spurred on the Germans to harden their defences, turning all their deep-water ports in northern France into fortresses. The most useful charts available to the Admiralty at the time dated back to 1875.

With the experiences the Americans had had before 1944 in the Mediterranean and in the Pacific, they favoured an amphibious beach invasion until a Normandy port could be secured. The British planners wanted a reliance on artificial harbours. An unfathomable amount of supplies would need to be brought ashore early on in an invasion to support and maintain the proposed three Divisions that would be the main force to secure the beachhead on 6 June. This would increase to ten Divisions on D-Day+5 and then an additional Division would land each day until the required twenty Divisions were ashore to mount the land campaign to advance through occupied France.

It was not until the Quebec Conference in August 1943 that an agreement was reached, giving tacit approval for the creation of two massive Mulberry harbours (Mulberry A – the US planned harbour, and Mulberry B – the British harbour) which would have to operate for around ninety days, withstand wind speeds exceeding Force 6 on the

Beaufort Scale and be the size of Dover harbour. The whole of the Normandy coastline needed to be surveyed and intelligence gathered as to where these harbours could be constructed. Vessels the size of the Landing Ships Tank (LST) measuring over 300 ft and weighing over 4,000 tonnes could easily ground on a beach which had too shallow a shelf. Detailed intelligence of the beach topography was critical to the operation.

Set up in 1943 by the Hydrographer of the Navy, Vice Admiral Sir John Edgell, a small survey unit basing itself out of HMS (a block of flats in West Cowes) was charged with the task. This small cadre of talented and brave men, who revisited the beaches and coastline time and again, created the most comprehensive and complete intelligence picture ever achieved of a landing area. Could the road leading off the beach be sufficient to carry tanks? Would the Roman-era peat workings on some of the Normandy beaches scupper the tanks coming ashore? The only way to find out was to survey the beaches. Lieutenant Commander Frank Berncastle was appointed as Commander for the operations, with his able assistant Commander Nisbet Cunningham Glen.

Berncastle, nicknamed 'Snooze' for his ability to fall asleep, was born in Croydon in July 1912, the son of an Australian doctor. His father was also an ex-merchant seaman and he encouraged Frank to pursue a merchant navy career, starting off on the River Thames on the training vessel . He was to sail all over the world during his early career with ships from the British India and Indo-Chinese Steam Navigation Company and P&O. In 1936 he met some survey officers in Chatham from the Royal Navy who mentioned that the branch was looking for recruits. He applied and was commissioned into the Royal Naval Reserve (RNR).

His first survey work was undertaken off New Zealand on the , under the command of Rear Admiral Sir Guy Wyatt, who would later become the Hydrographer of the Navy. When World War II started, Berncastle was reassigned to the minesweeping branch of the Royal Navy until Wyatt saw the opportunity for him to work under the Chief of Combined Operations (CCO), Lord Louis Mountbatten, in order to make the hydrography work of the Navy more professional.

Berncastle was invited to SHAEF HQ at Norfolk House on 21 October 1943 for a meeting chaired by the head of British Naval planning cell for Overlord, Rear Admiral Creasy. It was at this meeting where the priorities for intelligence and reconnaissance were laid out. The first priority was for reconnaissance of the site for the two Mulberry harbours.

Six joint beach survey operations took place from early 1943 to January 1944 to survey the significant sites for the Normandy landings, including most importantly the siting of the two Mulberry and supplementary Gooseberry artificial harbours. Three operations were dedicated to the survey soundings for the Mulberry and Gooseberry harbours whilst the other three were run to collect sand samples using COPP divers from the beach itself and to run soundings in support of the Overlord landings.

The mainstay of these operations was a newly developed 32-ft long small motor boat – the Landing Craft Personnel (Large) or LCP(L), which were ideally suited and specially adapted to do this type of beach survey work. The vessels were trialled for the task in the seas around Dover and they established a unit, the 712th Landing Craft Personnel (LCP) (Survey) Flotilla, which was manned largely by British, American and Australian reservists. It was formed 'for the purpose of obtaining information on the enemy held beaches in Normandy prior to the Allied landings'. The single-engine vessels had an exhaust below the waterline to subdue any engine noise and fumes and had a low silhouette on the sea. The engines could muster a speed of up to 10 knots, but at the lower speed of 3 knots required for sounding they did not perform well.

The vessels were fitted with a light-tight canopy so that the crew could work covertly at night without emitting any light – essential as these vessels were going so close inshore that the risk of compromise by the German defenders could be high. A typical complement for a hydrographic survey LCP was one officer, one motor mechanic, one coxswain and two seamen. They were poorly armed, and were only fitted with a stripped Lewis machine-gun, which was largely ineffective anyway when the vessels were rolling in the swell. Crews often carried supplementary pistols and grenades as a confidence boost. The LCP(L)s were typically paired up with a more heavily armed and manoeuvrable Motor Gun Boat (MGB) from the 1st Coastal Force Flotilla. They towed the LCP(L) to a designated drop-off point and would loiter at a prearranged location whilst the LCP(L) undertook their survey work. This was often at speeds of just 3 knots, which made the piloting of the craft difficult in shallow rough seas.

The teams used the Echo-Sounding Taut Wire (or ESTW) procedure to measure beach gradients off the enemy's coast. This involved anchoring one vessel while another craft pulled a taut wire between the two in differing directions to measure the distance, in parallel with talking depth measurements through echo sounding equipment. The boats were also fitted with a naval version of an RAF radio positioning system referred to as QH, which were routinely next to useless.

On many occasions the crews would get extremely close to the beach itself in full sight of the enemy defensive positions. These surveys were vital to Overlord and the intelligence provided by the crews on these vessels made a significant contribution to the collection effort and knowledge of the beach topography. It helped confirm or deny other sources of intelligence. As reported in the Operation KJD survey report, 'there are no appreciable discrepancies between the information obtained from these traces and that taken from Mosaic No. 2 (M) 122 and French chart No. 847 which seems to indicate that these publications can be accepted as reliable guides in planning landing operations on this stretch of coast.

'The traces show that the rocks near the Low Water (LW) line would form a disastrous barrier to any craft attempting to land near LW. In the case of trace No. 2 the rocks do not show even at LW springs, nor moreover are they shown on the chart, but they are there, and would undoubtedly bring to grief any craft endeavouring to land.'

The first survey operation (Operation KJD) mounted using these landing craft was on the night of the 27–28 February 1943 involving LCP(L) 154 under the command of Sub Lieutenant Scott RNVR with its escort MGB 317 which set out from the Solent at 2110hrs at a steady 10 knots to Cap Barfleur alongside its partner LCP(L) 201 with Sub Lieutenant Tew RNVR at the helm.

Just after midnight the vessels sighted potential enemy ships and they halted. At 0039hrs they ascertained the ships to be part of an enemy convoy 2 miles south of the St Marcouf Islands including a merchant vessel, a tug towing some barges and four other small craft.

At 0042hrs the enemy challenged the British vessels with a blue light, and then opened fire with tracer ammunition from 4,000-5,000 yards away.

The crews did not panic or deviate from their mission. At 0130hrs a taut wire was streamed and soundings run to measure the beach gradient. The operational report stated, 'this was about 50 yards from the beach which appeared to be steep with a small breakwater a few yards in front of a cluster of houses which were apparently formed at the junction of a road with the beach itself.'

Operation KJF had the objective of the Rocher du Calvados area of Normandy (the area which was to be the site of the Arromanches Mulberry harbour) on the night of the 26–27 November 1943 using the LCP(L) vessels 177, 190 and 283 accompanied by their usual MGB escorts and tows. Setting course at 2120hrs, they arrived at their

Map of the beach selected for Mulberry 'B' at Arromanches – shallow and sandy with a small island of rock outcrop offshore. (C.4840 British official Air Ministry graphic)

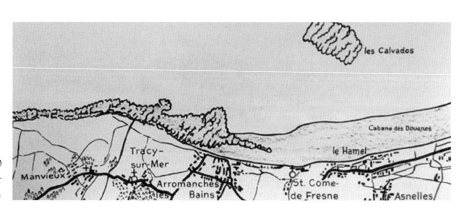

stated objective and started taking echo soundings while proceeding away from their marker boats. However, their efforts were marred by the ineffective use of the gear as the crew struggled to use the kit on the confined small LCP(L) craft due to their lack of experience: 'the traces were poor due to the difficulty of making the boat go slow enough to get a decent trace'.

In the official KJF report written by Lieutenant Commander Berncastle, 'No interest was aroused from the shore and there is no reason to suspect that our presence was detected.' Final locational positions were taken through bearings to the church in St Come-de-Fresne. It was apparent that the beach was contoured inshore of the low water line which would never have shown up from aerial photographs or the panoramic mosaics that were being produced at Medmenham and the ISTD.

Soundings were completed by 0400hrs and the LCP(L)s made their designated and pre-arranged rendezvous with their MGBs, assisted by the firing of some green Verey lights.

Operation KJG took place on the night of 1–2 December 1943 with the same officers and men who took part in the previous operation. The force included LCP(L) 190, 177 and 283 from the 712th LCP(L) Flotilla with their escorts, the MGBs 312, 316 and 326. The LCP(L)s formed up and proceeded at 2100hrs from Cowes for Pointe de la Percée and the French coast near the town of Vierville-sur-Mer on a clear and still night. It was this area of the Normandy coastline that was to be the site of the second Mulberry harbour used by the American forces. The LCP(L) vessels were towed close to the shoreline by their MGB marker boats. The crew had studied oblique aerial photographs prior to departure to orientate themselves with the local coastline. During the night, as they neared the coast, the crews fixed positions routinely using taut wire and echo soundings, and subsequently returned to Newhaven. They also took the opportunity to reconnoitre the coastline for prominent features but as stated in the official report, 'little can be given to supplement the oblique photographs as an aid to recognising at night this stretch of coast which is particularly lacking in distinctive features'.

Tidal streams were an area of focus for all the surveys undertaken off the French coast. It was necessary to gauge how strong the tides were around the invasion beaches and the flotilla achieved this using a 15-ft long pole running alongside the vessel and bottom samples were taken using an armed lead weights derived from 1-inch shell cases fixed to the flukes of the marker boat's anchor.

'The operation was carried out with skill and resolution in face of considerable difficulties.' This included problems with the measuring gear on the LCP(L) 190 vessel which had a defect to its echo sounding gear 'which was repaired by giving the amplifier a sharp blow'. This was routinely administered with a fist.

The force was under the command of the Senior Officer 1st Coastal Force Flotilla, but ultimately the KJG landing craft came under the direction of Lieutenant Commander Frank Berncastle.

After the mission, the LCP(L)s rendezvoused with their MGB escorts at position 'KK' at 0800hrs. A W/T watch was established with the senior officer LCP(L) carrying a portable W/T radio set to maintain communications between the MGB (call sign Pumic) and LCP (call sign Patchett) vessels.

It was also noted during Operation KJG that 'undue fatigue was caused by lack of hot food or drink during the long return passage in bad weather. It is considered that self-heating soups might be carried to obviate this.'This was duly organised by the Flotilla staff for future excursions to France, but only after Admiral Vian, the Commanding Officer at Cowes, intervened. The tins of soup should have carried a health warning, as they had a habit of exploding!

Copies of the KJG report went to the COSSAC Reconnaissance Committee and the operation played a vital role in successfully surveying beach areas where the Allies established the two Mulberry harbours off Arromanches and St Laurent, Omaha. However, KJG was not ultimately a success. The misidentification of the Vierville church spire for a tower at Pointe de la Percée caused a significant margin of error of over 2,000 yards from the objective. The error was only discovered as dawn approached and there was insufficient time to repeat the measuring procedures. Most of the failings were attributed to the unreliable QH equipment which was dependent on operator vigilance at the transmitters.

Berncastle was drafted in to support the hydrographic work for Mountbatten's staff at COHQ. He and other officers began training and operating out of Dover in early 1943. The COHQ Scientific advisor, Professor J.D. Bernal, had found some useful oblique aerial photographs indicating some potential obstructions on the Courseulles Beach, which looked like rocks where there should not have been any. These showed at the height of the tide when the aerial sortie had taken place to obtain the image. It transpired that the rock was actually just a kelp-seaweed bed.

Operation Bellpush Able involved LCP(L) 177, 190, 290 and 292 on the night of the 25–26 December 1943. The vessels had set a course for the Pointe de Ver lighthouse, which was first sighted at 2150hrs. It was this area which was later to become the Gold and Juno beaches of Overlord. Just before midnight, LCP(L) 292 anchored up about 1 ½ miles offshore under the command of Sub Lieutenant Waters RNVR. It was their task to measure the strength and direction of the tidal stream. The

Landing Craft
Personnel (Large) or
LCP(L) at sea from
starboard quarter
(© IWM London
Photographic
Archive – reference
A12067)

Landing Craft
Personnel (Large)
or LCP(L) at sea
(© IWM London
Photographic
Archive – reference
A24658)

teams had problems with the piano wire drums for taut wire measurements on three of the vessels. It was a difficult task to coordinate with the piloting done at the front of the boat and the wire streaming from the back of the vessel in pitch darkness. At the last attempt to measure a final set of soundings the vessel turned sharply, emitting an audible exhaust emission towards the shoreline. A few minutes later the Germans fired a star shell in the air to illuminate the area, followed by two more in quick succession. Fortunately for Berncastle and his men, they were not spotted. Two men from the COPP6 team came with the LCP(L) boats with the intention of launching a kayak and going ashore to undertake some beach reconnaissance but when the Germans extinguished the Pointe de Ver lighthouse the team abandoned any hope of this mission succeeding. At 0245hrs a course was set to rendezvous with their MGB escorts at a preset position before returning to Cowes.

A few days later, the follow-on Operation Bellpush Baker took place on the night of the 28–29 December 1943 using the same force and personnel from Bellpush Able. In addition, two members of COPP6, Lieutenants Amer and Wild, were brought along with a two-man kayak to get directly ashore onto the beach and investigate the nature of the beach.

Directly after this, Operation KJH took place using LCP(L) 290 and MGB 312, 316 and 317 on 31 December 1943 with Lieutenant Commander Clogstoun-Willmott as the Senior Officer from COPP1. The force was also complemented with Lieutenants Glen and Wild from COPP6 and Major General Scott-Bowden and Sergeant Ogden-Smith from COPP1. They also had a standby craft – LCP(L)292 with a COPP1 diver onboard, Lieutenant Galwey RNVR. The vessels were deployed against three significant Normandy locations: Ouistreham, Pointe de Ver and Port-en-Bessin. They used a primitive 'Heath Robinson' technique to gauge improvised markings using a short pole tied with handkerchiefs at intervals. The two COPP swimmers, Ogden-Smith and Scott-Bowden, swam ashore from nearly 500 yards out and were picked up a short while later, after carrying out their beach tasks: 'they were both somewhat exhausted from the battle with the surf'. For his role in this survey operation, Lieutenant Commander Nigel Clogstoun-Willmott was awarded a Mention in Dispatches (MiD).

There had been other COPP teams carrying out beach reconnaissance missions on different parts of the European coastline. Some of them were taken prisoner. COPP began training for operations around September 1943. Scott-Bowden was aware of the risks, 'we knew that reconnaissances were getting to be necessary on the Normandy beaches, over and above hydrographical reconnaissance, which were already being done and all the air photographic surveys that were being done and being utilised to try to work out the pilotage problem, which in the plateau, the Calvados area, was really extensive'.The teams at the time were not privy to the location being Normandy

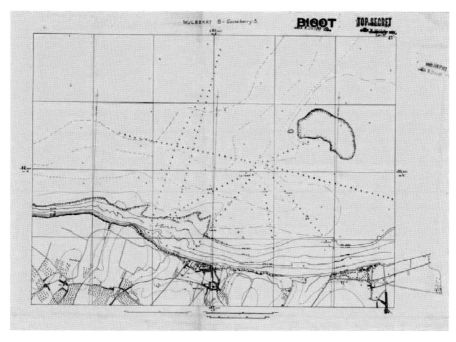

145 Operation KJF survey lines (from OP KJF report 26/27 November 1943)

but they appreciated that this was the beginning of the campaign to open up a second front.

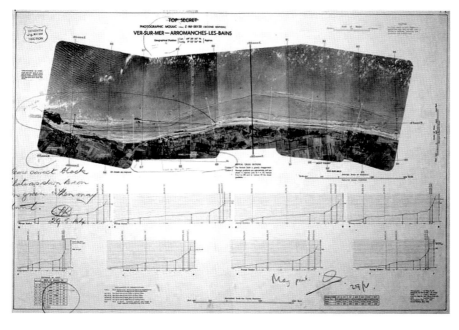

145 Operation KJF survey lines (from OP KJF report 26/27 November 1943)

'… there was great concernment about the beach-bearing capacity of the beaches, particularly on the British side, because there's been considerable erosion over a period of 2,000 years of the coastline, and original port on the plateau of Calvados, the Roman port, was 2 kilometres out from the shoreline today, and in that area, it was known that there were extensive peat reserves. Professor Bernal, who was the Chief Scientific Officer to Chief Combined Operations, read up the geological history of the Normandy beaches, in five languages … including Latin!'

Another expert in weight-bearing capacity of sand who was involved at the time was Major Sir Malcolm Campbell, due to his involvement in numerous land speed record-breaking attempts with . He often visited the COPP teams at their depot at Hayling Island and he was very much involved in the technical planning for this major combined operation.

Scott-Bowden stated, 'it was reckoned that there was about 14 inches of sand, above clay or peat, and where there is peat there is generally clay underneath the peat …

'… it was thought that, although it wasn't the dark period just passed, that New Year's Eve wouldn't be a bad time to do a quick reconnaissance of one of the British beaches … and we were briefed to go in over on New Year's Eve, 1943–1944, going in an MTB, towing a little craft used for hydrographical survey and certain hydrographical surveys had been done to establish the beach profile, and very good work had been done by a brilliant chap … Berncastle … and we were to have this craft. We were using the same technique that she'd been using for his surveys, his craft slipped its tow and did its reconnaissance and then was later picked up by an MTB.

'I spent hours studying air photographs, and their interpretation, at 21st Army Group Headquarters and St Paul's in London … one was very thoroughly briefed … the navigational pilotage problem we were really thoroughly briefed on by the Naval Headquarters and Admiral Sir Philip Bowen.

'… knowing that it was going to be in Normandy was an appalling burden … and knowing it for more than six months before the invasion took place, well it tended to be the topic of conversation, although its frightfully difficult for people nowadays to realise how wonderfully security-minded the whole nation was at that time, which helped one to keep one's mouth very firmly shut … we had proper security arrangements in our small unit, and things were really well-locked away in the safes, such as we had to have.

'We made sure we kept below the high-water marks, so that our tracks could be obscured by the rising tide that was still coming in.

'We also came across an outcrop of peat, which was suspected from air photographs, and so we confirmed that there is peat there. People were interrogated about beaches, the full length of the coast from the Pyrenees to Denmark, who'd sent in photographs which they were asked to do, and they all were concentrated in a place in Oxford, with an intelligence unit there we visited from time to time. We weren't surprised by this peat, but beneath it, of course there might be clay somewhere. But by and large, we knew that the area we did was going to turn out all right from the point of view of bearing capacity.

'We were each carrying a bandolier with a dozen tubes, but we didn't fill that amount … we've each got, I think, about eight.

'… the breakers were quite heavy, and we were positively bogged and tattered up with the bandolier and all our other kit, and we had a go at getting out and were flung back … we sat as far out in the water as we could, there were smaller waves coming over us, and watched the rhythms of these breakers until such time as we could time it, the difficulty being when you get out of your depth … we got separated a bit, and we swam like hell to make sure we weren't going to be pitched back in again.

'We got to a point where we started flashing out torches, and of course you've always got to be careful that in quite a rough sea that you don't get slung around and flash in the wrong direction … and after what seemed rather a long time, we saw the craft coming in to pick us up, but it wasn't long, really.'

The final joint survey operation mounted between the MGBs of the 1st Coastal Flotilla and the 712th LCP(L) Flotilla took place on 30 January 1944. Codenamed Operation Bellpush Charlie, it comprised of LCP(L) 291, 290 and 281 with the objective of the Calvados area of the Normandy coast, halfway between Cap Manvieux and the western edge of the town of Arromanches. The weather conditions were good, with no significant swell and good visibility – probably too good. As the vessels approached the Normandy coastline, the crews encountered a fog bank. At around 2 miles offshore, their visibility had been reduced to 50 yards.

During Bellpush Charlie it was the inexperienced crew members that hampered the survey work on the beaches 'while manoeuvring into position ready to stream taut wire they lost sight of the mark boat. This was the boat officer's first operational experience and he has had no training under such adverse conditions … it appears incredible that the mark boat was not sighted and can only be accounted for by the density of the fog.'

The poor visibility hampered this operation significantly, to a point where LCP(L) 281 and 291 collided, sustaining only minor hull damage. The Commanding Officer recommended that stern lights be fitted for future missions where poor visibility may be encountered. The operation achieved little and in the words of the official Bellpush Charlie report 'that so little was achieved is attributed to the unfortunate weather experienced, mechanical breakdowns, and the fact that although the personnel of the flotilla have had considerable operational experience, they have not had the opportunity for the training necessary to carry out such specialised work under such adverse conditions'.

Berncastle was erudite with his thoughts on his own operations and the vital role they played in the outcome for D-Day: 'It was not all success. We were undoubtedly lucky to have achieved so much on the first operation on 26/27th November 1943, and there can be no doubt that this contributed to the success of the Arromanches Mulberry Harbour and consequently to the whole Allied landings. Whether the error in positioning on the second operation contributed to the failure to build the second Mulberry Harbour to be used by the Americans, I do not know. It is a fact that we found nothing new that was not already known or available from the existing charts but we certainly confirmed them and added more detail. If we had discovered something different then the question of accuracy which I emphasise in the account would have been even more pertinent.'

When all these survey operations were completed by early 1944, Allied intelligence had a wealth of knowledge on the geography of the Normandy landing beaches. The Royal Navy proposed moving the crews to Iceland due to the secret and valuable knowledge they had accrued. But this knowledge was too valuable to be lost for Overlord, so the craft were employed in the initial assault phase on Neptune as pathfinders, marking the waypoints and channels for the vast armada of Allied naval vessels.

Major Fred Shotton played a significant role in the surveying and mapping support to the Normandy operations in his role as a senior military geologist. After a stint in Egypt, exercising his knowledge on hydrogeology to find water supplies for the Allied forces in North Africa, he was brought back in October 1943 to support the geology work for Normandy, working alongside physicists Professor Bernal and Lieutenant Colonel Johnson.

Just before Bellpush Charlie was mounted, the COPP diver teams were tasked with utilising a new entry method for beach survey, using an X-Craft midget submarine. The crews had been training for months with the COPP teams up at HMS on the shores of Loch Striven in Scotland. The craft, the X20 departed on 17 January 1944 for Operation Postage Able from Portsmouth, towed by the trawler HMS . The crew comprised three members of COPP1/Naval Party 750 – Clogstoun-Willmott, Scott-Bowden from the Royal Engineers and Ogden-Smith from the East Surrey Regiment and Special Boat Section (SBS). The X-Craft itself was manned by a skeleton crew of just two – Lieutenant Ken Hudspeth RANVR from the Australian Navy and Sub Lieutenant Bruce Enzer. In the words of Clogstoun-Willmott, who was in overall command of the operation:

'We were released about half-way across the Channel and made our own way under our own steam, as it were, from there on. I was on the bridge, more or less literally strapped to a post. Where one sat was not a conning tower, just the sort of top of the control room. You had a telephone which didn't work very well down to the control room and I was sitting like this and the sea was about there, so it was a very wet job. And you clung to this snorkel thing and they had some other sort of stanchion that came up that you were strapped to and eventually I sighted the coast and we took bearings on it so we knew where we were. It was getting on for dawn at this stage. We were heading for a point to the west of Port-en-Bessin and Verveuil and all that stretch of beach and cliffs, along there up to the next cliffs ... the first place you could see very clearly Port-en-Bessin.

'It was pretty near daylight by then and again one wondered would anyone see us, but we were such a tiny speck and were about 2 miles out, I think, and not going very fast. I wanted to get in on the surface because once we were submerged, our maximum speed was about three knots. Surface speed, we could do about seven or eight, it made a big difference, if we had to go too far under the surface, the batteries would soon run out so it was important to get there. So I risked staying on the surface for longer than I should have done. What you do is always a choice of one evil against another. Anyway, it was rather interesting seeing Port-en-Bessin and the cliffs each side of it, quite clearly in daylight. Anyway, we started creeping in and looking at the defences and points that we could make out at night, because you've got to be able to have some points of reference and be able to take bearings and know exactly where you are at night. We did that by day, through this tiny periscope, which was about as thick as a man's thumb. So we did a lot of that during that day and I think we had a little sleep during the afternoon. The days were spent peering through the periscope ... and making observations in our notebooks. We did quite a lot, because we went in quite close, I should think, as close as 100 yards from the edge of the water, depending on the depth because you had to have enough depth to remain submerged. We could see people on shore, you could see them bulldozing and improving their defences, making ditches. You could make out people quite easily most of the time. When we were at our "innermost" you could certainly see people.

'That night we surfaced and I think we had to charge batteries. That meant going out quite a long way, so that the noise of diesel (engines) wouldn't be heard and charged the batteries for about two to three hours, immediately after dark and then came in, extremely full of electricity and crept in carefully to the beach, in fact I think we grounded on purpose. I was determined to touch the soil of France. We had a long, sounding pole type of thing, marked and I remember making soundings as we went in. We were on the surface, I was on the casing, in fact, I was conning the boat in and the only other person on the casing was Scottie, all dressed up in his swimming gear and his sergeant because they were going to do the same thing again. It was fairly calm that night, much calmer than the first operation and he went in and messed around on the beach and took his samples. We went off about a couple of hundred yards and took current samples, tidal stream and some soundings all of which were noted down and he had a sortie schedule, we all had sortie schedules, which you memorised, to come back on alternative bearings.

'So I knew roughly where he ought to come back, abreast some bluff or other and sure enough, we saw the little blue light shining. The trouble of all these rendezvous was that people were inclined to dash in and across each other. This happened more than once on exercises and there was a fellow flashing out to seaward and a submarine waiting for him further in.

'A ridiculous situation but one that happened very easily, so we were very strict about depths of soundings. Anyway, it was all quite successful because we were all fairly well practiced by then. We picked him up without any real difficulty and he had had a moderately adventurous time. Again, he was nearly trodden on by a sentry and was in quite good form. Then there was this awful business of getting him out of his suit. He was exhausted and so was his sergeant and it was an awful business. We were in a space that was about that deep, rather like doing everything under a dining room table where people were swilling beer on top and it was all dripping through. It was wet, very wet in those subs and terrible condensation. They were unlined and so it was a job to get everything off … it was very hard work and they were exhausted.

'Anyway, we did the same thing next day, looking around further along the beach. These all turned out to be American beaches in the end, of course we didn't know that at the time. Much the same happened the second night except that when we came to laying the anchor, we anchored either whilst Scottie was inshore, probably while he was inshore because it was difficult to make sure you were in the right position unless you … anchor. When we did, we found it a hell of a job to weigh the anchor, because I was the only man and we had this fairly heavy cable, not chain of course, but a heavy rope thing. I couldn't weigh the bloody thing, it was too much for me, so I got old Ken Hudspeth up from below and together we managed it, with his hands … I was very thankful.

'During daylight, whilst we were wandering around the bay, trying to take observation and bearing, suddenly I saw a fishing boat within about 8 feet of us, buzzing past. We found we were surrounded by them and every other one had a German soldier on board to make sure the French fishermen did not decamp over the Channel and that sort of thing. We had the periscope up which is how we saw them. We pulled it down quickly and dived, it was rather alarming.

'We hadn't seen them before, should have seen them of course … we did do a circular search like subs always do but they must just have come round the point or something … we could see quite well the cliffs and anything higher, but a fishing boat, being very low, the periscope went that much above the water and always being covered by waves.

'… the next thing we heard was a sort of "whang, ping" and it sounded like an instrument string being twanged and after a bit, we noticed little spurts of spray and we reckoned we were being fired at. This was during the second or third day. Maybe it happened once or twice on the second day and it happened quite a lot on the third day. And we thought, well, they must have discovered us and were sending MTBs and trawlers and anti-sub vessels and God knows what and all that aircraft around which might have seen us through the water which was very shallow. After the second lot of firing which went on for about half an hour and then stopped and then started again … they probably hadn't taken alarm but thought it was a good thing to practice their musketry on. We reckoned the soldiers were just having a go at a good aiming mark and didn't realise it was a sub. You see we were moving so slowly, there was no feather of water and just a little stick sticking up like that and if we moved at all, it was about half a knot, so it probably didn't look like what they assumed was a periscope. Anyway, they didn't have any luck (they were firing small arms, maybe half-inch machine guns, not an anti-tank arms).

'We were anything from 200-500 yards offshore at this point and the ping was the sound of the bullet hitting the water, though it sounded as if it had hit us, though it didn't, luckily because we would have been blind if it had. Anyway, after a bit this got too much … we were going to do another night's recce but there wasn't really very much point in it, we thought. Ken Hudspeth and I thought, time to go, after all there was a great deal to be lost if we were caught, torture probably … we had a rather phoney cover story. I had a picture of myself with a French identification card disguised as "apache" which was a bit thin, though I did speak French, not good enough, but I could say I was a Breton or something. I spoke very bad French fairly fluently, but I don't think the others did. I didn't realise at the time that there was an elaborate cover plan along all those beaches right up to Calais where commando soldiers went in, in rubber boats and deliberately dropped compasses and dividers and various bits of navigation stuff, anchors and stuff. In fact a cousin of mine was doing it although I didn't know it at the time, it was such an elaborate plan that even if he had been caught, it wouldn't have mattered as much as we thought it would.

'I thought it would be a success because I knew we had good equipment.... I didn't want to know too much, but I had to know quite a bit about the landing craft otherwise I couldn't judge whether they could be beached there or not, or what. I thought it would be a fairly bloody show, but I thought we would get in all right. Actually, it was rather less bloody on the British beaches than I'd expected, but the American beaches were worse. We thought, whether we were right or not, that if they had accepted COPP help more than they had – they refused to have these midget subs acting as beacons to bring them in onto the correct beaches and sure enough, they didn't land on the correct beaches, they landed about a mile wrong and they couldn't get off the beaches and they were slaughtered on the beaches by the German fire.'

Using all the sources at their disposal – British Military Intelligence and the JIC assessment teams were sifting through the industrial scale aerial reconnaissance imagery, the holiday photographs from the British public, the auger samples from the cover COPP diver operations on to the beaches, even taking part in their own aerial sorties over the Normandy beaches in an adapted Mosquito reconnaissance aircraft. Accurate mapping and scale models were being developed through their work in order to aid the military planners and deploying forces.

CHAPTER NINETEEN

DISPERSE

*'Military intelligence is always out of date … there is a built in time-lag.
Better the best half-truth on time than the whole truth too late … in battle we
deal not with the true but with the likely. Speed is therefore of the essence of
the matter.'*

Brigadier Sir Edgar Williams,

General Bernard Montgomery's Chief Intelligence Officer 21st Army Group,

August 1942

From June 1942 an intelligence cell was established in a bleak basement office
called the 'Martian Room' in Storey's Gate, off St James's Park in London. It was to be
responsible for the distribution of top-secret intelligence summaries to a tight circle
of cleared military planners for D-Day. The group, which was known as the Theatre
Intelligence Section (TIS), was headed up by the tall and bespectacled Oxford don,
Professor John L. Austin, who was a Lieutenant Colonel by early 1944. The TIS was to
become the leading authority on proceedings in Normandy. It was owned originally

Professor John
Austin (c/o
Mark Rowe)

by the British Home Forces but command was later transferred to COSSAC via the 21st Army Group, where the intelligence section was being chronically underused. It became subsumed into the SHAEF G-2 planning cell by February 1942 and in the lead-up to D-Day it was a vital cog in the Allied intelligence machine, expanding its size to nearly 500 personnel to cope with the demand for its product.

The reports were nicknamed 'Martian' reports and they encompassed all sources of intelligence except ULTRA. These routine reports were published weekly and later daily, listing the changes in German military dispositions. The TIS had been busy from 1942 in sifting through intelligence from the French Resistance for interesting intelligence snippets for the benefit to the Air, Army and Naval departments. The Naval Intelligence Division (NID) was to rely heavily on the work of the TIS for intelligence on the German beach obstacles, the beach and cliff topography, RADAR stations and coastal defensive positions, and for assistance in developing target lists for Naval bombardment during the Neptune naval phase.

The TIS was to move locations as planning evolved for Overlord. It became a joint US-British unit and based itself out of the top floor offices of Peter Robinson's store on Oxford Street, London. The section was to accumulate a vast array of intelligence on the German coastal defences in Normandy on the supply lines, formations and transport systems which supplied them and on the German military organisation and disposition in this part of northern France.

Much of the seemingly trivial intelligence reports the TIS was to receive on the Normandy defences – such as the unfamiliar mechanisms of the captured French artillery in the coastal batteries to the lack of steel protective doors in the front of these gun emplacements – that had not arrived from Germany all had to be pieced together like a jigsaw. It has been estimated that over 50,000 eyewitness reports on the German defences in Normandy were provided by the French Resistance, which would have worked their way to the TIS office in London.

Austin was always very positive about the intelligence contributions made by the members of the French Resistance in Normandy, often at huge risk to themselves. 'I think that whatever the defences, we should ultimately have landed where we did – the beaches decided that. But this plan, certainly one of the most memorable ever furnished by the Resistance, gave enormous confidence by showing the fixity and weakness of the defence systems well in advance.'

The TIS had responsibility for a number of intelligence subjects:

(i)   Enemy order of battle
(ii)   Enemy land defences
(iii)   Beaches, inundations, roads, rivers and airfields

(iv)   Terrain and topography

(v)   Enemy lines of communication including military roads, military control of railways, troops and supply movements, rates of reinforcements, motor transport concentrations, fuel supply and dumps in conjunction with the Air War Office

(vi)   Signal installations, in relation to defence systems, and order of battle in conjunction with Military Intelligence War Office

(vii) Military supplies and supply installations

(viii) Local resources, electric power, and water supply

(ix)   Civil administration, organisation and control in occupied countries, insofar as it would affect the work of the intelligence staffs of army groups

(x)   German Air Force intelligence, limited to the following: German Air Force – Intelligence concerning strength and location of ground personnel which might affect ground operations, Flak-Intelligence concerning flak and airfield defences which might be used in a ground role.

One of the men that served with Austin at the time, Professor Beattie, commented: 'He was an outstanding authority on all branches of intelligence work, and they soon depended on his advice far more than would normally have been considered proper in any headquarters.'

The TIS was responsible for the production of pocket guides for the troops landing on the beaches of Normandy, referred to as the *Invade Mecum* booklet. Austin had quirkily named the booklet after his time at Shrewsbury School where new pupils were issued with a guidebook called the *Vade Mecum* (or 'Invade with me') which they were to carry on their person at all times. These regional field intelligence handbooks were issued to individual units, down to platoon level, and could fit easily in a pocket. They provided maps, town streetplans, roadsigns, communications and water sources for eight regions, from Cherbourg to Paris and Châteaudun, covering the projected invasion route through northern France. In some cases, the TIS could even provide the names of the mayors and Director of Utilities in some of the French towns and hamlets they were to pass through.

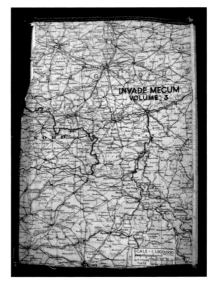

The *Invade Mecum* D-Day guide for landing assault units, produced by the TIS

It has been said of Austin that 'he was more than anybody responsible for the lifesaving accuracy of D-Day intelligence'. This well-compiled and comprehensive digest projected years of hard-won intelligence into the hands of individual units coming ashore on 6 June 1944. It was a masterstroke. They were an invaluable resource to the combat teams.

Maps are an integral part of any military operation, and the scale of Overlord meant the demand for good-quality mapping was often at the core of much of the intelligence collection effort by aerial reconnaissance, French Resistance or the ISTD in Oxford. The TIS was to produce fifty original 1:25,000 maps of the Normandy coast illustrating the German fortifications and defensive positions.

It was also integral in the production of the *Neptune Monograph*, which laid out all the knowledge Allied intelligence had on the beach defences and fortifications in Normandy, down to detailed individual sketches of the casemates and gun emplacements. It would even include details on the tides, currents and astronomical data.

As D-Day crept closer and was just a few days away, an intelligence officer from 21st Army Group visited GC&CS staff at Bletchley Park to convey the operational planning for Overlord. It helped convey to staff how their individual sections would work with the various liaison teams on board the Naval vessels or actually ashore with the advance forces. They were made aware of the importance of their work, and how it would contribute to the campaign and, most significantly, it gave them some idea of the scale and volume of traffic they would have to work through to meet demand.

Signals intelligence would be passed from Bletchley Park to Special Liaison Units (SLU) which were assigned to strategic military command level headquarters via Typex encrypted links referred to within a Special Communication Unit (SCU). These SLU teams were in essence the outward end of the ULTRA chain and could be found with 21st Army Group, 2nd Tactical Air Force (2nd TAF), US 3rd Army (with General Patton), US 1st Army (with General Omar Bradley) and one with the Canadian Forces, under General Henry Crerar.

Out of all the Special Liaison Units (SLU) for D-Day, the most significant was SLU8, which was assigned to Montgomery's 21st Army Group HQ. One of the team, RAF Flight Sergeant Gordon Rosenberg, had the responsibility of using the Typex machine to decipher ULTRA reports received from Bletchley Park. These messages were first passed to his chief of intelligence Brigadier Edgar Williams. In the run-up to D-Day they were billeted at Southwick House, near Portsmouth, alongside the senior officers General Eisenhower, Sir Arthur Tedder and General Montgomery. On D-Day+3 the SLU was deployed to Arromanches with General Montgomery to provide that direct ULTRA intelligence link in the fields and forests of France.

ONI APPENDIX VII. ANNEX A
JUNO AREA
DESCRIPTION OF BEACH DEFENCES (ST AUBIN sur MER to LA RIVIERE inclusive)

1. <u>On the Beaches</u>
   (a) <u>A line of fortified Beach strongpoints</u>
   These are widely spaced and are limited to the towns of ST AUBIN, BERNIERES, COURSEULLES (two strongpoints, one East and one West of the harbour) and LA RIVIERE. COURSEULLES, as the only place with a harbour on this stretch of coast, is the most strongly defended; there is also a strongpoint in rear of the town at 968849. The remainder of the coastline is protected by obstacles (see below) and weapons are sited to provide flanking fire in front of the obstacles as much as frontal fire out to sea. On artillery support, see below para 4.
   Between the strongpoints there are no fortifications, apart from a small post at 949863, midway between COURSEULLES and LA RIVIERE. The strongpoints are roughly of platoon size (30-50 men each if fully manned); the defence works present no unusual features except that they contain a large number of pillboxes and fortified houses on the seafront; Beach exits in the towns are thoroughly blocked & may also have fixed flame throwers to protect them.
   (b) <u>Obstacles</u>
   There is a continuous line of steel underwater obstacles along the entire beach. This consists mainly of two to four rows of steel hedgehogs, at a height of 12ft to 20ft above chart datum. AT COURSEULLES, however, the obstacles are thicker than elsewhere and extend further down the beach: Element C and large pyramids made of timber stakes are used here as well as hedgehogs. There is wire along the entire beach. Details are unknown: coiled wire and apron fence are most likely. As a rule there is only one belt of wire.
   Behind the beach, in the spaces between the strongpoints there are minefields up to 200 yards deep. These consist of both anti-tank and anti-personnel mines. There are narrow belts of anti-personnel mines surrounding the strongpoints.
   In rear of the minefields, the remainder of the low-lying ground is liable to flooding. It has been kept in a saturated condition by the Germans so as to form an obstacle to all vehicles and make movement difficult for Troops on foot. Roads and tracks through the flooded area are passable but are likely to be mined. In addition to the coastwise flooding the valley of the SEULLES is flooded up to 2 miles inland.

2. The only fortified positions inland are the following, which are connected with the beach fortifications:
TAILLEVILLE	003823 – a coast artillery HQ controlling Artillery in this area
DOUVRES-la-DÉLIVERANDE	0080 – a large RADAR station
COURSEULLES	968849 – possibly HQ for the COURSEULLES strongpoints

   There is also an OP in the church-tower at GRAYE-sur-MER 959850; but the town of GRAYE-sur-MER is NOT strongly defended.
MONT FLEURY	924863 – a RADAR station

3. <u>A line of field works on the rising ground behind the beaches</u>
   This consists of revetted dugouts and weapon-pits. It is built mainly on forward slopes at a height of 60-100 feet above sea level. It commands the coastal minefields and inundations, and supports the beach fortifications. This line is at present weak; but may be quickly increased and strengthened, especially by last minute laying of wire and mines.
   Similar field works have been built across the PROVENCE valley on the Northern outskirts of CREPON 9083, also across the SEULLES Valley protecting REVIERS 9681

4. <u>Artillery Positions</u>, in rear of the beach are echeloned up to three miles inland. Some are in concrete casemates, others are field positions only.
   MONT FLEURY 918861 – four field guns in casemates. Role coast defence, unlikely to bear on this beach unless guns are moved out of the casemates. Battery light defences support LA RIVIERE strongpoint
   VER-sur-MER 919842 – four medium howitzers in casemates. Role beach defence, in front of and on beaches at COURSEULLES
   REVIERS 972808 – four field gun howitzers. Role beach defence, all along JUNO beach, but principally towards COURSEULLES.

   Certain batteries near OUISTREHAM and in the area West of ARROMANCHES may also be brought to bear on this beach, if they are NOT otherwise committed.

The SLU teams were fitted out with US Dodge ambulances at Little Horwood and Whaddon in Buckinghamshire. Within SCU1 of Section VIII at Whaddon, a small team of engineers, which were referred to as the Mobile Construction team, led by Dennis Smith were responsible for fitting-out these vehicles with communications equipment in the grounds of Whaddon Hall. Eight of these ambulances were fitted out with a HRO receiver, a Mark III transmitter and power pack, operated by a team of two or three operators and a driver. Specialist RAF cipher staff attached to the unit would be housed in an additional vehicle. The teams had previously used Packard cars built by the Leonard Williams firm in Brentford but they had been deemed unsuitable for Overlord. In the early part of 1944, eight Guy 15-cwt vans were fitted out for Normandy to be used as the communication vans for the deployed SCU/SLU teams as part of SCU8, attached to the various Army Groups.

Six miles from Bletchley was Whaddon Hall, the main SIS W/T communications centre known as a Government Communications Centre (GCC). It was run by Brigadier Gambier-Parry (referred to in this context as Controller of Special Communications or CSC) who oversaw SIS agent communications, the Radio Security Service (RSS) and the PWE black propaganda broadcasting effort. Attached to Whaddon was SCU1, which ran a transmitting station in the village called Windy Ridge. With fixed teleprinter links from Hut 3, the site was responsible for transmitting Bletchley Park SIGINT reports directly to Allied commanders in the field and was the control hub for all SCU/SLU operations globally.

Colour photograph of a seven-man Lancaster bomber crew at RAF Waddington with two yellow pigeon boxes (© IWM London Photographic archive – reference TR186)

Mainline, the wireless transmission site at Whaddon Hall (© Geoff Pigeon)

SLU Guy 15-cwt Vans and personnel in the grounds of Whaddon Hall, being fitted out in April 1944 for deployment in the British and Canadian sectors on D-Day (© Geoff Pigeon)

The messages that were transmitted out of Windy Ridge to the deployed SLU teams had a priority scheme referred to as the Zs:

Z = Routine
ZZ = Important
ZZZ = Urgent

If a message had 4 or 5 Zs they were of maximum priority and would have gone direct to the operational commander, for example Montgomery or Patton.

Just before D-Day, Windy Ridge had around twenty staff on each watch, from all three service arms. The transmitters for the site were down the road at Tattenhoe Bare Farm, which was to avoid any interference with the sensitive receiving aerials at Whaddon.

General Patton's 3rd Army HQ was codenamed Lucky Forward with its attached SLU – which was referred to as Zeta – encompassing a Humber Super Snipe estate car which contained the cipher equipment and a Dodge van with all the rest of the equipment. The SCU would have in the region of sixteen staff, a Sergeant, two drivers and three W/T operators. The cipher teams would have used One-Time Pads (OTP) printed at the Oxford University Press. The 3rd Army went ashore on 4 July 1944 into the Cherbourg Peninsula via Utah beach.

SCU10 was formed in late 1943 and was based at Seawalls House in Bristol, also equipped with the Humber Super Snipe vehicle and a Bedford 3-tonne Control vehicle equipped with radio transmitter and receiver equipment, aerials and a Typex machine. Six SCU10 vehicles would be deployed with the 21st Army Group on Overlord. They were linked via W/T and under the operational command of Chief Counter Intelligence officer at the 21st Army Group HQ, as they were responsible for mobile W/T detection once ashore in Normandy. When in France they found themselves augmenting what the 30 Assault Units were tasked to undertake and unearthed numerous German radio workshops and stores, often returning German radio equipment back to England by air for assessment.

The SIS Section VII teams at Whaddon were not just fitting-out mobile vehicle communications units for Normandy, they also had a role in fitting out the Motor Gun Boats (MGB) and Motor Torpedo Boats (MTB) attached to the 15th MGB Flotilla operating out of Kingswear on the River Dart, a stone's throw from Dartmouth. In the weeks before D-Day these fast craft were used to drop SOE, SIS and MI9 to work with the French Resistance and reconnoitre the German defences. The Whaddon radio fits were crucial for the communications on these vessels.

Not long after the outbreak of World War II, an effective pigeon service came into being to supply birds for the relaying of intelligence between Britain and the continent. Pigeons were used extensively to convey secret messages between the French Resistance, SOE and Special Forces teams, like the Jedburgh units deployed into northern France. The Germans also found value in the use of pigeons. Each German intelligence section operating in and around Normandy used its own section of pigeons to relay information and secret messages. By 1942, the British deployed a falconry unit on the Isles of Scilly to intercept any suspect German pigeons that

Abwehr agents in England might be despatching.

NID prepared a generic questionnaire that was sent with pigeons to Resistance fighters in France. The questionnaire was a list of intelligence requirements for Allied planners. They wanted information on:

1. Address of German HQ
2. Address of place where German crews sleep
3. Names of ships sunk by our action
4. German preparation for invasion
5. Positions of German guns
6. German arrangements for coast watching or patrolling by day and night
7. German wireless stations
8. Morale of population
9. Morale of German crews
10. Alterations at docks and dock building
11. Coast and beach defences
12. Places of storage of mines, torpedoes and ammunition
13. Air raid damage – particularly damage to port facilities
14. AA defences
15. Amount and methods of oil transport
16. Extent of barge and shipbuilding
17. Movements of merchant ships and types of cargo
18. Amount and methods of oil storage including whereabouts of petrol dumps
19. Extent of listening to broadcasts

A total of nearly 200,000 pigeons were supplied from British pigeon breeders to the Armed Services and Intelligence agencies for their operations throughout the war. One of their major uses was for Operation Columba, using pigeons to gather intelligence from German occupied territory. Pigeons were used to provide an agent with a communications link back to Britain, after they had been dropped in German-occupied territory. It was an arrangement the RAF had with the French Resistance, to scatter pigeons in strategic sectors of France, often to ease the overloaded wireless networks.

They were often dropped at low altitude by parachute over enemy occupied territories with instructions and a questionnaire outlining the Allies information requirements for the finder. Their losses were large, as many of the birds were found by the enemy or collaborators. If anyone was found with a British pigeon they could have faced a death sentence. One such agent who was shot was Louis Berrier on 3

1.

2.

The National Pigeon Service

22, CLARENCE STREET,
GLOUCESTER.

Dear Sir,
I thank you for your communication informing me

that you have......10......birds ready for dispatch.

Will you kindly forward birds to:

.....Wing House.....

.....

on......1st Oct......if possible.

Enclosed please find (a) O.H.M.S. label for attaching to basket; (b) Railway Carrier's Notes, which kindly hand to booking clerk when dispatching birds.

Your basket will be sent back to you by return of rail.

Thanking you for your kind co-operation.

For the N.P.S. Committee.

J Selby - Thomas.

Secretary.

3.

Message No. 50

Pigeon No. 163 sent from Cambridge on 9.7.1941
Returned to Sandwich on 14.7.1941
With following message in French from Normandy or Brittany dated 13.7.1941
Transmitted to M.I.14 etc.

This Weston Super Mare bird strayed and was caught by Sandwich Police. Message forwarded to Sigs via Air Ministry Pigeon Officer.

Impossible to give any troop identifications.

We listen to all B.B.C. news and talks as do 95% of the people. The emissions on 49 metres and 41 metres are very much disturbed. Everything interests us but speak clearly and loud. We hear especially well "Jean (? Marien) in spite of the disturbances.

(a) There are no important concentrations of troops and no embarkation practices.

(b) Small detachments of artillery but of not much importance.

(c) The moral of the troops is very bad; they refuse to sing on returning from exercises and refuse to do manoeuvres, - there only been one during the last 3 days.

(d) No troop movements by rail.

(e) Nothing to report concerning aviation.

4.

Copy No. 4.   Army Form G.968.

ARMY PIGEON SERVICE
CONSIGNMENT NOTE   № 41006

This form with items 1 to 4 completed, should be retained as record by
O.C. Unit receiving pigeons mentioned below.

(1) Please receive (a)_____birds from the loft of (b)_____
Address (c)_____in (d) Basket No._____

Ring Particulars	COLOUR	SEX	Ring Particulars	COLOUR	SEX

(3) Collected by (a) Signature_____ (b) Rank_____
(4) Signature of Consignee (a)_____ (b) Rank_____ (c) Date_____
(5) Name of Command (a)_____ (b) Signature of Command Pigeons
Officer_____

1. Picture of Gustav, an RAF Coastal Command pigeon (©IWM London Photographic archive – reference CH13321)

2. Pigeon brings first D-Day news – Gustav, war correspondent's dispatch (© IWM London Photographic archive – reference CH13323)

3. NPS pigeon request note (© RPRA)

4. Example of returned pigeon message (from TNA – ADM 199/2475)

5. Army Pigeon Service, consignment note (© RPRA)

5.

August 1941 in the town of Ernes, southeast of Caen. The German counter-espionage teams in Normandy opened up their own pigeon school in Saint-Lô, which scuppered much of the RAF and French Resistance plans to expand the use of British pigeons.

The operation by the National Pigeon Service (NPS) occurred over the space of three-and-a-half years, and in total some 16,554 pigeons were sent for drops over Europe, of which only 1,842 returned to the shores of Britain. In the build up to Overlord, the intelligence requirements for northern France were vast, and pigeons provided photographs, diagrams and critical information of the Normandy region in broadening the understanding and locations of the German defensive positions.

During the war 7,556 unique reports were provided to the Services from the Air Ministry Pigeon Section, including three of the earliest insights of the D-Day landings. Many British pigeon lofts in southern England supplied nearly 47,000 birds to the Signals Corps of the US Army, some of which landed on the beaches of Normandy on 6 June with US troops.

There were some standout pigeons:

Commando (NURP.38.EGU.242) bred by Sid Moon in Haywards Heath. This bird made three trips to occupied France with SOE agents in 1942. He was awarded the Dickin Medal, but his work for the SOE was so secret at the time that his citation for the medal read: 'For successfully delivering messages from Agents in Occupied France on three occasions: twice under exceptionally adverse conditions, while serving with the NPS in 1942.'

Kenley Lass (NURP.36.JH.190) bred by W.H. Torkington from Paynton. This bird was the first to be used for secret communications from enemy occupied France. Its first mission was a parachute jump with an agent. On landing in France, the agent had to walk 9 miles on foot at night with the bird concealed on his person. The pigeon was then further detained for eleven days in a house whilst the agent collected the intelligence she was to carry home. She was released at 0820 hrs on 20 October 1940, arriving in Kenley at 1500 hrs the same day, covering over 300 miles. A few months later, on 11 February 1941 she was sent on a parallel task, except she was only confined in a house for four days this time and homed in an excellent time with more vital information. She was awarded the Dickin Medal from the PDSA for her work. Her citation reads: 'For being the first pigeon to be used with success for secret communications from an agent in enemy occupied France while serving with the NPS in October 1940.'

Gustav (NPS.42.31066) bred by NPS member F.E. Jackson in Corsham, who had been previously used with the Resistance in Belgium. For Normandy he was one

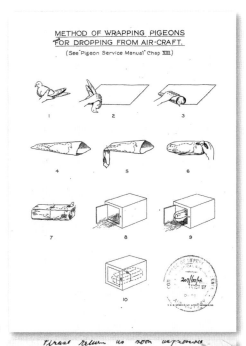

Procedure for wrapping pigeons for parachuting/carrying by agents (© RPRA)

NPS Authorisation for a Deputy Pigeon Supply Officer (PSO) (© RPRA)

of a group of six birds given to a Reuters correspondent, dispatched from a landing craft off the beach during one of the first landing waves. The weather was bad on D-Day but Gustav managed to fly the 150 miles to his home loft at RAF Thorney Island in a time of five hours and sixteen minutes, carrying the first message of the Normandy landings. Sergeant Harry Halsey removed the message from Gustav's container on his leg and the message read: 'We are just 20 miles or so off the beaches. First assault troops landed 0750. Steaming steadily in formation. Lightnings, Typhoons, Fortresses crossing since 0545. No enemy aircraft seen.' He was also awarded the Dickin Medal and his citation reads: 'For bringing the first message from the Normandy beaches from a ship off the beachhead while serving with the RAF on 6 June 1944.'

Duke of Normandy (NURP.41.SBC.219) was dropped with paratroopers from the 21st Army Group on D-Day and had spent six days in a basket while the troops secured the beachhead. On his eventual release, he managed to fly back to his loft in Britain in a journey that lasted twenty-seven hours. His Dickin Medal citation reads: 'For being the first bird to arrive with a message from Paratroops of 21st Army Group on D-Day, 6 June 1944, while serving with APS.'

Paddy (NPS.43.9451) was bred in County Antrim. He was just one of the several hundred birds, both Service and civilian, which were used on Overlord. Paddy achieved the fastest recorded flight time (four hours and fifty minutes) from Normandy. On 15 March 1944, he was selected for the Overlord campaign and moved to lofts at a south coast RAF station to train and prepare for D-Day. His trainer, Sergeant McLean,

German poster advertising the sentencing of French national Louis Berrier, killed by firing squad for possessing a British pigeon

Ministry of Food, NPS priority ration card WWII (© RPRA)

described the pigeon as of 'exceptional intelligence'.

The birds were supplied through local agreement with selected lofts by the NPS and trained by NPS Special Section groups, which were bolstered by reinforcements from NPS breeders all over the country. The Special Section was created to maintain secrecy for Overlord, with 'the greatest care being taken to ensure that the least possible information was available to the loft owners regarding the work being undertaken'.

By 1942 a new system was introduced by the NPS, in establishing groups of fanciers under a Pigeon Supply Officer (PSO) largely to meet the demand put upon the service. In southern England around 1,300 lofts were training and supplying pigeons. When the birds were used for operations by the SOE or the Jedburgh teams, the fanciers would receive a small rent in the form of a payment for service flights, however many of the birds did not return. The pigeons that were selected for service were collected from the loft owners, often just the day prior to despatch and taken to the airfield where they were fitted with their green message containers and packed into single bird containers with a parachute attached. They were also packaged up with enough corn for ten days, some instructions and the questionnaire.

Once found in a field or garden by a willing Frenchman, he was instructed not to free the bird in adverse weather or at dusk but to keep hold of it until the weather was good. They were to be fed an eggcup of corn every day and watered frequently. The pigeon would need to be placed on a tree when the time was right for despatch. There was advice on fitting the questionnaire and any other paper into the canister and on to the bird's leg. In one such case, a bird returned from France with a message containing over 5,000 words and 15 sketch maps.

German troops in northern France were encouraged to shoot pigeons flying overhead, and they even employed specialist falconry teams to intercept the birds in the Pas-de-Calais region.

The unpaid PSO kept training records of all the nominated birds, so on receipt of a service's request which typically arrived ten days prior to an operation, they would know which pigeons had the requisite training to home from France. Most fancier groups in southern England were capable of supplying around 1,000-2,000 birds per month if the need arose. In the summer of 1944, some 28,000 pigeons were in training, readying the supply for the invasion of Europe. The groups were not just supplying British troops and agents, they also supplied the Signals Corps of the US Army with a few hundred pigeons for Overlord, mostly from designated lofts in Portsmouth and Plymouth.

Bletchley Park also maintained an active pigeon loft under the management of a local fancier, Charles Skevington. He was responsible for training and preparing the pigeons that were given to SOE agents at RAF Tempsford airfield when they were deployed to Europe. Skevington had been excused military service, as he worked for a corn merchant which during the war was a 'reserved occupation'.

Special Section was formally closed down in January 1945, although the reality was the final push into Europe needed no further requirement from the NPS.

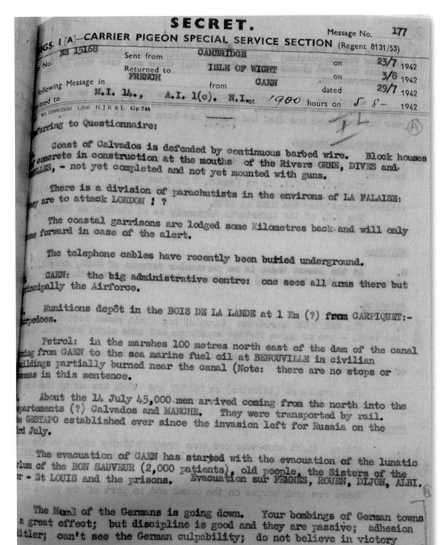

SECRET.

[A] CARRIER PIGEON SPECIAL SERVICE SECTION (Regent 8131/53)

Message No. **177**

HGS. I

NS 15168

No.	Sent from	CAMBRIDGE	on	23/7 1942
Returned to	ISLE OF WIGHT	on	3/8 1942
following Message in FRENCH	from CAEN	dated	29/7 1942
itted to M.I. 14., A.I. 1(c). N.I.	at 1900 hours on 5 8 - 1942

Referring to Questionnaire:

Coast of Calvados is defended by continuous barbed wire. Block houses of concrete in construction at the mouths of the Rivers ORNE, DIVES and VILLES, - not yet completed and not yet mounted with guns.

There is a division of parachutists in the environs of LA FALAISE: they are to attack LONDON ! ?

The coastal garrisons are lodged some Kilometres back and will only come forward in case of the alert.

The telephone cables have recently been buried underground.

CAEN: the big administrative centre: one sees all arms there but principally the Airforce.

Munitions depôt in the BOIS DE LA LANDE at 1 Km (?) from CARPIQUET:- torpedoes.

Petrol: in the marshes 100 metres north east of the dam of the canal going from CAEN to the sea marine fuel oil at BENOUVILLE in civilian buildings partially burned near the canal (Note: there are no stops or commas in this sentence.

About the 14 July 45,000 men arrived coming from the north into the departments (?) Calvados and MANCHE. They were transported by rail. The GESTAPO established ever since the invasion left for Russia on the 3rd July.

The evacuation of CAEN has started with the evacuation of the lunatic asylum of the BON SAUVEUR (2,000 patients), old people, the Sisters of the Poor - St LOUIS and the prisons. Evacuation sur FEGNES, ROUEN, DIJON, ALBI.

The Moral of the Germans is going down. Your bombings of German towns a great effect; but discipline is good and they are passive; adhesion Hitler; can't see the German culpability; do not believe in victory

Sample report from 1942 from Normandy transmitted via pigeon (© ADM 199-2475)

Date	Despatches	Returned	%
Beginning of Service to September 1941	616	139	22.5
October 1941–March 1942	74	14	19
April 1942–September 1942	1,342	267	20
October 1942–March 1943	1,664	113	7
April 1943–September 1943	3,793	528	14
October 1943–March 1944	2,819	161	5.75
April 1944–September 1944	6,246	620	10
TOTAL	16,554	1,842	1

The US 21st Army Group in conjunction with the NPS and others generated a plan called Operation Columba for the creation of mobile pigeon lofts which would go into France with the invasion force once the bridgehead was established. Each of these mobile sections could carry 720 pigeons, with a reserve of 1,400 birds held back in England to replenish the mobile sections when required.

As stated in a Columba summary report from January 1944, 'it is recommended that direct consultation begin between 21 Army Group and the Special Section with a view to ensuring that intelligence requirements are fully covered and coordinated in all stages of operations'.

There were essentially three components to the success of the NPS/Special Section support in the build up to D-Day:

1. Constant supply of pigeons which were capable of homing from across the Channel from distances up to 300 miles.
2. Means of delivering these birds in good condition to the users in areas where information was required.
3. The presence of people with the courage and will to use them.

In terms of intelligence value, pigeons have stood the test of time in all wars. This can best be surmised from a PID statement from L.J. Beck from the French section, who wrote of the value of the pigeon service to the work of the SOE and the PWE:

a) The information contained in these extracts does not duplicate information from other sources.

Headquarters   25th August, 1945.
United Kingdom Base
APO 413, US Army

The Secretary,
National Pigeon Service,
22, Clarence Street,
Gloucester.

Dear Sir,

         On behalf of the Signal Corps, United
States Army, I would like to express sincere
appreciation to the members of the National Pigeon Service
for the help and co-operation which they have so
generously extended.

         During the operations of our forces in
the European Theatre, British pigeon fanciers furnished
46,532 pigeons for our use.   Some of these birds
landed with American troops on D-day and communication
by pigeon continued until the final surrender of Germany.

         We well recognise that this abundant
supply of carrier pigeons would not have been possible
without the splendid assistance of the many civilian
breeders of your organization, who without cost to us,
kept our needs constantly supplied.

         It would be impossible to express our
gratitude personally to each member of the National
Pigeon Service who participated, so that I am taking this
method of conveying our thanks to the entire group.

         Yours very truly,

         Signed:- F. S. STRONG, JR.,
         Brigadier General USA.
         Commanding.

Letter of thanks from the US Army to the NPS, August 1945

b) The messages have this unique advantage over practically all other sources that they are speedy and detailed with regard to geographical location.

c) The matters which are always of interest to us and which form in many ways an essential part of our intelligence are:

    i) Information regarding the audibility and reactions to the BBC

    ii) Living conditions

Air Ministry,

King Charles Street,

Whitehall,

S.W.1.

31st May, 1945.

Sir,

   I am commanded by the Air Council to express their appreciation of the valuable services rendered by the Committee and Members of the National Pigeon Service during the war against Germany.

   The British Army, the Royal Air Force and the Army of the United States have made the fullest use of the pigeons supplied by the National Pigeon Service, and highly-trained birds given or lent by your members have also been employed on special missions and by the Resistance Movements of our Allies. Furthermore, the assistance of pigeon owners in carrying out the measures of control instituted in this country has been an important contribution to security.

   The Council are most grateful to all those who have contributed their time and experience to these various activities in support of the war effort.

    I am, Sir,
     Your obedient Servant,

     Signed:- A.W. Street.
     Permanent Under-Secretary of State.

The Secretary,
 The National Pigeon Service Committee.

Letter of thanks from the Air Ministry to the NPS, May 1945

  iii) The names of collaborators

 d) Complete destruction.

Overlooking Portsmouth harbour on the Portsdown escarpment are five historic Victorian forts, known as the Palmerston Forts. One of these, Fort Southwick, played a critical role in the execution of D-Day through the relay of information and intelligence directly to the Allied invasion fleet. In February 1942, work began to excavate a huge underground complex 100 ft below the surface of the Fort. 172 Tunnelling Company, Royal Engineers were charged with the task of excavating an array of tunnels that was to eventually house over 700 staff from all three services, although the majority of staff were women from the WRNS. It was one of the main communications hubs for Overlord and was connected to the outside world via an array of teleprinter networks which reached out to the Admiralty, Southwick House and other locations.

Over 1,000 staff were based above ground in the Fort itself and the access to the secret tunnel complex was via three staircases. Because of the D-Day connection, its location and work underground were very closely guarded secrets.

Linked to Fort Southwick was a secure underground radio station built into the Paulsgrove chalk pit half a mile away, which acted as the transmitting and receiving station for the underground headquarters. The distance between would have avoided any attention from the *Luftwaffe* flying in the area. The complex is dominated by a main tunnel running east to west, which is 112 ft long.

NAVAL SECTION – BLETCHLEY PARK

Graphic showing the chain of communication for intelligence during Overlord from the Naval Section in Hut 3 at Bletchley Park and how intelligence was conveyed to the ANCXF Admiral Bertram Ramsay

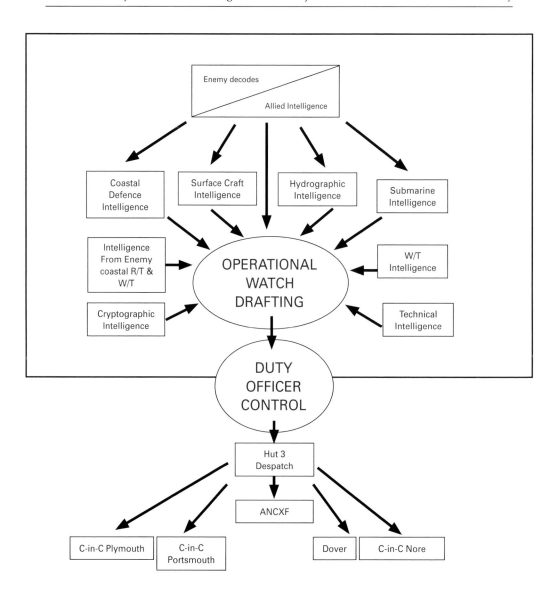

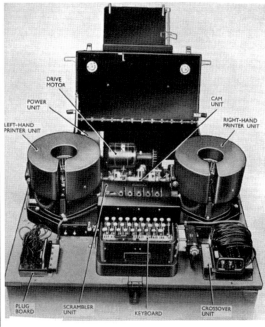

TOP LEFT: Typex No. 1 (© Crown Copyright, by kind permission of Director GCHQ)
TOP RIGHT: Typex Mark 22 (© Crown Copyright, by kind permission of Director GCHQ)
BELOW: Whaddon Hall and Mainline radio station to the rear

CHAPTER TWENTY

FINALE

'Intelligence for Neptune was the outcome of years of research with unequalled resources by large and specialised inter-service bodies. It was complete and detailed.'

Admiral Sir Bertram Ramsay, ANCXF, Eisenhower's Naval Commander

~~~

As the thin periscope slowly broke the surface of the warm June Atlantic swell from the X-Craft midget submarine X23 parked less than a mile offshore, the crew on board fell silent with nervous anticipation. They pulled their eyes away from monitoring their instruments and concentrated their gaze on their boss, Lieutenant George Honour, as he gazed through the eyepiece. The rays of afternoon sunshine glistened on the swell of the waves and cast rainbows across his line of sight. His mouth dropped as he concentrated hard on what he could see, 'Oh my God … there're Germans. They're playing bloody football on the beach!' A ripple of smiles and nervous laughter passed around the close-knit team in the hot, humid and dank submarine. 'I can't believe it, they're playing bloody football!'

This did not just signify that the beach near the Orne Estuary was full of Germans who liked football, but more importantly it meant that the beach itself was not mined. It was a clear indication that the beach should not pose any significant obstacle to the assault force in the coming days.

This fact had not escaped the rest of the crew, who were eagerly awaiting their turn to peer through the periscope eyepiece. They all wanted to see this for themselves. There was a palpable tension beginning to arise amongst the team, as this was the first time they had set eyes on the beach, their goal and target during some three months of arduous training and preparation. Their loneliness and isolation were subdued by the reality of being, now, at the vanguard of the Allied invasion of Europe.

The crew of these midget submarines was restricted to just four, due to the space and air restrictions when submerged. The June operation would see this count rise to five, to allow for the minimal X-Craft manning of three plus the two COPP (Combined Operations Pilotage Parties) divers. X23 was manned by a crew who had grown accustomed to each other during the rigorous training programme in northwest

COPP team members picture outside Hayling Island Yacht Club

Scotland and at the depot at Hayling Island. Lieutenant George Honour was the Commanding Officer for the boat but in reality he was subservient to the orders of the COPP/9 diver and officer Lieutenant Geoff Lyne, who was more affectionately known as 'Thin Red'. He was a regular Royal Navy officer and was a Navigation Specialist, a role much sought after in the Navy at the time, but 'Thin' had volunteered for 'Special Service'.

Thin looked gaunt but wired, no doubt as the Benzedrine was working its way through his system. Benzedrine, or 'Bennies' as they were more affectionately called by the crew, were issued to keep the men alert and keep them going on missions such as this. They were a powerful amphetamine.

Thin's COPP/9 colleague was Lieutenant Jim Booth RNVR, who had come into the COPP teams via a circuitous route. Born in London in 1921, his family had moved to Leicestershire, where his father had been previously based with the Leicestershire Yeomanry during World War I. He had joined up in November 1939 without telling his parents, just a couple of months after enrolling on a Science degree at Trinity College, Cambridge. Many of his university friends had aspirations of being swish Spitfire pilots but Jim had decided on another path and sought service with the Royal Navy.

His first ship was HMS *Hussar*, a fleet minesweeper based out of the port of Harwich. At the time Hussar had responsibility for clearing an east coast sea passage to Scapa Flow, which had to be cleared of mines daily as the German Navy was well aware of its strategic importance to the British Navy. During Booth's service on this ship he witnessed the ship being hit by a *Luftwaffe* bomb.

On his next vessel, the cruiser HMS *Kenya*, Booth travelled further afield to the shores of West Africa and he quickly won promotion to Able Seaman. He had loved his time on the *Kenya* but as with all servicemen he endured long periods of abject boredom. HMS *Kenya* was the only cruiser to survive the war intact, and famously pursued the *Bismarck* after HMS *Hood* was sunk.

George Honour had been briefed about the D-Day mission only three weeks prior to sailing from HMS *Dolphin*. He had become so paranoid about the potential compromise of the mission that he had prevented himself from going out drinking prior to the mission with the hope that his orders would remain in his head. This had not stopped Booth and Hodges from going ashore for a quick pint.

The crew of X23 had been stationed at Fort Blockhouse in Gosport (HMS *Dolphin*) since the D-Day preparation exercises had been completed. Each of the two midget submarines had been packed with supplementary oxygen canisters, supplied ironically from the *Luftwaffe*. Twelve cylinders would allow for an extra day's oxygen if required. It had been found that the *Luftwaffe* oxygen cylinders were well designed and ideal for the job on submarines and had been stockpiled from downed aircraft. Both craft had been modified for the operation by the removal of the usual explosive side-cargoes to add in welded buoyancy cylinders to compensate for the additional weight in the submarine.

As the X23 cut away its mooring ropes from the quay heading out towards East Gate in Portsmouth harbour, the deafening sound and choking fumes from the Gardner diesel engines meant that Lieutenant Honour had to shout through the hatch to get Lieutenant Booth to steer correctly. It was a full three days before the scheduled D-Day landings were to take place under the amphibious plans of Operation Neptune.

It was not long before the boat linked up with its tow outside Spithead, the trawler HMS *Grenadier* under the command of Lieutenant Day.

The crew used to joke about the engines being the same four-cylinder engines that were used in London buses. Needless to say, this engendered fond affection when it kicked into life on the surface. Below surface the hum of the electric motors helped with the haphazard sleep arrangements. There was only one sleep suit, effectively a sealed sleeping bag, laid out over the battery compartment. It was always a short and restless two- to three-hour sleep but the enduring hum of the motor helped.

The crew of X23, or 'Xiphias' as she was christened by the Royal Navy, had come together months before in the midget submarine training grounds of northwest Scotland. The three-man X-Craft crew of Lieutenant George Honour, Sub Lieutenant

Jimmy Hodges and ERA George Vause had gelled well with their two COPP diver crewmen, Lieutenant Geoff 'Thin Red' Lyne and Lieutenant Jim Booth.

The twenty-six-year-old George Honour had volunteered for hazardous service whilst serving in the Western desert with the Royal Naval Volunteer Reserve. Lieutenant Jimmy Hodges was an experienced diver and was the only member of the crew who had been trained to cut submarine netting, something they knew they should not have to deal with on this operation.

The codename assigned to the mission was Operation Gambit, referring to a chess move where

COPP diver and swimsuit

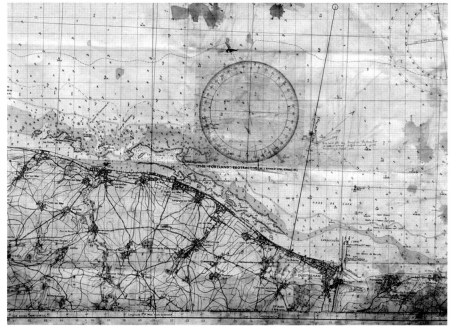

168 The Operation Gambit navigational chart used by Lieutenant Geoff 'Thin Red' Lyne RN

353

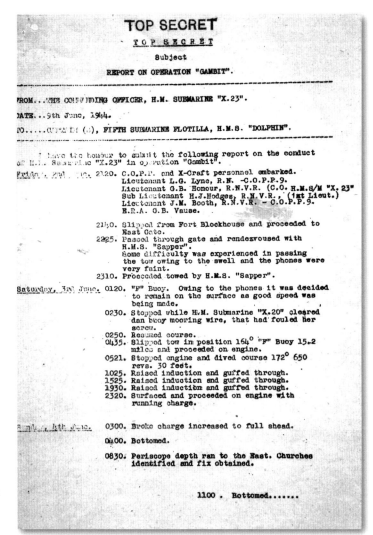

TOP SECRET

TOP SECRET

Subject

REPORT ON OPERATION "GAMBIT".

FROM...THE COMMANDING OFFICER, H.M. SUBMARINE "X.23".

DATE...9th June, 1944.

TO.....CAPTAIN (S), FIFTH SUBMARINE FLOTILLA, H.M.S. "DOLPHIN".

I have the honour to submit the following report on the conduct of H.M. Submarine "X.23" in operation "Gambit".

Friday, 2nd June. 2120. C.O.P.P. and X-Craft personnel embarked.
Lieutenant L.G. Lyne, R.N. -C.O.P.P.9.
Lieutenant G.B. Honour, R.N.V.R. (C.O. H.M.S/M "X.23"
Sub Lieutenant H.J.Hodges, R.N.V.R., (1st Lieut.)
Lieutenant J.M. Booth, R.N.V.R. - C.O.P.P.9.
E.R.A. G.B. Vause.

2140. Slipped from Fort Blockhouse and proceeded to East Gate.
2225. Passed through gate and rendezvoused with H.M.S. "Sapper".
Some difficulty was experienced in passing the tow owing to the swell and the phones were very faint.
2310. Proceeded towed by H.M.S. "Sapper".

Saturday, 3rd June. 0120. "F" Buoy. Owing to the phones it was decided to remain on the surface as good speed was being made.
0230. Stopped while H.M. Submarine "X.20" cleared dan buoy mooring wire, that had fouled her screw.
0250. Resumed course.
0435. Slipped tow in position 164° "F" Buoy 15.2 miles and proceeded on engine.
0521. Stopped engine and dived course 172° 650 revs. 30 feet.
1025. Raised induction and guffed through.
1525. Raised induction and guffed through.
1930. Raised induction and guffed through.
2320. Surfaced and proceeded on engine with running charge.

Sunday, 4th June. 0300. Broke charge increased to full ahead.

0400. Bottomed.

0830. Periscope depth ran to the East. Churches identified and fix obtained.

1100 . Bottomed......

'Extract from Lieutenant Geoff 'Thin Red' Lyne Operation Gambit report

your opening pawns are sacrificed. It was very much a reflection of the nature of the operation that these two midget submarines would guide the way to the invasion force but may well be lost in the process. They were ultimately to be the first elements of the Allied Expeditionary Force to be in position off the coast of Normandy.

The crews arrived at their destination on 4 June 1944, X20 off Juno Beach and X23 off Sword Beach. Once they had fixed their positions within sight of the French coast, they sank to the bottom awaiting their orders that night. They surfaced at 2315hrs to receive their pre-arranged BBC radio message from the powerful Niton transmitter on the Isle of Wight, and to their consternation received the radio transmission at

0100hrs stating, 'For Padfoot, unwell in Scarborough.' Which meant the operation was postponed for twenty-four hours due to the poor weather conditions. It would mean another day at the bottom awaiting the BBC message to proceed with the plan. On the night of 5 June they received the BBC message that the invasion was on. The logbook of X23 read:

> '2315. Surfaced and commenced wireless watch. Message received operation taking place, but reception was very difficult and master gyro had to be stopped during the period the message was coming in. This unsettled the compass and caused it to be unreliable. However, during the period of wireless-watch the craft had already reached and anchored in her marking position, so the compass defection did not prove as serious as it might have done.'

At 0415hrs on 6 June 1944 the crews of X20 and X23 surfaced and rigged up their 18 ft telescopic masts with its attached seaward light. They would also employ an echo sounder and radio beacon to guide in the navigational Motor Launches (ML), which were to lead the invasion force on to the beaches.

In the early morning summer light, as the crew worked feverously to rig the masts, they were treated to a display of Naval shore bombardment that is recorded as the heaviest and most sustained in history. George Honour was to reflect after the event that he found the Naval bombardment 'reassuring'. This was to subdue when the over-the-horizon bombardment stopped. As the midget submarine bobbed up and down in the heavy swell there was an eerie silence. Lieutenant Jim Booth spoke of his fear and trepidation of being all alone. They were close to shore, in broad daylight and the Germans were emerging from their defensive positions. But it was not long before the Allied armada, one of the biggest invasion fleets in the history of war, appeared on the horizon.

A few years after the war Lieutenant George Honour recalled: 'It was unbelievable. Although I knew they were on our side it was still a frightening sight. One can only imagine what the enemy must have felt, waking up to this awesome spectacle and knowing that they were the targets.'

Divided into Charlie, Dog, Easy and Fox zones, the beach, which was to become known as Omaha, was a 6-mile long beach running between Sainte-Honorine-des-Pertes and Vierville-sur-Mer. It was the responsibility of the US 1st Army, 5th Corps to assault.

On the British sector the guiding lights and echo soundings emanating from the X-Craft brought the Allied vessels on to the right zones of their allocated beaches. This was not the case for Omaha, however. American planners had refused the offer

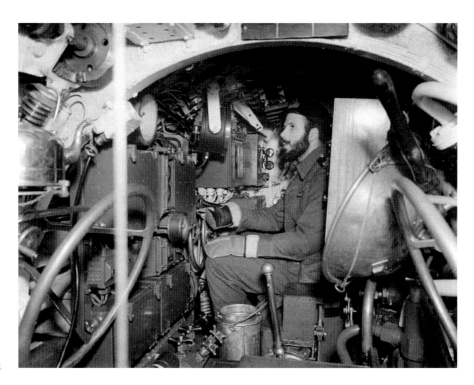

Interior of X-Craft

of inshore markers, and only accepted the use of pilot craft. This was ironic, as Omaha Beach had had the most detailed reconnaissance undertaken by Clogstoun-Willmott and his COPP teams in the earlier reconnaissance missions. The Americans were concerned it might alert the German defences. Major General Scott-Bowden explains, 'they had little pilot boats which went in front on each divisional sector to take in the amphibious tanks, and for each divisional sector on Omaha Beach, there were eight LCTs, each with four amphibious tanks in them, total of thirty-two tanks on each sector, and I was with the right hand sector, which I think was the 1st Division. The decision had to be made, in that case, at fifteen hundred yards, as to whether to launch the DD tanks or whether to take the LCT straight on in and beach … there were beach obstacles all over the place, including these very unpleasant large calibre shells on poles with raised fuses sticking out seawards … it was certainly getting very rough on Omaha Beach, and I was with the Naval Lieutenant Navigator responsible for making this decision, and to assist in case conditions had been bad, to assist with the pilotage onto the beach, and Bruce Ogden-Smith was with the other Naval Lieutenant on the other boat on the left hand sector, and he decided, quite rightly, that it wasn't feasible to launch these amphibious tanks, and we went straight on in with them and put them on the beach, but it wasn't very long before they were being picked off left right and centre, and very little we could do except pick up some of the crews. By that time, the infantry landing craft were coming through and off-loading their chaps and getting the wounded chaps on to the outgoing infantry landing craft. On the left-hand sector, where it wasn't quite so rough, they decided to give it a go, and launched the amphibious tanks…. I think all but a handful sunk, so they never did get ashore … the casualties were appalling … they brought in the battleship *Texas*, which was firing from a twelve-inch gun, point blank into the concrete defences built into the hillside, ahead of an attacking infantry platoon. It was the most phenomenal sight. Nobody could ever have been braver than the American soldiers fighting on Omaha Beach. They were the most experienced, highly trained, efficient and brave chaps you could possibly have witnessed, possibly have seen, and gradually and gradually, they succeeded in capturing the whole of this honeycomb of concrete emplacements which were terribly well concealed.'

The most western of the landing beaches was the 3-mile long stretch between Pouppeville and La Madeleine, which was known as Utah. This was assigned to the US 1st Army, 7th Corps and was separated into Tare Green, Uncle Red and Victor zones.

The American forces landing on Utah Beach had also declined the offer of having the midget submarines act as waymarkers for the naval fleet. Consequently the strong winds and tides were to push the landing forces a significant distance west of their objectives, landing in the wrong places on the beach. The landing craft were pushed on to areas of the beaches that were more heavily defended.

General Dempsey was to lead the British 2nd Army, landing three divisions on the beaches north of the main Normandy town of Caen. To the right of the British landings was the American 1st Army, under the command of General Omar Bradley. These beach landings would be bolstered by drops of Airborne troops from two divisions behind the German defensive line. The Allies' immediate objectives once ashore would be to assault the Normandy towns of Bayeux, Isigny, Caen and Carentan. As each of these were taken, the Americans would advance onto the Cotentin Peninsula and aim for Cherbourg.

The 6-mile long beach either side of Courseulles-sur-Mer from La Rivières to St Aubin-sur-Mer became known as Juno Beach. This was the responsibility of the Canadian 3rd Infantry Division and the British 2nd Army, 1st Corps. It was divided into Love, Mike and Nan sectors.

The British 2nd Army, 1st Corps (alongside French/British Commandos) were assigned to the 5-mile long beach between St Aubin-sur-Mer and Ouistreham at the mouth of the River Orne, which was known as Sword.

Years of painstaking reconnaissance and intelligence collection by hundreds of specialist intelligence personnel and highly trained commandos culminated in a wealth of knowledge of the Normandy beaches and their dominant German defences. The *Luftwaffe* airfields in northern France had been hit hard by the Allies for three weeks prior to D-Day to nullify any effect it would have on the invasion. The key to Normandy was the path to the beaches. The SHAEF commanders needed to be certain the troops and supplies would have a safe passage across the Channel. Over the course of the twelve hours before H-Hour on 6 June, ten dedicated channels were swept by 287 Allied minesweepers, clearing the way to the beach approaches. It was the greatest number of minesweepers ever assembled for a single Naval operation. The measure of success of this operation was that only one Allied destroyer was hit by mines during the whole of the Neptune operation.

For the Overlord assault to be a success and for the Allied forces to get a grasp of the beachhead, the thousands of obstacles on the beaches and hinterland needed to be cleared. This was undertaken by a dedicated and highly skilled team of Royal Marines and Royal Engineer divers and explosives/ordnance specialists in a British team called the Landing Craft Obstacle Clearance Units (LCOCU) or American Naval Combat Demolition Units (NCDU). The unit was made official on 20 January 1944 and was under the overall command of Lieutenant Robert Billington RNVR. They were to be the first men ashore 6 June 1944.

The LCOCU teams, all 'special duties' volunteers, were trained at HMS *Appledore* in Fremingham camp at the junction of the Taw and Torridge rivers in North Devon. The base was to become known as the Combined Operations Experimental Establishment (COXE). Their initial training included a stint down at HMS *Dolphin*, the Gosport submarine base, where they were trained in the use of the prototype Davis Submarine Escape Apparatus (DSEA), which had been designed for submarine escape rather than shallow water diving. Over time, the units were to adopt the more refined oxygen re-breather Dunlop Underwater Swimming Breathing Apparatus (UWSBA). It was worn on top of a new purpose-built rubber diving suit, also made by the Dunlop Rubber Company in Birmingham. Training was under the command of a former Boom defence commando, Lieutenant Commander E.C. Davis RNR, assisted by Chief Petty Officer D.P. Reid. The unit was divided into ten separate teams, each with twelve men, comprising one officer and eleven other ranks.

They also spent time at the aptly named HMS *Volcano*, a bomb-disposal facility based at Holmrook Hall in Ravenglass, Cumbria. Here they were taught demolition techniques and the defusing of bombs and devices.

Each man in the unit undertook the standard intensive eight-week long course, and the area around Appledore and Instow were ideal for learning beach drills. The information from the COPP reconnaissance teams earlier in 1944 on the Normandy

Frogmen of the LCOCU (© IWM London Photographic Archives – ref A28997)

Frogmen of the LCOCU changing into their shallow water diving suits (©IWM London Photographic Archives – ref A28997)

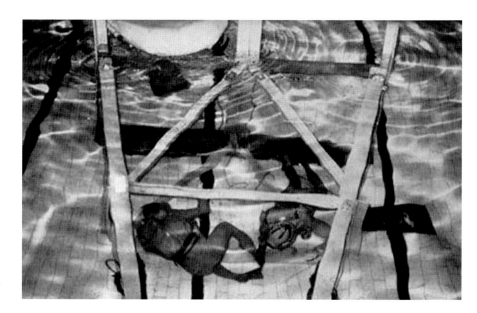

LCOCU divers
training on
'Belgian Gate'
in Ilfracombe
swimming baths,
1944

beaches enabled the Admiralty to commission a 150-yard wide reconstruction at North Burrows Bay of some of the German beach obstacles they would be facing in June 1944. The LCOCU diver teams would rehearse on this mock-up frequently.

During the spring of 1944, the LCOCU divers could be seen every day at the salt-water swimming baths in Ilfracombe, as the Admiralty had constructed a replica Belgian Gate for them to practise their demolition techniques, wearing their new Dunlop rubber diving suits and UWSBA equipment. This particular obstacle was a formidable task for the demolition teams. They had established it would require thirty-six individual pieces of the almond-smelling Plastic Explosive (PE) to reduce the 2.5 tonne steel mass to a height of just 2 ft. On the day itself, the intent was to set off the explosives, using time-delay fuses, to coincide with the Naval bombardment to fool the Germans into thinking the explosions were the result of the Naval gunfire rather than the highly trained divers operating on the shoreline.

The teams were to meet an array of intricate and well-designed obstacles on the beaches of Normandy. Many of them were mined, often with the common German Teller mine which had the advantage for the LCOCU teams by not doing well when submersed for long periods in seawater. The knowledge of the Teller mine and the smaller *Schu-mine* had been gleaned from many sources. The Tarbrush and Hardtack commando raids on the French coast over previous years had captured intact Teller mines, and the CSDIC POW interrogation intelligence had yielded all the information the Allies would need to develop trained and skilled bomb disposal experts.

The US equivalent of the LCOCU was the Naval Combat Demolition Units

(NCDU), which were created to take on the challenge of Omaha and Utah beaches. Each NCDU comprised a nine-man team augmented with three US Naval seamen who were brought down from Scotland for Overlord. Intensive training programmes were developed around the Assault Training Centre in Woolacombe, North Devon from mid April 1944.

They were integrated into the US Army Combat Engineers to form thirteen-man 'gap' assault teams with a total NCDU complement of thirty-two teams deployed for the operation. Their role was to clear 50-yard wide gaps through the obstacles to be subsequently marked by the Army Demolition Group.

On 6 June the NCDU teams suffered heavy losses on the American sector beaches. They lost thirty-seven men, with seventy-one wounded, a staggeringly high casualty rate of 52 per cent – making D-Day the most fateful day in US Naval special forces history.

The four Royal Navy and six Royal Marine LCOCU teams were deployed at H-Hour on D-Day using inflatable boats from Landing Craft Assault (LCA) platforms. Gold Beach was the responsibility of LCOCU teams 3, 4, 9 and 10, Sword Beach had allocated LCOCU teams 7 and 8, whilst Juno had LCOCU teams 1, 5, 11 and 12. Their specific mission was to clear the obstacles from the range of 3 m to 1.4 m depth, the Royal Engineers having the responsibility for the shallower zone and beach itself. Their aim was to clear a 1,000-yard wide path through the beach obstacles, waymarked by the Royal Navy Beach Commandos who would lay out flags where the beach sections had been cleared of mines and obstacles.

For such a small, tight unit as the LCOCU, it suffered high casualty rates with two killed and ten wounded, some seriously. One of the LCOCU teams was led by Lieutenant H. Hargreaves DSC, a twenty-one-year-old cotton salesman from Burnley. After D-Day he reflected:

'The invasion of Normandy to the average person was the greatest combined operation that had ever taken place, and that in fact was the truth. However, few people know of the work carried out by small, special units, both before the operation, and during the initial assaults. We were one of the small units which had this particular role to play. A role which was not easy, and from which many of us did not expect to return, but one which we were determined to carry out until our work was completed. For the invasion of Normandy the Force Commanders used approximately a hundred and twenty officers and men of the LCOCU units divided into ten parties, or units. Each unit had an officer and eleven men, and each was allotted to its own beach and had its own particular job to do. In my case, and that of a brother officer, we found ourselves detailed to deal with the obstacles on a beach near the village of La Rivière.

'We were supposed to go in at H Hour, which was the very beginning of the assault … and went hell-for-leather for the beach and arrived hoping to find the front row of obstacles on the water's edge, and not in the water, but discovered some two or three feet of water over them. We left our craft and got to work at once on posts with mines secured to the tops of them, specially constructed wooden ramps, which were mined, and steel hedgehogs with mines and anti-aircraft shells on top of them, and we were subjected the whole time to quite a hot fire from rockets, shells, and bombs.

'We must have been about four hundred yards from the beach when the firing first started, and they didn't forget to inform us that they knew we were coming. When we finally got on the beach we discovered that we were being systematically sniped, not only with rifles but also by odd bursts of machine-gun fire – a most unpleasant experience but one we soon got used to. As time went on we almost forgot about it until we realised that opposition was dying down because in the meantime the Army had landed and was dealing with machine-gun posts, mortar posts, and all the other unpleasant places Jerry had prepared for us.

'The weather was very much worse than anyone would have expected in June, and we had the greatest difficulty working in a very heavy surf. It was hard going and we soon got pretty tired, but in the meantime the obstacles were being slowly but systematically destroyed. As we made an initial gap for the landing craft to come through, so we increased the size of the gap as time went on. We succeeded in clearing the whole of the beach some thousand yards in length, with obstacles going out to over four hundred yards, by the end of D-Day.

'That didn't end our work, of course, although the worst was over. Landing craft of all shapes and sizes were simply pouring on to the beach, and in the meantime, having cleared that beach, we had to proceed to another beach and get rid of the obstacles there. In all, we successfully disposed of over two thousand five hundred obstacles, practically every one mined: in addition to this – as a sort of savoury – we cleared the explosives out of half a dozen beetle tanks.

'Not long before D-Day a special jacket had been invented to protect us against that terrible blast which can be experienced when a mine or shell explodes underwater. This jacket was known as a "Kapok Jacket" and was worn underneath our swim-suits. It proved to be a most wonderful thing and saved the lives of no less than three of my men. One of my petty officers, who was working in about six feet of water, had a shell or mortar bomb explode in the water quite close to him, and although he was completely knocked out, and

TOP AND
BOTTOM:
Commandos from
LCOCU clearing
beach obstacles
at La Rivières,
9 June 1944
(©IWM London
Photographic
Archives – ref
A23993)

in fact paralysed for several hours, he had no injuries whatever, and no after-effects. A Royal Engineer who was swimming towards the beach from one of the landing craft and was some distance farther away from the explosion than the petty officer, was killed outright, and I have no doubt that many men suffered the same fate on that day.

'I would like to make it quite clear that we don't in any way look upon ourselves as supermen, or heroes, or anything like that at all, and we did not by any means clear all the obstacles off the beaches in time for the landing craft to get in. There were nowhere near enough of us to have hoped to do it. What we could and did do, was to clear an initial gap for the landing craft to beach safely, and to increase that gap as quickly as possible until the beach was entirely free from obstacles.

'Consequently many of the landing craft who didn't use the gap, because of the simple fact that there just wasn't room for them, struck obstacles, or had holes blown in them or their bottoms torn out, with the result that many men had to swim ashore with full equipment.

'When our original job had been completed we had to keep our reputation as "Jack the Handyman" by doing many jobs to assist on the beaches, such as winching drowned vehicles out of the water. We did this by taking a wire with a hook on the end, right out to sea in our swim-suits and breathing-sets, hook up the vehicle, come to the surface, and signal to the operator ashore to start up his winch, which he did, and pulled the drowned vehicle up high and dry. We helped to unload stores, we cleared mines, we assisted the Royal Engineers, in fact we did everything except mind the babies, and if there had been any there we would have done that too.'

The LCOCU teams were full of former bank clerks, engineers, carpenters, clerks and students who admirably acquitted themselves on D-Day. They were to go ashore at H-Hour, 0725hrs during the first assault wave. On Gold Beach alone there were in the region of 2,500 obstacles on the stretch of the 3¼-mile long beach. The intelligence gathered in the years prior on the beach obstacles was to be critical to this clearance task. Without the knowledge of the Element C, the tetrahedrons or the Teller landmines gathered from years of intelligence collection, many more of these LCOCU divers and the following waves of assault troops would have been killed.

A few days before D-Day, Admiral Ramsay's Intelligence staff levied a requirement on the Admiralty Operational Intelligence Centre (OIC) to send ULTRA decrypts direct to them, obfuscating the OIC. They wanted the raw and undigested intelligence direct from Bletchley Park, something that the OIC and its founder, Admiral Sir Norman Denning opposed vehemently. It was a significant departure from the well-established protocol, but it was trialled for a few days. In less than ten days the ANCXF Intelligence staff had become overwhelmed with the volume of traffic from Bletchley that the

Fighter Direction Tender, the converted LST 216 (©IWM Archive reference A21922)

decision was revoked and the OIC was reinstated as the processing hub for Bletchley ULTRA traffic.

The OIC had been involved with much of the preliminary planning for Neptune, most notably on the minefields and approach lanes to the allocated Normandy beaches. These approach routes changed frequently before D-Day, and numerous aerial and naval reconnaissance missions were mounted in the final days to make sure the current intelligence on the River Seine basin was as current as it could be.

For the Normandy landings the Royal Navy introduced three Fighter Direction Tenders (FDT) whose mission was to protect the beachhead. They had been converted from the most suitable ships available at the time to the Royal Navy, HMS *Boxer*, *Bruiser* and *Thruster*, and were to be the Allies eyes and ears in the crucial period of Neptune. In essence, they were the command and control centres for the entire invasion fleet. In the early stages of the landings, the three FDTs (FDT13, FDT216 and FDT217) were to be responsible for providing immediate tactical intelligence from radio intercept to the Controller of Fighters back in England. Their role was vital for the RAF and USAAF to dominate the airspace above Normandy to protect the huge logistical chain from the south coast of England. The *Luftwaffe* had been decimated through a concerted bombing campaign in northern France in the preceding weeks, and they had less than 300 operational aircraft by D-Day. The *Luftwaffe* 3rd Air Fleet, under the command of Field Marshal Hugo Sperrle, based in northern France had just 172 fighters, fifty-nine reconnaissance aircraft and eighty-eight bombers at its disposal. All air operations had been suspended just before D-Day due to the weather conditions.

The Allied Expeditionary Air Force (AEAF) had decided that RAF mobile RADAR could provide early warning and Ground Control Intercept (GCI) for German *Luftwaffe* aircraft. The disastrous raid on Dieppe had shown that low-grade signals intelligence needed to be interpreted at one central hub before being assessed and presented to senior military commanders. For Overlord, the Air Section at Bletchley Park was to act as this focal point. Dieppe had also shown how easy it was for a breakdown in communications to occur between the forces taking part in the invasion. Allied commanders were to moot the idea of having a Headquarters ship which would act as a command and control communications centre for the three services taking part in Overlord. It would need to be located close to the Normandy coast and have deployed SIGINT staff on board to collect and intercept German military signals during the battle but also to receive timely SIGINT from back in Britain, produced by the Y Services and Bletchley Park.

Fitting out each of the three FDTs with the most sophisticated communications and RADAR equipment available began in earnest from February 1944. Crucially, the fits included the new Type 11 RADAR which could operate on German frequencies and was situated on the deck with a rotating gantry. The success of the Bruneval raid (Operation Biting) in February 1942 had led to the Type 11 development. These vital raids on the French coast had provided unique dividends for the Overlord forces. It was this Type 11 which was used most off the Normandy coast during Overlord. Each FDT had in the region of 250 highly trained military staff, most of whom were RAF RADAR and communications specialists.

One role the FDT teams would play would be as a deployed Y Service collection platform to intercept German wireless communications from ashore, most notably those command and control communications between ships, between *Luftwaffe* ground control to airborne pilots, or from ship to shore. Overlord had learnt many lessons from the Dieppe raid in 1942, and Allied planners had understood that an operation the size and scale of Overlord would require very effective command and control communications, and effective RADAR and radio counter-measures plan.

A former passenger liner, HMS *Hilary*, was also employed as a HQ and SIGINT ship for the Commander of Naval Force 'J' attacking Juno Beach. Personnel from No. 4 Ship Signal Section were deployed on *Hilary*, alongside Army signallers to provide radio links between the HQ and the troops ashore. *Hilary* had some other HQ sister ships – HMS *Largs* (operating off Sword Beach with Force S), HMS *Bulolo* (operating off Gold Beach with Force G). These three vessels were referred to as Headquarters Landing Ships (HQLS). They were responsible for the control and management of the Neptune landings and of all the Naval vessels taking part in the operation into their designated zones and beaches. Similar to the FDT ships, they had mixed crews, but mostly RAF personnel and Royal Navy. These HQLS were vital for choreography in the chaos of war – ensuring there were effective lines of communication between the units ashore on the beaches with the landing craft, HQ ships, FDTs and other HQ elements back in England to make sure up-to-date information was being communicated across the chains of command. It was the *Hilary* that would distribute air raid warnings over the invasion fleet with intelligence gleaned from the FDT Y Service teams. But it was considered that 'these warnings might better be promulgated from the Fighter Direction Tender or Ship, which has better knowledge of the position of friendly and hostile aircraft than an HQ ship, which has no proper air warning RADAR'.

The ships were in place on 6 June 1944. FDT217 positioned itself about 5 miles off Juno, Sword and Gold beaches, covering the Eastern (British & Canadian) section of the assault area, whilst FDT216 was off Omaha and Utah beaches covering the Western (US) part of the assault area. FDT13 was located 40 miles off Gold Beach in the main shipping channels for convoy protection. They were in position by 0430hrs and sequenced to have their full RADAR operating capability by 0725hrs, breaking their radio silence. FDT217 was to be the Master Control vessel, choreographing Allied fighters dependent on the disposition of and the threat from *Luftwaffe* fighters operating in the region.

On that first vital day, 6 June 1944, it was these FDT vessels that would make sure there was continuous daytime low-level air cover for the five beaches. This was affected through a rolling wave of aircraft sorties whereby Spitfires would arrive after an outward journey from an English airfield, spend fifteen minutes patrolling the beaches, and then return for the necessary refuelling and rearming. During the night around forty fighters were on continual patrol in the area, all equipped with Airborne Interception (AI) RADAR. This was all interwoven with the hundreds of Allied bombers who were operating in the area, striking key German defensive targets.

The FDT ships were to stay in position for seventeen days after D-Day, providing this vital activity supporting the Allied push into the hinterland, and it has been estimated that seventy-six German aircraft were destroyed as a result of the FDTs. Of equal importance was the function these FDTs played in the collection of tactical intelligence for the Allied force. The intelligence Y Group sections on board each of the three FDTs were critical in listening to the German wireless communications and conveying their significance in near real time to the Commanders on the ground or on board ships. Some of the radio intercepts by the Y teams merged with their own

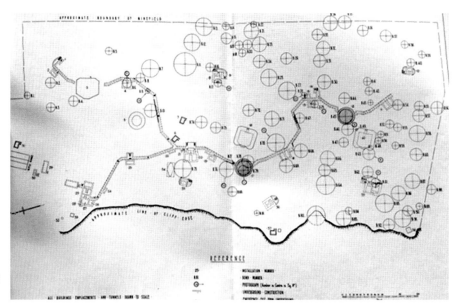

Le Havre – Le
Clos des Ronces
170mm Coastal
Battery showing
individual
emplacements and
tunnels to scale

Direction Finding (D/F) capability onboard resulted in successful interdceptions of enemy aircraft. It was a huge advantage having deployed Y Service capability onboard to give advance warning of German *Luftwaffe* attacks and as an aid to identification. On ship the Y Office opened out into the Air Control Room, which during the restless early days of Overlord allowed 'priceless last-minute information to be passed to the directing officers and via them to their aircraft without delay'.

The main duty of the FDTs were to prevent the enemy attacks firstly on the Allied shipping and secondly on the beaches. Their success could be gauged by the fact that the only loss caused by German bombing was that of the Lawford.

The commander of Force J and the Eastern task force for D-Day, Admiral Sir Phillip Vian conveyed a signal after D-Day to the returned COPP teams at Blockhouse. The signal read 'CONGRATULATIONS TO THE VANGUARD OF OVERLORD.' It was a fitting tribute to the COPP and X-Craft crews of X20 and X23. They were the vanguard of a mighty assault force, but in the years prior to Overlord taking shape there were many men who formed the vanguard for Overlord.

The secrecy behind Overlord enabled its successful outcome. There were very few incidents where the secrets behind BIGOT and the Normandy invasion had leaked. In May 1944, Captain Edward Miles from the US Navy drank a considerable amount of alcohol at a party and had conveyed a lot of top-secret information to others at the venue whilst inebriated. He was given a one-way ticket back to America, along with one of his compatriots, Major General Henry Miller, who was BIGOT-cleared and had the role of Quartermaster to the 9th US Airforce. At a dinner party on 18 April 1944, organised at Claridges by the US Army's chief intelligence officer in Britain, Brigadier General Edwin Sibert, Miller informed his audience of Red Cross nurses that the invasion of Europe was to begin before 15 June. Even though he was a personal friend of Eisenhower, he was demoted to Lieutenant Colonel and sent back to the US, having narrowly escaped a court martial.

There were further breaches of security during the lead-up to D-Day. Brigadier Harris, a British staff officer in charge of SHAEF communications, reported the loss of the SHAEF communications plan containing all the radio networks and cipher plans for Overlord during his journey home. It was found outside Waterloo Railway station by a taxi driver, who picked it up noticing the top secret and BIGOT markings and duly took it to the Metropolitan Police headquarters at New Scotland Yard.

In the summer of 1943 a copy of an Overlord plan blew out of the SHAEF office window at Norfolk House in St James's Square. The papers were handed in by an elderly gentleman who professed his eyesight was so bad he could not read any of the information. Sergeant Thomas Kane, a secretary to the Ordnance Supply Section of SHAEF Headquarters, inadvertently sent a parcel containing top-secret BIGOT documents to his sister who lived in in Chicago. The parcel exposed its classified contents at the Chicago sorting office to at least a dozen postal staff at the office, all of whom had to be kept under strict surveillance until D-Day.

Overlord was achieved by an industrial-scale intelligence collection effort that is probably unique in warfare. It was of an unprecedented scale and complexity. SIGINT and the ULTRA traffic were hugely significant in the insight they provided into the strategic and operational thinking of the German High Command. The situational awareness it provided through the SLU teams to Allied commanders during the Normandy campaign undoubtedly saved many lives. To give some idea of scale, by September 1944 Hut 8 at Bletchley Park was undertaking over 2,200 German Naval decrypts per day.

Many of the German intelligence operations in early 1944 had been characterised by poor management and oversight, along with signs of complacency across the command chain. Hitler and his Supreme Command had a dysfunctional command structure which diluted the ability for strategic decision-making across many levels of the military structures. *Feldmarschall* Gerd von Rundstedt (*Oberbefehlshaber West* OBW) as the main land commander in Normandy had no direct control over the German *Luftwaffe* or *Kriegsmarine*. The senior *Luftwaffe* officer, *Feldmarschall* Hugo Sperrle would get his orders direct from the *Oberkommando der Luftwaffe* (OKL). This confusion was furthered by the fact that the senior *Kriegsmarine* Admiral Theodor Krancke, who controlled the *Marinegruppe West* would take his orders from the Navy

High Command, *Oberkommandomarine* (or OKM). Even von Rundstedt felt powerless to authorise strategic changes to the defence of Normandy.

The Germans' apparent lack of awareness of the Assault, and its size and scale until it was too late has been on occasion attributed to an incompetent German Y Service who had not separated fact from deception. The Allied deception campaign and bogus wireless transmissions had fooled its enemy. It was more due to the lack of correlation and assessment of all sources of intelligence and information.

It had taken time, but the British had learned eventually how significant the intelligence collected by one service could be to another. Overlord had drawn the three services' intelligence arms together with a collective voice. A key lynchpin for the Allied Commanders was Brigadier E.T. 'Bill' Williams, designated as General Staff (Intelligence) or GS(I) for 21st Army Group under General Bernard Montgomery. Williams, an ex-Oxford don from Merton College, had excelled in his role in North Africa whilst deployed with the 1st King's Dragoon Guards (KDG). He had served on Colonel Freddie de Guingand's intelligence staff in Cairo in his role of Director of Military Intelligence in the Middle East.

Between February and June 1944 some of the most critical but routine intelligence reports that were issued were referred to as the 'Weekly Neptune Intelligence Reviews', which Williams orchestrated. He would have access to all secret intelligence, including ULTRA reporting from Bletchley Park. The reports were distributed not only to Montgomery but also to General Eisenhower and his planning teams at SHAEF HQ, and to the subordinate commands of 1st US Army under General Omar Bradley and the British 2nd Army under Lieutenant General Sir Miles Dempsey. The influence of these reports was well respected even across the British intelligence community, largely as 21st Army Group dominated a lot of the Overlord planning.

Montgomery was to reflect on the value Williams brought to Overlord: 'He saw the enemy picture whole and true – he could sift a mass of detailed information and deduce the right answer.'

The Salerno landings in Italy nine months before the Normandy landings had showed what could be achieved through overwhelming force. But D-Day and the Normandy offensive was to be very different from Italy. It was to be the first time the Allies launched an assault against a major defended coastline, and Hitler's fabled Atlantic Wall. Intelligence was at the core of this operation at all levels. The meticulous planning and logistics choreographing would aim to put two million men ashore in just two months, with their accompanying 500,000 vehicles and 3 million tonnes of supplies.

British intelligence had collected aerial photographs from sorties by the RAF and USAAF, they had collected sand, German mines and soil samples from covert raids and reconnaissance missions, and they had surveyed the beaches and their topography

Naval Signal Distribution Office in the CHQ Fort Southwick, in one of the wider tunnels (© Bob Hunt/ Portsdown Tunnels)

Naval Cypher Office, CHQ Fort Southwick underground CHQ (© Bob Hunt/ Portsdown Tunnels)

over countless missions, resulting in excellent knowledge of the currents, beach gradients and tide tables. There were some noted gaps in the intelligence picture, such as the gun emplacements on the Pointe du Hoc cliffs, the whereabouts of the 352nd Infantry Division or the 21st Panzer Division or the capabilities of the Merville battery,

Naval
Teleprinting
Office, CHQ
Fort Southwick
underground
complex (©
Bob Hunt/
Portsdown
Tunnels)

Naval
Teleprinting
Office, CHQ
Fort Southwick
(© Bob Hunt/
Portsdown
Tunnels)

but these mistakes were almost insignificant in comparison to the wider requirements of Overlord.

As a result of years of intelligence collection on Normandy defences from every strand of intelligence effort, the Allied Supreme Commander would know more

Fort Southwick/
UGHQ,
operations
Room, 1944
(© Bob Hunt/
Portsdown
Tunnels)

about the Atlantic Wall and its defensive fortifications than the Germans who had constructed it.

Normandy was an intelligence operation unparalleled in the depth of its detail, scale and accuracy of the final picture, and the ingenuity of its deception and propaganda measures. The success of the Naval phase of Neptune and ultimately the triumph of Overlord could be attributed to the comprehensive intelligence and reconnaissance work undertaken from 1940 onwards. The triumph was a reflection of robust inter-service teamwork, which may have seemed an impossible thing to attain in the earlier stages of the war. Over the course of a year it was to drive the Germans out of occupied Western Europe and culminate in the defeat of the Third Reich.

Through concerted effort over many years, Allied intelligence had sought to provide its commanders with all the intelligence and information it could for Normandy. There can be no doubt that a military commander had ever gone into battle better prepared or informed than Eisenhower. But wars are ultimately not won by reconnaissance, deception or intelligence. In the case of Overlord, the beaches were taken by the ordinary marines, sailors, soldiers and airmen who ultimately won the fight for Normandy.

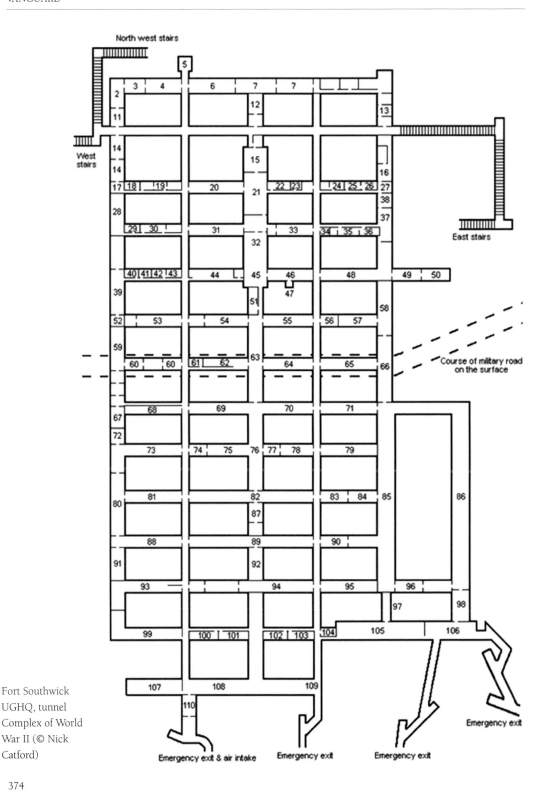

Fort Southwick
UGHQ, tunnel
Complex of World
War II (© Nick
Catford)

Fort Southwick/UGHQ Tunnel Complex – Key to some of the rooms:

2. Logistics & Ground Damage

3. Fire point
4. Logistics
5. Damage Control HQ No. 2
6. Plans
7. Intelligence Office

11. Logistics
12. Intelligence Communications
13. Records Office
14. Commander in Chief's
15 Communications Records
15. Plotting Room
16. Commander in Chief
17. Assistant Chief of Staff

18. Submarine & Naval Air

19. Flag Officer Netherlands

20. Records Room
21. Main Operations Room
22. Operations Office
23. Staff Office Operations
24. COAS
25. Assistant Chief of Staff
25. Operations
26. Secretary to COAS
27. Flag Lieutenant
28. Conference Room
29. Maritime Air Liaison Officer
30. Shipping Plans
31. Trade Records
32. Trade Plot
33. National Shipping Authority
33. & Military Movements
34. Assistant Chief of Staff Plans
35. Chief of Staff
36. Secretary to Chief of Staff
37. Channel Committee
38. Secretariat

38. Secretary
39. Spare
40. Senior Office Mine

41. Senior Officer Naval

42. SONCS (H)

43. Assistant to Chief of Staff

44. Q Message Room
45. Mine Warfare Plot
46. Mine Records
47. Clock Control
48. Office
49. Typing Pool
50. Top Secret Registry
51. Command Signals Officer
52. Fire Point
53. Netherlands Crypto Office
54. Crypto Office
55. Wireless Telegraphy

56. Operations PBX
57. GPO Relay Set/Frame

58. GPO Battery Room
59. Meteorological Office
60. Spare
61. Cleaners Store
62. Couriergram Office
63. Main Signals Office
64. MSO Records
65. Administration PBX
66. GPO Power Room
67. Crypto Stores
68. Crypto Workshop
69. Teleprinter Room
70. Teleprinter Room
71. Spare
72. Wardroom Store
73. Wardroom
74. Lamson Tube Exchange

75. Teleprinter Room
76. Teleprinter Room
77. Lamson Tube Motors
78. Electrical Engineering

79. Teleprinter Switchboard

80. Galley
81. Wardroom
82. Spare
83. GPO
84. GPO
85. GPO V/F Room
86. GPO Carrier Room
87. Electrical Engineering

88. Store
89. Ratings Mess
90. Dormitory
91. Galley store
92. Dormitory

93. Officers Lavatories
94. Dormitory

95. Dormitory
96. GPO
97. Secondary Lighting

98. Air Conditioning Room
99. Ratings Lavatories
100. Engineers Workshop
101. Engineers Store
102. Boiler room
103. Damage Control HQ

104. Coke hold
105. Diesels
106. Coolers
107. Female Lavatories
108. Air Conditioning Plant
109. Police Keyboard
110. B Adit intake tunnel

POSTSCRIPT

'… the history of warfare knows no other like undertaking from the point of view of its scale, its vast conception and its masterly execution'.

Stalin, message to Churchill, 11 June 1944

~~~

Battles, or indeed wars, cannot be won by intelligence alone. Intelligence only provides an insight to military commanders about the intent and capabilities of an enemy. As its nature, intelligence is always continuous and as so is never complete, and there will always be gaps in the intelligence picture. By June 1944, the Allies had a far superior aerial reconnaissance and imagery intelligence service through RAF Medmenham, much more significant signals intelligence and espionage capabilitie than that of the Germans.

The centralisation of intelligence under a single committee with an effective hierarchical flow of intelligence and assessment is one of the critical principles of an effective organisation. The work Churchill had undertaken in overhauling the role of the Joint Intelligence Committee (JIC) during World War II had a significant effect on how Allied intelligence generated such valuable intelligence assessments of the Normandy defences. Information had to flow across many agencies and command layers, and timely assessments needed to be undertaken. It was the JIC that had the total view of how Overlord would evolve. Overlord succeeded, and at a much smaller cost than many had anticipated at the time.

One of the major issues that affected German intelligence in 1944 was the lack of collaboration between the German signal intelligence agencies. The inter-service collaboration on cryptographic analysis varied widely and often relationships were not cordial. There was regularly duplication of effort between the agencies and no real or effective intelligence cooperation between the six agencies. Intelligence sharing did occur; for example, in early 1944 around a third of all Supreme Command Armed Forces Signals Intelligence Agency (OKW/Chi) product would have made its way to Goering's Research Bureau (FA). There was better collaboration in the field, with the exchange of personnel and equipment, and the sharing of intelligence between the three services' signals intelligence agencies. Hitler, however, had a deep-seated mistrust for signals intelligence.

The Germans had struggled to get aerial reconnaissance over southern England during the build-up to D-Day. German intelligence had only a handful of agents operating in Britain at the time, most of whom had been turned into double agents and were working for the Allies. The High Command, and Hitler himself, were blind to Overlord.

Signals intelligence was one of the most crucial aspects for gathering intelligence on the German military dispositions and intentions. It had been recognised since the North Africa campaign in 1942 how important ULTRA had become. Colossus had the ability to decrypt Hitler's High Command enciphered messages within hours of them being sent, as opposed to weeks. This was a key strategic bonus for Allied intelligence before D-Day. There was a recognition, then, of the importance of intelligence to the outcome of a battle. The Normandy campaign reinforced this message.

As has been highlighted, the work of the British Y Services, Radio Security Service (RSS) and Bletchley Park laid the foundation for what was to be a fully informed and briefed invasion force. The value of SIGINT to the operation could also be looked at through a different lens. In the summer of 1944 the Americans were to set up the Target Intelligence Committee (TICOM). A number of teams were put together of highly trained specialists, notably cryptologists drawn from Bletchley, to capture documents, technology and personnel of the six main German signals organisations. They had learned the value of covert intelligence collection teams on the ground from the experiences of 30 Assault Unit, especially in Paris. The SIGINT component of 30 Assault Unit's work was taken over by TICOM. The other SIGINT targets outside Paris on the Black List of 30AU were all evacuated well ahead of the Allied advance and yielded little of intelligence value.

The very fact these teams were being established showed the value that SIGINT had to military command and control. It was an arms race, much like the race for missile or nuclear technologies.

When meeting any ageing veterans of any conflict, be it World War II or combat missions in Helmand Province, Afghanistan, you can always be touched by the humility of service personnel and how dismissive they can be of the roles they have played in history. In writing this book, it has been both an honour and a privilege to meet some of the surviving veterans from D-Day – men like Lieutenant Tony Byrd from the 15th Flotilla operating out of Dartmouth, or Lieutenant Jim Booth who has assisted me greatly in reconstructing the detail behind the Operation Gambit mission. As he recalled, 'when you're a young man, and part of a good team of like-minded extroverts, you just think it's all an exciting adventure, and you never imagine that you might not survive'.

All military veterans of all conflicts shape their memories around both their good and bad experiences, and some of the most abounding memories of all are those 'dits' or funny anecdotes.

Throughout the war, whilst serving with the clandestine units like COPP/9, Jim was sworn to secrecy. It must have run in the family. When on leave he often got into stunted conversations with his sister, Cecilia. She was serving with the FANY (First Aid Nursing Yeomanry) teams of the Princess Royal's Volunteer Corps (PRVC). She served as a radio operator doing clandestine operational work running agents in Norway in conjunction with the Special Operations Executive (SOE).

The months after D-Day saw Jim's COPP team posted to the Far East to undertake further clandestine missions against Japanese positions along the coast of Burma, often using two-man canoes that had been launched from submarines. Jim often mentioned this stint of the war was much more exciting and dangerous than anything he did in 1944.

After the war, Jim spent 1945–7 still in the Royal Navy, serving on minesweepers clearing mines in the Aegean Sea out of Malta. Jim was to meet his future wife, Bertha, in 1946 on the island, after a blind date between friends. They married in 1951, shortly after Jim was invalided out of the Navy due to lung damage. He subsequently went into farming in Devon, owning a series of livestock farms in the county, including the 320-acre West Bowerland farm outside Okehampton. One day whilst out working on the farm, he wanted to take his Massey Ferguson tractor up to the top of the farm to cut some straw bales. He took his trusty Fairburn-Sykes Commando dagger that had served him well during his COPP service. Neatly emblazoned on the brass handle are his initials and service details: 'JCMB' and 'COPP No. 9 Normandy 1944 Burma 1945'. Whilst at the top of the farm he lost the knife after it had fallen out of his tractor. In 2014 his son Charles, who was born at the farm, returned to reconnect with his roots and spoke at length to the current farmer Mr Jewel.

'Your father served in the Navy during the War didn't he?' questioned Mr Jewel. Charles confirmed this and Mr Jewel shuffled off to a nearby barn. Whilst sorting through some scrap tools in a bucket he came across the knife which he had found fifteen years earlier at the top of the farm. He had gone up to the farm to sort out an ash tree that had blown over, to cut up for firewood. He had spotted something metallic in the rootball and discovered Jim's Fairburn-Sykes dagger. Jim is now reunited with his World War II dagger. We could call this circumstance, or chance, but clearly that knife was meant to be returned to its rightful owner.

It is important to conclude how war-fighting may have changed in the years since D-Day. But the intelligence preparation of the battlefield was as important then as it was at Waterloo to how it is used now on the streets of Basra in 2004, to the Sangin compounds in Helmand Province. Operation Overlord is a classic example of what can be achieved through meticulous planning, effective reconnaissance and full spectrum intelligence-gathering prior to the onset of fighting. Vanguard exemplifies that hundreds of specialists dedicated to their craft helped shaped the strategic understanding of German defences in northern France in 1944. Overlord would not have achieved its ends without the bravery and courage of those dedicated individuals assigned to special duties who helped pave the way for the biggest military invasion in modern history.

Shelves of books have been written about D-Day. As a military operation it stands out as probably been the most well-known in history. This is a reflection of the complexities and scale of such an invasion. To give an idea of scale, on 6 June 1944 the Allies landed 156,000 troops into Normandy. This comprised 73,000 US forces who landed at Utah Beach and Omaha Beach, and also the contingent of airborne troops who landed at various drop zones around Normandy. In the British and Canadian sectors, a total of 83,115 troops were landed at Gold Beach, Sword Beach and Juno Beach.

To support the Allied landings on 6 June, some 11,590 aircraft were made available. On D-Day itself Allied aircraft flew some 14,674 sorties and 127 were lost.

Operation Neptune involved a huge naval task force of 6,939 vessels, which included 1,213 naval combat ships, 4,126 landing ships and landing craft, 736 anciliary craft and 864 merchant vessels. Over 195,700 personnel were assigned to the Neptune armada.

Five days after D-Day, on 11 June, some 326,547 troops, 54,186 vehicles and 104,428 tonnes of supplies had made its way onto the beaches of Normandy. The logistics behind the invasion force is almost unfathomable in its scale, reach and complexity but vital to maintain the Allied foothold in northern France and to sustain the new Second Front that had opened on that one day in history.

However, the cost was immense. Naval losses alone totalled twenty-four warships and thirty-five merchantman or auxillaries sunk, and a further 120 vessels damaged. It has been estimated that in the run-up to Overlord, in April/May 1944 the Allied air forces lost nearly 12,000 men and over 2,000 aircraft in operations which paved the way. On the beaches themselves there were huge casualties, with the 1st Infantry assault on Omaha being the worst. Of all the Allied troops that had landed by nightfall, there were 2,400 casualties. The British landed 29,000 men at Sword but with 630 casualties. The joint British and Canadian landings at Juno yielded 1,200 casualties. At Utah Beach the US forces had the lightest casualties with only 197 men killed or wounded out of the 23,000 troops that landed. All military success comes at a cost.

Many veterans are asked, 'Why do you old men revisit cemeteries year after year? Why do you return to the site of some of your worst experiences?' There is no simpler answer beyond, 'If you were there, you do not need telling; if you were not, then no amount of words would ever help you understand.'

I would like to end this book with a salient D-Day quote from US Admiral Chester Nimitz: 'They fought together like Brothers-in-Arms, they died together and now they sleep side by side. To them we have a solemn obligation.'

ACRONYMS AND ABBREVIATIONS

AA Anti-Aircraft

ACAS (I) Assistant Chief of the Air Staff (Intelligence)

ACIU Allied Central Interpretation Unit (formerly CIU)

AEAF Allied Expeditionary Air Force

AI Air Intelligence or Airborne Interception (RADAR)

ANCXF Allied Naval Commander-in-Chief Expeditionary Force

ANX Advanced Navigation Exercise

APID Aerial Photographic Interpretation Department

APIS Army Photographic Intelligence Section

APX Advanced Penetration Exercise

ATS Auxiliary Territorial Service

AU Amplifier Unit

BBC British Broadcasting Corporation

BCRA *Bureau de Contre Espionnage Renseignements et d'Action – the Central Office of Information and Action*

BEF British Expeditionary Force

BIOS British Intelligence Objectives Sub-Committee

BP Bletchley Park

BTM British Tabulating Machine company

BUF British Union of Fascists

CAD *Comite d'Action contre la Deportation*

CCO Chief of Combined Operations

CH Chain Home (RADAR)

CHIS Covert Human Intelligence Source

CIC Combined Intelligence Committee

CIO Central Intelligence Officer

CIS Combined Intelligence Section

CIU Central Interpretation Unit

CNR *Conseil National de la Résistance*

CO Commanding Officer

COHQ Combined Operations Headquarters

COMNAVEU Commander Naval Forces Europe

COPP Combined Operations Pilotage Parties

COSSAC Chief of Staff to the Supreme Allied Commander

COXE Combined Operations Experimental Establishment (HMS *Appledore* in North Devon)

CP Command Post

CRR Compilation and Records Room (Beaumanor)

CSC Controller of Special Communications

CSDIC Combined Services Detailed Interrogation Centre

DASV *Deutscher Amateur Sende und Empfangs Verein*

DD Duplex Drive (Amphibious tanks)

Deputy Director Operations Division (Irregular) or DDOD(I)

D/F Direction Finding

DGER *Direction Générale de Études et Recherches*

DISC Defence Intelligence and Security Centre

DNI Director Naval Intelligence

DNR Department of Naval Research

DPWI Director of Political Warfare Intelligence

DSEA Davis Submarine Escape Apparatus

DZ Drop Zone

EMFFI *Etat Major des Forces Francaises de l'interieur*

ERA Engine Room Artificer

ESTW Echo Sounding Taut Wire

ETO European Theatre of Operations

ETOUSA European Theatre of Operations, United States of America

FANY First Aid Nursing Yeomanry (now PRVC Princess Royals Volunteer Corps)

FDT Fighter Direction Tenders

FFI *Forces Francaises de l'intérieur*

FIAT Field Information Agency Technical

FIU Forward Interrogation Unit

FMC Forward Maintenance Centre

FOB Forward Officers, Bombardment

FORDE Foreign Office Research and Development Establishment (Knockholt)

FUSAG First United States Army Group

GAF German Air Force

GCC Government Communications Centre

GC&CS Government Code & Cipher School

GCWS Government Communications Wireless Station (Knockholt)

GCI Ground Control Interception (RADAR)

GFP *Geheim Feld Polizei*

GHQ General Headquarters

GPO General Post Office

GSGS Geographical Section General Staff

GS(I) General Staff (Intelligence)

HDML Harbour Defence Motor Launch

HFDF High Frequency Direction Finding

HUMINT Human Intelligence

HQLS Headquarters Landing Ship

HSSPF Höhere SS-und Polizeiführer (Higher SS and Police Commander)

HW High Water

IAU Intelligence Assault Unit

IFF Identification Friend or Foe

IMINT Imagery Intelligence

IPB Intelligence Preparation of the Battlefield

ISIS Inter-Service Information Series

ISSB Inter-Service Security Board

ISTD Inter-Services Topographical Department

ITX Initial Training Exercise

IWIO Illicit Wireless Intercept Organisation

JCS Joint Chiefs of Staff

JIC Joint Intelligence Committee

JIS Joint Intelligence Staff

JNCO Junior Non-Commissioned Officer

JPS Joint Planning Staff

KDG King's Dragoon Guards

KdS *Kommandeur der Sipo*

LCA Landing Craft Assault

LCOCU Landing Craft Obstacle Clearance Unit

LCP(L) Landing Craft Personnel (Large)

LCS London Controlling Section

LCT Landing Craft – Transport

LRC London Reception Centre

LRDG Long Range Desert Group

LST Landing Ship Tank

LW Low Water

MARES *Marine Einsatz Kommando*

MEW Ministry of Economic Warfare

MF Medium Frequency

MGB Motor Gun Boat

MI Military Intelligence

MIRS Military Intelligence Research Section

MRATHS Malvern RADAR and Technology History Society

MTB Motor Torpedo Boat

NCDU Naval Combat Demolition Unit

NCO Non-Commissioned Officer

NID Naval Intelligence Division

NID6 Naval Intelligence Division 6 (forerunner to ISTD)

NPS National Pigeon Service

OCM *Organisation Civile et Militaire*

OIC Operational Intelligence Centre (Admiralty)

OKH *Oberkommando des Heeres*

OKL *Oberkommando der Luftwaffe*

OKM *Oberkommando der Kriegsmarine*

OKW *Oberkommando der Wehrmacht*

ORBAT Order of Battle

OSS Office of Strategic Services (forerunner to the CIA)

OT *Organisation Todt*

OTP One-Time Pads

OTU Operational Training Unit

OUP Oxford University Press

OWI Office of War Information

PE Plastic Explosive

PI Photographic Interpretation

PID Political Intelligence Department (covername for the Political Warfare Executive)

PIU Photographic Interpretation Unit

PLUTO Pipeline Under The Ocean

POW or P/W Prisoner of War

PR Photographic Reconnaissance

PRU Photographic Reconnaissance Unit

PSO Pigeon Supply Officer

PWD Psychological Warfare Division (SHAEF)

PWE Political Warfare Executive

PWIS Prisoner of War Interrogation Section

RADAR RAdio Detection And Ranging

RAF Royal Air Force

RCA Radio Corporation of America

RCM Radio Counter Measures

RE Royal Engineers

RM Royal Marines

RMBPD Royal Marines Boom Patrol Detachment

RN Royal Navy

RNR Royal Naval Reserve

RNVR Royal Naval Volunteer Reserve

RO Radio Operator

RSS Radio Security Service

RU Research Unit

SACSEA Supreme Allied Commander, South-East Asia

SAS Special Air Service

SBS Special Boat Section

SCU Special Communications Unit

SD *Sicherheitsdienst*

SFHQ Special Forces Headquarters

SHAEF Supreme Headquarters Allied Expeditionary Force

SIGINT Signals Intelligence

SIPO *Sicherheitspolizei*

SIS Secret Intelligence Service (GB) or Signal Intelligence Service (USA)

SIU Special Intelligence Unit [forerunner to 30 RN Commando (Special Engineering Unit)]

SLO Special Liaison Officer

SLS Special Listening Service/Section

SLU Special Liaison Unit

SNCO Senior Non-Commissioned Officer

SO Special Operations

SOE Special Operations Executive

SOG Special Operations Group

SOTB Special Operator Training Battalion

SP *Stool Pigeon*

SPRI Scott Polar Research Institute

SSB Secret Service Bureau

SSRF Small Scale Raiding Force

STS Special Training Schools

SWOPS Special Wireless Operators

T/A Traffic Analysis

TAF Tactical Air Force

TDS Theatre Documents Section

TICOM Target Intelligence Committee

TIS Theatre Intelligence Section

TRE Telecommunications Research Establishment

USAAF United States of America Air Force

USNR United States Naval Reserve

UWSBA Underwater Swimming Breathing Apparatus

VI Voluntary Interceptor

W&D Wet and Dry (X-Craft compartment)

WD War Department

WOYG War Office Y Group

WRNS Women's Royal Naval Service (informally Wrens)

W/T Wireless Telegraphy

WU Wireless Unit

WWII World War Two

BIBLIOGRAPHY

Chapter 1 – Great Crusade

Remarks at Clifton College, Friday 29 May 1953 by General Omar Bradley, Chairman of the Joint Chiefs of Staff (c/o Clifton College Archives)

Ralph Bennett, *Behind the Battle: Intelligence in the War with Germany 1939–1945*, Chapter – Set Fair in the West, the Autumn Showers, p. 244

H. Hinsley, *British Intelligence in the Second World War Volume I*, Chapter 15 – Developments in the Organisation of Intelligence

SHAEF/2FX/1/DT – SHAEF (INT) *Directive No.10 for Placename codewords*, issued 10 March 1944

SHAEF, 13 February 1944, Constitution and activation of Supreme Headquarters, Allied Expeditionary Force Copy no. 72

Michael S. Goodman, *The Official History of the Joint Intelligence Committee. Volume I: From the approach of the Second World War to the Suez Crisis* (Routledge, 2014)

NID UD Report No. 287, 25 January 1943, *German preparations to defend ports in Northern France and low countries*

Antony Beevor, *D-Day – The Battle for Normandy*, Penguin-Viking

Tristan Lovering MBE, *Amphibious Assault – Manoeuvre from the sea. From Gallipoli to the Gulf – a definitive analysis* (Seafarer Books, 2007)

The Times Publication, *D-Day – The Story of D-Day through Maps* (HarperCollins Publishers, 2014)

Report of the General Board. United States Forces, European Theatre. Organisation and Operation of the Theatre Intelligence Services in the European Theatre of Operations, File 320.2/57 Study #14 http://usacac.army.mil/cac2/cgsc/carl/eto/eto-014.pdf

Walter Bedell Smith letter to Brigadier General Joe Sweet from the Military Service Publishing company, 7 March 1952, CREST document archive. Ref CIA-RDP80R01731R003100190064-2

Stephen Badsey, *D-Day – From the Normandy Beaches to the Liberation of* France (Colour Library Books Ltd, 1993)

Max Hastings, *Overlord – D-Day and the Battle for Normandy 1944* (Michael Joseph Limited - Pan Grand Strategy Series, 1984)

Chapter 2 – Bluff

ADM 202/599 *30 Assault Unit* Photographs

F.H. Hinsley, *British Intelligence in the Second World War: Volume 4, Security and Counter-Intelligence* (Cambridge University Press, 1990), Volume 4, p. 295

Richard Collier, *Ten Thousand Eyes* (London: Collins, 1958)

Desmond Young, *Rommel* (London: Book Club Associates, 1950)

Terry Henson, *Porky's War – the story of a real-life Freddie the Frogman* (Menin House, an imprint of Tommies Guides Military Booksellers, 2012)

George Forty, *Fortress Europe: Hitler's Atlantic Wall* (Ian Allan Publishing House, 2002)

Stephen Badsey, *D-Day – From the Normandy Beaches to the Liberation of France* (Colour Library Books Ltd, 1993)

ON1 Appendix VII: Annex C – Text and Diagrams of Neptune batteries, Copy No. 1952

ON1 Appendix VII: Annex A - Assault Beach Defence Maps, Copy No. 2949

ON1 Appendix VII: Annexe D – Text and Traces of Coast Defences (to fit chart maps 1013-1017), Copy No. 2959

Jock Haswell, *The Intelligence and Deception of the D-Day landings* (B.T. Batsford Publishers Ltd, 1979)

Chapter 3 – Pinprick

James D. Ladd, *Commandos and Rangers of World War II* (Battle Standards, 1978)

Paul Winter, *D-Day Documents* (Bloomsbury Publishers, 2014)

Operation Tarbrush: Details of individual operations 3, 5, 8 and 10 from office of Flag Officer Commanding, Dover ADM 179/401 1944

WO 205/220 *Operation Tarbrush: Outline plans, information on beach mines and obstacles* [former reference 437/1/OpsA]

Private papers of Captain R. Wooldridge MC – IWM London Archives (Documents 19880)

Captain Scott-Bell DSC RN, *Operation 'Force Regulator', An account of an aborted raid before D-Day* (The Royal Marines Historical Society – The Sheet Anchor) Volume XXXVI, No. 1

http://www.mirror.co.uk/news/uk-news/ww2-astonishing-meeting-nazi-4665275

Damien Lewis, *Churchill's Secret Warriors – The Explosive true story of the Special Forces desperadoes of WWII* (Quercus Publishers, 2014)

Ian Dear, *10 Commando* (Pen & Sword Publishers, 1987)

PORMG reference 5511A, *An interview with George Lane MC of No. 4 Commando*, series of interviews carried out by Russell Miller c. 1989–91 for *Nothing less than Victory* (Portsmouth History Centre, 1993)

James D. Ladd, *SBS – The Invisible Raiders. The History of the Special Boat Squadron from World War Two to the present* (Book Club Associates, 1993)

Winston S. Churchill, *The Second World War: Volume V – Closing the Ring* (Penguin Books Ltd/Book Club Associates, 1985)

Chapter 4 – Racket

M.R.D. Foot, *SOE 1940-1946: An outline History of the Special Operations Executive*, Chapter VII – Security and Penetration, pp. 143-4.

http://www.telegraph.co.uk/news/obituaries/1318954/Leo-Marks.html

Leo Marks, *Between Silk and Cyanide* (London: Harper Collins, 1998)

E.H. Cookridge, *Inside SOE – The Story of Special Operations in Western Europe 1940–1945* (Arthur Barker Ltd, 1966)

Richard Collier, *Ten Thousand Eyes.* (London: Collins, 1958)

HS6-614 Volume 227 Yeo-Thomas Passy & Brossolette missions March 1943–May 1944

HS9/1458 N238 Yeo-Thomas FFE DOB 17/6/01

HS7/126 History of EMFFI (*Etat Major des Forces Francaises de l'interieur*) DRP/151 Appreciation of Strength and Organisation of the French *Maquis* as at 26.1.1944

IWM Documents Reference 12848 – Private papers of AAG Staggs – a W/T Operator with F Section SOE in the FARMER circuit

David Stafford, *Secret Agent – The True Story of the Special Operations Executive* (BBC)

Pierre Lorain and David Kahn, *Secret Warfare – The Arms and techniques of the Resistance* (Orbis Publishers, 1984)

Lloyd Bott CBE DSC, *The Secret War from the River Dart – The Story of the Royal Navy's 15th Motor Gunboat Flotilla 1942–1945* (Dartmouth History Research Group, 1997), Paper 23

Charles Milner, Guy Hamilton and Ronald Seddon, *HMMTB718 'Something Special' – The Story of MTB718* (York Publishing, 2014)

Brooks Richards, *Secret Flotillas – Clandestine Sea Operations to Brittany 1940–44* (Pen & Sword Maritime, 2012)

Pierre Duffoir – SOE Personal File

Maurice Rouneau – SOE Personal File

www.soe-french.co.uk

Chapter 5 – Persuaders

www.chichester.co.uk/news/local/hero-fred-92-handed-highest-honour-by-french-government-1-7157091#ixzz3zMWye73w

Colin Beavan, *Operation Jedburgh – D-Day and America's first shadow war*

The *Daily Telegraph*, Jeanette Guyot, obituary, 26 April 2016

SUSSEX Operation 1943–1944. Colonel Heflin notes – FPM responsible for planning, mounting and launching. Francis Pickens-Miller Collection. George C Marshall Research Library (c/o Portsmouth History Centre archives, Portsmouth Central Library)

IWM Interview with Fred Arthur Bailey http://www.iwm.org.uk/collections/item/object/80011495 catalogue number 11752, production date 11 December 1990

'Jedburgh operations support to the French Resistance in Eastern Brittany from June-September 1944' Major Ralph Nichols USA Masters 1993 thesis presented to the Faculty of the US Army Command and General Staff College, Fort Leavenworth, Kansas

www.plan-sussex-1944.net

Phillip M. Williams, *OSS Station Victor: Hurley's Secret War*

Interview transcript, Sgt Fred Bailey

Interview transcript, Sgt John Sharp

SAS Brigade Operation Instructions No. 2, Copy No. 8, 29 March 1944, Operation Overlord, from files WO218/114

Martin W. Bowman, *The Bedford Triangle – US undercover operations from England in World War 2* (Patrick Stephens Publishing, 1988)

Chapter 6 – Cages

Helen Fry, *The M Room: Secret Listeners who bugged the Nazis* (CreateSpace Independent Publishing Platform, 2013)

WO208/4970 The History of CSDIC (UK)

WO219/4717A Some observations on the morale of the Wehrmacht, 19 July 1944

WO208/3478 The Interrogation of Prisoners of War

ADM 202/599 30 Assault Unit Photographs

Falko Bell, *One of our most valuable sources of Intelligence: British intelligence and the Prisoner of War system in 1944* (Intelligence and National Security, 2016) Vol. 31, No. 4, pp. 556-78

Wilton Park: A very special POW camp www.ajr.org.uk/index.cfm/section.journal/issue.Aug09/article=3213

WO 208/3458 'Coordination arrangements for the interrogation of P/W', 17 July 1939

WO 208/3458 'Coordination arrangements of the interrogation of prisoners of War taken in the United Kingdom', 21 July 1939

www.mi5.gov.uk/bad-nenndorf

CAB 79/9, COS (41) 58th Meeting, 17 February 1941

CAB 79/9, JIC (41) 68, 11 February 1941

CAB81/93 JIC (45) 54 (O), 15 February 1945

WO 208/3583 CSDIC Interrogation report SIR 52 PW M1859 deserted from Le Havre

WO 208/3584 CSDIC Interrogation reports SIR 99 PW M329 and PW M323 from 24 Panzer Division

WO 208/3585 CSDIC Interrogation reports SIR 136 of PW M 359, Unteroffizier 146 Infantry Regt and SIR127 PW M358 Gefreiter from 10 Coy, IR 145

WO 208/3720 RPS Interrogation reports – Informant of MI 19(RPS)/1945

WO 208/3588 CSDIC Interrogation reports SIR 253

WO 208/3590 CSDIC Interrogation reports SIR 314 German defences at Caen from PW KP/2 (M) Gundlach

Chapter 7 – Black List

Nick Rankin, *Ian Fleming's Commandos*

ADM 223/500 *Proposal for Naval Intelligence Commando Unit*

ADMI/15798 XC4262 memo from Lt. T.J. Glanville RNVR, 31 October 1944

XC4262 – DEFE2/1109 Minutes from meeting to discuss the Intelligence Assault Unit (Special Engineering Unit), No. 30 Commando held at COHQ, Room 412 on 31 December 1943

http://globalnews.ca/news/274605/breaking-german-codes-real-reason-for-1942-dieppe-raid-historian/

BBC WW2 People's War entry contributed by BBC Radio Norfolk Action Desk L/Sgt Rogers MM http://forum.commandoveterans.org/cdoForum/posts/list/3953.page#14484, Dennis Solly story, 21 November 2005 [BBC–WW2 People's Archive]

Guy Allan Farrin, *The History of 30AU*, pp. 84-8

ADM 202/599 30 Assault Unit Photographs

ADM 202/308 Report on activities of Pikeforce D-Day to D+8

Interview with 30AU veteran, Royal Marine Patsy Cullen, April 2016

ADM223/213 *History of SIGINT operations undertaken by 30 Commando/30AU*, from the Godfrey Archive, Volume 10A

ADM1/15798 *Report of activities of Operation Woolforce* – 30AU in Paris during 1944

30 Assault Unit at Littlehampton (December 1943–October 1944), jottings by Major Freddie Townsend OBE RM (retd), 21 June 1989, accessed in Littlehampton Museum archives

European axis signal intelligence in World War II as revealed by 'TICOM' investigations and by other Prisoner of War interrogations and captured material, principally German, DOCID 3560861 declassified and approved for release by NSA on 6 January 2009 pursuant to EO12958, pProduced by Army Security Agency, 1 May 1946. www.nsa.gov/news-features/declassified-documents/european-axis-sigint/assets/files/volume_1_synopsis.pdf

Captain The Reverend D.A. Farquharson-Roberts RM, *Royal Marines and D-Day – Some Personal Reminiscenses* (Royal Marines Historical Society Special Publications, 1994), No. 16, Second Edition 2012

Chapter 8 – Listeners

CAB301/77 *Organisation and Funding of British Intelligence – SIGINT and Codebreaking*, History of SIGINT in WWII, Appendix IV, p. 842, p. 916 – Attachment 2

Joan Nichols, *England Needs You: The Story of Beaumanor Y station World War Two* (2000)

Neil Webster, *Cribs for Victory: The Untold Story of Bletchley Parks Secret Room* (Polpero Heritage Press, 2011)

Ralph Bennett, *ULTRA in the West – The Normandy Campaign of 1944–45* (Hutchison & Co., 1979)

Interview with Y Service Officer Guy William Hugh Waters, IWM Interview, reference 10870

John Pether, *Funkers and Sparkers – Origins & Formation of the 'Y' Service*, Bletchley Park Trust report No. 14, January 2011

Another Bit of Bletchley – A Personal memoir by Sir Arthur Bonsall, Bletchley Park Trust report No. 17, September 2009

European axis signal intelligence in World War II as revealed by 'TICOM' investigations and by other Prisoner of War interrogations and captured material, principally German, DOCID 3560861 declassified and approved for release by NSA on 6 January 2009 pursuant to EO12958, produced by Army Security Agency, 1 May 1946 www.nsa.gov/news-features/declassified-documents/european-axis-sigint/assets/files/volume_1_synopsis.pdf

Albert Praun, Principal Author former General of the German Signal Corps, *German Radio Intelligence*, abridged copy of MSP-038, Department of the Army, Office of the Chief of Military History, Reference ID A56914, approved for release by NSA pursuant to EO13526, reference ID A56914

Gordon Welchman, *The Hut Six Story – Breaking the Enigma Codes* (M & M Baldwin Publishers Ltd, 1997)

Chapter 9 – Rhubarb
ADM 202/599 30 Assault Unit Photographs

R.V. Jones, *Most Secret War* (Hamish Hamilton Ltd Publishers, 1978)

James D. Ladd, *Commandos and Rangers of World War II* (David & Charles Publishers, 1989)

G Section PRJ296 Document Historical records G Section, c/o RAF Medmenham Collection archives

Taylor Downing, *Spies in the Sky: The Secret Battle for Aerial Intelligence during World War II* (Abacus Publishers, 2012)

Official summary of WWII Reconnaissance activities, RAF Medmenham collection

Roy Conyers Nesbit, *Eyes of the RAF – A History of Photo-Reconnaissance* (Bramley Books, 1996)

Ground Controlled Interception RADARs in Operation Neptune/Overlord. 'The Allied Invasion of France June 1944.' The story of the Fighter Direction Tenders used during the 'D-Day' Assault and the Mobile RADAR Convoys that landed on the beaches, prepared by Horace Red Macauley. www. rquirk.com/cdnradar/cor/chapter11.pdf

Sinclair McKay, *The Secret Life of Bletchley Park – The WWII codebreaking centre and the men and women who worked there* (Aurum Press Ltd, 2011)

Chapter 10 – Jellyfish
Michael Smith, *Station X – Codebreakers of Bletchley Park* (Pan Grand Strategy Series, Channel 4 books

1998)

Gordon Welchman, *The Hut Six Story* (M&M Baldwin Publishers, 1997)

T.H. Flowers, '***D-Day at Bletchley Park'***, in Copeland, B.J. (ed) ***Colossus: The Secrets of Bletchley Park's Codebreaking Computers*** (Oxford University Press, 2006).

Ralph Bennett, *Ultra in the West: The Normandy Campaign 1944–45* (London: Hutchinson & Co Publishers)

The Influence of ULTRA in the Second World War, annual Liddell Hart Centre for Military Archives Lecture by Professor Harry Hinsley, King's College London, 18 February 1992

http://www.456fis.org/ULTRA.htm

Introduction: The influence of ULTRA in the Second World War' Codebreakers: The Inside Story of Bletchley Park, edited by F.H. Hinsley and Alan Stripp (Oxford University Press 1993), pp. 12-13

www.hertfordshirelife.co.uk/out-about/places/decodingtheenigmainletchworth

http://www.colossus-computer.com/colossus1.html

http://www.ellsbury.com/ultrafirstcomputers.htm

Alan Turing's Automatic Computing Engine: The Master Codebreaker's Struggle to Build the Modern Computer, edited by B.J. Copeland (Oxford: Oxford University Press, 2005)

ADM202/599 30 Assault Unit Photographs Volume 2

Sinclair McKay, *The Secret Life of Bletchley Park – The WWII codebreaking centre and the men and women who worked there* (Aurum Press Ltd, 2011)

Chapter 11 – Magic
Michael Smith, *Station X – Codebreakers of Bletchley Park* (Channel 4 Books, Pan Grand Strategy Series, 1998)

http://ciphermachines.com/purple

www.nsa.gov/public_info/_files/crypto_almanac_50th/baron_oshimas_contributions.pdf DOC-ID 3866295 Approved for release by NSA on 26 May 2010. FOIA Case #60395

Mary Barbler, *D-Day Deception: Op Fortitude and the Normandy Invasion*

HW12/295 Item reference 126329, Japanese Berlin – Ambassador's interview with Ribbentrop, December 1943

Mockler-Ferryman, *Military Intelligence Organisation*, P.134 in CAB 121/380. SIC File D/France/6/6, COS (43)63rd(o) Meeting of 1 April, 111th and 112th (o) meetings of 25 and 26 May; JIC (43)181(o) of 21 April, JIC (43)217 of 20 May

http://www.washingtonpost.com/archive/politics/1998/05/26/japans-unwitting-d-day-spy/9309f2b9-dd69-4ee3-8eaf-b9b4754631d8/

Michael Smith, *The Secrets of Station X – How the Bletchley Park Codebreakers helped win the war*

Michael Smith, *The Bletchley Park Codebreakers*

Max Hastings, *The Secret War: Spies, Codes and Guerillas 1939–1945* (William Collins Publishers, 2015)

Carl Boyd, *Hitler's Japanese Confidant: General Oshima Hiroshi and MAGIC intelligence, 1941-1945* (Lawrence: University Press of Kansas, 1993)

Ben MacIntyre, *Double Cross – The True Story of the D-Day Spies* (Bloomsbury Publishing, 2012)

Leonard Mudloff and the Oshima intercept, from www.citizensforfauquier.org

David Kahn, *How I Discovered World War II's Greatest Spy – and other stories of Intelligence and Code* (CRC Press – Taylor & Francis Group, 2014)

Lieutenant General Hiroshi Oshima, covering period October 1938 to August 1944, WO 208/4703

TIS Threat Intelligence Section dossiers WO219/1899. Ref TIS/RI/Def/6.1 account of Visit of Italian Mission to German Defences on the Channel coast.

Chapter 12 – London Calling

H817.1990 BBC Radio broadcasts

HS8/445 TNA documents on April 1943 BBC *messages personnels* broadcasts

SOE Memo 17 March 1944, Ref DRP/723 titled *'BBC Messages'*

SOE/SO HQ Memo to BGS Plans, HQ 21 Army Group, 9 March 1944, *'Issue of Operational Instructions to Resistance groups by means of BBC messages'*

Leo Marks, *Between Silk and Cyanide – the Story of SOE's Code War* (London: Harper Collins, 1998)

Code messages to the French Resistance Movement, 1 January–30 July 1944, BBC Written Archives, Ref 10190

Foreign General – Code Messages 1941–1945, BBC Written Archives, Ref E2/90

Anatol Goldberg, The Ears of Britain at War: Personal impressions of the BBC Monitoring Service in Wartime, September 1945, BBC Written Archives, C73 Compilations, A/C Number 46245, Ref 830/698a

Compilations selected documents on Monitoring 1938–1941 (Account No. 70,156)

Publicity – BBC Monitoring Service 1939–1946, R44/276/1, includes BBC Monitoring Service structure/sections, BBC Written Archives (Account no. 8853)

Departmental External Services Monitoring Service: Establishment File 5, 1939–1945, BBC Written Archives R13/169/8, Formerly 830/696

Sam Bassett, *Royal Marine – The Autobiography of Colonel Sam Bassett CBE RM* (London: Peter Davies Publishers, 1962)

Chapter 13 – Fourth Arm

'The Fourth Arm' memorandum, 19 August 1940 – TNA, AMD 223/447

Lee Richards, 'Rainbow in the Dark: Assessing a century of British Military Information Operations', from Defence Strategic Communications, Journal of NATO Strategic Communications Centre of Excellence, Volume 1 Number 11, Winter 2015

www.bbc.co.uk/threecounties/peoples_war/beds_secret_war.shtml#propaganda

TNA FO 898/45 – Project Number Two for ASPIDISTRA BLACK

www.psywar.org/delmer/8420/1001

Policy – Propaganda – Axis Communications 1942, BBC Written Archives R34/625 (Account no. 32589/8)

Policy-Propaganda, Counter-Propaganda File IA (first part of two files) 1939 (formerly 830/687), BBC Written Archives

FO 954/23 (The National Archives) 15 October 1941, pp. 89-92

Policy-Propaganda: Directive R34/654/1, French Service, PWE 1941, PWE Directive for BBC French Service Week 39 (1941) Monday 29 September 1941, BBC Written Archives (Account no. 10102)

Policy-Propaganda: Directive R34/654/2, French Service, PWE January 1944, BBC Written Archives (Account no. 48847) PWE 43/11/26a, PWE/43/11/27, 3–16 January 1944

Policy-Propaganda: Directive R34/654/3, French Service, PWE January–March 1944 (Account no. 48848), Reference PWD/44/12/1a

www.cheddington.org.uk/organisations/1944

Report on Special Operations during 'Overlord' – to Chiefs of Staff, SHAEF

Falling Leaf – The Journal of the Psywar Society, Winter – January 2003, No. 179

Falling Leaf – The Journal of the Psywar Society, Spring – May 2004, No. 181

Falling Leaf – The Journal of the Psywar Society, Winter – January 2006, No. 187

Falling Leaf – The Journal of the Psywar Society, Winter – January 2010, No. 202

David Garnett, *The Secret History of PWE – The Political Warfare Executive 1939–1945* (St Ermin's Press, 2002)

WO 219/4827 ZF.2, dissemination log – French transport workers leaflet & ZF.4 Dissemination log – Eisenhower warning leaflet

John A. Taylor, *Secret Sisters of Bletchley Park – Psychological Warfare in World War II* (Magic Flute Publications, 2015)

Psychological Warfare Division SHAEF FO 898/489, *Leaflet Operations in the Western European Theatre 1944–1945* (1945)

MUS/901/154, dated 29 June 1943 – Planning with PWE and BBC

WO 171/168, after action report 'SUBJECT: Operations of No. 13 Amplifier Unit against the Cherbourg Garrison on 26-27 June 1944' by Major Gordon Shepherd

12th Army Group – Latest Reports of Leaflet reactions, No. 11-T

Chapter 14 – Deceit

DEFE 2/502, diagram showing RADAR counter-measures for Operation Overlord, 5/6 June 1944.

Lance Corporal Heinz Herbst of the German Army Signals Intelligence Service, interview transcript from Russell Millar 1989–92 collection for his book *Nothing but Victory* (Portsmouth History Centre), ref PORMG – 5495A

John Nichol, *After the Flood – What the Dambusters did next*

Ben MacIntyre, *Double Cross – The True Story of the D-Day Spies* (Bloomsbury Publishing, 2012)

Ben MacIntyre, *Operation Mincemeat* (Bloomsbury, 2010)

F.H. Hinsley, *British Intelligence in the Second World War – Volume 5: Strategic Deception*, Appendix 2 (Cambridge University Press, 1990)

F.H. Hinsley, *British Intelligence in the Second World War – Volume 2: Its Influence on Strategy and Operations*, Appendix 13 (Cambridge University Press, 1988)

Stephen Tatly, *Agent Garbo: The Brilliant, Eccentric Secret Agent who Tricked Hitler and Saved D-Day* (Houghton Mifflin Harcourt, 2012)

John Strawson, *Hitler as Military Commander* (B.T. Batsford Ltd, 1971)

Mary Kathleen Barbier, *D-Day Deception: Operation Fortitude and the Normandy Invasion* (Stackpole Books, 2007), Military History Series

WO219/308 Operation Fortitude, cover plan for Overlord, including details of deceptive lighting plan and wireless deception. Minutes of meeting at Norfolk House Friday 14 January 1944 to discuss provision of real, decoy and deceptive lighting in coastal areas

HW43/76 Allied SIGINT Policy and Organisation – written by Nigel de Grey

REPORTS ON THE WIRELESS DECEPTION & SECURITY MEASURES TAKEN BY THE THREE SERVICES IN CONNECTION WITH OPERATION NEPTUNE JULY 1944. OPERATION NEPTUNE – RADIO DECEPTION. REF: CLH/A.160-172/44 Dated 7 July 1944 [Marked as TOP SECRET – but now declassified/non-published]

Chapter 15 – Dicing

Taylor Downing, *Eyes In the Sky* (Abacus Publishers, 2011)

Roy Conyers Nesbit, *Eyes of the RAF – A History of Photo-Reconnaissance* (Bramley Books, 1996)

MED: PRJ 296 'History of G Section at Medmenham', written July 1945

Medmenham Collection-Historical Record/Biography and Interview – Mr Frederick Mason. Ref KHG 338

World War Two Photo Intelligence by Colonel Roy Stanley – Page 3

ADM 202/599 30 Assault Unit Photographs

Thirty-Four Wing: An unofficial Account (Portsmouth History Centre archives)

David Kahn, *How I Discovered World War II's Greatest Spy – and other stories of Intelligence and Code* (CRC Press – Taylor & Francis Group, 2014)

Alastair W. Pearson, *Allied Military Model Making during World War II* (Cartography and Geographic Information Science, 2002), Vol. 29, No. 3, pp. 227-41

A.B. Clough, *The Second World War 1939–1945. Army, maps and survey* (War Office, London, 1952)

The Times Publication, *D-Day – The Story of D-Day through Maps* (HarperCollins Publishers, 2014)

Chapter 16 – Contact Register

Nicholas Rankin, *Ian Fleming's Commandos* (Faber & Faber, 2012), Chapter 7 – Mapping the Future, pp. 137-42

Paul Winter, *D-Day Documents* (Bloomsbury Publishers, 2014)

C. Pareyn and E.P.F. Rose, 'Part VII: Field Guides to World War battlefields in Northern France', in *Geology and Warfare – Examples of the Influence of Terrain and Geologists on Military Operations*, Chapter 15 – A Field Guide to British Military applications of Geology in Normandy during 1944, ed. by Edward Rose and Paul Nathanail (Geological Society, 2000)

Don Chapman, 'The Holiday Snapshots Invasion', *Oxford Times*, 6 June 1984,

Edward P.F. Rose, Jonathan C. Clatworthy and Paul Nathanail, 'Specialist Maps Prepared by British Military Geologists for the D-Day Landings and Operations in Normandy, 1944', *The Cartographic Journal*, July 2006, Vol. 43, No. 2, pp. 117-43

http://www.bassettbranches.org/

Bassett, *Royal Marine – the Autobiography of Colonel Sam Bassett CBE RM* (London: Peter Davies Publishers, 1962)

Colonel E.P.F. Rose, *Secret Sappers – Terrain intelligence by the Geological Section ISTD During World War II* by in Bugle & Sabre IX The Military History of Oxfordshire and Buckinghamshire, p. 44

TNA WO 252/583, ISIS *Report on France: Normandy West of the Seine, Volume 2 – Inter-Service Topographical Department, Part VIII(A) Photographs of Part V(A) Coast, Beaches and Exits, April 1943*

Hugh Clout and Cyril Gosme, 'The Naval Intelligence Handbooks: a monument in geographical writing', *Progress in Human Geography* 27, 2 (2003) pp. 153-73

History of the Geological Section – Inter Services Topographical Department, October 1943–June 1946, WO402378

Obituary of H. Clifford Darby FBA, extract from Proceedings of the British Academy

ISIS Report on France: Normandy West of the Seine, Volume 2 – Inter-Service Topographical Department, Part VIII(A) Photographs of Part V(A) Coast, Beaches and Exits, April 1943 [TNA WO 252/583]

H.C. Darby (ed.) Naval Intelligence Division, Geographical Handbook, France Vol. 1 (London: Hodder and Stoughton, 1942)

Donald McLachlan, *Room 39 – Naval Intelligence in Action 1939–1945* (London: Weidenfeld & Nicholson, 1968)

Chapter 17 – Sand

http://www.coppheroes.org/

Donald McLachlan, *Room 39 – Naval Intelligence in Action 1939–1945* (London: Weidenfeld & Nicholson, 1968)

Logan Scott-Bowden interview transcript – 5530A/PORMG (Portsmouth History Centre). Transcript from series of interviews undertaken by Russell Miller in 1990–91 for his 1993 book *Nothing less than Victory*

Lieutenant Commander Nigel Clogstoun-Wilmott RNVR interview transcript – 5479A/PORMG (Portsmouth History Centre). Transcript from series of interviews undertaken by Russell Miller in 1990–91 for his 1993 book *Nothing less than Victory*

Lieutenant George Honour RNVR, Commander of X23, interview transcript – 5503A/PORMG (Portsmouth History Centre). Transcript from series of interviews undertaken by Russell Miller in 1990–91 for his 1993 book *Nothing less than Victory*

www.warmemorialtrustnorwich.com/70th-anniversary-of-the-d-day-landings

Soil investigations relating to the stability of a clay beach under traffic: report to the War Office WO/21/DJM December 1943, Department of Scientific and Industrial Research – Road Research Laboratory (from Shotton Archive, University of Birmingham)

Colonel E.P.F. Rose, *Secret Sappers – Terrain intelligence by the Geological Section ISTD During World War II* by in Bugle & Sabre IX The Military History of Oxfordshire and Buckinghamshire, p. 44

Lieutenant Commander C. Brunning RNVR, Commander of HMS *Darthema* typescript – PORMG 1990/661 (Portsmouth History Centre)

Claude Pareyn and Edward P.F. Rose, 'A field guide to British military applications of geology in Normandy during 1944', in *Geology and Warfare – Examples of the Influence of Terrain and Geologists on Military Operations* (Geological Society, 2000), Part 7, Chapter 15, pp. 413-89

C.E.T. Warren and James Benson, *Above Us the Waves – The Story of Midget Submarines and Human Torpedoes* (Pen & Sword Military Classics, 2006)

ADM179/323 Operation Postage Able, *Reconnaissance of French Coast using X Craft*, 25 December 1943, Reference 0302/45/15

Paul Kemp, *Underwater Warriors – The Fighting History of Midget Submarines* (Cassell & Co Military Paperbacks, 1996)

Pamela Mitchell, *The Tip of the Spear – The Midget Submarines* (Richard Netherwood Ltd, 1993)

Bill Strutton and Michael Pearson, *The Secret Invaders* (New York: British Book Centre, 1959)

Ian Trenowden, *Stealthily By Night – Clandestine Beach Reconnaissance and Operations in World War II* (Crécy Books, 1995)

Chapter 18 – Survey

Lieutenant Commander Nigel Clogstoun-Wilmott RNVR interview transcript – 5479A/PORMG (Portsmouth History Centre). Transcript from series of interviews undertaken by Russell Miller in 1990–91 for his 1993 book *Nothing less than Victory*

IWM Documents, reference 12534, Private papers of Lieutenant Commander Frank M. Berncastle RN, including his publication 'Sounding in the Dark: The Hydrographic Surveying of Beaches for use by Assault Craft and Prior to the Landings on the Coast of Normandy, 1944'

ADM 179/318 report submitted to HMS *Vectis*, 13 December 1943, note to IO/ANCXF only

Lieutenant Commander Frank Berncastle obituary www.telegraph.co.uk/news/obituaries/1404607/Lieutenant-Commander-Frank-Berncastle.html

'As it Was', by an Old Hydrographer Commander Nisbet Cunningham Glen www.hydro-international.com/content/article/as-it-was-27

Logan Scott-Bowden interview transcript – 5530A/PORMG (Portsmouth History Centre). Transcript from series of interviews undertaken by Russell Miller in 1990–91 for his 1993 book *Nothing less than Victory*

Chapter 19 – Disperse

ADM199/2475 Director of Naval Intelligence files – degaussing, captured German Harbour book, German preparations for invasion, Combined Intelligence Committee and Carriers Pigeon Service reports

John Langshaw Austin FBA (1911–60), extract from *Proceedings of the British Academy*, obituary by G.J. Warnock (PBA 49, 350-351)

Bletchley Park Magazine, Issue No. 6, Spring 2016

Pigeons in Two World Wars – a Racing Pigeon Double Volume, Part II, 'Pigeons in World War Two' edited by Major W.H. Osman

Special Section – Royal Signals 1940–1945, War Office London Publication

Columba Summary – No. 11 dated 7 Jan 44. MI 14.d/00/4/44 (WO206 files)

TNA ADM 199/2475 MI14 and Pigeons

John A. Taylor, *Secret Sisters of Bletchley Park – Psychological Warfare in World War II* (Magic Flute Publications, 2015)

Geoffrey Pigeon, *The Secret Wireless War – The story of MI6 Communications 1939–1945* (Arundel Books, 2008) www.prestige-press.com

A brief history of the Special Communications Units of Royal Signals 1939–1946 with reference to their origins in the Radio Security Service, and association with the Army 'Y' Service and Special Liaison Units. Compiled by RT Jenks in 1992, IWM Documents 2024

Report of the General Board. United States Forces, European Theatre. Organisation and Operation of the Theatre Intelligence Services in the European Theatre of Operations. File 320.2/57 Study #14. http://usacac.army.mil/cac2/cgsc/carl/eto/eto-014.pdf

Chapter 20 – Finale

ADM179/475 *Operation NEPTUNE Employment of X20 & X23 1944* May–June

http://www.combinedops.com/FDTs.htm

C.E.T. Warren and James Benson, *Above Us the Waves – The Story of Midget Submarines and Human Torpedoes* (Pen & Sword Military Classics, 2006)

Bill Strutton and Michael Pearson, *The Secret Invaders* (New York: British Book Centre, 1959)

Pamela Mitchell, *The Tip of the Spear – The Midget Submarines* (Richard Netherwood Ltd, 1993)

Paul Kemp, *Underwater Warriors – The Fighting History of Midget Submarines* (Cassell & Co Military Paperbacks, 1996)

Ian Trenowden, *Stealthily By Night – Clandestine Beach Reconnaissance and Operations in World War II* (Crécy Books, 1995)

Interview transcript – Lieutenant George Honour RNVR, Portsmouth History Centre archives

Interview transcript – Lieutenant Jim Booth RNVR

T.J. Waldron and James Gleeson, *The Frogmen – The Story of the Wartime Underwater Operators* (London: Pan Books, 1950)

Terry Henson, *Porky's War – the story of a real-life Freddie the Frogman on D-Day* (Menin House, an imprint of Tommies Guides Military Booksellers, 2012).

'Frogmen: First ashore on D-Day', *DIVER Magazine*, December 2014 www.divernet.com/commercial-military-diving/p302479-frogmen:-first-ashore-on-d-day.html

Logan Scott-Bowden interview transcript – 5530A/PORMG (Portsmouth History Centre). Transcript from series of interviews undertaken by Russell Miller in 1990–91 for his 1993 book *Nothing less than Victory*

Harry Hinsley, *British Intelligence in the Second World War: Its influence on Strategy and Operations*, Volume I – Appendix 13, Intelligence before and During the Dieppe Raid (1979)

DEFE 2/1226, *Fighter Direction Ships* CR-12817-43 Equipping of Boxer, Bruiser and Thruster as FDS (LSF)

WO 244/12, *A report on the role and operation of British Headquarters Ships and Fighter Direction Tenders in the assault on the continent of Europe June 1944* (Headquarters AEAF, September 1944) A7573

AVIA 6/14431, *Suppression of RADAR interference in communication receivers on Fighter Direction Tenders* by HFC Williams Tech.Note No. Rad. 208 May 1944. RAE Ref: Rad.S4730/96

Ground Controlled Interception RADARs in Operation Neptune/Overlord. 'The Allied Invasion of France June 1944.' The story of the Fighter Direction Tenders used during the 'D-Day' Assault and the Mobile RADAR Convoys that landed on the beaches. Prepared by Horace Red Macauley. http://www.rquirk.com/cdnradar/cor/chapter11.pdf

Badsey, *D-Day – From the Normandy Beaches to the Liberation of France* (Colour Library Books, 1993)

Sinclair McKay, *The Secret Life of Bletchley Park – The WWII codebreaking centre and the men and women who worked there* (Aurum Press Ltd, 2011)

WO205/532 GSI Weekly Neptune review, covering 1 February 1944–30 June 1944

INDEX

Page numbers in *italics* refer to photographs, illustrations and tables.